P9-DEP-143

Glen Oaks College Library
Centreville, Michigan

SHRUBS OF MICHIGAN

CECIL BILLINGTON

CRANBROOK INSTITUTE OF SCIENCE

Bulletin 20, Second Edition, second printing 1968

Copyright 1943, 1949 ©

Cranbrook Institute of Science
Bloomfield Hills, Michigan 48013

Second Edition, revised and enlarged
Second printing 1968

Lithographed by Kingsport Press from type set by

The Cranbrook Press

Preface

To the Second Edition

The first edition of this bulletin was published December 1, 1943. Twenty-five hundred copies were printed. Toward the end of 1946 the Director of the Institute advised me that at the rate of sale then obtaining the edition would be exhausted before the end of 1947 and requested that the preparation of a second edition be undertaken.

The reception accorded the first edition has been most gratifying both to the Cranbrook Institute of Science and to me. To have thus supplied an evident need is an important step in the fulfillment of the purposes of the Institute.

In preparing a new edition, I have taken advantage of constructive criticism received from reviewers and users. The main objection to the first edition was that the nomenclature followed Gray's 'Manual of Botany,' Seventh Edition, which was published in 1908. Since that time many changes have been made in the rules governing botanical nomenclature, and much work has been done by specialists to bring the names of our plants into harmony with these rules. These changes, which have resulted in annuling much of the literature previously published, are scattered through a vast array of botanical publications, making it difficult, if not impossible, for anyone other than a professional botanist to keep abreast of them.

A botanical manual such as Gray's or Britton's is a listing in one place of the plants growing within a certain limited geographical range, with names in accordance with the prescribed and accepted nomenclatorial procedure. As intimated above, application of the rules by which botanical nomenclature is governed at the present time has changed many of the names used in the Seventh Edition of Gray's Manual. It has been my contention that a work such as the present bulletin, designed principally for amateur use, should be supported by a recognized botanical manual so that any interested person wishing to go further in his studies would be able to do so without being confronted by an entirely different set of names. As desirable as this would be, however, it is not possible to accomplish it at this time. An eighth edition of Gray's Manual has been in preparation for some time and, while it is nearing completion, the editors are not able to say definitely until it is actually published what the name of any particular plant is to be. Under present conditions anyone is privileged to name and publish a new species, variety, or form of any plant, which then becomes a part of our taxonomy, no matter how trivial or undesirable it may be. The disposition of the thousands of such names imposes a terrific burden on those endeavoring to bring about an orderly and workable nomenclature.

In selecting the names for the plants here included all known recent authoritative publications have been reviewed and where it has seemed desirable the names therein published have been adopted. Where these names differ from those given in the first edition of this bulletin, the name used in that edition will be found in parenthesis following the new name. It is hoped that when the new Gray's Manual is published the names here used will be in reasonably close accord with those to be found in it.

In preparing this second edition the aim has been not only to furnish the user with current authentic botanical names for the shrubs but also to give other interesting information concerning them. Numerous new species, varieties, and forms of shrubs, as well as of other plants, have been named since the Seventh Edition of Gray's Manual was published in 1908. A number of the new shrubs are found in Michigan and these, together with several species which had been previously known from the state but which did not come to light during preparation of the first edition, are now included.

Another important change is the inclusion in this edition of a number of plants which were previously excluded because they did not seem to meet fully the definition of a shrub. They are discussed in greater detail in the Introduction.

The net result of these changes is that 46 shrubs have been added to the 161 given in the first edition, making a total of 207 with descriptive text, illustration, and distributional map. Supplementary to those so treated in the first edition a number of species, varieties, and forms were briefly referred to in the appropriate text. In the present edition this category also has been considerably expanded.

In the first edition I invited anyone having knowledge of the location of a shrub not given therein to furnish the information for use in possible future editions. Several have responded, and the distribution record has been altered accordingly. Also, all sources of distributional information used in the previous edition and such other sources as have since come to light have been checked for possible further records. I repeat the invitation to report the finding of plants in locations not herein given.

To save space and paper the introduction to the first edition is not reprinted in its entirety in this edition. Portions have been deleted, and the balance edited to conform to the changes herein referred to.

The keys to the genera have been altered to include the several new shrubs added. Likewise, the Index, Bibliography, Glossaries (both pictorial and textual), and the information concerning authors and generic and specific names have all been enlarged to cover the added species.

Since the publication of the first edition, Michigan's botanical circle has been depleted by the death of Dr. Oliver A. Farwell, at his home in Lake Linden, September 18, 1944. Dr. Farwell bequeathed his herbarium of some 40,000 sheets to Cranbrook Institute of Science, where it is now housed. Time has not permitted its complete incorporation into the Institute herbarium, but as far as possible the wealth of information it contained has been drawn upon in the preparation of this edition.

It is a most fortunate circumstance that Mr. Thomas Cobbe, the artist who furnished the drawings of the species illustrating the first edition, returned safely to civilian life after serving in the Army during World War II, and has again contributed his talents in supplying the cuts for several added species. It is equally fortunate that Mrs. Marcelle R. Hatt, who made the drawings for the pictorial glossary in the first edition, was again available to make additions and revisions.

It is hoped that the several additions and the various changes in this edition will contribute materially to the value of the book and intensify the enjoyment and satisfaction of those who use it in exploring our fields and woods.

CECIL BILLINGTON

October 12, 1948

Preface

To the First Edition

When the Director of the Cranbrook Institute of Science, Dr. Robert T. Hatt, assigned to me the task of compiling a work on the shrubs of Michigan as one in the series of popular bulletins to be published by the Institute he doubtless had in mind that a layman can best write for laymen. Be that as it may this book has been prepared with the idea that it will be most useful to those who cannot be professional botanists, but who have the taste and desire to observe and enjoy the beauties which nature has distributed about us and which are so abundantly represented by the shrubs. Technical terms have been used, but the writer has had in mind the oft-repeated statement of various friends who have said that their interest in higher education cooled completely when they reached botany with its aggregation of seemingly meaningless and unpronounceable words. It is quite impossible to describe the various parts of plants without using the names which have been assigned to them in general usage. The apparent difficulty of these will disappear with a little close study.

To those who desire to go beyond the range of this little volume in the study of shrubs or other forms of plant life a great variety of material is available. In seeking to make this bulletin popular, scientific accuracy has not been sacrificed, but a consistent effort has been made to give the reader the most precise information possible concerning the shrubs of Michigan expressed in relatively simple terms.

CECIL BILLINGTON

Bloomfield Hills, Michigan
September 1, 1942

Contents

Introduction

The first step in compiling this bulletin on the shrubs of Michigan consisted in ascertaining the proper definition of a shrub. To do a job it is necessary to know what the job is.

On first thought it seems easy to define a shrub. Shrubs are all about us, along the roads, in the woods and planted for ornamental purposes around our homes. Various sources were consulted from which the following are quoted:

> "A woody perennial plant smaller than a tree. The line of demarcation between shrub and tree in the matter of size is somewhat indeterminate; but if the plant is a vine, or if it is a bush, that is, consists of a number of small stems from the ground or branches from near the ground, it is called by botanists a shrub. In popular language a shrub is a bush."—*New Standard Dictionary*, Funk and Wagnalls.

> "The line between shrubs and trees is not very definite. A shrub generally has a number of stems springing from the ground and a tree usually has a single trunk, but this is not uniformly true in either case."—*Cyclopedia of American Horticulture*, Bailey.

> "A shrub generally has several stems from the same root, or a single crooked or leaning stem, not large enough for a fence post, and seldom more than three inches in diameter. Shrubs are as a rule most abundant in poorer soils; and they usually grow slowly or are much shorter-lived than trees."—*Economic Botany of Alabama*, Harper.

> "Shrubs are woody plants of bushy habit in varying sizes, developing several stems instead of a single trunk as does a tree."—*The Garden Encyclopedia*.

> "Shrub. A woody perennial, smaller than a tree, usually with several stems."—*Gray's New Manual of Botany*, Seventh Edition.

> "Shrub. A woody plant usually less than 20 feet high and generally with several stems from a common base."—*Trees and Shrubs of Minnesota*, Rosendahl and Butters.

The definitions are fairly well in agreement, but I know of one soft maple, which in no sense could be defined as a shrub, having nine trunks some of which are at least a foot in diameter, all springing from one common center, at the ground. Multiple-trunk trees are by no means uncommon, particularly in second growth areas, and there are many instances where ordinary shrubs have grown far beyond anything usually thought of as a shrub. I have seen on Cranbrook old staghorn sumacs from fifteen to twenty feet tall and with trunks nine inches in diameter at the base, and seven inches in diameter three feet from the ground. Plants being unpredictable in the nature of their variations, however, there seems to be nothing we can do but make our writings fit the circumstances as they exist, and in this bulletin an average definition has been attempted.

Although the word vines does not appear in the title of this bulletin woody vines, after consideration, were included in the first edition and are continued in this. There are not many of them, and they answer all the specifications for shrubs with the one exception that they require some form of support. One would have no hesitation in including poison ivy as a shrub, and yet it might with equal reason be classed as a vine. When a fence post or a tree is convenient it acts as a vine and climbs, sometimes to considerable heights. Lacking such support it does not trail on the ground as a grape vine might do, but grows in regulation shrub-like form.

An important change in this edition is the inclusion of several plants which, as explained in the introduction, were omitted from the first edition because they did not fully meet the definition of a shrub. Among these are *Clematis virginiana, Menispermum canadense, Decodon verticillatus, Solanum Dulcamara* and *Chiogenes hispidula.* There has been no uniformity in the treatment of these border-line plants. Some authors include one or more of them among the shrubs, but hardly any two authors include the same ones. In the first edition I included *Epigaea repens* and *Gaultheria procumbens,* exactly the same sort of plants as those mentioned above. For what reason I included them I do not know, except possibly that they are such well-known and popular members of our flora. They did not meet the definition of a shrub any better than those that were omitted. Now, to be more consistent, I am going against all observed precedent and including this whole group in the second edition. Also, the little dwarf mistletoe, a very diminutive shrub, parasitic on conifers, omitted before is here included. In justification of this procedure I can only plead that it will tend to make the second edition a more useful catalog of our shrubs than the former one was.

While the position of the shrub may be secondary to that of the tree, it none the less occupies a very important place. A great deal of the beauty which meets our eyes as we drive about the country is derived from the shrubs. They are everywhere along our roadsides and streams. Sometimes they are regarded as a nuisance and if given a chance some species will quickly take possession of an abandoned field to the exclusion of practically everything else.

Our native shrubs bear flowers in myriad forms and colors; some in bold panicles, others in delicate racemes and some singly. These are followed by an equally interesting and colorful assortment of fruits ranging from the delicate translucent red berry of the yew, the pale blue berries of the silky dogwood and the huckleberries to the dry flat seeds of the wafer ash, the greatly inflated pods of the bladder nut and the pyramidal red bobs of the staghorn sumac. Many of these fruits remain on the shrubs until far into the winter, furnishing a bright and inter-esting note in a generally drab landscape.

The leaves of our shrubs are equally interesting to the student and the nature lover. They run the gamut of botanical descriptions from those of the yew, which are thin and narrow, the juniper, still narrower with tips as sharp as needles, to the compound leaves of the prickly ash, the elder and the sumac. In the autumn these same leaves add their quota of beauty to the landscape. The autumnal coloring of the sumacs is particularly noteworthy and there is scarcely a more beautiful sight than a swamp of poison sumac after the first frost in the fall. The leaves take on a brilliant scarlet and crimson hue brightened with yellow and orange—an irresistible beauty to many unsuspecting persons who gather the leaves for decorations, only later to find themselves afflicted with a most severe case of poisoning.

The beauty of our native shrubs does not entirely disappear with the leaves. In the leafless season a mass of shrubbery is enveloped in a hazy mist and exhibits many interesting patterns of form and color adding much of beauty to the winter landscape. Although less brilliant than the flowers and leaves, the bark of our native shrubs exhibits a wide range of colors. From the yellow and green of the willows, which gleam in the winter sunshine, to the dark red of the red-osier dogwood which becomes a bright purplish-red when the cold weather comes, there are myriads of shades and tints. In March and early April the twigs of the red-osier, anticipating the return of spring and the growing season, be-come bright red and glow in the increasing sunshine.

It would be strange indeed if in a group as numerous as our native shrubs there should not be found a few freaks and renegade members. In the former class may be mentioned the witch-hazel which, reversing the usual procedure, blooms in the autumn at the moment its leaves are falling. The flower buds appear in August, expand in October and November giving to the shrub the aspect of April. Then there is the leatherwood, or moosewood, a peculiarity of which is its thick, porous bark. This is soft and pliant, yet its tenacity and toughness are aston-ishing. It is practically impossible to separate a limb from the bush with unaided hands. Its fibers furnish a wonderful example of natural string, and the Indians used it for bow strings, fish lines and in the manufacture of baskets. The renegades are the two prominent nuisances, poison ivy and poison sumac.

Poison sumac is our most poisonous plant. Its juices are extremely dangerous to some persons, who cannot even pass the bush with impunity, while others enjoy a complete immunity. It is hazardous to experiment with it recklessly. The poison shows itself in long continued swellings upon the surface of the body and many will attest their painful nature. Poison ivy is a woody vine climbing by numerous aerial rootlets, the stem sometimes two or three inches in diameter. It climbs trees and fence posts, lacking which it assumes a shrubby growth. It grows in too great abundance throughout Michigan, and instead of becoming extinct, partly because of its general immunity from disturbance, it is increasing. Unlike poison sumac, which grows only in very wet places where it can be avoided by the majority of people, poison ivy is found in every situation, too frequently where it is not wanted.

The shrubs, perhaps, do not have as many ingenious ways of dispersing their seeds as the herbaceous plants, but a number of the different methods are represented. For example, the witch-hazel ripens its last year's nutlets at the time it blooms in October, and finally sends them out from their woody pods with a projectile force which carries them several yards. The thin, nearly round seeds of the wafer ash are wind-borne and young shrubs spring up in great profusion in the vicinity of the parent bush. Other shrubs depend upon the birds to broaden their distribution.

In holding the fallen leaves in place in our woods the shrub performs a great economic service; it aids in transforming them into humus, an indispensable part of fertile soil, and it conserves the water supply.

In addition to the many merely interesting attributes of our shrubs it is only fair to mention some of their more utilitarian uses. The juniper, willow, witch-hazel, sumacs, wintergreen and viburnums are used in medicines and the industries, while those whose fruit is used as food include the following: huckleberries and blueberries, elderberry, raspberries, blackberries, plums, viburnums and the hazelnut. Our native shrubs also include many species which are extensively planted as ornamentals in landscaping. In this class may be mentioned the yew, juniper, willow, alder, spice bush, witch-hazel, nine-bark, spiraea, roses, cherries, sumacs, bittersweet, bladder nut, dogwoods, buttonbush, viburnums and elders. It would be possible to go on indefinitely enumerating interesting features concerning the majority of our shrubs. In most cases as far as practicable these will be mentioned in connection with each species, and it is hoped that the foregoing will serve to instill in the reader the

Millie Reynolds

VIRGIN'S BOWER (*Clematis virginiana*)

Douglas T. Grubb

RED CURRANT (*Ribes triste*)

Walter P. Nickell

BLACKBERRY (*Rubus* sp.)

Walter P. Nickell

AROMATIC WINTERGREEN (*Gaultheria procumbens*)

necessary interest and curiosity to cause him to go further in the study of this most interesting group of our native plants.

In writing the descriptions in this bulletin technical terms of the parts of flowers have been used, but the descriptions have not been carried quite as far as in the professional manuals. Such terms as are included have been used advisedly. In many cases they could have been translated into common language, which the glossary attempts to do. However, if the beginner wishes to carry on the study here begun it will be necessary to master these terms sooner or later, and in this as in other things there is no time like the present.

The metric system of measurements has been used because it is in almost universal use in botanical manuals. The meter (m.) equals 39.37 inches, or approximately 3.3 feet, the decimeter (dm.) is approximately 4 inches, the centimeter (cm.) ⅖ of an inch and the millimeter (mm.) ¹⁄₂₅ of an inch.

The principal objective of the scientific naming of plants is the establishment of a stable nomenclature. Actually, however, no such stability exists and single species have been known under many names. This has resulted chiefly from changes of ideas regarding relationship and from lack of agreement among investigators on the proper limits of genera and species. For instance, a plant which one botanist considers merely a species under an established genus, another botanist, equally competent, feels is sufficiently different to be placed in a separate genus. One botanist studying the large amount of variation among willows may recognize many species in one area. Another would consider them as local variants unworthy of a special name, or as merely hybrids. It all depends upon the investigator. Those who wish to erect a large number of species have been termed "splitters" and those who take the opposite view "lumpers." In the interests of the amateur for whom this bulletin has been produced I have tried to lean toward the conservative side.

Also, most of the plants have a number of synonyms which have been discarded in arriving at the name given here. In the preparation of monographs it is obligatory to list all such synonyms, with the authors and place of publication, but in the interests of simplicity and avoidance of confusion they are not given in this bulletin. In a few instances when it seemed of possible interest, reference is made to them in the comment following the formal description of the plant, or, as in the case of those names used in the first edition and now superseded, they are given in parenthesis following the new name.

In compiling this bulletin information and material for the descriptions have been drawn from a great variety of sources, all of which have been more or less freely consulted and compared. In addition the herbarium of the Cranbrook Institute of Science has been examined in special cases and my practical experience over a long period of field work largely influenced the accounts. The works consulted are listed in the bibliography at the end of this volume.

Although this edition has been considerably enlarged as compared with the first, it still does not pretend to be a complete catalog of every shrub which has been described from Michigan. Long lists of plants, particularly in the Rose family, which is an extremely polymorphic group, have been omitted. Generally these omissions have been referred to under the proper genera.

The primary purpose of this volume is still to awaken and stimulate an interest in our native flora and to create a desire to know more about it.

Identifications—To aid in quickly locating a shrub, keys, simplified as much as possible, have been provided. Only characters which are present during the normal summer season on mature specimens are used. For those who wish to study the shrubs in winter, books giving keys based on winter characters are obtainable. As this bulletin is primarily intended for the amateur a few words of instruction in the use of keys may be helpful.

To the extent possible those characters which stand out and tend to catch the eye are used. Two alternatives are given, either a character is or is not present. In the keys the two opposed characters are given the same number. The following will serve as a simple illustration:

1. Leaves linear or scale-like, persistent
   2. Leaves flat, sharp-pointed, not over 2 mm. wide, green beneath................*Taxus*
   2. Leaves in whorls of three, needle-like, with a white line beneath................*Juniperus*
1. Leaves not linear or scale-like, deciduous
     3. Leaves simple
       4. Petioles with stipules and glands; fruit a drupe................*Viburnum*
       4. Petioles without stipules and glands; fruit a samara................*Acer*
     3. Leaves compound
       Etc. etc.

To use the keys let us suppose branches from two different shrubs have been gathered, both of which have leaves and fruit. With the specimens in hand reference is made to the key to the genera. The first division calls for linear leaves. The specimens to be identified have simple, broad leaves and are clearly deciduous. Obviously they do not belong under the first classification. On consulting the key and examining the branches it will be noted that the petioles of one of them has both stipules and glands at the base and that the fruit is a drupe or berry. Of the two specimens *Viburnum* is plainly the genus to which this one belongs. The other branch is found not to have stipules and glands at the base of the petioles and the fruit is a samara having two broad, spreading wings. This leads to the genus *Acer*. If the leaves had been linear or scale-like the shrubs would have come under the first division and the process would have been the same.

After determining the genus the next step is to turn to the page indicated and in the same manner determine the species. In constructing the keys it is literally impossible not to use botanical terms. To aid in their understanding and render identification easier explanatory illustrations and a glossary of terms have been appended. These should be consulted whenever doubt arises as to the meaning of a word or phrase.

Accurate observation of the structure in question and correct interpretation of descriptive terms is essential to the successful working of the keys. The beginner is bound to encounter difficulties no matter how carefully he works. Nature scarcely ever produces identical forms, and there will usually be difficulty in deciding how fully a phrase may typify a character. However, when once a general insight is gained these questions disappear and the study of shrubs or any branch of our native flora becomes an absorbing pastime.

A small hand lens will be found exceedingly helpful in the work of identification. One with magnifying powers of 8-12 diameters is sufficient. Several makes are available.

The keys to the genera used herein have been patterned after the very efficient and easily used 'Keys to Woody Plants' by W. C. Muenscher, published in 1936, the author having given his permission to so use them.

Among the shrubs are a number of genera which are very difficult even for the professional botanist. These include the willows which hybridize naturally, making the determination of the different species very difficult, the blackberries, roses, and the hawthorns or *Crataegus*. The most the amateur can hope to do is know the marked types of these genera. Many species, varieties and forms which have been named in each of these groups will not be included in this bulletin. In the event the student wishes to pursue his study of one or more of these genera beyond the scope of this work, there are, in addition to the manuals, monographs which may be obtained for the purpose. Investigators in these special fields are continually bringing out new works and almost any university or college can supply an up-to-date bibliography.

Shrubs and the Conservation of Wildlife—A volume dealing with our native shrubs would hardly be complete if it failed to mention their usefulness in conserving our wildlife. Our streams are usually lined with shrubs which anchor the banks and shade the waters, conditions upon which much of the fish life and its food are dependent. Food and shelter are first essentials in conservation of land animals, and shrubs are one of the most important elements in providing these essentials. They constitute the cover for wildlife, both bird and mammal, which corresponds to barns and sheds for domestic animals; they afford shelter from the elements and refuge from enemies, not to mention food of a variety of classes including browse, mast, fruit and seed. Places to feed, hide, rest, sleep, play and raise young have been specified as constituent parts of habitable range. Shrubs forming low thickets are invaluable for the protection of quail, pheasants and other ground birds, and vines in combination with shrubs give extra security to these same birds. Without cover, wildlife cannot remain on an area, and there is abundant reward for leaving patches of shrubs in fence rows or other convenient places, for the farm with some shrubbery, greenery and wildlife is a much more satisfactory place on which to live than one completely devoid of such life.

It is desirable that cover plants produce food as well as shelter. Wild grapevines, plums and haws are outstanding in this respect, and under winter conditions the mechanical protection offered by a thorny bush or a dense tangle of grapevines often represents the only chance quail or other ground birds have of dodging their enemies. Almost any farmer can testify that these are easy to grow in fence rows or on other waste lands.

So far in this discussion of shrubs in relation to conservation of our wildlife the emphasis has been upon the broader areas of farm lands and the preservation of our native shrubs as cover for ground birds and animals. There is another division of our wildlife which is attractive and valuable equally to the farm and city dweller. Reference is here made to the smaller non-game or song birds. The economic value of these birds has long been recognized. The song birds are not only beautiful in themselves, but they help to maintain the beauty of our ornamental shrubs, trees and vines by feeding on destructive insects. In doing landscape planting about our homes the dual purpose of beautifying the grounds and attracting the birds should be borne in mind. The selection of plants should be made discriminately so that they will not only add to the beauty of the premises, but also provide food and cover for the birds. A variety should be planted to avoid monotony and give a diversity of fruits over the longest possible period. Shrubs, trees and vines should be planted for summer flowering and for autumn fruiting, including some species which will hold their fruit through the winter. To attract the widest variety of birds it is necessary to have shrubs and trees which appeal to the seed-eating as well as for the fruit-eating species.

[8]

Shrubs for landscape planting—In commenting upon the individual shrubs reference has been made in some cases to their value from an avian standpoint. However, many of the native shrubs do not take kindly to civilization and, while their fruits make splendid food for the birds, they cannot readily be used in landscaping. In the following list some shrubs sold by nurseries and not native to Michigan have been included. They are primarily for landscape planting, but many of them will naturalize readily and fit appropriately into the native scene. No attempt is here made to offer suggestions for ornamental planting. In order to be successful, shrubs or other plants must be situated in suitable habitats. Nurserymen or landscape architects can advise in this respect. It is probable that the fruits, berries and seeds of wild plants are more relished by the birds than those of cultivated varieties and wild plants should be used whenever possible.

The plants here listed are given in alphabetical order by genera and without descriptions simply to serve as a guide in the selection of materials for an ornamental or naturalized planting attractive to our native birds. The United States Fish and Wildlife Service (Biological Survey) and the United States Bureau of Plant Industry have made extensive investigations of this entire subject and have literature available upon request.

Acer pennsylvanicum, Striped Maple

Acer spicatum, Mountain Maple

Alnus rugosa, Speckled Alder

Amelanchier humilis, Low Juneberry

Aralia spinosa, Hercules' Club

Arctostaphylos Uva-ursi var. *coactilis*, Bearberry

Aronia melanocarpa, Black Chokeberry

Aronia prunifolia, Purple Chokeberry

Berberis japonica, Japanese Barberry

Berberis Thunbergii, Thunberg's Barberry

Berberis vulgaris, Common Barberry

Betula glandulosa, Dwarf Birch

Betula pumila, Swamp Birch

Celastrus scandens, Climbing Bittersweet

Cornus alternifolia, Alternate-leaved Dogwood

Cornus asperifolia, Rough-leaved Dogwood

Cornus obliqua, Silky Cornel

Cornus racemosa, Panicled Dogwood

Cornus rugosa, Round-leaved Dogwood

Cornus stolonifera, Red-osier Dogwood

Crataegus Crus-galli, Cock-spur Thorn

Crataegus mollis, Red-fruited Thorn

Crataegus punctata, Large-fruited Thorn

Empetrum nigrum, Black Crowberry

Euonymus americanus, Strawberry Bush

Euonymus atropurpureus, Burning Bush

Euonymus obovatus, Running Strawberry Bush

Gaultheria procumbens, Teaberry, Checkerberry

Gaylussacia baccata, Black Huckleberry

Gaylussacia frondosa, Blue Tangle, Dangleberry

[9]

Ilex verticillata, Winterberry
Juniperus communis var. *depressa,*
Prostrate Juniper
Juniperus horizontalis, Creeping
Juniper

Lindera Benzoin, Spice Bush
Lonicera canadensis, American Fly
Honeysuckle
Lonicera dioica, Smooth-leaved
Honeysuckle
Lonicera hirsuta, Hairy Honeysuckle
Lonicera involucrata, Involucred
Fly Honeysuckle
Lonicera oblongifolia, Swamp Fly
Honeysuckle

Mitchella repens, Partridge-berry
Myrica cerifera, Wax Myrtle
Myrica Gale, Sweet Gale

Parthenocissus inserta, False Grape
Parthenocissus quinquefolia, Virginia
Creeper
Prunus americana, Wild Yellow Plum
Prunus nigra, Wild Plum
Prunus pumila, Sand Cherry
Prunus susquehanae, Appalachian
Cherry
Prunus virginiana, Choke Cherry
Ptelea trifoliata, Shrubby Trefoil
Quercus prinoides, Shrub Oak
Rhamnus alnifolia, Alder Buckthorn
Rhamnus caroliniana, Indian Cherry
Rhus aromatica, Fragrant Sumac
Rhus copallina var. *latifolia,* Dwarf
Sumac
Rhus glabra, Smooth Sumac
Rhus typhina, Staghorn Sumac
Ribes americanum, Wild Black Currant
Ribes Cynosbati, Prickly Gooseberry
Ribes gracile, Missouri Gooseberry
Ribes oxyacanthoides, Northern
Gooseberry
Rosa acicularis, Prickly Wild Rose
Rosa blanda, Smooth Rose
Rosa carolina, Pasture Rose
Rosa palustris, Swamp Rose

Rosa rubiginosa, Sweetbrier
Rubus allegheniensis, High-bush
Blackberry
Rubus canadensis, Millspaugh's
Blackberry
Rubus flagellaris, Dewberry
Rubus hispidus, Hispid Blackberry
Rubus idaeus var. *aculeatissimus,*
Wild Red Raspberry
Rubus occidentalis, Black Raspberry
Rubus odoratus, Purple-flowering
Raspberry
Rubus parviflorus, Salmon Berry

Sambucus canadensis, Common Elder
Sambucus pubens, Red-berried Elder
Shepherdia canadensis, Canadian
Buffalo Berry
Smilax hispida, Hispid Greenbrier
Smilax rotundifolia, Common Green-
brier
Symphoricarpos albus, Snowberry
Symphoricarpos occidentalis,
Wolfberry
Symphoricarpos orbiculatus, Indian
Currant

Taxus canadensis, American Yew

Vaccinium corymbosum, High-bush
Blueberry
Vaccinium macrocarpon, Large
Cranberry
Vaccinium myrtilloides, Sour-top
Vaccinium ovalifolium, Tall Bilberry
Vaccinium Oxycoccos, Small
Cranberry
Vaccinium pennsylvanicum, Low
Sweet Blueberry
Vaccinium stamineum, Deerberry
Vaccinium uliginosum, Bog Bilberry
Vaccinium vacillans, Late Low
Blueberry
Vaccinium Vitis-Idaea, Cowberry
Viburnum acerifolium, Mapleleaf
Virburnum
Viburnum cassinoides, Withe-rod

Viburnum dentatum, Arrow-wood
Viburnum lantanoides, Hobble-bush
Viburnum Lentago, Nanny-berry
Viburnum pauciflorum, Squashberry
Viburnum prunifolium, Black Haw
Viburnum pubescens, Downy Arrow-wood

Virburnum trilobum, High-bush Cran-berry
Vitis aestivalis, Summer Grape
Vitis labrusca, Northern Fox Grape
Vitis riparia, River-bank Grape
Vitis rotundifolia, Muscadine
Vitis vulpina, Frost Grape

Collecting—In the section on Rare Species reference is made to the fact that it would be highly desirable for the beginner to collect certain shrubs and supply specimens to our principal state herbaria. This would necessitate having collecting equipment adequate for the purpose, and a few words of instruction as to what to get and how to use it follow.

A botanizing outfit may be as simple or as elaborate as one's pocket-book permits. The following list will prove adequate for all practical purposes in collecting specimens. If the student wishes to establish an herbarium for his specimens he will need mounting papers and genus covers, labels, gummed cloth, etc. However, if he merely collects the specimens for others they may be sent to the herbarium without mounting.

1. Vasculum or collecting case. A tin box in the shape of a flattened cylinder, with a hinged opening the entire length to permit of entering the plants with the minimum of bending or breaking. The secret of keeping plants fresh lies in keeping them from the air and these tin boxes do this admirably.

2. Small pruning shears. For shrubs these are essential. A sharp pocket knife is a reasonably good substitute. (In collecting herbaceous plants, where it is desirable to include the roots, a trowel is necessary.)

3. Botanical plant press. Plant presses are varied, but a simple one consists of two perforated boards of equal size and thickness, a little larger than the mounting paper, and a number of sheets of drying paper, or blotters to fit them. Slatted presses, almost as easy to make as perforated boards, provide better ventilation, hence quicker drying. The whole is kept in place by a double strap which may be tightened or loosened according to the number of plants and drying sheets in the press.

4. Drying papers and folders. Regular botanical drying paper may be purchased or thick blotting paper may be procured and cut to proper size. For the folders old newspapers cut as long as the mounting papers and twice as wide, so that when folded once over they form covers the same size as the sheets, are sufficient. The specimens to be pressed are placed in these covers. It is then possible to move them to change the dryers without disturbing them. Instead of old newspapers plain news-paper stock can be procured and cut to size at a nominal cost.

[11]

5. Ventilators. Sheets of corrugated board, cut the size of the blotters serve an important function in helping the work of blotters between which they are interspersed.

6. A small quantity of cotton-wool to be used in the form of pads to equalize the pressure around woody stems or large flower heads. Instead of the wool I use small pieces of newspapers torn to fit the requirements, which prove very satisfactory. The pieces can be dried and used repeatedly.

This about completes the list of necessary equipment for collecting and pressing botanical specimens. The plants should be pressed as soon as possible after gathering and enough specimens should be made for all required purposes. The plants should be arranged in the folders as nearly as possible in a natural manner, and the pressure equalized around the thick stems and heads with bits of newspaper or cotton-wool. One or more drying papers should be used between each two folders. When all the plants have been put in the folders between the blotters and ventilators, the press should be strapped and left to dry. At first the dryers should be changed at least each twenty-four hours and the damp dryers dried out and stored for future use.

There are botanical supply houses which furnish all the above equipment and supplies. Their names will be supplied upon application to the publisher.

One of the most important points to remember in connection with collecting plants of any kind is to have complete data with every specimen. Data should include exact location, township, county, etc., habitat, date, character of plant, color of blossom, collector and any information which would be useful in its study. Two methods are used. One is to prepare full notes in the field. These are given a number and the same number is affixed to the plant in the press and follows it, even into the herbarium. Usually plants are not named in the field, but are studied after the drying process is completed. The alternative plan is to place in the folder, slips giving the necessary data, or the information may be written on the folder itself.

A specimen in an herbarium without proper data is almost worthless. Data are fully as important as a name. In checking herbaria for distribution records during the compilation of this bulletin a great many specimens were found without the location given. For example some specimens revealed that they were collected at "Mud Lake." The collector knew at the time where Mud Lake was located, but as there are probably a hundred Mud Lakes in Michigan the information was of no practical value. The collector knew where it was; but collectors die, are not always available when wanted, and they also forget. The only safe way is to be sure that all necessary data are on every specimen at the time it is collected or mounted.

Acknowledgments—I wish to testify to the valuable assistance which has been rendered so freely by others in compiling this bulletin and in revising it for a second edition. At the time the first edition was written I was employed, and Mrs. C. L. Lundell in my stead thoroughly searched the herbarium at the University of Michigan for distributional records. Valuable suggestions were also received from Dr. Lundell. For the revision, I am especially indebted to Drs. E. B. Mains, Rogers McVaugh, and Bessie Kanouse, all of the University of Michigan herbarium, for the use of the collections, for assistance with a number of difficult problems, and for the loan of specimens for study and from which to produce several of the species illustrations.

I received the same cordial welcome and ready assistance at Michigan State College in checking the herbarium there for distributional records, and to Drs. Bessy, Darlington, and Drew of that institution I say a sincere thank you.

Thanks to Messrs. R. R. Dreisbach, of Midland, and C. A. Bazuin, of Grand Rapids, for making their private herbaria available to me. A large number of additional distributional records were secured in checking these two excellent collections. And also to Mr. William J. Gilbert, of Albion College, who placed the herbarium of the college at my disposal and provided unusually fine working quarters.

To Dr. M. L. Fernald, of Gray Herbarium, Harvard University, I am especially indebted for calling attention to several Michigan shrubs omitted from the first edition, and to Dr. C. A. Weatherby, of the same institution, for most valuable advice concerning nomenclature; also to Dr. Robert C. Foster, Acting Curator of the Herbarium, for the loan of mounted specimens.

Dr. Henry K. Svenson, Brooklyn Botanical Garden, read critically certain portions of the first edition, and to him I am indebted for correction of errors which otherwise might have been carried over into the second.

Mr. William K. Kelsey furnished the heading for the personal statement which closes this volume. Many thanks for this assistance.

I found it a difficult matter to assemble all the information concerning the authors of the various plant names which I wanted to include in the second edition. I am very much indebted to the following persons for promptly answering my correspondence concerning this phase of the work and providing the desired answers to my inquires: Dr. Ethel Zo Bailey, Curator, Bailey Hortorum, Cornell University; Dr. Norman C. Fassett, University of Wisconsin; Dr. Elbert L. Little, Jr., Dendrologist, U. S. Forestry Service; Dr. Ernst J. Palmer, Arnold Arboretum; Dr. H. W. Rickett, Bibliographer, The New York Botanical Garden; and Dr. C. O. Rosendahl, University of Minnesota.

Dr. Charles C. Deam, the veteran botanist of Indiana and America, was more than generous in contributing sage advice from his own experience gained during a lifetime of intensive botanical labors.

Mrs. Marjorie T. Bingham assisted with many useful suggestions and contributed generously of her time in smoothing out certain rough spots during the preparation of the first edition.

To Mr. and Mrs. Perry J. Reynolds, Walter P. Nickell, Douglas T. Grubb, and Edward O. Eichstedt I am indebted for the submission of excellent color photographs of shrubs, four of which appear facing pages 4 and 5 of this second edition.

To Mr. Thomas J. Cobbe, who prepared the figures for the species of plants, and to Mrs. Marcelle R. Hatt, who prepared those used in the pictorial glossary, go my grateful thanks for the excellent drawings which illustrate the volume. The color frontispiece is by Dr. Robert T. Hatt, and the late Dr. Paul McPharlin designed the attractive cover for the book.

It seems proper to give credit here to those amateur field botanists with whom I tramped the fields and woods now many years ago while laying the foundation for an undertaking such as compiling this bulletin. They were an enthusiastic lot, and from earliest spring to snowfall they were searching every week-end for rare plants and making collections of the local flora for their own personal pleasure and information. To Mr. John M. Sutton must be given credit for introducing me to them, and for many years he was an enthusiastic member of the group. At that time Mr. C. K. Dodge was a frequent visitor to Detroit and accompanied us on our trips. Also Dr. Oliver A. Farwell was in Detroit, and we all felt distinctly honored when he came along. Messrs. Benjamin Chandler and Bruno Gladewitz were exceptionally able amateur botanists and contributed greatly to my education in field work. Chandler has been dead these many years, but his memory lives on in the fine specimens he made, which are now deposited in various herbaria about the state. The same is true of Mr. Dodge. Mr. Branson A. Walpole, at that time in Ypsilanti, author of the 'Flora of Washtenaw County' was often in our party. Mrs. Billington, who for many years was a week-end botanical widow, should come in for her fair share of the credit, and it is here freely given.

Without her ready cooperation this opportunity would not have come to me.

The foregoing has a modern counterpart in the group of enthusiastic amateur workers who are contributing so freely of their time and resources to the upbuilding of the herbarium of Cranbrook Institute of Science. Messrs. Dale J. Hagenah, N. W. Katz, Clarence J. Messner, Paul W. Thompson, George W. Thomson, and in most cases their wives, meet at the Institute once a week and carry on the work which in a larger institution would be done by employees. This is in addition to their field trips, which have contributed many specimens to the collections. I cannot single out any one of them in particular for credit, but I am sure the distributional records and other details in this bulletin are much more complete than would have been the case in the absence of their valuable assistance.

Thanks are due to Mr. William L. Wood, superintendent of the Cranbrook Press during the printing of the first edition, and to Mr. George E. Migrants, filling the same position during the production of the second edition, for their willing cooperation and efficient assistance in solving the many typographical problems.

There are doubtless others not here enumerated who in one way or another contributed to the production of this bulletin and its revision. Although they may remain nameless they will understand that I nonetheless fully appreciate their interest and help.

And last but by no means least I here give special recognition and thanks to those two members of the staff of Cranbrook Institute of Science with whom I have recently been closely associated, Drs. Robert T. Hatt and Stanley A. Cain. Because of this close association they have been called upon frequently in connection with my problems. It was Dr. Hatt, Director, who suggested that I undertake the work. He has been exceptionally patient and understanding in dealing with the many complicated situations and problems which have arisen in connection with both editions, and to him must go the major credit for the production of the book. Dr. Cain, Staff Botanist, because of his position, naturally has had to stand the brunt of my detailed questioning. He was not available at the time the first edition was published, but I have consulted with him in reference to almost every phase of the revision; he has spent endless hours in critically reading and correcting the manuscript, and if the present edition is an improvement over the first, as I am sure it is, much of the credit must go to him.

Mr. A. N. Goddard and the Michigan Sportsman's Fund, administered by Mr. Gustavas D. Pope, contributed generously to the publication fund for the first edition. The second edition is financed from the revolving publication fund of Cranbrook Institute of Science. Together these sources must be credited with such educational influence as this work may have in fostering an interest in our native shrubs and instilling an appreciation of their importance in conserving our natural resources.

Ecology

Michigan is known as the Peninsula State and is divided into two parts called the Upper and Lower Peninsulas. From east to west the Upper Peninsula measures 318 miles. In width it varies from 30 to 164 miles. The greatest length of the Lower Peninsula is 277 miles from north to south and its extreme width is 259 miles. The total area of both peninsulas is 58,915 square miles and, situated as it is within the waters of the Great Lakes, the state has a coast line of over 1600 miles.

The Upper and Lower Peninsulas are strikingly different in many respects. In the western portion of the Upper Peninsula are located the copper and iron bearing rocks which have made Michigan famous as a mining state. The eastern portion of this peninsula is underlaid with stratified sedimentary rocks, and large portions of both sections are covered with glacial drift.

The Lower Peninsula is generally level or rolling. The entire surface is covered deeply with glacial drift consisting of sand, gravel and clay variously intermixed, and the topographical outlines are due to joint action of moving ice and flowing water during and following the glacial period. The peninsula is divided by lateral moraines into certain more or less clearly marked floral regions. All parts of the state are abundantly watered by its many small rivers and by some 5000 lakes which for the most part were left in the wake of the retreating glaciers. These geological factors are briefly mentioned because of their marked influence upon the vegetation of the state. In the bogs and marshes of Oakland County for example are to be found many species which are distinctly alpine. Here these species found a congenial habitat as the ice departed and have maintained themselves ever since.

Plants growing naturally group themselves into communities. This grouping is brought about by the character of the environment, certain plants thriving best under a given set of conditions of soil, moisture, etc. Thus plants requiring the same conditions will tend to grow together in the locality where those favorable conditions exist. The study of these communities is known as plant ecology, the science of the interrelations of plants and their environments. This is essentially an outdoor study and one of the most practical of the divisions of botany, since ecological principles form the basis for the practice of agriculture and forestry. Michigan has a great variety of soils and surface conditions which create a large number of well marked plant communities. Among the most prominent may be mentioned the following:

Sand dunes	Oak-Hickory forests
Jack Pine plains	Hemlock forests
Cedar-Tamarack bogs	Meadows
Beech-Maple forests	Lake shores

Each of these situations has its characteristic plants. For example, the Trailing Juniper is found mostly along the rocky shores of the northern counties. Likewise the Jack Pine plains have their quota of distinctive shrubs and other plants, which are found growing in greater abundance there than in other localities.

However, it is not the function of this bulletin to treat of the ecological side of our native shrubs. Those readers who may wish to pursue the subject further will find ecology a most interesting and entertaining study.

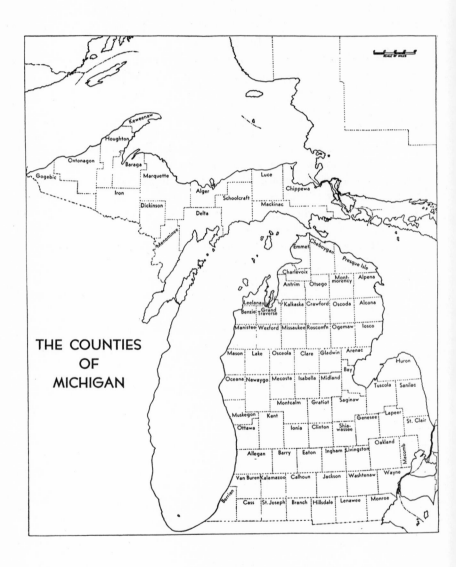

THE COUNTIES
OF
MICHIGAN

Keweenaw
Houghton
Ontonagon
Baraga
Gogebic
Marquette
Iron
Dickinson
Delta
Menominee
Alger
Schoolcraft
Mackinac
Luce
Chippewa

Emmet
Cheboygan
Presque Isle
Charlevoix
Mont-morency
Alpena
Antrim
Otsego
Leelanau
Benzie
Grand Traverse
Kalkaska
Crawford
Oscoda
Alcona
Manistee
Wexford
Missaukee
Roscom'n
Ogemaw
Iosco
Mason
Lake
Osceola
Clare
Gladwin
Arenac
Bay
Huron
Oceana
Newaygo
Mecosta
Isabella
Midland
Tuscola
Sanilac
Montcalm
Gratiot
Saginaw
Muskegon
Kent
Genesee
Lapeer
St. Clair
Ottawa
Ionia
Clinton
Shia-wassee
Allegan
Barry
Eaton
Ingham
Livingston
Oakland
Macomb
Van Buren
Kalamazoo
Calhoun
Jackson
Washtenaw
Wayne
Berrien
Cass
St. Joseph
Branch
Hillsdale
Lenawee
Monroe

SCALE OF MILES

Distribution

The general distribution of each species is given in connection with its botanical description. Likewise in connection with each shrub will be found its range in Michigan. For example, *Rubus occidentalis* L., the Black Raspberry, is "common throughout"; *Empetrum nigrum* L., Black Crowberry, is "Upper Peninsula"; and *Quercus prinoides* Willd., Dwarf Chestnut Oak, is "infrequent, central and southern." This information has been taken from Beal's 'Michigan Flora' and other available sources.

In addition to the general probable Michigan range the accompanying maps set forth by counties the actual record as evidenced by herbarium specimens and published lists. The lists checked in compiling these maps are starred in the Bibliography.

The herbaria of the University of Michigan, Michigan State College, Albion College, and the Cranbrook Institute of Science were carefully checked. Many important private collections have been incorporated in these herbaria, and it is felt that taken together they present an adequate cross section of the distribution of our Michigan flora. My own herbarium has been given to the Cranbrook Institute of Science, where it is now housed. In addition to the foregoing, the private herbaria of Mr. R. R. Dreisbach, Midland, and Mr. C. A. Bazuin, Grand Rapids, Michigan, were checked for the second edition. Also I am indebted to Professor Heber W. Youngken for informing me of the record of a specimen of the hobble-bush in the herbarium of the Massachusetts College of Pharmacy.

It is certain that some or all of the shrubs are to be found in more localities than are here listed, but no such specimens are deposited in our principal state herbaria and they are not listed in any of the well-circulated published lists. Large areas of the state are under cultivation and obviously such areas are not particularly attractive to field botanists. This fact no doubt accounts for the scarcity of records in some instances. Michigan has not been as fortunate as Indiana, where Mr. Charles C. Deam, over a period of forty years, traveled 125,000 miles to collect in each of the 1016 townships of the state. It is doubtful if ever before the flora of an entire state has been so thoroughly studied as was that of Indiana. I have botanized as an avocation for some twenty-odd years, during which time I covered considerable territory, but compared to the whole, scarcely scratched the surface. Other botanists both amateur and professional have collected in various sections of the state, publishing lists of plants found, all of which have been consulted in compiling the maps. It is realized, however, that by far the greater areas of the state have not been botanized and that the distribution of any or all of the species may be much greater than is indicated. Also some of the records were made many years ago. Great changes have taken place, even in the last quarter century, and it would be strange indeed if some of the older stations had not been wiped out entirely. Marshes have been drained, forests removed and great areas burned over so frequently that the only wonder is there is any vegetation left at all. In a sense the distribution as shown by the maps is historical and the collector need not be surprised if plants which are recorded in a certain locality can no longer be found there.

Rare or Infrequent Species

In every given locality there are a number of plants which apparently may be classified as rare. The reasons for this are twofold; the plant may actually be rare, or it may be that insufficient field work has been done to establish the facts.

The following list of shrubs has been selected for special mention because, so far as the records go, they are rare in Michigan. The beginning field botanist may do a really worthwhile piece of work by thoroughly exploring the theoretical range of these plants and establishing definitely whether they really are rare or whether their rarity is only apparent for the reason above stated. It is well known that amateur astronomers discover many of the new comets which visit our solar system from time to time, and also that they carry on an important work in connection with the cataloguing of stars and other astronomical endeavors. It seems to me that there is an equally important field for the beginning systematic botanist in determining the distribution of our native plants. Such a work would provide a worthy objective, the results of which would add much of value to the sum of human knowledge. Our great botanical manuals have been built up from the investigations of a large number of individuals carried on over a long period of time and the greater the number of investigators continuing the work the more accurate and thorough our records will become. In the list below, many blanks in our knowledge of shrub distribution are noted and the filling in of these is a practical and worthy opportunity for the amateur botanist.

In checking the three large state herbaria for distribution records many gaps were found. If this is true of such prominent plants as the shrubs, it is probably even more true of other plants. Well-prepared specimens, properly labeled, would be welcome in any herbarium; while the laboratory botanist is engaged with his students in the classroom or struggling with profound problems in cytology or morphology the collector may be roaming the fields and woods in the fresh air and sunshine, surrounded by the trees, shrubs, flowers and birds, at the same time carrying on an important work of investigation—a truly ideal combination.

Among the rare or little-known species are:

Arceuthobium pusillum Bieb. This little dwarf parasite may not be particularly rare, but it is so small and so difficult of detection that attention is directed to it here. Perhaps it is not confined to the northern counties, and it may be looked for wherever conifers are present.

Clematis verticillaris DC. Very few records of this vine are available. Its general range includes the entire state, and it should be looked for and reported when found.

Asimina triloba Dunal. The Papaw reaches the northern limit of its range in the southern portion of the state. It has been collected in Gratiot County. Is this the most northerly station?

Rosa Lunellii Greene. This rose is another of those plants with such disjunct distribution that it has attracted attention generally among botanists and geologists. For discussion see reference under the species, page 175. Only one station is recorded, Keweenaw Peninsula. Specimens would be welcome at all state herbaria if any user of this bulletin is lucky enough to find the plant.

Ceanothus sanguineus Pursh. Prof. M. L. Fernald called my attention to the omission of this shrub from the first edition. It is one of those rare plants which seems to be far from home in Michigan, the nearest station in its regular distribution being in South Dakota. So far it is recorded from only five stations in Michigan, all in Keweenaw County.

Empetrum nigrum L. Here is a plant the range of which is clearly northern. Only three stations are recorded, Keweenaw, Alger and Schoolcraft counties, all in the northern peninsula. It must be scattered all through this section and further records would be helpful in establishing its distribution in the state.

Oplopanax horridum (Sm.) Miq. This is truly a rare plant. The only station known in this part of the country is Isle Royale, Keweenaw County, where it is at least seven or eight hundred miles east of its principal range. Its presence here presents a problem in the distribution of species for the beginner to work on. A theory has been proposed. See if you can discover it. Incidentally the plant might be looked for in other counties along Lake Superior in the Upper Peninsula.

Lyonia ligustrina (L.) DC. Here is a shrub which, according to the authorities should not be in Michigan at all. Gray's Manual gives its range as "central Maine to central New York and southward." Beal's 'Michigan Flora' records it as follows: "Keweenaw Point, Dr. Robbins." Another record is from Newaygo County, where it was found in 1915 by Dr. Henry T. Darlington. One station is at the extreme northern tip of the Upper Peninsula and the other about the middle of the Lower Peninsula. One would expect that a thorough botanizing of the intervening territory would bring to light other stations, and specimens with proper data would be welcome. Only by such field work can the exact distribution of our flora be ascertained and future manuals reflect the facts.

Vaccinium stamineum L. This apparently is a very rare huckleberry. In checking the herbaria and lists for this bulletin the only record discovered was from Washtenaw County.

Vaccinium uliginosum L. When the first edition was published only two stations were discovered for the Bog Bilberry, Isle Royale and the mainland of Keweenaw County. The present edition gives two other counties, Chippewa and Emmet.

Vaccinium caespitosum Michx. Beal's 'Michigan Flora' lists the Dwarf Bilberry as follows: "Shores of Lake Superior and westward, A. Gray, Flora of North America; Lyons, U. P." It will be noted that specific localities are not given. At the time the first edition was published no record of the species in Michigan was discovered. It has since been recorded from two counties, one in the Upper Peninsula and the other in the northern part of the Lower Peninsula. It is still a rare species, and it would be a worthwhile piece of work to locate it and supply specimens to the various state herbaria.

Vaccinium Vitis-Idaea L. var. *minus* Lodd. This arctic plant is called the Rock Cranberry. Its general range as given in Gray's Manual is as follows: "Arctic America, south to the mountains of Maine, New Hampshire and Vermont, Lake Superior, etc.; and along the coast to Cape Ann, Mass." The only Michigan record of it is from Isle Royale, made by A. E. Frost in 1868, and it has not been collected since. Beal does not list it in his 'Michigan Flora,' and it is included in this bulletin with the idea that some beginning systematic botanist may have the thrill of re-discovering it and establishing it firmly as a member of our flora.

Lonicera involucrata (Richards.) Banks. The only records of this honeysuckle are from Keweenaw and Washtenaw counties, about as far apart in the state as it is possible to have them. Is it to be found in other localities?

Viburnum lantanoides Michx. In checking the distribution of Michigan shrubs for this bulletin no specimen of the Hobble-bush was found, though Whitney (1851) reported the species common in the Upper Peninsula. Dr. Heber W. Youngken has kindly informed me that he collected a specimen August 12, 1938, at Pentwater, Oceana County, Michigan. This specimen is in the Massachusetts College of Pharmacy. I have found it at Muskoka Lakes in Ontario and specimens from this station are in the Cranbrook herbarium. Michigan is well within the species' range, and a thorough search will doubtless discover other stations. One such was reported from adjoining Muskegon County by a user of the first edition.

Viburnum pauciflorum Raf. This viburnum is recorded only from Isle Royale, Keweenaw County. The range for it in Gray's Manual is given as follows: "Newfoundland and Labrador to Alaska, south to the mountains of Cape Breton Island, Northern New England, Allegheny County, Pennsylvania, northern Michigan, Minnesota, Colorado and Washington." Rosendahl and Butters in 'Trees and Shrubs of Minnesota' give the distribution of this species in their state as follows: "In cold woods north of Lake Superior." Minnesota extends out over Lake Superior and comes very close to Isle Royale. Although this island is a part of Michigan it is much closer to Minnesota than to the state of which it is a part and it is possible that *Viburnum pauciflorum* does not grow on the mainland of Michigan. It would be interesting to have this determined definitely and it is hoped that some beginning systematist may get the inspiration to make the necessary search from his perusal of this bulletin.

[23]

Plant Names and Their Authors

The naming of plants today is based on the binomial system, which was established by Linnaeus in 1753. Before that time plants had been studied and named, but they had no accepted or uniform short definite technical names. The pre-Linnaean botanists used what really amounted to a brief description of the plant. In this connection it should be remembered that most of those who wrote of plants then were known as herbalists and were primarily interested in the healing virtues of plants. There were some, however, who were interested directly in the study of plants with a view to identifying them, much as is done by our systematists of today, and many generic and other names which were in use prior to 1753 were adopted by Linnaeus.

In this volume as a matter of interest to the student, these pre-Linnaean authors' names are indicated by the use of a square bracket [ ]. Since the time of Linnaeus the naming of plants has proceeded at an accelerated pace. In order to conserve space in the manuals there has grown up a system of abbreviations of authors' names. For example instead of using the full name of Linnaeus it is abbreviated by using simply the capital L. after the binomial name of the plant, or in some cases the surname is given in full without initials, as Gray for Asa Gray, the great American botanist.

As a matter of information and possible interest to the reader, there follows a complete list of the authors who named the shrubs in this bulletin, together with the abbreviations used in each case and the period in which they worked. In a few instances it has been impossible to secure all the desired information regarding the individual. Apparently records were inadequately kept or the authors did not publish widely enough to attract the attention of the chroniclers. These omissions have been noted at the proper point.

Adans.—Adanson, Michel; 1727–1806.
Ait.—Aiton, William; 1731–1793.
Anders.—Andersson, Nils Johan; 1821–1880.
Ashe—Ashe, William Willard; 1872–1932.
B. & H.—Bentham, George; 1800–1884; Hooker, Joseph Dalton; 1817–1911.
Bailey—Bailey, Liberty Hyde; 1858– .
Banks—Banks, Joseph; 1743–1820.
Barratt—Barratt, Josef; 1797–1882.
Bart.—Barton, William P.C.; 1786–1856.
Bebb—Bebb, Michael Schuck; 1833–1895.
B. Ehrh.—Ehrhart, Balthasar; 1700–1756.
Bess.—Besser, Wilibald Swibert Joseph Gottlieb; 1784–1842.

Best—Best, George Newton; 1846–1926.
Bickn.—Bicknell, Eugene Pintard; 1859–1925.
Bieb.—Bieberstein, F. A. M. von; 1768–1826.
Bigel.—Bigelow, Jacob; 1787–1879.
Blake—Blake, Sidney Fay; 1892– .
Blanch.—Blanchard, William Henry; 1850–1922.
Blume—Blume, Carl Ludwig; 1796–1862.
Britt.—Britton, Nathaniel Lord; 1859–1934.
Bush—Bush, Benjamin Franklin; 1858–1937.
Butters—Butters, Frederick King; 1878–1945.

C. A. Mey.—Meyer, Carl Anton von; 1795–1855.

Camp—Camp, W. H.; 1904– .

Coult.—Coulter, John Merle; 1851–1928.

Coult. & Evans—Coulter, John Merle; 1851–1928; Evans, Walter Harrison; 1863–1941.

Cov.—Coville, Frederick Vernon; 1867–1937.

Cov. & Britt.—Coville, Frederick V.; 1867–1937; Britton, Nathaniel Lord; 1859–1934.

Crép.—Crépin, François; 1830–1903.

Dcne.—Decaisne, Joseph; 1807–1882.

Dcne. & Planch.—Decaisne, Joseph; 1807–1882; Planchon, Jules Emile; 1823–1888.

DC.—DeCandolle, Augustin Pyramus; 1778–1841.

Deane—Deane, Walter; 1848–1930.

Desf.—Desfontaines, René Louiche; 1750–1833.

Dill.—Dillenius, Johann Jacob; 1684–1747.

Donn—Donn, James; 1758–1813.

Dougl.—Douglas, David; 1799–1834.

Drescher—Drescher, Aubrey A.; 1910–.

Dunal—Dunal, Michael Felix; 1789–1856.

Du Roi—Du Roi, Johann Philipp; 1741–1785.

Eat.—Eaton, Amos; 1776–1842.

Eggl.—Eggleston, Willard Webster; 1863–1935.

Ell.—Elliott, Stephen; 1771–1830.

Engl.—Engler, Heinrich Gustav Adolph; 1844–1930.

Erlan.—Erlanson, Eileen Whitehead; 1899–.

Evans—Evans, Walter Harrison; 1863–1941.

Fabric.—Fabricus, Phillip Conrad; 1714–1774.

Farw.—Farwell, Oliver Atkins; 1867–1944.

Fern.—Fernald, Merritt Lyndon; 1873– .

Fern. & Macbr.—Fernald, Merritt Lyndon; 1873– ; Macbride, J. Francis; 1892– .

Fern. & Weath.—Fernald, Merritt Lyndon; 1873– ; Weatherby, Charles A.; 1875– .

Flügge—Flügge, Johann; 1775–1816.

Forbes—Forbes, James; 1773–1861.

Fritsch—Fritsch, Karl; 1864–1934.

Fuller—Probably Fuller, Andrew Samuel; 1828–1896.

G. N. Jones—Jones, George Neville; 1904–.

Goldie—Goldie, John; 1793–1886.

Grauer—Grauer, a pupil of George Heinrich Weber, 1752–1828. Apparently no other information available in the United States.

Gray—Gray, Asa; 1810–1888.

Greene—Greene, Edward Lee; 1842–1915.

Gronov.—Gronovius, Jan Fredrik; 1690–1762.

Hanes—Hanes, Clarence R.; 1874–.

HBK—Humboldt, F. Alexander von; 1769–1859; Bonpland, Aimé; 1773–1858; Kunth, C. S.; 1788–1850.

Heller—Heller, Amos Arthur; 1867–1944.

Hermann—Hermann, Frederick J.; 1906– .

Hook.—Hooker, William Jackson; 1785–1865.

H. Winkl.—Winkler, Hubert; 1875–1941.

Jacq.—Jacquin, Nicolaus Joseph; 1727–1817.

J. F. Gmel.—Gmelin, Johann Friedrich; 1748–1804.

J. Lange—Lange, Johan Martin Christian; 1818–1898.

Kalm—Kalm, Pehr; 1716–1779.

Kern.—Kerner, Marilaun Anton Josef von; 1831–1898.

K. Koch—Koch, Karl Heinrich Emil; 1809–1879.

Knerr—Knerr, Ellsworth Brownell; 1861–1942.

L.—Linnaeus, Carolus; 1707–1778.

L. f.—Linnaeus, Carl von (the son); 1741–1783.

Lam.—Lamarck, J. B. A. P. Monnet; 1744–1829.

LeConte—LeConte, John Eaton; 1784–1860.

L'Hér.—L'Héritier de Brutelle, C. L.; 1746–1800.

Lindl.—Lindley, John; 1799–1865.

Link—Link, Heinrich Friedrich; 1767–1851.

Lodd. Loddiges, Conrad L.; 1738–1826.

Loud.—Loudon, John Claudius; 1783–1843.

Ludw.—Ludwig, Christian Gottlieb; 1709–1773.

Macbr.—Macbride, J. Francis; 1892– .

Mackenzie—Mackenzie, Kenneth Kent; 1877–1934.

Marsh.—Marshall, Humphrey; 1722–1801.

Maxim.—Maximowicz, Carl Johann; 1827–1891.

Medic.—Medicus, Fredrich Casimir; 1736–1808.

Michx.—Michaux, André; 1746–1802.

Mill.—Miller, Philip; 1691–1771.

Miq.—Miquel, Friedrich Anton Wilhelm; 1811–1871.

Moench—Moench, Konrad; 1744–1805.

Muhl.—Muhlenberg, G. H. E.; 1753–1815.

Munson—Munson, Thomas Volney; 1823–1913.

Nash—Nash, George Valentine; 1864–1919.

Neck.—Necker, Noel Joseph de; 1730–1793.

[25]

Glen Oaks College Library
Centreville, Michigan

Nees—Nees von Esenbeck, Christian Gott-
fried; 1776–1858.
Nutt.—Nuttall, Thomas; 1786–1859.
Oeder—Oeder, Georg Christian von; 1728–
1791.
Pall.—Pallas, Peter Simon; 1741–1811.
Palmer—Palmer, Ernest Jesse; 1875– .
Peck—Peck, Charles Horton; 1833–1917.
Pers.—Persoon, Christian Hendrik; 1761–
1836.
Planch.—Planchon, Jules Emile; 1823–
1888.
Poir.—Poiret, Jean Louis Marie; 1755–
1834.
Porter—Porter, Thomas Conrad; 1822–
1901.
Pursh—Pursh, Frederick Traugott; 1774–
1820.
R. & S.—Roemer, J. J.; 1763–1819; Schul-
tes, Joseph August; 1773–1831.
Raf.—Rafinesque-Schmaltz, C. S.; 1783–
1840.
Regel—Regel, Eduard August von; 1815–
1892.
Regel & Tiling—Regel, E. A. von; 1815–
1892; Tiling Heinrich Sylvester; died
1871.
Rehd.—Rehder, Alfred; 1863–.
Reichenb.—Reichenbach, Heinrich Gottlieb
Ludwig; 1793–1879.
Richards.—Richardson, John; 1787–1865.
Rob.—Robinson, Benjamin Lincoln; 1864–
1935.
Robbins—Robbins, James Watson; 1801–
1879.
Roem.—Roemer, Johann Jacob; 1763–1819.
Rowlee—Rowlee, Willard Winfield; 1861–
1923.
Rydb.—Rydberg, Per Axel; 1860–1931.
Salisb.—Salisbury, Richard Anthony; 1761–
1829.

Sarg.—Sargent, Charles Sprague; 1841–
1927.
Scheele—Scheele, Georg Heinrich Adolph;
1808–1864.
Schneid.—Schneider, Camillo Karl; 1876– .
Schrad.—Schrader, Heinrich Adolph; 1767–
1836.
Sm.—Smith, James Edward; 1759–1928.
Small—Small, John Kunkel; 1869–1938.
Spach—Spach, Edouard; 1801–1879.
Spreng.—Sprengel, Kurt; 1766–1833.
Syme—Boswell-Syme, John Thomas; 1822–
1888.
T. & G.—Torrey, John; 1796–1873; Gray,
Asa; 1810–1888.
Tausch—Tausch, Ignaz Friedrich; 1793–
1848.
Thory—Thory, Claude Antoine; 1759–
1827.
Thunb.—Thunberg, Carl Peter; 1743–
1828.
Torner—Torner, Eric, a pupil of Linnaeus.
Apparently no other information available
in the United States.
Torr.—Torrey, John; 1796–1873.
Tourn.—Tournefort, Joseph Pitton; 1656–
1708.
Trel.—Trelease, William; 1857–1941.
Vent.—Ventenat, Etienne Pierre; 1757–
1808.
Walt.—Walter, Thomas; 1740–1789.
Wang.—Wangenheim, F. A. J. von; 1749–
1800.
Wats.—Watson, Sereno; 1826–1892.
Weath.—Weatherby, Charles A.; 1875–
1949.
Wendl.—Wendland, Johann Christoph;
1791–1869.
Wieg.—Wiegand, Karl McKay; 1873–
1942.
Willd.—Willdenow, Carl Ludwig; 1765–
1812.
Wood—Wood, Alphonso; 1810–1881.

Plant Names and Their Origin

As stated above, plant names are now generally made up of two words. The first word represents the genus to which the plant belongs and is a noun. It is always written with a capital letter. The second word, which indicates the species, is an adjective or a noun and is rarely capitalized. Examples are: *Taxus canadensis* Marsh., *Rosa blanda* Ait., *Salix candida* Flügge. In some instances varieties are recognized and named. When this is the case the name of the plant consists of three words and it is written thus: *Rubus allegheniensis* Porter var. *Gravesii* Fernald; which means simply that Mr. Fernald has studied a *Rubus allegheniensis* which he feels is entitled to varietal rank and has named it after Mr. Graves. Some authors recognize smaller variations than are entitled to varietal designation. These are called "forma" or "form." In the interest of simplification the inclusion of varieties and forms has been somewhat limited in this bulletin. The species are gathered into genera, the genera into families, the families into orders, the orders into classes and the classes into divisions. The study of all these is highly interesting, but beyond the scope of this bulletin.

Generic names sometimes represent a character belonging to the entire group of species. Sometimes such names are ancient, having been in use prior to the time of Linnaeus and adopted by him. Others are fanciful and have no reference to the character of the plant named, while others seek to render imperishable the name of some man. A splendid example of the latter is the Twin-flower, which is named *Linnaea borealis,* being dedicated to Linnaeus, who first pointed out its characters and with whom it was a special favorite. Another is *Kalmia,* the laurel, dedicated to Pehr Kalm, a pupil of Linnaeus who traveled in America.

Here follows a list of all the generic names used in this bulletin, with a brief statement of their origin. Names in use before Linnaeus are referred to as ancient or classical.

Acer. The classical name, from the Celtic *ac,* hard.

Alnus. The ancient Latin name derived from the Celtic, in allusion to the growth of these plants along streams.

Amelanchier. The French name for the Medlar, a related plant.

Amorpha. From the Greek word meaning deformed, because of the absence of four of the petals.

Andromeda. Named by Linnaeus for Andromeda of Greek mythology. An example of fanciful naming above referred to.

Aralia. The derivation of this name is unknown.

Arceuthobium. From two Greek words, juniper and life, in reference to its living on conifers.

Arctostaphylos. Name composed of two Greek words meaning bear and cluster (of grapes).

Aronia. Slightly modified from *Aria,* the name of the beam tree of Europe.

Asimina. From the Indian name *Assimin.*

Benzoin. So named because of its odor, which resembles that of benzoin, an Oriental gum.

Berberis. The Latin form of *Berberys,* the Arabic name of the fruit.

Betula. The ancient name.

Ceanothus. An obscure name used by Theophrastus, probably misspelled.

Celastrus. Greek name of an evergreen tree.

Cephalanthus. Name composed of two Greek words meaning a head and a flower, head-flower.

Chamaedaphne. From two Greek words, on the ground and laurel; low laurel.

Chimaphila. Greek: winter-loving, in reference to the evergreen character of the plant.

Chiogenes. Name from two Greek words meaning snow and offspring, in reference to the snow-white berries.

Clematis. Greek: A name of Dioscorides for a climbing plant with long lithe branches.

Comptonia. Named for Bishop Compton, of Oxford.

Cornus. From the word *cornu,* a horn, in reference to the toughness of the wood.

Corylus. Name Greek, from the helmet-like involucre.

Crataegus. Named from a Greek word meaning strength, because of the hardness and toughness of the wood.

Decodon. Name a combination of two Greek words meaning ten-toothed, referring to the calyx.

Diervilla. A name given as a compliment to Dr. N. Dierville, who first carried the plant from Canada to Joseph Tournefort, the author of the genus.

Dirca. Name of uncertain derivation, but probably so called from a fountain in Thebes.

Empetrum. An ancient name derived from two Greek words meaning upon a rock.

Epigaea. Name composed of two Greek words meaning upon and the earth, referring to the trailing growth of the Arbutus.

Euonymus. Name from the ancient Greek words good and name.

Fatsia. From the Japanese vernacular name of one of the species.

Gaultheria. Named in honor of Dr. Hugues Gaulthier, a naturalist and physician of Quebec in the middle of the 18th century.

Gaylussacia. Named for the celebrated chemist, Gay-Lussac.

Grossularia. Resembling small, unripe figs.

Hamamelis. Greek, at the same time as the apple, the flowers and fruit being borne together.

Hudsonia. Named in honor of William Hudson, an early English botanist.

Hypericum. An ancient Greek name of obscure meaning.

Ilex. The ancient Latin name of the Holly Oak.

Juniperus. The classical name.

Kalmia. Dedicated to Pehr Kalm, pupil of Linnaeus, who traveled in America.

Ledum. Greek: *ledon,* the plant now called *Cistus Ledon.*

Lindera. Named for John Linder, a Swedish botanist of the 18th century.

Linnaea. Named by Gronovius for Linnaeus, with whom the plant was a special favorite.

Lonicera. Named in honor of Adam Lonitzer, a German botanist and explorer of the southern Allegheny Mountians.

Lyonia. Named for John Lyon, early American botanist and explorer of the southern Alleghenies.

Menispermum. Name from two Greek words, moon and seed.

Mitchella. Named in honor of Dr. John Mitchell, an excellent botanist who resided in Virginia and who early corresponded with Linnaeus.

Myrica. The ancient Greek name of the Tamarisk or some other shrub; or perhaps from the word meaning to perfume.

Nemopanthus. Name stated by the author to mean flower with a filiform peduncle.

Oplopanax. Greek: armor, armed, armed panax; referring to the densely bristly stems.

Parthenocissus. Derived from two Greek words, virgin and ivy.

Physocarpus. Name derived from two Greek words meaning a pair of bellows and fruit.

Potentilla. Diminutive of *potens,* powerful, from the medicinal properties of some species.

Prunus. The ancient Latin name of the plum tree.

Psedera. Name supposed to be a contraction of two Greek words, false and *hedera,* the ivy.

Ptelea. The Greek name of the elm, applied in this instance to a plant with similar fruit.

Pyrus. Latin name of the pear tree; classical spelling, *Pirus.*

Quercus. The classical Latin name of probable Celtic derivation meaning beautiful tree.

Rhamnus. The ancient Greek name.

Rhus. The ancient Greek and Latin name.

Ribes. The Arabic name, *ribes.*

Robinia. Named for John Robin, herbalist, and his son, Vespasin Robin, who first cultivated the locust tree in Europe.

Rosa. The ancient Latin name.

Rubus. The Roman name of the bramble, from *ruber,* red.

Salix. The classical Latin name.

Sambucus. Ancient Latin name of the elder.

Shepherdia. Named for John Shepherd, once curator of the Liverpool Botanical Gardens.

Smilax. An ancient Greek name of obscure meaning.

Solanum. Ancient Latin derivation, probably from *solor,* to quiet, referring to the plant's medicinal qualities.

Spiraea. From a Greek word meaning to twist, because of the twisting of the pods in some of the original species.

Staphylea. From the Greek word meaning a cluster.

Symphoricarpos. Name composed of two Greek words meaning to bear together, and fruit; referring to the clustered berries.

Taxus. The classical name, probably from the Greek name, a bow, the wood having been used for bows.

Vaccinium. Ancient Latin name of obscure derivation; perhaps blueberry.

Viburnum. The ancient Latin name.

Vitis. The classical Latin name.

Zanthoxylum. Derived from two Greek words meaning yellow and wood.

Specific names more generally refer to some distinctive peculiarity of the plant. Occasionally, however, as with generic names, the author has sought to honor some friend or famous person by naming a plant after him. A good example of this is *Cornus Baileyi* Coult. & Evans, which was named for L. H. Bailey, the eminent American author of horticultural works. For the most part, however, specific and varietal names refer to some outstanding character of the plant, its habit or the locality from which it was first described. These names are all Latinized in one form or another, the endings varying with the gender of the preceding generic noun.

In order that the student may gain an understanding of their meaning the following glossary of the Latin specific terms used in this bulletin is included.

abactus. To drive away, referring to the thorns.

acerifolium. Leaves like the maple.

acicularis. Slender, needle-shaped or needle-pointed.

aculeatissimus. Thorny, prickly or pointed.

aestivalis; aestivale. Summer-flowering.

affine. Related to others; with an affinity for.

alba; albicans; albinus; albus. Dead white, without luster.

albinervium. Whitish, pale.

allegheniensis. Growing in the Allegheny Mountains.

alnifolia; alnifolium. Leaves like the alder, or alnus.

Alnobetula. Two generic names modified and combined to make one specific name.

alternifolia. Leaves alternating on opposite sides of the stem.

americana; americanum; americanus. From America.

amoenum. Pleasing; nice.

Amomum. Referring to the acrid seeds of the shrub.

angustata; angustifolia; angustifolium. Narrow-leaved.

aquifolium. With pointed leaves.

arbutifolia. Leaves like the arbutus.

argentifolia. With silvery tinted foliage.

aromatica. Referring to the spicy smell of the leaves when crushed.

asperifolia. Rough-leaved.

asplenifolia. Like the fern genus *Asplenium.*

associus. Associated with. So named because found with other plants rare to the locality.

atrococcum. Having black fruit.

atropurpurea; atropurpureus; atropurpureum. Dark purple.

attractus. To draw to; attraction.

aureum. Golden-yellow color.

avellana. Latin, a filbert, drab, the color of the shell of the hazelnut.

avipes. Bird-footed.

baccata. Berry-like.

Baileyi; Baileyanus. Honoring L. H. Bailey, the eminent horticulturist and botanist.

balsamifera. Producing balsam.

Bartramiana. Honoring the early American botanist, William Bartram.

Bebbiana. Named in honor of Michael Schuch Bebb, 1833–1895, a distinguished student of willows.

bellobatus. A beautiful bramble.

Benzoin. So named because of its odor, which resembles that of benzoin, an Oriental gum.

bicolor. Two-colored.

bifarius. Arranged in two rows.

blanda. Smooth; agreeable; pleasant; charming.

borealis; boreus. Northern.

Bourgeauiana. Honoring Eugene Bourgeau, botanist, 1813–1877.

Brighamii. Named for H. C. Brigham, who discovered the plant near Toledo, Ohio.

Brittonii. Honoring Nathaniel Lord Britton, author of Britton's 'Manual of Botany,' 1905, and co-author of Britton & Brown's 'Illustrated Flora,' 1913.

caespitosum. Growing in tufts; matted.

caerulea. True blue; sky-blue.

calcicola. Referring to the habitat of the plant, marly swamps and limestone rocks.

calva. Bare; naked; without hairs.

calyculata. Having bracts resembling, or imitating, an outer calyx.

canadense; canadensis. Canadian.

candida. White; hoary.

canescens. Grayish-white; hoary.

canina. Pertaining to a dog; the dog-rose.

caprifolium. Literally goat-leaved; the honeysuckle plant.

carolina. From Carolina.

cassinoides. Helmet-shaped.

cathartica. With purging effect.

cauliflorus. Referring to the flower stalk.

centifolia. Hundred-leaved; many-leaved.

chiococcum. White-berried.

chrysocarpa. Yellow-fruited.

cinnamomea. Cinnamon-like, possibly referring to the fragrance of the flower.

circinata. Round-leaved.

cisatlantica. This side of the Atlantic.

coactilis. Felt-like; close pubescent.

coccinea. Scarlet.

communis. Growing together, or in society; common.

complex. Latin: closely connected.

conabilis. Latin: difficult.

conjuncta. Joined; united.

copallina. Yielding gum-copal.

cordata. Heart-shaped, referring to the leaves.

cordifolia. Having heart-shaped leaves.

cornuta. Latin: a horn; horned or spurred.

corymbosum. Arranged in corymbs (flat-topped clusters).

crinitum. With long hairs.

crispa. Curled closely.

Crus-galli. Cock-spur.

cuneata. Wedge-shaped.

Cynosbati. Dogberry.

Deamii. Honoring Charles C. Deam, the noted Indiana botanist.

denudata. Bare.

dentatum. Toothed, as saw teeth.

depressa. Flattened; lying down flat.

dioica. With the stamens and pistils in separate flowers on different plants.

discolor. Two-colored; having different colors.

dissensus. Not in harmony with the others.

distinctus. Decidedly different.

Dodgei. Named for Charles Keene Dodge, distinguished Michigan botanist, 1844–1918.

Douglasii. Named for David Douglas, botanist 1798–1834.

Dulcamara. The ancient name, probably composed of *dulce,* sweet, and *amare,* bitter; or, transposed, bittersweet, a common name for the plant.

Eamesii. Honoring Dr. Edwin H. Eames.

Emersoniana. Named for George Barrell Emerson, author of 'Trees and Shrubs in Massachusetts,' 1875.

eriocephala. Woolly-headed.

flagellaris. Whip-like, in reference to the long, slender stems.

Florenceae. Dedicated to Mrs. Florence Hanes, Schoolcraft, Michigan.

floridum. Bearing flowers; flowering.

Frangula. Latin name during ancient times.

frondosa; frondosus. With abundant foliage.

fruticosa; fruticosus. Bushy; shrubby.

Gale. An aromatic plant.

gallica. Of French origin.

gaspensis. Referring to place of original collection, the Gaspé Peninsula.

glabra. Smooth; without hairs.

glabrifolia. With smooth foliage.

glandulifera. Having small glands.

glandulosa; glandulosum. Glandular.

glaucescens. Covered with a gray bloom; glaucous.

glaucocarpa. Bearing glaucous fruits.

glaucophylla. Having gray-blue leaves.

glaucophylloides. Bearing glaucous leaves.

globosom. Ball-shaped; globe.

gracile; gracilis. Slender, slight in form.

grandiflorus. With flowers larger than usual.

groenlandicum. From Greenland.

Grossularia. Resembling small unripe figs.

Hanesii. Honoring Mr. Clarence R. Hanes, Schoolcraft, Michigan, who with Mrs. Hanes, furnished Dr. Bailey with many new species of the genus.

Hermanni. Named in honor of Frederick J. Hermann, a contemporary worker.

heteradenius. Having different kinds of glands.

hirsuta. Rough, hairy; having long distinct hairs.

hirtellum. Minutely hairy; pubescent.

hispida; hispidula; hispidus. Having stiff hairs or bristles.

horizontalis. Level; horizontal.

horrida, horridum. Horrible; offensive.

hudsonianum. In reference to Hudson Bay.

humilis. Low-growing.

huronensis. Referring to location, vicinity of Lake Huron.

hypoglauca. In reference to the glaucous underside of the leaves.

hypomalaca; hypomalacum; hypomalacus. Soft pubescent underneath.

hyporhysa. Wrinkled underneath.

idaeus. From Mount Ida, in reference to European origin.

incana. Gray with age; hoary.

inserta. Connected; supported; referring to mode of attachment.

interior. Inland, away from the coasts.

intermedia; intermedium; intermedius. Intermediate between two forms.

intonsa. Having hairs; bearded.

intricata. Entangled; intricate.

involucrata. With an involucre.

japonica. From Japan.

jejunus. Poor; small.

kalamazoensis. Named for Kalamazoo County, Michigan.

Kalmianum. Named for Pehr Kalm.

keweenawensis. Named for the Keweenaw Peninsula of Michigan.

labrusca. A very old name pertaining to the wild grapevine.

laciniatus. Cut into narrow lobes.

lacorum. Of the lakes.

lacustre. Living by the lake.

laetabilis. Attractive; graceful.

laevigatum; laevigatus. Smooth; slippery.

Lamarckii. Named in honor of the early botanist, J. B. A. P. Monnet Lamarck.

lanceolata. Leaves narrow, tapering to each end, like a lance.

lantanoides. Resembling mountain-sage, lantana.

latifolia. With broad leaves.

latisepala. With broad sepals.

Lentago. Ancient Latin name of a shrub.

leucocarpa; leucocarpum. Bearing white fruit.

licens. Growing vigorously, or luxuriantly.

ligustrina. Privet-like; resembling privet.

limulus. Somewhat askew; oblique.

localis. Of, or belonging to a place.

longifolia. Bearing long leaves.

Lonicera. Named for Adam Lonitzer, a German botanist, 1526–1586. The honeysuckle.

lucida. Shining; glistening.

Lunellii. Honoring Joel Lunell, botanist, 1851–1920.

Lyoni. Honoring John Lyon, an early American botanist.

macrocarpon. Bearing large fruit.

macrosperma. With large seeds, referring to the nutlets.

maculata. Spotted.

Margaretta. Named for Mrs. William Willard Ashe.

mediocris. Ordinary; in a middle state between too much and too little.

melanocarpa. Bearing dark or black fruit.

membranaceum. Being of the texture of membranes.

meracus. Latin: pure; unmixed.

michiganensis. Named for Michigan.

microphylla. Small-leaved.

minus. Small; less.

missouriense; missouriensis. Missouri, the original collection having been made in that state.

mollis. Soft; tender.

Morrowi. Named for Dr. James Morrow, who travelled extensively in Japan.

mucronata. Having a stiff and sharp point.

multiflora. Many-flowered.

myrtilloides. Resembling *Vaccinium myrtillus,* whortelberry.

neglectus. Insignificant; unobserved.

nigra; nigrum. Black.

nigricans. Turning black.

notatus. To note; designate.

obliqua. Oblique, probably referring to a character of the stone.

oblongata. Longer than broad; sides nearly parallel (of leaves).

oblongifolia. With oblong leaves.

obovalis; obovatus. Reversed ovate, attached at smaller end (of leaves).

occidentalis. Western.

odoratum; odoratus. Sweet-smelling; fragrant.

officinalis. Medicinal.

oligocarpa. Bearing but little fruit.

opulifolius. Having leaves like the snowball bush, *Virburnum Opulus.*

Opulus. Snowball; cranberry.

orbiculatis. Circular.

ovalifolium. Bearing oval leaves.

ovatum. With ovate leaves.

ovatus. Ovate, the broader end toward the base.

oxyacanthoides. Resembling the hawthorn, with sharp spines.

Oxycoccos. Bearing acid berries; cranberry.

padifolia. Leaves as in *Prunus Padus,* Black Dogwood.

pallidum; pallidus. Pale in color.

palustris. Bog-loving; growing in swampy ground.

paniculata. Having panicles of flowers.

parviflorus. Bearing small flowers.

pauciflorum; pauciflorus. With few flowers.

pauper. Poor; moderate; meagre.

pedatifidus. Divided in a pedate manner (nearly to the base).

pedicellaris. With distinct flower stalks.

pedicellata. Referring to the pedicel.

pellita. In reference to the fine pubescence.

pennsylvanicum. From Pennsylvania.

peracer. Very sharp, alluding to the thorns.

peregrina. Exotic; foreign; strange.

pergratus. Latin; very pleasant.

perspicuus. Clear; evident; growing in large colonies.

petiolaris. Stalked; petioled.

philadelphica. Named for the locality from which the plant was first collected.

plausus. Latin: approved; excellent.

plus. Possessing additional qualities.

Polifolia (Andromeda). Smooth-leaved.

polifolia (Kalmia). With leaves like the Germander, *Teucrium Polium.*

potis. Vigorous; flowers many and large.

pratincola. Meadow- or prairie-growing.

prinoides. Resembling *Quercus Prinus.*

procumbens. Lying along the ground; trailing.

prolificum. Prolific.

prostratum. Lying flat on the ground.

pruinosa. Having a waxy, powdery secretion on the surface.

prunifolia; prunifolium. Bearing leaves like the plum tree.

pubens; pubescens. Pubescent; downy with soft short hairs.

pumila. Low; dwarfish; little.

punctata. Marked with dots.

pusillum. Small; weak; slender.

pyracanthifolia. Leaves narrow, as in *Pyracantha.*

quadrangularis. Four-angled; cut square.

quinquefolia. Five leaflets.

racemosa; racemosus. Bearing racemes.

radicans. Rooting.

Rappii. Named for Mr. Fred W. Rapp, who discovered the plant near Vicksburg, Michigan.

repens. Creeping and rooting.

rigida. Stiff; inflexible.

rigidiuscula. Somewhat rigid.

ringens. Gaping open, in reference to the flower.

riparia. Growing on the banks of rivers or streams.

Rosa. Rose-like.

rostrata. Having a beak.

rotunda. Rounded in outline.

rotundifolia. Having round leaves.

rubiginosa. Rust-colored; rusty.

rugosa. Wrinkled.

Rydbergii. Honoring Per Axel Rydberg, noted contemporary botanist.

salicifolia. Bearing leaves like the willow.

sanguinea; sanguineus. Blood-red; bloody.

sativum. Sown or planted for crops.

Sayiana. Dedicated to Thomas Say, eminent naturalist.

saxosum. Rocky, in reference to the habitat.

scandens. Climbing.

Schoolcraftianus. Dedicated to the memory of Henry Rowe Schoolcraft, explorer, 1793–1864.

Schuetteana. In commemoration of Joachim Heinrich Schuette.

sempervirens. Evergreen; persistent during the winter.

sera. Late growing, or flowering.

sericea. Silky.

serissima. Late-fruiting.

setigera. Bristle-bearing.

setosum. Beset with bristles.

Solonis. Named for Dr. David Solon Chase Hall Smith, who first discovered the plant in 1815.

sphaerocarpum. Bearing ball-like fruits.

spicata; spicatum. Spike-like; pointed.

spinosa. Bearing spines; spiny.

spinosissima. Very spiny; most spiny.

stamineum. With prominent stamens; stamen-like.

stolonifera. Bearing suckers or runners.

strigosus. Closely covered with pointed bristles.

succulenta. Referring to the soft character of the pomes.

suffulta. Supported beneath.

superioris. Surpassing in quality; finer; higher grade.

susquehanae. In reference to the original locality, the banks of the Susquehanna River.

syrticola. Growing on a sand bank.

tantalus. So little; so small.

tatarica. From Tartary, referring to the place of origin.

tenuicaulis. With thin stalks.

tenuifolia. With fine or slender leaves.

textoris. Woven; referring to the use of the twigs in making baskets.

Thunbergii. Named in honor of the early botanist, Carl Pehr Thunberg.

tomentosa. Covered with short, soft matted hairs; woolly.

Toxicodendron. Poison-leaved.

triflorus. Three-flowered.

trifolia; trifoliata. With three leaflets; three-leaved.

triloba; trilobum. With three lobes.

tristis; triste. Dull-colored; sad; gray.

typhina. Shaped like antlers.

typica. Having the distinguishing features of a type.

uliginosum. Growing in mud.

umbellata. Bearing umbels.

Uva-ursi. Bearberry.

uvidus. Juicy, referring to the berries.

vacillans. Swaying; unsteady.

vagus. Uncertain; not clear; inconstant.

variispinus. With variable spines.

Vernix. Varnish.

versicolor. Changing color; different colors.

verticillata; verticillatus; verticillaris. Whorled.

villosa; villosus. Downy; with shaggy hairs.

virginiana. Virginian.

viridis. Green.

viscosa. Sticky; clammy.

vitaceae. Vine-like; like the grape vine.

Vitis-Idaea. Very ancient name of doubtful application.

vulgare; vulgaris. Common.

vulpina. Fox-like; alluding to the reddish-brown color of a fox.

Wheeleri. Named for Dr. C. F. Wheeler, an early Michigan botanist.

Woodsii. Honoring Alphonso Wood, noted botanical writer, 1810–1881.

Xylosteum. The ancient name.

The Form and Structure of Shrubs

A pictorial glossary of the principal terms used in
describing the shrubs included in this bulletin

When I informed a friend that I was compiling a bulletin on the shrubs of Michigan, he instantly asked if sufficient pictures were being used to make the work useful to beginners, stating that no amount of words could take the place of illustrations. Concurring in the idea, although the usual glossary had already been prepared, I decided to include illustrations for those descriptive terms which would permit of such treatment and which illustration would make more understandable. The illustrations are arranged alphabetically in accordance with the usual practice for glossaries, and it is hoped they will prove useful to the student .

In the descriptions of the shrubs there will be found many combinations of the terms herein listed and illustrated. For example "crenulate-serrate" and "crenulate-denticulate." The terms are thus used to indicate a combination of forms somewhat modified. Teeth which are crenulate-serrate would be neither purely crenulate nor serrate, but an intergrading of the two. The same applies to crenulate-denticulate.

In the shapes of leaves we have the same thing. A leaf may be too narrow to be classed as elliptic and still too wide to be strictly lanceolate. When this occurs it is called elliptic-lanceolate, a modification of the two forms. Linear-lanceolate is another combination of descriptive terms the meaning of which is obvious.

In the shape of the corolla will be found such descriptive terms as long-campanulate. In this case the corolla is bell-shaped, but the tube is somewhat longer than in a strictly campanulate form.

The same principle holds true in describing fruits, where we find the term subglobose to describe a berry which is slightly less than a globe in form.

The student will have no difficulty in mastering these combined terms. They are too inexact to translate into satisfactory illustrations and are further evidence of the great variability of plants and the difficulty experienced by man in trying to fit descriptions accurately to them.

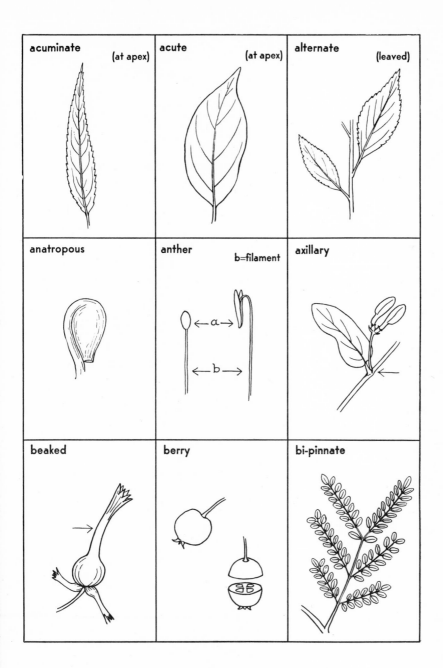

acuminate (at apex)

acute (at apex)

alternate (leaved)

anatropous

anther b=filament

axillary

beaked

berry

bi-pinnate

[35]

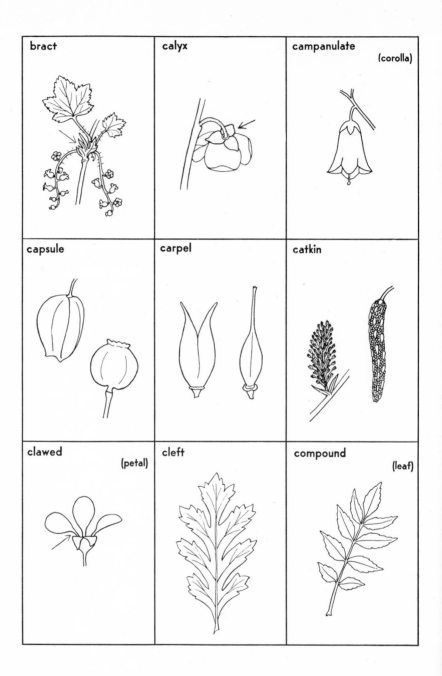

bract	calyx	campanulate (corolla)
capsule	carpel	catkin
clawed (petal)	cleft	compound (leaf)

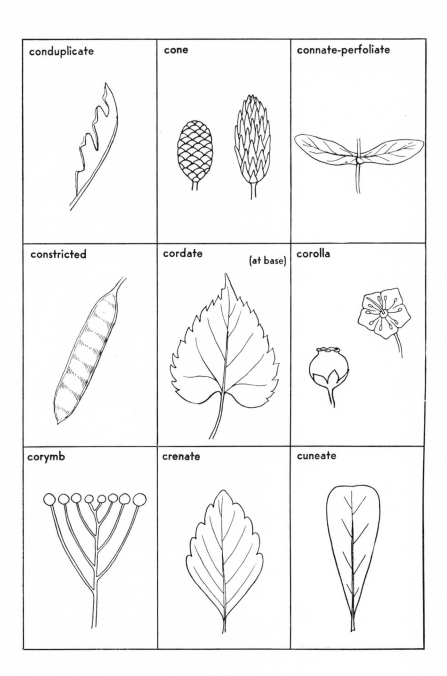

conduplicate

cone

connate-perfoliate

constricted

cordate (at base)

corolla

corymb

crenate

cuneate

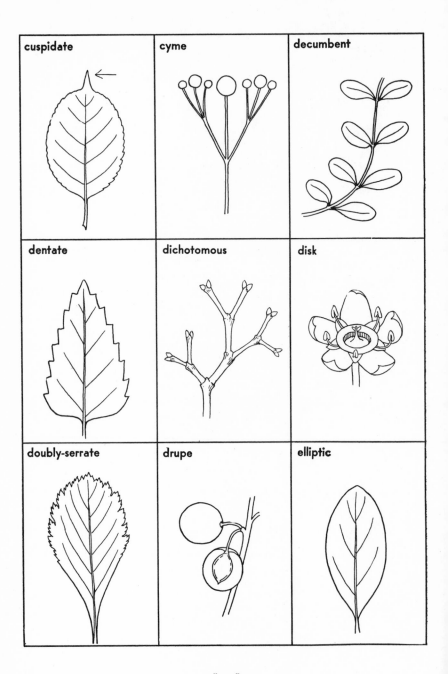

cuspidate	cyme	decumbent
dentate	dichotomous	disk
doubly-serrate	drupe	elliptic

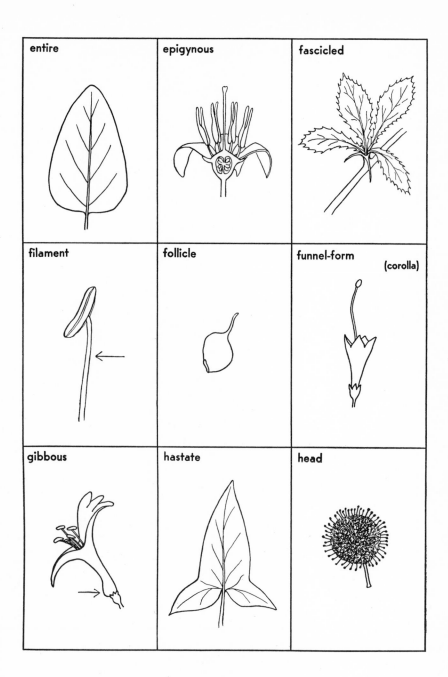

entire

epigynous

fascicled

filament

follicle

funnel-form
(corolla)

gibbous

hastate

head

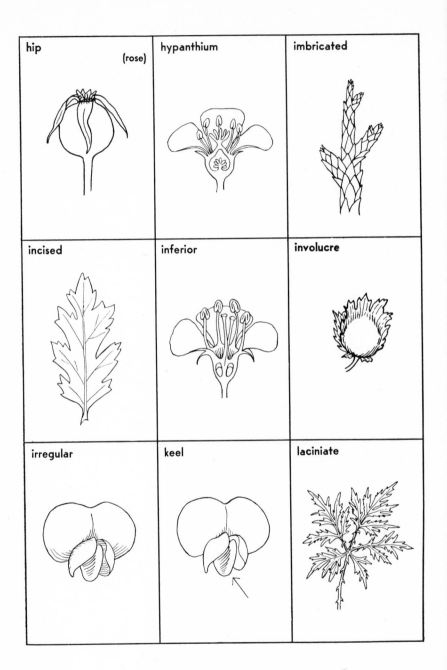

hip (rose)	hypanthium	imbricated
incised	inferior	involucre
irregular	keel	laciniate

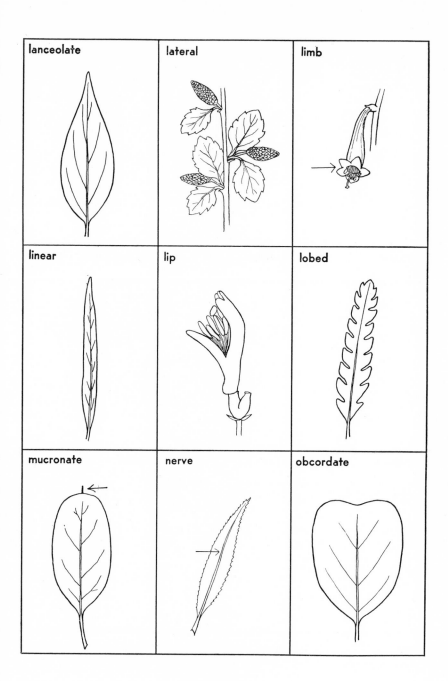

lanceolate	lateral	limb
linear	lip	lobed
mucronate	nerve	obcordate

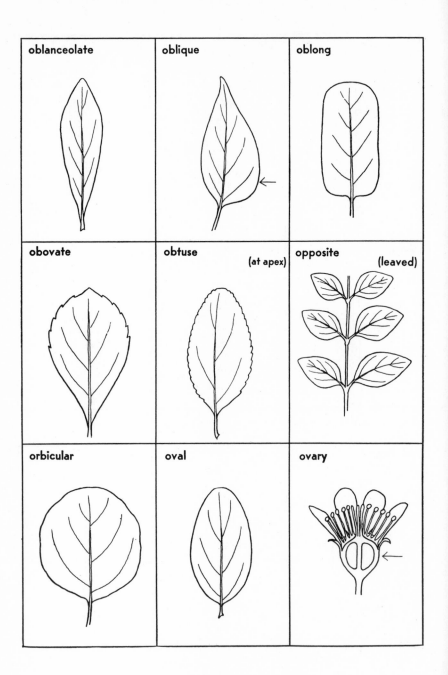

oblanceolate	oblique	oblong
obovate	obtuse (at apex)	opposite (leaved)
orbicular	oval	ovary

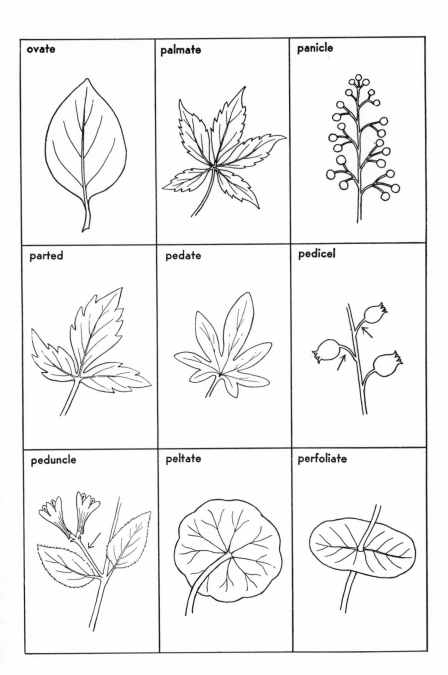

ovate

palmate

panicle

parted

pedate

pedicel

peduncle

peltate

perfoliate

[43]

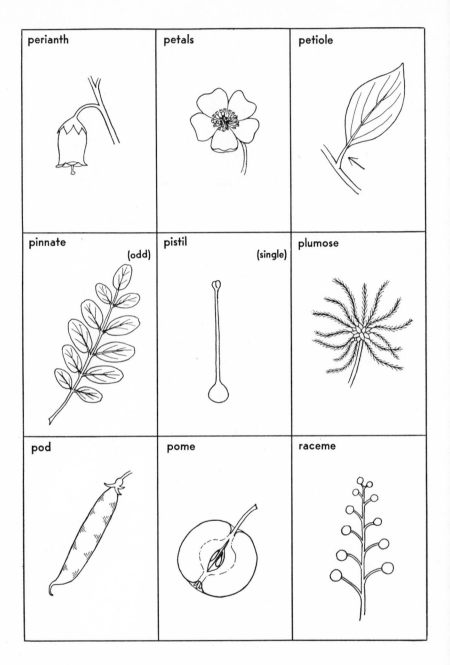

perianth	petals	petiole
pinnate (odd)	pistil (single)	plumose
pod	pome	raceme

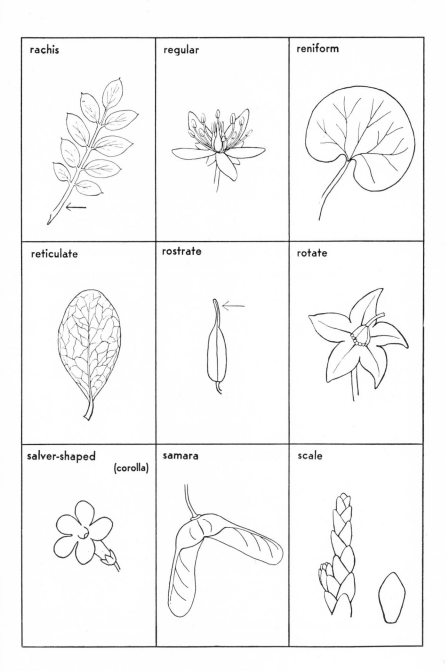

rachis	regular	reniform
reticulate	rostrate	rotate
salver-shaped (corolla)	samara	scale

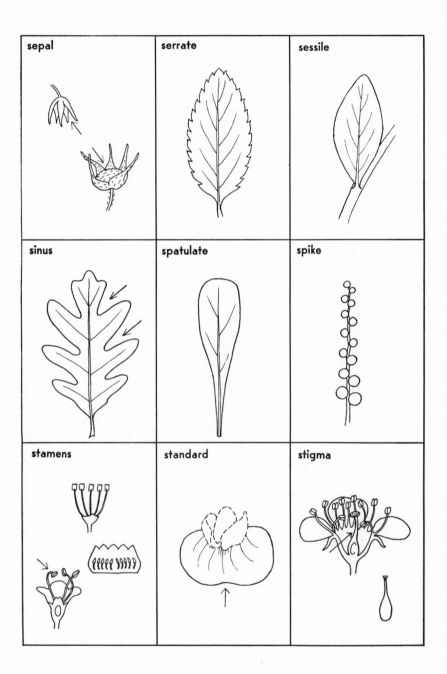

sepal

serrate

sessile

sinus

spatulate

spike

stamens

standard

stigma

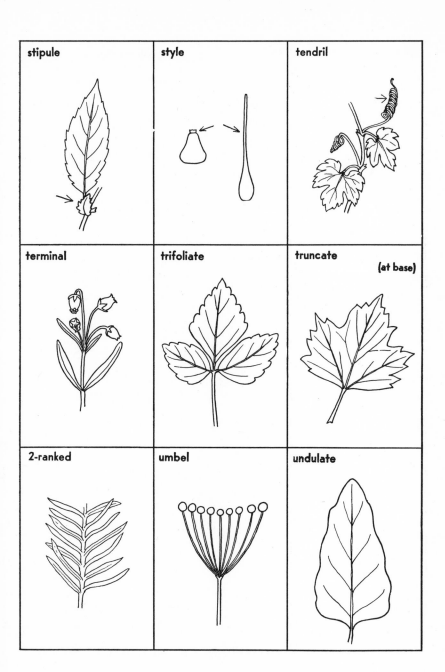

stipule	style	tendril
terminal	trifoliate	truncate (at base)
2-ranked	umbel	undulate

urceolate

vein

whorled

winged

Keys to the Genera of Michigan Shrubs

These keys follow the general style of 'Keys to Woody Plants,' by W. C. Muenscher, 1936, Ithaca, N. Y.

KEY I

Shrubs with scale-like, linear or needle-like leaves.

1. Leaves alternate, scattered
    2. Leaves less than 3 mm. long, scale-like, close pressed and imbricated, densely pubescent; low shrub..*Hudsonia*, p. 229
    2. Leaves more than 3 mm. long, not scale-like
        3. Leaves strongly involute, blunt; fruit a red or pulpy berry-like drupe..*Empetrum*, p. 192
        3. Leaves flat, green beneath, sharp-pointed, not over 2 mm. wide; fruit red, drupe-like ....*Taxus*, p. 57
1. Leaves opposite or in whorls of 3
    4. Leaves opposite, connate, suborbicular, about 1 mm. wide; very small parasitic plants growing on coniferous trees; fruit a berry..*Arceuthobium*, p. 95
    4. Leaves in whorls of 3, needle-like, with a white line beneath, or sometimes scale-like on the same plant; terrestrial evergreen shrubs; fruit a berry-like cone.. ....*Juniperus*, p. 57

KEY II

Shrubs with opposite, compound leaves.

1. Leaflets 3
    2. Stems climbing or twining; vines; petioles bending and clasping; bark not white-striped; flowers cymose-paniculate; fruit an achene furnished with the persistent plumose style.................................*Clematis*, p. 97
    2. Stems not climbing or twining; shrubs; petioles long, not bending or clasping; older bark white-striped; flowers in drooping racemes; fruit a bladder-like inflated capsule...*Staphylea*, p. 208
1. Leaflets 5–11, oblong, or ovate-lanceolate; bark with large, raised corky lenticels; flowers in compound cymes; fruit small and berry-like..............*Sambucus*, p. 309

KEY III

Shrubs with alternate compound leaves.

1. Leaves bipinnately compound; stems prickly; fruit drupe-like......................*Aralia*, p. 233
1. Leaves once compound
    2. Leaves 3-foliate
        3. Stipules present
            4. Stipules attached to the petiole for at least half their length; fruit a fleshy hip...................................*Rosa*, in part, p. 169
            4. Stipules not attached to the petiole for half their length; fruit an aggregation of many small drupelets............*Rubus*, in part, p. 151
        3. Stipules absent
            5. Lateral leaflets not symmetrical; without tendrils; often climbing by aerial roots; fruit a whitish drupe........................*Rhus radicans*, p. 199
            5. Lateral leaflets symmetrical
                6. Petioles 1–3 cm. long, leaf margins crenate; fruit a red drupe..*Rhus aromatica*, p. 199
                6. Petioles 5–10 cm. long; leaf margins entire or serrulate; fruit a winged samara..*Ptelea*, p. 191
    2. Leaves more than 3-foliate

7. Leaves palmately compound
  8. Stems with spines or prickles; biennial; fruit a collection of small
      drupes on a spongy receptacle...*Rubus,* in part, p. 151
  8. Stems without spines or prickles; a vine climbing by branched
      tendrils; perennial; fruit a berry...*Parthenocissus,* p. 219
7. Leaves pinnately compound
  9. Stems without thorns, prickles, or bristles
    10. Leaflets entire
      11. Leaflets 21–51, about 1–1.5 cm. long, white-canescent;
          fruit a pod..*Amorpha,* p. 185
      11. Leaflets fewer, not subtended by stipels
        12. Leaflets 5–7, about 1 cm. long, silky; low shrub with
            shreddy bark; petals yellow; fruit a collection
            of dry achenes...*Potentilla,* p. 149
        12. Leaflets 7–13, about 4–11 cm. long, mostly glabrous;
            tall shrub with smooth bark; petals greenish-yellow;
            fruit a small whitish drupe....................................*Rhus Vernix,* p. 197
    10. Leaflets dentate, or only a few-toothed toward the apex, opposite,
        nearly sessile; axis of leaf wing-margined in one species;
        sap milky; fruit a sort of dry drupe....................................*Rhus,* in part, p. 193
  9. Stems bearing thorns, prickles, or bristles
    13. Stipules present; leaflets not dotted with pellucid glands
      14. Stipules small and spiny; margin of leaflets entire,
          elliptical; fruit a dry several-seeded pod.............................*Robinia,* p. 187
      14. Stipules large, not spiny
        15. Stipules attached to the petiole half their length
            or more; margin of leaflets evenly serrate;
            fruit a fleshy hip...*Rosa,* in part, p. 169
        15. Stipules attached at the base of the petiole only;
            margin of leaflets generally coarsely and unevenly
            toothed or doubly serrate; fruit an aggregation
            of many small drupelets.................................*Rubus,* in part, p. 151
    13. Stipules absent; leaflets dotted with pellucid glands,
        margins entire; wood yellow; fruit a capsule
        with strong lemon flavor..*Zanthoxylum,* p. 191

KEY IV

Shrubs with opposite or whorled simple leaves.

1. Leaves with lobes
  2. Petioles usually with stipules and glands; fruit a drupe......*Viburnum,* in part, p. 297
  2. Petioles without stipules and glands; fruit a samara...............................*Acer,* p. 209
1. Leaves without lobes
  3. Stems climbing, creeping, prostrate, or forming low mats
    4. Leaves deciduous
      5. Leaves connate, entire, sessile, or on stalks less than 8 mm.
          long, green beneath; flowers large, 2-lipped, yellow or red;
          fruit a berry; seeds not red....................................*Lonicera,* in part, p. 283
      5. Leaves oblanceolate, finely serrate, nearly sessile; flowers small,
          regular, disc-shaped, dark-maroon; fruit a rough
          capsule; seeds red...*Euonymus,* in part, p. 205
    4. Leaves persistent
      6. Leaves entire or slightly undulate, base cordate or rounded,
          glabrous; fruit a red berry...*Mitchella,* p. 279
      6. Leaves crenate, rounded-oval, contracted at the base,
          pubescent; fruit a capsule...*Linnaea,* p. 296
  3. Stems erect or ascending
    7. Margin of leaves entire
      8. Leaves and twigs covered with rusty scales. ....*Shepherdia,* p. 231
      8. Leaves and twigs not covered with rusty scales

9. Leaves with pellucid dots; low shrubs; fruit a capsule....................................*Hypericum*, p. 227
9. Leaves without pellucid dots
   10. Twigs 2-edged, flattened or winged; leaves sessile or practically so,
      leathery, lower surface glaucous, margin serrate...................*Kalmia polifolia*, p. 253
   10. Twigs not 2-edged, flattened or winged; leaves with distinct petioles
      11. Leaves persistent, tending to be crowded toward the end of the
         season's growth, often in whorls of 3, leathery;
         fruit a capsule..*Kalmia*, in part, p. 251
      11. Leaves deciduous, opposite or verticillate
         12. Stems semi-herbaceous, woody at base, forming aerenchyma,
            sometimes rooting at the tip; flowers in axillary cymes.....*Decodon*, p. 232
         12. Stems entirely woody, not forming aerenchyma and
            never rooting at the tip
            13. Lateral buds above the axils, imbedded in the bark;
               leaves often in whorls of 3;
               fruit a head of nutlets......................................*Cephalanthus*, p. 280
            13. Lateral buds axillary, not imbedded in the bark;
               leaves opposite; fruit a berry or drupe
               14. Bark of stems and branches loose, peeling
                  off in shreddy pieces; fruit a berry
                  15. Twigs very slender; low shrub, 3–10 dm.
                     tall; bundle-scar 1......................*Symphoricarpos*, p. 293
                  15. Twigs of medium thickness; tall shrubs,
                     over 1 meter in height;
                     bundle-scars 3...............................*Lonicera*, in part, p. 283
               14. Bark of stems and older branches smooth, not
                 peeling off in long shreds; fruit a drupe
                  16. Leaves with lateral veins running somewhat
                    parallel with margin and meeting
                    near the apex................................*Cornus*, in part, p. 237
                  16. Leaves with lateral veins ending near the
                    margin and not running
                    to the apex................................*Viburnum*, in part, p. 297
7. Margin of leaves not entire, usually serrate or dentate
   17. Opposite bases of petioles connected by a distinct transverse line or ridge
      18. Buds naked or with 1 pair of visible bud scales;
         fruit a fleshy drupe...*Viburnum*, in part, p. 297
      18. Buds not naked, with several overlapping scales;
         fruit a dry capsule...*Diervilla*, p. 281
   17. Opposite bases of petioles not connected by a distinct transverse
     line or ridge; leaves glabrous on upper surface; petiole 5–18 mm. long;
     branchlets green; fruit a smooth capsule..........................*Euonymus*, in part, p. 205

KEY V

Shrubs with alternate simple leaves.

1. Leaves with lobes
   2. Stems climbing or twining
      3. Leaves with one or more lateral lobes on each side of midrib;
         crushed leaves and stems with rank odor;
         fruit a red berry..*Solanum*, in part, p. 277
      3. Leaves palmately-lobed and veined; crushed leaves and stems
         without rank odor; fruit a berry or drupe
         4. Stems provided with coiled tendrils; leaves not peltate,
            lobes acute; fruit a berry..*Vitis*, p. 220
         4. Stems twining, tendrils absent; leaves peltate near the edge,
            lobes rounded; fruit a drupe....................................*Menispermum*, p. 99
   2. Stems erect

5. Leaves distinctly palmately lobed
   6. Older bark separating in numerous thin layers
      7. Leaves and twigs glandular-clammy;
         fruit an aggregation of drupelets................................*Rubus,* in part, p. 151
      7. Leaves and twigs not glandular-clammy;
         fruit an inflated pod...*Physocarpus,* **p. 119**
   6. Older bark close, not separating in layers
      8. Leaves glandular beneath; petiole short; spines generally
         present; fruit a smooth or prickly berry....................................*Ribes,* p. 104
      8. Leaves not glandular beneath, 1–3 dm. in diameter;
         spines present on midrib; petioles long; flowers greenish-
         white in panicles; fruit a 2-seeded drupe.........................*Oplopanax,* p. 235
5. Leaves not as above
   9. Leaves pinnately lobed
      10. Leaves with numerous deep, rounded lobes on each side of the
         midrib, sweet-scented shrubs; fruit small, nut-like..........*Comptonia,* **p. 85**
      10. Leaves with few to several shallow, rounded or pointed lobes
         on each side of the midrib; not sweet-scented
         11. Leaves 1–2 dm. long; buds clustered at ends
            of branches; fruit an acorn................................*Quercus,* in part, p. 93
         11. Leaves 2–13 cm. long, buds not clustered at ends of
            twigs; fruit a small pome............................*Crataegus,* in part, p. 134
   9. Leaves not pinnately lobed, but irregularly lobed;
      buds scaly...*Crataegus,* in part, p. 134
1. Leaves without lobes
   12. Leaves with entire margins
      13. Leaves generally with a pair of tendrils at base of the petiole;
         stems usually with spines or prickles, green and climbing;
         fruit a blue or black berry...*Smilax,* p. 61
      13. Leaves without tendrils at base of petiole; stems spineless
         14. Leaves persistent, leathery, and sometimes revolute
            15. Stems creeping, prostrate, or forming dense low mats
               16. Stems covered with brown hairs
                  17. Leaves 0.5–1.5 cm. long with coarse
                     brown scale-like hairs on lower surface;
                     fruit a white berry...............................*Chiogenes,* p. 259
                  17. Leaves 2–8 cm. long, oval oblong, rugose,
                     glabrous or pubescent; fruit a capsule........*Epigaea,* p. 256
               16. Stems not covered with brown hairs
                  18. Leaves glaucous on lower
                     surface..............*Vaccinium,* in part (cranberries), p. 273
                  18. Leaves green on the lower surface
                     19. Leaves with black dots on the lower
                         surface, thick and leathery, 5–18 mm.
                         long, oval or obovate.....*Vaccinium Vitis-Idaea,* p. 273
                     19. Leaves without black dots on the lower
                         surface, 1–1.5 cm. long,
                         obovate-spatulate......................*Arctostaphylos,* p. 259
           15. Stems erect
               20. Lower surface of leaves covered with dense, woolly,
                 rusty-brown hairs; fruit a capsule.........................*Ledum,* p. 249
               20. Lower surface of leaves not densely
                 covered with rusty-brown hairs
                  21. Leaves white on the lower surface,
                     linear-lanceolate, revolute; low shrubs;
                     fruit a subglobose capsule.....................*Andromeda,* p. 253
                  21. Leaves light green on lower surface,
                       leathery, slightly revolute, fruit a
                     subglobose capsule...........................*Kalmia,* in part, p. 251
         14. Leaves deciduous, not revolute

22. Bark and leaves aromatic; flowers yellow, before the leaves, which are
oblong-obovate and pale beneath; fruit a red obovoid drupe.....................*Lindera*, p. 103
22. Bark and leaves not spicy-aromatic
   23. Vines or scrambling shrubs; leaves ovate, base often cordate or lobed;
crushed leaves and stems with strong disagreeable odor;
fruit a red berry...*Solanum*, in part, p. 277
   23. Erect shrubs
      24. Branchlets enlarged at the nodes; bark very fibrous and leathery;
flowers before the leaves, which are oval-obovate;
fruit a red ovoid drupe..*Dirca*, p. 229
      24. Branchlets not enlarged at the nodes
         25. Lateral veins running parallel to the margins of the leaf and
ending near the apex; leaves ovate, obovate or oval, 5–9 cm.
long, clustered at the ends of the branches;
fruit small, globose, blue when ripe.......................*Cornus*, in part, p. 237
         25. Lateral veins not running parallel to the margin of the leaf
            26. Leaves 1.5–3 dm. long, not crowded at the ends of the lateral
branches; fruit 7–13 cm. long, pulpy when ripe......*Asimina*, p. 99
            26. Leaves smaller; fruit not as above
               27. Each bud covered with a single hood-like scale;
flowers in catkins...*Salix*, in part, p. 63
               27. Each bud covered by more than one scale; flowers not in catkins
                  28. Petioles 6–12 mm. long; apex of leaf
mucronate; fruit red, drupe-like
on long pedicels....................................*Nemopanthus*, p. 203
                  28. Petioles less than 1 cm. long, or none
                     29. Lower surface of leaves covered with
yellow resinous dots
                       30. Leaves when crushed sweet-scented;
apex of leaf rounded, often with a few
teeth; fruit a waxy drupe....*Myrica*, in part, p. 85
                       30. Leaves not sweet-scented
                           31. Fruit a capsule.........*Lyonia*, in part, p. 255
                           31. Fruit a berry......*Gaylussacia*, in part, p. 261
                     29. Lower surface of leaves not covered
with yellow resinous dots
                       32. Branchlets greenish or reddish and
minutely white-speckled or hairy;
fruit a berry.............. ...*Vaccinium*, in part, p. 263
                       32. Branchlets with gray or brownish
shreddy bark, not white-speckled
or hairy; fruit globular capsules
in leafless racemes..............*Lyonia*, in part, p. 255
12. Leaves with margins not entire, generally dentate, serrate, etc.
   33. Shrubs with thorny branches, stems, or twigs
      34. Twigs and branches armed with branched spines; inner bark
and wood yellow; fruit red, berry-like..............................*Berberis*, p. 101
      34. Twigs and branches armed with thorns; inner bark and
wood not yellow; fruit a drupe or pome
         35. Petioles with glands near the upper end;
fruit a drupe...*Prunus*, in part, p. 180
         35. Petioles without glands near the upper end;
fruit a pome...*Crataegus*, in part, p. 134
   33. Shrubs without thorny branches, stems, or twigs
      36. Stems climbing or twining; vines; leaf margins crenate-serrate;
lateral veins not straight; fruit an orange capsule.................*Celastrus*, p. 207
      36. Stems erect; shrubs

37. Stems low, 1–2 dm. tall, almost herbaceous, from subterranean creeping stems; leaves persistent, glossy, coriaceous, clustered near the end of the new growth
    38. Leaves oval, with wintergreen flavor; fruit red, berry-like................*Gaultheria*, p. 257
    38. Leaves oblanceolate or with main veins of lighter green, without wintergreen flavor; fruit a capsule.................................*Chimaphila*, p. 247
37. Stems higher, more than 2 dm. tall
    39. Leaves with 3 nearly equal veins from near the base; much branched shrubs; fruit a capsule.............................*Ceanothus*, p. 215
    39. Leaves with 1 main vein, and otherwise not as above
        40. Buds with distinct stalks
            41. Leaves crenate-dentate to wavy, base oblique; fruit a 2-celled, woody pod...*Hamamelis*, p. 115
            41. Leaves serrate or doubly serrate; base not oblique; fruit small nutlets in a persistent cone-like woody structure..*Alnus*, p. 90
        40. Buds without distinct stalks
            42. Buds naked, leaf base slightly or not at all oblique; fruit berry-like...*Rhamnus*, in part, p. 211
            42. Buds with scales
                43. Each bud covered with one hood-like scale.........*Salix*, in part, p. 63
                43. Each bud covered with two or more scales
                    44. Leaves variously lobed or coarsely serrate
                        45. Leaves short and broad; shrub thorny; fruit a pome..................................*Crataegus*, in part, p. 134
                        45. Leaves elongated; shrub not thorny; fruit an acorn..................................*Quercus*, in part, p. 93
                    44. Leaves not as above (see next line, new paragraphing)
46. Base of leaf broad, rounded, cordate or subcordate
    47. Petioles with one or more glands near the upper end.............*Prunus*, in part, p. 180
    47. Petioles without glands
        48. Leaf margins evenly and simply serrate, dentate, or crenate
            49. Leaves 1–7 cm. long, not waxy on the upper surface, midrib not glandular above; flowers in racemes; petals narrow; fruit small, berry-like, sweet and pleasant......*Amelanchier*, p. 123
            49. Leaves 4–8 cm. long, waxy on the upper surface, midrib glandular above; flowers in cymes; petals roundish; fruit small, berry-like, not sweet and pleasant.............................*Aronia*, in part, p. 122
        48. Leaf margins unevenly and mostly doubly serrate or dentate
            50. Bark on young stems with transversely elongated lenticels; fruit a samara in cone-like catkins..*Betula*, p. 89
            50. Bark without lenticels; fruit a nut within a husk-like involucre...*Corylus*, p. 87
46. Base of leaf tapering or acute
    51. Lower surface of leaves covered with yellow glands, scurf, or dots
        52. Leaves sweet-scented when crushed, mostly entire towards the base, lower surface covered with yellow resinous glands; fruit a waxy drupe...*Myrica*, in part, p. 85
        52. Leaves not sweet-scented and otherwise not as above
            53. Leaves coriaceous, persistent, lower surface covered with yellowish scurf; fruit a capsule in one-sided leafy racemes..*Chamaedaphne*, p. 256
            53. Leaves not coriaceous, deciduous, lower surface covered with yellowish resin globules; fruit berry-like............*Gaylussacia*, in part, p. 261
    51. Lower surface of leaves not covered with yellow glands, scurf, or dots

54. Twigs glabrous or more or less pubescent in lines, rugulose; leaves lanceolate, elliptical, or oval, mostly serrulate with bristle-tipped teeth........*Vaccinium*, in part, p. 263
54. Twigs and leaves not as above
    55. Midrib of leaf with dark glands on the upper surface; fruit a berry-like pome..*Aronia*, in part, p. 122
    55. Midrib of leaf without dark glands; fruit a drupe or capsule
        56. Fruit fleshy
            57. Stipules small, sharp and persistent, nearly black; petals somewhat united at base, oblong, obtuse; fruit red......................................*Ilex verticillata*, p. 201
            57. Stipules not as above, ephemeral; petals small, short-clawed, notched at end, or wanting; fruit black..*Rhamnus*, in part, p. 211
        56. Fruit a dry capsule or follicle
            58. Leaves serrate or doubly serrate; fruit follicular, in corymbs or panicles...*Spiraea*, p. 121
            58. Leaves serrulate; fruit a 5-valved capsule borne in clusters...*Lyonia*, in part, p. 255

The Shrubs of Michigan

TAXACEAE—Yew Family

Trees or shrubs with alternate, evergreen, linear leaves; flowers dioecious, or rarely monoecious, borne on short scaly peduncles, the sterile flowers globular, consisting of a few naked stamens with anther cells, the fertile consisting of an erect ovule which becomes a bony-coated seed, furnished with a fleshy outer disk.

Only the following genus occurs in Michigan.

Taxus [Tourn.] L.—Yews

Taxus canadensis Marsh. (American Yew, Ground Hemlock). Fig. 1. A low, straggling evergreen shrub, rarely more than 1 meter tall; leaves flat, pointed, 10–25 mm. long; 1–2 mm. wide, rigid, green on both sides, bitter, spiral on the branches, appearing two-ranked. Flowers in early spring, dioecious or monoecious, solitary in the axils of the leaves of the previous year's growth. Fruit a nut-like chestnut-brown bony seed, about 5 mm. long, nearly enclosed when ripe in a coral-red, pulpy, berry-like cup; ripe in midsummer.

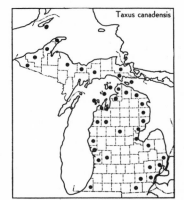

Taxus canadensis

Commonly in evergreen woods from Newfoundland to Virginia, west to Iowa and Manitoba. Michigan, throughout.

In Michigan the American Yew is often found in deep cedar swamps and bogs, like some of our herbaceous plants, apparently entirely out of its natural habitat. The generic name *Taxus* is derived from the Greek word *taxon*, meaning bow. It is said that the Indians often made their bows of its wood. The American Yew characteristically appears to be healthy and vigorous, and when bearing the translucent red fruits artistically arranged among the dark green leaves it makes a most beautiful appearance.

PINACEAE—Pine Family

Mostly evergreen trees, or rarely shrubs, with resinous juice; leaves mostly awl-shaped or needle-shaped, entire; flowers monoecious or rarely dioecious, borne in or having the form of scaly catkins, of which the fertile become cones or berry-like; ovules 2 or more at the base of each scale.

Juniperus is the only genus of this family in Michigan which includes plants that may be classified as shrubs.

Juniperus [Tourn.] L.—Junipers

Decumbent; leaves in whorls of 3, linear-subulate, prickly-pointed; catkins axillary..*J. communis* var. *depressa*, p. 59
Trailing; leaves mostly opposite, sometimes awl-shaped and loose, sometimes scale-shaped, appressed-imbricated; catkins terminal..*J. horizontalis*, p. 59

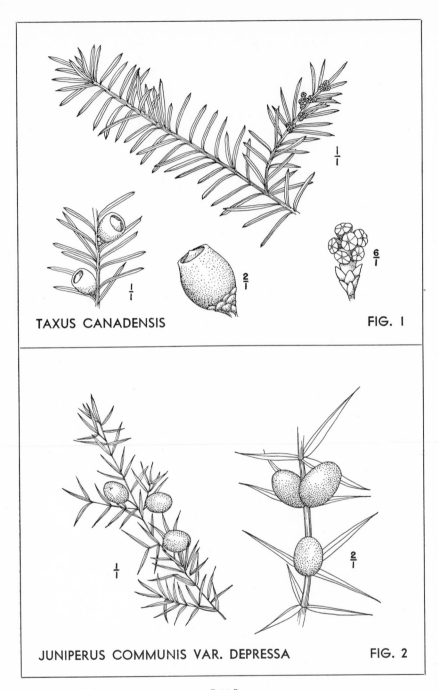

TAXUS CANADENSIS $\frac{1}{1}$ $\frac{2}{1}$ $\frac{6}{1}$ FIG. 1

JUNIPERUS COMMUNIS VAR. DEPRESSA $\frac{1}{1}$ $\frac{2}{1}$ FIG. 2

Juniperus communis L. var. *depressa* Pursh. (Prostrate Juniper). Fig. 2.
Low spreading evergreen shrub about 1 m. tall and often several m. in

diameter; leaves 8–13 mm. long, 1–1.5 mm. wide, straight or nearly so, sharp-pointed with a white stripe beneath; flowers in the axils of the younger branches, opening in the early spring; fruit resembling a berry, 6–10 mm. in diameter, sweet, fleshy, aromatic, ripening in the autumn of the third year.

Common in poor rocky soil and pastures from Labrador to British Columbia, south to Massachusetts and New York, along the Great Lakes and in the Rocky Mountains to Colorado and Utah. Michigan, throughout.

The seeds of the Prostrate Juniper seem to germinate easily and a community of these shrubs is apt to contain a large proportion of young plants in all sizes which are easy to transplant. The berries are used in making gin. They also have medicinal qualities and are used as a diuretic.

Juniperus horizontalis Moench. (Creeping Juniper). Fig. 3. Prostrate, evergreen shrub, sometimes spreading over a considerable area; leaves bluish-

green, scale-like, with a sharp point, or occasionally awl-shaped on young strong-growing shoots; flowers, early spring; fruit a dark fleshy berry, ripening during the second summer.

Rocky or sandy shores and banks, borders of swamps, etc., Newfoundland to New England, New York, northern Michigan, Minnesota and northward. Michigan, shores of Upper Peninsula and the northern part of the Lower Peninsula.

To those who are accustomed to thinking of evergreens only as trees or upright shrubs it is a curious sight to see the long, creeping branches of this juniper spreading among the other vegetation near the shores of the lakes and swamps of the northern Michigan counties. It belongs strictly to the north and unlike some other such species it seems never to have adopted the bogs of our southern counties as a habitat.

LILIACEAE—Lily Family

Herbaceous or woody plants and vines; leaves deciduous, alternate, simple, various in outline; flowers regular, mostly perfect, with a 6-parted perianth arranged in two circles; stamens 6, one before each of the divisions of the perianth; carpels 3, united; ovary 3-celled; fruit a few- to many-seeded pod or berry.

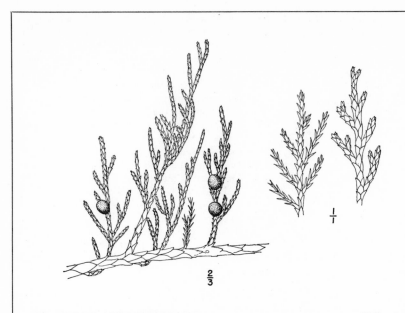

$\frac{2}{3}$

$\frac{1}{1}$

JUNIPERUS HORIZONTALIS   FIG. 3

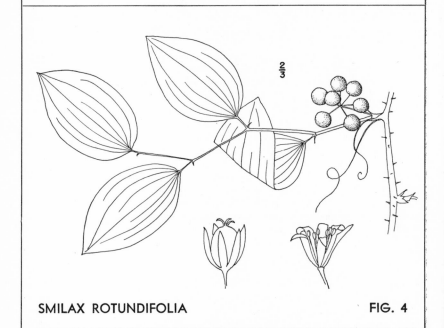

$\frac{2}{3}$

SMILAX ROTUNDIFOLIA   FIG. 4

The Lily family is represented by many genera and species in Michigan. Only the following genus, however, contains plants which may be classified as shrubs.

Smilax [Tourn.] L.—GREENBRIERS

Leaves rounded or lanceolate, 5-nerved; peduncle about the length of the petiole or shorter; stem prickles scattered, stout; berries blue-black with a bloom...*S. rotundifolia,* p. 61

Leaves ovate, 7-nerved, peduncle 2-4 times as long as the petiole; stem prickles usually numerous; berries black without a bloom........................*S. hispida,* p. 61

Smilax rotundifolia L. (Common Greenbrier, Horse Brier). Fig. 4. Climbing woody vines, the stems and branches terete, prickly with scattered spines

Smilax rotundifolia

up to 1 cm. in length, glabrous; branchlets zigzag, more or less 4-angular; leaves deciduous, simple, alternate, ovate or round-ovate, often broader than long, slightly cordate at the base, acute or acuminate at the apex, entire or obscurely denticulate, 5 nerved, 5-15 cm. long, green both sides, thick and shining when mature; petioles 6-12 mm. long with a pair of tendrils at their base by which the plant climbs; flowers dioecious, in 6–25-flowered umbels, small, greenish or yellowish, regular, the perianth segments all distinct and deciduous, pubescent at the tip; filaments 2-3 times as long as the anthers; peduncles flattened, generally shorter than the petioles; pedicels 2-8 mm. long; berries blue-black with a bloom, 6–8 mm. in diameter, 1–3-seeded. Flowers, June; fruit ripe, October and November.

Moist thickets and in woods, Nova Scotia, Ontario to Minnesota, Florida and Texas. Michigan, infrequent in southern peninsula.

This *Smilax* is very variable, passing into the named variety *quadrangularis* (Muhl.) Wood., which has branches and especially branchlets 4-angular, and

Smilax hispida

is more common westward. I have collected the variety in Berrien County and the branches were square enough to have been mechanically shaped.

Smilax hispida Muhl. (Hispid Greenbrier). Fig. 5. Stems glabrous, long and climbing, the lower and older parts generally thickly beset with long and weak blackish bristly prickles, the flowering branchlets mostly naked; leaves deciduous, simple, thin, dark green and shining both sides, ovate, abruptly acute and cuspidate at the apex, obtuse or subcordate at the base, 7-nerved, 5-13 cm. long, rough-margined; petioles 8-18

[61]

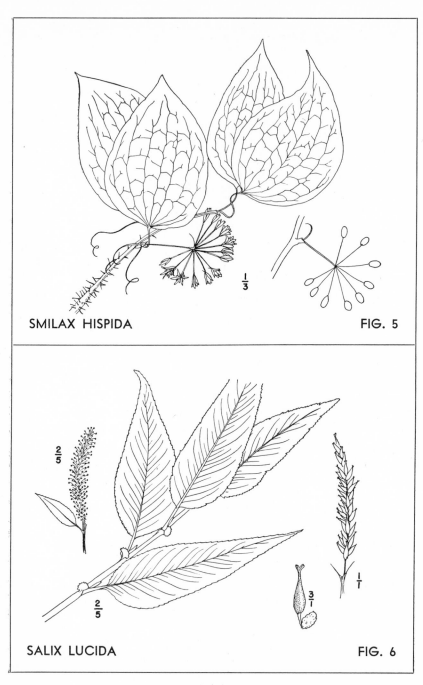

SMILAX HISPIDA $\frac{1}{3}$ FIG. 5

SALIX LUCIDA $\frac{2}{5}$ $\frac{2}{5}$ $\frac{3}{1}$ $\frac{1}{1}$ FIG. 6

mm. long, tendril-bearing; flowers dioecious in 6–25-flowered umbels, small, greenish or yellowish, regular, the perianth segments lanceolate, nearly 6 mm. long, distinct and deciduous; filaments a little longer than the anthers; peduncles flattened, 2–4 times as long as the petioles; pedicels 4–10 mm. long; berries globose, black without a bloom, 6–8 mm. in diameter; 1-seeded, or rarely with 2 seeds. Flowers, June; fruit, October, November.

Moist thickets, Connecticut to Virginia, west to Ontario, Minnesota, Kansas and Texas. Michigan, throughout.

The Hispid Greenbrier is widely distributed in both peninsulas of Michigan and is a familiar vine in thickets generally. The attractive fruit is frequently used in winter bouquets.

SALICACEAE—Willow Family

Trees or shrubs with bitter bark and alternate, simple leaves; flowers dioecious, both kinds in catkins, each flower subtended by a bract, without perianth, the staminate with two to many stamens, the pistillate with a single compound pistil composed of two carpels and two more or less divided stigmas. At maturity the pistil opens, setting free the small seeds, which are furnished with long silky down. The family includes two genera, *Salix*, the willows, and *Populus*, the aspens and poplars or cottonwoods. None of the latter is classed as a shrub in Michigan and they are therefore not treated here.

Salix [Tourn.] L.—Willows
Key to the Genus *Salix*
Based on a combination of floral and vegetative characters

1. Scales of the catkins pale or yellowish, caducous
    2. Stamens 3–5 or more
        3. Leaves green both sides, ovate-lanceolate, long-acuminate; stipules small, generally persistent; fruit mature early summer; capsule conic-ovoid, 4.5–6.5 mm. long..*S. lucida*, p. 67
        3. Leaves paler or white beneath, oblong-lanceolate, short-acuminate; stipules none; fruit mature in autumn; capsule conic-subulate, 7–10 mm. long..*S. serissima*, p. 67
    2. Stamens 2; leaves nearly sessile, linear, tapering at each end, remotely denticulate; stipules small, lanceolate, deciduous; capsule blunt, short..*S. interior*, p. 69
1. Scales of catkins mostly brown to black, persistent
    4. Capsules and ovaries glabrous
        5. Stipules persistent, conspicuous (see also *S. syrticola*)
            6. Leaves dull above, the young pubescent with early deciduous soft hairs
                7. Pistillate aments in anthesis with widely divergent ovaries; leaves oblong-lanceolate, subcordate, rounded or tapering at base, 1/8–1/3 as broad as long; fruiting aments with widely divergent capsules; pedicels as long as, to much longer than the bracts..*S. rigida*, p. 69
                7. Pistillate aments in anthesis with appressed ascending ovaries; leaves broadly oblong-lanceolate to ovate, mostly strongly cordate, about 1/2 as broad as long; fruiting aments with capsules crowded; pedicels shorter than to barely exceeding the bracts..*S. cordata*, p. 71
            6. Leaves glossy above, glabrous from the first, ovate or obovate to oblong-lanceolate, base broadly rounded, short-acuminate, glandular-serrate; aments dense; capsules attenuate-beaked, 9–11 mm. long..*S. glaucophylloides* var. *glaucophylla*, p. 71

5. Stipules obsolete or minute (except *S. syrticola*)
   8. Leaves glabrous or quickly glabrate
      9. Leaves short-oval to oblong-lanceolate, base broadly rounded, usually subcordate, slightly glandular-serrate; petiole 6–12 mm. long; staminate aments very silky, 2–3 cm. long; pedicels 6–8 times the length of the scale..*S. balsamifera,* p. 72
      9. Leaves oblong-linear to elliptic-obovate, base acutish, entire; petiole 2–5 mm. long; staminate aments sparingly pubescent or glabrate, 1–2 cm. long; pedicels twice the length of the scale..*S. pedicellaris,* p. 73
   8. Leaves covered with long silky tomentum on both sides, ovate or broadly lanceolate, finely serrate, teeth gland-tipped; stipules conspicuous, ovate-cordate, glandular-serrate; aments leafy-peduncled; capsule 5–8 mm. long, subsessile..*S. syrticola,* p. 73
4. Capsules and ovaries pubescent
  10. Catkins naked at base, appearing before the leaves
     11. Mature leaves glabrous or glabrate beneath
       12. Leaves lanceolate to elliptic, acute at the apex, irregularly crenate-serrate; stipules large, sharply toothed or entire; capsules narrowly conic, tomentose..................................*S. discolor,* p. 75
       12. Leaves narrowly lanceolate, acuminate at apex, finely and evenly serrate; stipules minute, deciduous; capsule conic-ovoid, silvery pubescent..*S. petiolaris,* p. 75
     11. Mature leaves pubescent, at least beneath
       13. Leaves dull, grayish-tomentose, undulate-crenate or subentire, capsules slender-beaked
         14. Leaves oblanceolate or oblong-lanceolate, 5–15 cm. long; stipules medium-sized, semi-ovate, entire or toothed..*S. humilis,* p. 77
         14. Leaves linear-oblanceolate, 1–5 cm. long; stipules minute, deciduous......................*S. humilis* var. *microphylla,* p. 79
       13. Leaves lustrous beneath with minute silky pubescence, narrowly lanceolate, finely serrate; capsule blunt.........*S. sericea,* p. 79
  10. Catkins leafy-bracted at base, appearing with the leaves
     15. Style filiform, longer than the stigmas; leaf-margins subentire
       16. Leaves white-tomentose beneath, oblong or oblong-lanceolate, green and loosely tomentose or becoming glabrate above; capsules ovoid-conic, acute, densely tomentose......................................*S. candida,* p. 81
       16. Leaves silvery-velvety beneath, lance-linear to oblanceolate, bright-green and glabrous above; capsule short-conic with rounded base, densely white-pubescent............................*S. pellita,* p. 83
     15. Style short or none; leaves obovate to elliptic-lanceolate, acute or acuminate, dull-green and minutely downy above, serrate, crenate, or subentire; capsule long-beaked; pedicels long and thread-like..*S. Bebbiana,* p. 81

Key to the Genus *Salix*

Based principally on mature foliage, and on branchlet and growth-habit characters

1. Leaves entire or subentire
   2. Leaves entire, 2.5–5 cm. long, obtuse or somewhat pointed, acutish at base, smooth on both sides, somewhat coriaceous when mature, revolute, reticulated, pale and glaucous beneath; low glabrous shrub, cold bogs..*S. pedicellaris,* p. 73
   2. Leaves subentire, 4–12 cm. long, lance-linear to oblanceolate, green and glabrous above, white-velvety to pale green and glabrate beneath; large shrub or small tree, river banks and swamps.......................................*S. pellita,* p. 83
1. Leaves toothed

[64]

3. Mature leaves glabrous
    4. Leaves less than three times as long as broad
        5. Mature leaves very thin, dull, dark green above, paler beneath; stipules obsolete or minute; much-branched shrub, rarely a small tree, low woods..*S. balsamifera,* p. 72
        5. Mature leaves thick, firm, dark green and shining above, glaucous beneath; stipules persistent, conspicuous; shrub or shrubby tree, sandy shores..*S. glaucophylloides* var. *glaucophylla,* p. 71
    4. Leaves three or more times as long as broad............................*S. rigida,* in part, p. 69
3. Mature leaves more or less pubescent
    6. Branchlets heavily villous or tomentose
        7. Margin of leaves not revolute
            8. Leaves even when fully grown long silky-tomentose on both sides, the tomentum later deciduous, ovate or very broadly lanceolate, cuspidate-acuminate, dull green both sides, very closely serrate with fine gland-tipped teeth; branchlets tomentose; large straggling shrub, shores of Great Lakes..*S. syrticola,* p. 73
            8. Leaves heavily villous when young, the hairs inclined to persist at maturity, broadly lance-oblong to oblong-ovate, long acuminate, tapering from below the middle, teeth at first gland-tipped, soon glandless; branchlets heavily villous; medium shrub, more northern..*S. cordata,* p. 71
        7. Margin of leaves revolute, leaves oblong to linear-lanceolate, 4–12 cm. long, rather rigid, downy above, becoming glabrate, white-tomentose below; branchlets densely white-tomentose.........................*S. candida,* in part, p. 81
    6. Branchlets glabrous, glabrate or puberulent, occasionally somewhat pubescent (except *S. candida*)
        9. Lower surface of leaves more or less tomentose, upper surface more or less rugose
            10. Leaves elliptical or oblanceolate to ovate
                11. Blade 2–3 times as long as wide, margin flat, the upper surface more or less pubescent; branchlets grayish-puberulent; shrub or small tree, moist or dry habitat.........*S. Bebbiana,* p. 81
                11. Blade 3–4 times as long as wide, margin revolute, the upper surface glabrous or glabrate; branchlets more or less puberulent or glabrate; shrub, 1–3 m. tall, dry habitat.....*S. humilis,* p. 77
            10. Leaves narrowly oblanceolate to linear-lanceolate
                12. Twigs very slender, 1–2 mm. in diameter, dingy puberulent; small tufted shrub, 0.5 m. tall or less, sandy habitat..................................*S. humilis* var.*microphylla,* p. 79
                12. Twigs moderately stout, 2–4 mm. in diameter, white tomentose; hoary shrub, 0.5–2 m. tall, cold bogs..*S. candida,* in part, p. 81
        9. Lower surface of leaves glabrous or silky, upper surface not distinctly rugose
            13. Lower surface of leaves green or only slightly paler than the upper, neither glaucous nor white-silky
                14. Leaves linear-lanceolate to linear, blade 8–20 times as long as wide, tapering at base, sessile or nearly so, teeth distant, 2–4 per cm.; shrub forming dense clumps, alluvial soils......................................*S. interior,* p. 69
                14. Leaves lanceolate to ovate, blade 2–7 times as long as wide
                    15. Leaves, especially on the sucker shoots, caudate-acuminate, lustrous; shrub or small tree, wet grounds, stream banks..*S. lucida,* p. 67
                    15. Leaves merely acuminate
                        16. Leaves mostly 4–20 mm. wide, acute or tapering at base; stipules lacking or ephemeral; low shrub, damp soil..*S. petiolaris,* p. 75
                        16. Leaves mostly 15–30 mm. wide, obtuse, rounded or subcordate, rarely acute at base

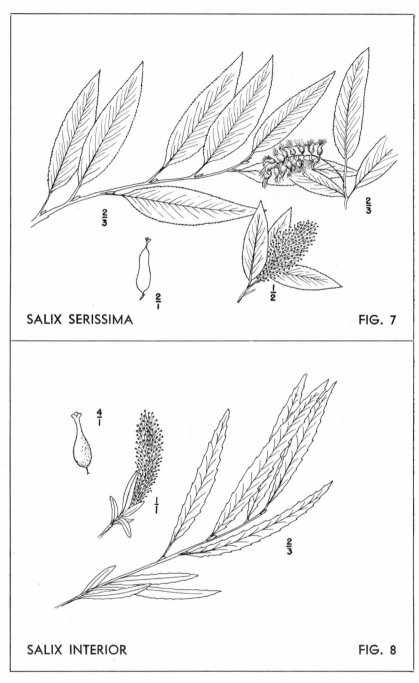

SALIX SERISSIMA   FIG. 7

SALIX INTERIOR   FIG. 8

17. Leaves firm, lustrous, teeth very fine, 10–20 per cm.; stipules early deciduous;
tall shrub; swamps..*S. serissima*, p. 67
17. Leaves thinner, not lustrous; teeth coarser, 3–8 per cm.; stipules usually
persistent; shrub, wet habitat..*S. rigida*, in part, p. 69
13. Leaves much paler on the lower surface, usually glaucous or white-silky
18. Leaves lanceolate to elliptic, 2–3.5 cm. broad, glaucous beneath in
maturity, margin irregularly wavy-toothed; stipules large, usually sharply
toothed and persistent; large shrub, low places..............................*S. discolor*, p. 75
18. Leaves narrowly lanceolate, 1–2 cm. broad, lustrous beneath with fine silky
pubescence, margin finely serrate; stipules narrow, deciduous; large shrub,
wet habitat...*S. sericea*, p. 79

Salix lucida Muhl. (Shining Willow). Fig. 6. Shrub, 1–3 m. tall;
bark brown, smooth or somewhat scaly; twigs yellowish-brown and glossy;

leaves alternate, simple, deciduous, ovate-lanceolate or narrower, 5–15 cm. long, finely and evenly serrate, rusty-pubescent when very young, in maturity thick, leathery, glabrous, green and shining on both sides; stipules small, oblong or semicircular, generally persistent; catkins appearing with the leaves on short leafy branches, the staminate 2–5 mm. long, the fertile becoming 3–5 cm. long in fruit; capsule rounded at base, 4.5–6.5 mm. long, pale brown or greenish; style about 0.5 mm. long, entire; stigmas short, thick. Flowers, April, May; fruit, June.

The Shining Willow is found along the banks of streams, lakes and in roadside ditches from Newfoundland to Manitoba, south to Pennsylvania, Illinois and Nebraska. Michigan, common throughout. This is a most beautiful willow and adds materially to our natural landscape.

The following variety has been separated and is reported by Hanes from Kalamazoo County: *Salix lucida* Muhl. var. *intonsa* Fern.

Salix serissima (Bailey) Fern. (Autumn Willow). Fig. 7. A shrub 1–4 m. tall; bark olive-brown and shining; stipules none; leaves simple, alternate, deciduous, elliptic or oblong-lanceolate, short-acuminate, rounded at the base, 4–8 cm. long, 1–3 cm. broad, closely serrulate, glabrous, dark green and shining above, pale or whitish beneath; catkins appearing with the leaves, on short leafy twigs, the staminate 1–1.5 cm. long, the fertile becoming loosely flowered, 2–3.5 cm. long, scales obovate, pale yellow; capsule narrowly conical, olive- or brown-tinged, 7–10 mm. long, glabrous, ripe in late autumn, the pedicel twice exceeding the gland; style short and thick. Flowers, June, July; fruit persistent until autumn.

The range of the Autumn Willow is from Quebec to New Jersey, west to

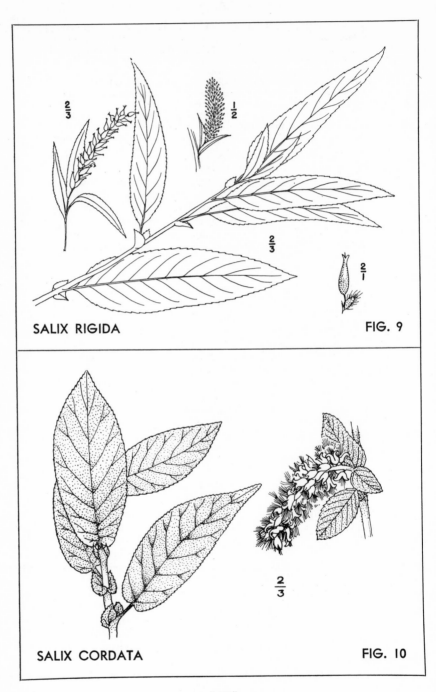

SALIX RIGIDA

FIG. 9

SALIX CORDATA

FIG. 10

$\frac{2}{3}$

Alberta and Minnesota. It is found in bogs and swamps, mostly in calcareous regions. Michigan, throughout.

The Autumn Willow is so named because of its late flowering.

Salix interior Rowlee. (Sandbar Willow, Longleaf Willow). Fig. 8. (*Salix longifolia* Muhl., Gray's Manual, 7th Edition, Shrubs of Michigan, 1st Edition.) A shrub with clustered stems 1.5–4 m. tall, or sometimes taller; bark grayish; branchlets reddish-brown, usually glabrous; stipules mostly lacking; leaves simple, alternate, deciduous, linear or oblong-lanceolate, 3–15 cm. long, 4–15 mm. broad, tapering at each end, nearly sessile, more or less silky when young, at length smooth and green both sides, the margin with widely spaced, slender, sharp teeth; catkins appearing with or after the leaves; the staminate clustered at the tips of slender branches, 1.5–3 cm. long, 5–8 mm. wide, the pistillate solitary at the ends of rather long leafy shoots, loosely flowered, scales lanceolate, thinly pubescent, yellow, deciduous; capsule short-pedicelled, blunt; stigmas large, very short, divided. Flowers, April, May; fruit into July.

This willow ranges from Quebec to Manitoba, south to Delaware and Louisiana. Michigan, common throughout.

The Sandbar Willow is usually found in rich alluvial deposits or in places subject to flooding and it is for this reason that it has received one of its common names.

Salix rigida Muhl. (Heartleaf Willow). Fig. 9. (*Salix cordata* Muhl., Gray's Manual, 7th Edition, Shrubs of Michigan, 1st Edition.) A shrub 1.5–3.5 m. tall, usually with several stems; twigs green or brown, puberulent or pubescent when young; stipules semi-cordate or nearly round; leaves alternate, simple, deciduous, oblong-lanceolate or narrowly lanceolate, 4–12 cm. long, 1–4 cm. wide, rounded to subcordate at base, sharply serrulate, dark green above, slightly paler beneath, strongly nerved with age; catkins appearing with the leaves, 2–6 cm. long, rather slender; fruiting aments with widely divergent capsules; scales generally very pubescent, persistent; capsule narrowly ovoid, glabrous, 4–5 mm. long, short-pedicelled. Flowers, April, May; fruit through May.

In wet places along streams and ditches from New Brunswick to Maryland, west to Manitoba and eastern Kansas. Michigan, common throughout.

This is a characteristic shrub of the water courses. It hybridizes freely and has

[69]

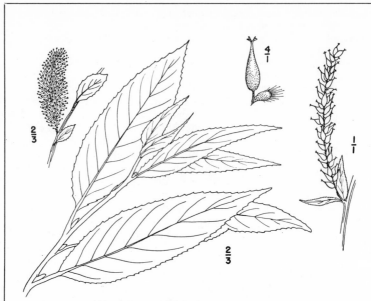

SALIX GLAUCOPHYLLOIDES VAR. GLAUCOPHYLLA FIG. 11

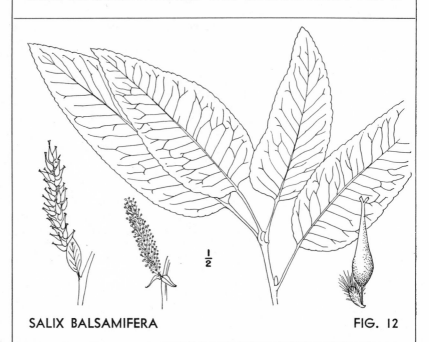

SALIX BALSAMIFERA   FIG. 12

several named varieties and forms. One of these varieties, *Salix rigida* Muhl. var. *angustata* (Pursh) Fern., with narrow leaves, has been reported from Washtenaw County.

Salix cordata Michx. (Heartleaf Willow). Fig. 10. Medium shrub with several stems; branchlets heavily villous when young, the pubescence inclined

to persist; leaves simple, alternate, deciduous, broadly lance-oblong to oblong-ovate, long-acuminate, gradually tapering from below or near the middle, mostly strong cordate, the mature ones 3–13 cm. long, 2–5.5 cm. broad, each margin with 25–90 forward-arching, mostly simple teeth, at first gland-tipped, soon glandless, heavily villous when young, the pubescence inclined to persist on the mature foliage; mature petiole 5–35 mm. long; mature and larger stipules with an average of 14 gland-tipped or mostly glandless teeth on the longer margin; staminate aments on leafy branchlets; leaves well-grown at anthesis; bracts blackish to brown, with white beard; pistillate aments in maturity 2–6 cm. long; bracts narrowly obovate, fuscous or brown, their bright white beard only slightly longer; ovaries in anthesis appressed-ascending, in fruit more spreading; pedicels shorter than, to barely exceeding the bracts. Flowers, April, May; fruit through May or early June

Southern Labrador Peninsula to James Bay, Ontario, south to Newfoundland, Nova Scotia, northern Maine, eastern Cape Cod, northern New York, Simcoe and Bruce counties, Ontario, and northern Michigan.

According to Fernald (1946): "*Salix cordata* Michx. has been wrongly guessed, ever since Willdenow, to be identical with the later *Salix cordata* Muhl." In Fernald's article he has assigned the willow heretofore passing as *Salix cordata* Muhl. to *Salix rigida* Muhl., stating that *Salix cordata* Michx. is a more northern plant, which includes northern Michigan in its range. This change has

been made so lately that only one county record is available at this time. The species should be looked for and reported.

In addition to their wind-blown seeds, willows growing on stream, lake and pond banks have another form of distribution. Their branches are brittle and break off easily. Falling into the water the fragments float to other localities along the shore, where they root easily and become permenently established.

Salix glaucophylloides Fern. var. *glaucophylla* (Bebb) Schneid. (Broadleaf Willow). Fig. 11. (*Salix glaucophylla* Bebb, Gray's Manual, 7th Edition, Shrubs of

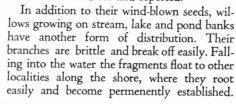

[71]

Michigan, 1st Edition.) A shrub 1–3 m. tall; stems clustered; twigs yellowish to dark brown, pubescent, becoming glabrous; stipules 3–10 mm. long, ear-shaped, serrate, persistent; leaves simple, alternate, deciduous, ovate, obovate, oblong-lanceolate, broadly rounded at the base, 4.5–12 cm. long, 2–4.5 cm. wide, short-acuminate at the apex, glandular-serrate, firm, dark green and shining above, white-glaucous beneath, glabrous throughout; petiole stout, 6–12 mm. long; catkins appearing before the leaves, with a leafy bract at the base, the staminate 3–5 cm. long, the pistillate 4–7 cm. long in fruit; bracts densely white-villous, persistent; style filiform; capsule slender-beaked, 9–11 mm. long, glabrous; pedicel slender, 2–4 mm. long. Flowers, April, May; fruit May and early June.

Found on sandy or alluvial shores of rivers and lakes, eastern Quebec and New Brunswick to Alberta, south to Maine, northern Ohio, Illinois and Wisconsin. Michigan, throughout, but mostly along the shores; rare in the interior.

The sand dunes and ridges of the Great Lakes are the chosen habitats of the Broad-leaf Willow. When growing in the shifting sand of the dunes it roots readily at the nodes, sending new shoots into the air while the roots take hold in the sand. It thus forms extensive thickets which are useful in holding the sand. Like most of the willows, it is not constant and several varieties have been named. Regarding this species, Fernald (1946) states: "Unfortunately the name of *Salix glaucophylla* Bebb (1881) is antedated by the same name for quite a different species by Besser (1822) and by Andersson (1851)." The typical *Salix glaucophylloides* is a coarse shrub or small tree up to 5 meters high which does not include Michigan in its range. The variety *glaucophylla* (Bebb) Schneid. is a low shrub localized about the Great Lakes.

Salix balsamifera Barratt. (Balsam Willow). Fig. 12. A much-branched shrub, 1–2.5 m. tall, or rarely a small tree up to 7 m. in height; bark of old stems smooth, dull gray, branches olive; young twigs glabrous, reddish-brown, shining; leaves alternate, simple, deciduous, elliptic, ovate-oval to oblong-lanceolate, thin, glabrous, broadly rounded and mostly subcordate at the base, acute or obtuse at the apex, dark green above, glaucous and strongly reticulate-veined below, 5–8 cm. long, 2–4 cm. wide, slightly glandular-serrate; petiole slender, 6–12 mm. long; stipules minute or wanting; catkins appearing with the leaves, leafy-bracted at the base, cylindric, the staminate about 2 cm. long, dense, the pistillate 5–7 cm. long, very lax in fruit; bracts villous, persistent; style very short; stamens 2; filaments glabrous; capsule very narrow, acute, 4–5 mm. long; pedicel long and slender. Flowers, May; fruit, June.

In swamps, low woods, thickets, Newfoundland, Labrador, to Manitoba and British Columbia, south to Maine, New York, Michigan and Minnesota. Michigan, throughout.

In flower the Balsam is one of the most beautiful willows. When growing in swampy grounds in full sunshine it produces large, broad clumps and when so situated assumes its finest form.

Salix syrticola Fern. (Furry Willow). Fig. 13. A straggling shrub, 1–3 m. tall, with short, tomentose twigs; stipules conspicuous, ovate-cordate, gland-

ular-serrate, exceeding the short, stout petioles; leaves simple, alternate, deciduous, broadly ovate to ovate or ovate-lanceolate, cuspidate-acuminate, cordate or broadly rounded at base, 4–8 cm. long, 1.5–3 cm. wide, very closely serrate with fine projecting gland-tipped teeth, clothed with a long, silky tomentum, even when full grown, deep green on both sides, prominent nerves beneath; catkins appearing with the leaves, on pubescent peduncles, 1–2.5 cm. long, bearing several small leaves; pistillate 2–4 cm. long in flower, 6–8 cm. long in fruit; capsule when mature 5–8 mm. long, glabrous; pedicel short, glabrous; stigma entire, scales all oblong, pale brown, densely covered with long hairs; staminate catkins 2-4 cm. long, stamens 2, filaments glabrous. Flowers, April, May; fruit, May, June.

Gray's Manual gives the range of this willow as: "Shores of the Great Lakes." In Michigan, all records except that from Kent are from counties bordering the lakes.

, The Furry Willow is well named, as the whole shrub is covered with a coat of woolly hairs which give it a very striking appearance.

Salix pedicellaris Pursh. (Bog Willow). Fig. 14. Low, subsimple or loosely branching shrub, glabrous throughout; bark on older stems brown; branchlets elongate, dark brown, strongly ascending; stipules obsolete; leaves simple, alter-

nate, deciduous, entire, obovate-oblong to broadly oblanceolate, obtuse or acutish at tip, narrowed at base, green on both surfaces, glabrous from the first, thickish, leathery when mature, 2.5–5 cm. long, 1–2 cm. broad; fertile catkins thick-cylindric, loosely few-flowered, borne on long, leafy peduncles, appearing with the leaves; scales obovate-oval, obtuse or acutish, glabrous or glabrate, greenish-yellow; capsules reddish or yellowish, ovoid at base, tapering gradually to the thick, blunt beak; pedicels 2–4 mm. long, twice exceeding the scale; stigmas short, thick, entire; stamens 2, filaments free. Flowers April, May; fruit, May, June.

Cold bogs, eastern Quebec to British Columbia, New Jersey, Pennsylvania, and northern Iowa; also Idaho and Washington. Michigan, throughout.

Two varieties of this willow have been named, one of which is recorded from Michigan: *Salix pedicellaris* Pursh var. *hypoglauca* Fern. Leaves green above,

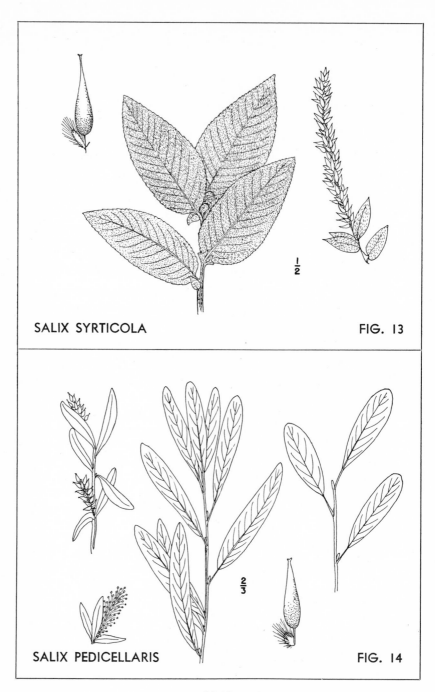

SALIX SYRTICOLA

$\frac{1}{2}$

FIG. 13

SALIX PEDICELLARIS

$\frac{2}{3}$

FIG. 14

glaucous beneath, the young reddish, thin, glabrous, in age subcoriaceous, 3–8 cm. long, 1–2.5 cm. broad; fertile catkins rather densely flowered; capsules purplish or yellowish, 5–8 mm. long, ovoid and thickish at base, obtuse at tip. Recorded from Mackinac, Chippewa, Keweenaw, and Houghton counties.

Salix discolor Muhl. (Pussy Willow, Glaucous Willow). Fig 15. Shrub, or sometimes becoming a small tree, bark thin, smooth, or somewhat scaly, dark gray; twigs light to dark brown, sometimes pubescent; buds large with glossy scales; stipules large and sharply toothed or entire; leaves simple, alternate, deciduous, lanceolate to elliptic, 5–10 cm. long, 2–3.5 cm. wide, smooth and

Salix discolor

bright green above, soon smooth and glaucous beneath, or sometimes pubescent when young, margin irregular wavy-toothed or nearly entire; flowers appearing before the leaves in very early spring; staminate catkins thick-cylindrical, sessile on the old wood, dense, with long silky hairs; pistillate catkins sessile or with a few small leaves on the peduncles, becoming 4–6 cm. long in fruit; scales persistent, long, silky-hairy; mature capsule 5–7 mm. long, tomentose; pedicel short, slender; styles short, but distinct. Flowers, April; fruit, May, June.

The Pussy Willow grows in swamps and wet places from Newfoundland and Nova Scotia south to Delaware, Kentucky, northern Missouri, west to North Dakota and Saskatchewan. Michigan, frequent throughout.

Two varieties have been reported, as follows: *Salix discolor* Muhl. var. *latifolia* Anders. (*Salix discolor* Muhl. var. *eriocephala* (Michx.) Anders. of Gray's Manual, 7th Edition), with fully grown leaves retaining a rusty-colored pubescence; aments more densely flowered and more silvery-silky. Oakland, Washtenaw, Kalamazoo, and St. Clair counties. *Salix discolor* Muhl. var. *prinoides* (Pursh) Anders., with narrow leaves; aments more loosely flowered and less silky; capsules more thinly tomentose; styles longer; stigma lobes laciniate. Oakland County (Bingham), and Kalamazoo County (Hanes). These varieties should be sought in other locations, as they have the same range as the species.

The furry catkins of this willow creeping out from under their protecting scales early in the spring is a cheerful sight, as they herald the arrival of spring. In common with all wind-pollinated plants, it bears a tremendous crop of pollen, and this pollen furnishes the honey bee with an abundant supply of 'bee-bread.'

Salix petiolaris Sm. (Slender Willow). Fig. 16. Shrub 1–3 m. tall, much branched; twigs slender, green to dark brown or purplish, glabrous to puberulent; leaves simple, alternate, deciduous, linear or narrowly lanceolate, taper-pointed, entire to short serrate-dentate, 2.5–10 cm. long, 3–20 mm. wide, slightly silky when young, soon smooth, finely reticulate on both sides in age; petioles 6–12 mm. long; stipules minute, caducous; catkins appearing before the leaves, the staminate obovoid, 1–2 cm. long, bracts yellowish or pale brown, the pistillate

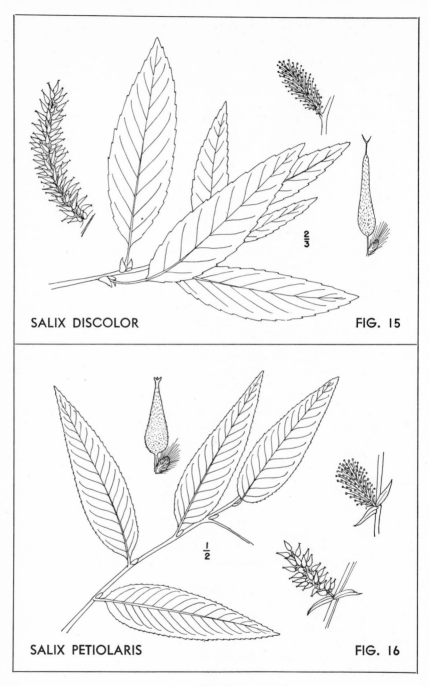

SALIX DISCOLOR $\frac{2}{3}$ FIG. 15

SALIX PETIOLARIS $\frac{1}{2}$ FIG. 16

ovoid-cylindric, at first 1–2 cm. long, in fruit broad and loose from the lengthening of the pedicels, becoming 2–4 cm. long; scales persistent, pubescent; capsule 4–6 mm. long, conic-ovoid, sparingly silvery-pubescent; pedicels slender, 1.5–3 mm. long; stigmas nearly sessile, lobed. Flowers, May; fruit, June.

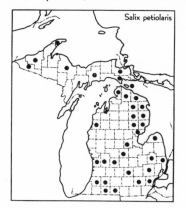

Damp soil, New Brunswick to the Great Lakes region and Manitoba, south to Tennessee. Michigan, frequent throughout.

During recent months the identity of this willow has been the subject of considerable discussion in botanical circles. On the one hand, it is set forth that the plant which J. E. Smith named *Salix petiolaris* was a British tree and not our low, slender-branched American shrub. Those holding to this view claim that our shrub is *Salix gracilis* Anders. Adopting this construction, Hanes in his 'Flora of Kalamazoo County, Michigan,' reports *Salix gracilis* Anders. var.*textoris* Fern. from that county. On the other hand, it is as definitely maintained that the reverse is true and that the material which Smith had originally came from this country. The various Michigan herbaria examined for distributional data contain many sheets of this willow named *Salix petiolaris* J. E. Smith, a large number of which were verified by specialists. Until the matter is definitely settled I decided to follow the nomenclature so long in use and continue the same treatment as used in the first edition.

Salix humilis Marsh. (Prairie Willow). Fig. 17. Shrubs with clustered stems, 1–3 m. tall; branchlets yellowish to brown, more or less puberulent or glabrate; stipules medium-sized, semi-ovate, entire or toothed; petioles distinct, 2–8 mm. long; leaves simple, alternate, deciduous, oblanceolate or oblong-lanceolate, 5–15 cm. long, 8–25 mm. wide, narrowed at base, acute or abruptly short-acuminate at the apex, entire or undulate, or undulate-serrate, revolute, downy above, becoming glabrate, glaucous beneath, rugose-veined and softly tomentose; catkins appearing before the leaves on the old wood, numerous, sessile, the staminate ovoid-cylindric, 1.5–2 cm. long, becoming 2–4 cm. long in fruit, which ripens almost before the leaves appear; scales persistent with long silky pubescence, capsule slender, long-beaked, 8–9 mm. long, tomentose; pedicel about as long as the scale; style very short, entire; stigmas short, divided. Flowers, April, May; fruit May.

The range of the Prairie or Upland Willow is from Newfoundland to Minnesota, south to Florida and Texas. Michigan, frequent throughout.

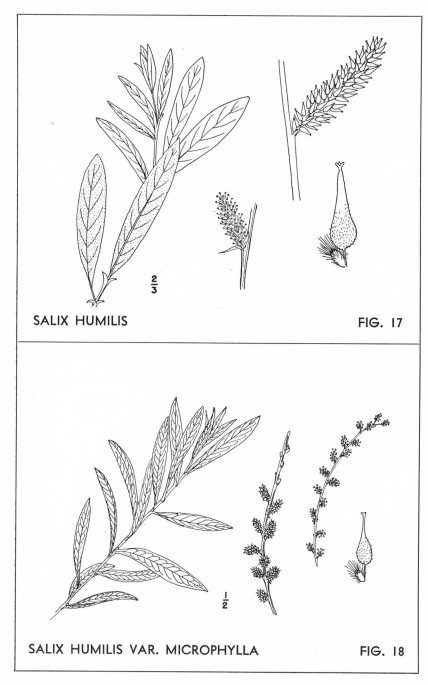

SALIX HUMILIS

FIG. 17

SALIX HUMILIS VAR. MICROPHYLLA

FIG. 18

As its common name indicates, this willow is a shrub of the dry plains and barrens. It is noted for the great variety in size and shape of its leaves, and several varieties have been separated and named. Of these, the following are found in Michigan: *Salix humilis* Marsh. var. *hyporhysa* Fern. (*Salix humilis* Marsh. var. *rigidiuscula* Anders. of Gray's Manual, 7th Edition), leaves glabrous or sparsely puberulent and rugose-reticulate below; fruiting aments 2–8 cm. long, Kalamazoo County (Hanes), Oakland County (Bingham); *Salix humilis* Marsh. var. *keweenawensis* Farw., "a low form growing amongst rocks, young leaves rotund, mature broadly obovate, densely tomentose," Keweenaw Peninsula (Hermann) and Isle Royale (Brown); *Salix humilis* Marsh. var. *microphylla* (*Anders.*) Fern., described below.

Salix humilis Marsh. var. *microphylla* (Anders.) Fern. (Sage Willow, Dwarf Upland Willow). Fig. 18. (*Salix tristis* Ait., Gray's Manual, 7th Edition, Shrubs of Michigan, 1st Edition.) Low

Salix humilis var. microphylla

shrub with numerous tufted stems 0.4–1 m. tall, closely resembling *Salix humilis*, except that it is smaller in every way; young twigs dingy-puberulent, older twigs dark yellow-brown and glabrate; leaves crowded, narrowly oblanceolate to linear-lanceolate, 1–5 cm. long, 5–12 mm. wide, narrowed at the base, obtuse or acute at the apex, entire with a revolute margin, green and more or less pubescent above, densely white-tomentose below; petiole very short; stipules minute, deciduous; catkins appearing before the leaves, numerous, crowded, 1–1.5 cm. long, sessile, naked, spreading, the fertile becoming 2 cm. long in fruit; scales 1–2 mm. long, hairy; capsule 6–7 mm. long, narrowly conic, with rounded base and long, slender beak; pedicel 1–2 mm. long; stigmas lobed, deeply cleft or nearly entire. Flowers, March, April; fruit, May.

Found on sandy uplands or borders of hillside thickets, roadsides, etc., from Massachusetts to North Dakota, south to Florida, Tennessee, Missouri, and eastern Nebraska. Michigan, infrequent; not recorded from the Upper Peninsula.

Concerning this willow the first edition had the following comment in the text: "Closely resembling *Salix humilis*, except that it is smaller in every way." Subsequent work upon the species has convinced Fernald (1946) that it is not sufficiently different to be given specific rank, and he now considers it a variety of *Salix humilis* Marsh. This construction is accepted for the second edition. However, the Sage Willow seems to be sufficiently important to warrant continuing the text, illustration, and distributional map under the new name.

Salix sericea Marsh. (Silky Willow). Fig. 19. Stems clustered, 1–3 m. tall, light brown to dark brown, glabrous or puberulent to pubescent when young; stipules narrow, deciduous; leaves simple, alternate, deciduous, narrowly lanceolate, 0.4–1 dm. long, 1–2 cm. broad, finely serrate, at first silky beneath, finely reticulate on both surfaces in age; catkins appearing before the leaves, narrowly

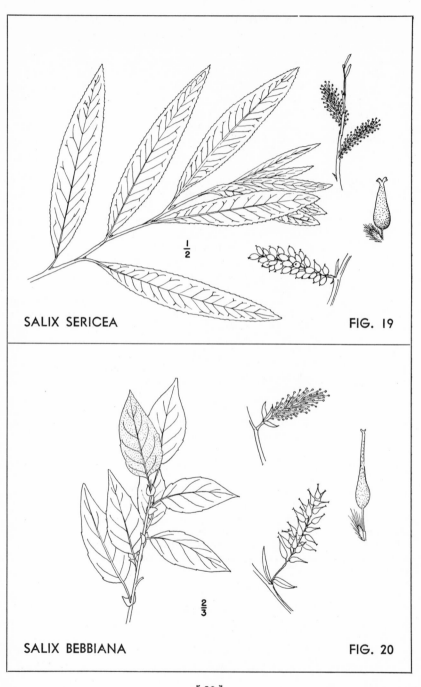

SALIX SERICEA

$\frac{1}{2}$

FIG. 19

SALIX BEBBIANA

$\frac{2}{3}$

FIG. 20

cylindrical, sessile to subsessile, peduncle sometimes with 2–3 small bracts, the staminate 1–2 cm. long, the fertile densely flowered, in maturity 2–3 cm. long;

scales ovate or oval and obtuse, dark brown, long pilose; capsule ovoid-oblong, 3–5 mm. long, blunt, silvery-pubescent, its pedicel about equaling the scale and twice exceeding the gland; style obsolete or very short; stigmas short, notched. Flowers, May; fruit, June.

Wet places, New Brunswick west to Michigan and eastern Iowa, south to South Carolina, Kentucky and southeastern Missouri. Michigan, very common in central portion of state, also in Upper Peninsula.

A tall willow with slender, purplish, somewhat downy twigs, growing in swamps and along streams.

Salix Bebbiana Sarg. (Beaked Willow, Bebb's Willow). Fig. 20. (*Salix rostrata* Richards., Gray's Manual, 7th Edition, Shrubs of Michigan, 1st Edition.) Shrub, or sometimes a small tree, 2–6 m. tall; stems few; branchlets

numerous, slender, yellowish to brown, grayish-puberulent; stipules when present semi-cordate, toothed, acute; leaves simple, alternate, deciduous, obovate to elliptic-lanceolate, 3–10 cm. long, 1.5–2.5 cm. broad, acute or acuminate, dull green and minutely downy above, pale to glaucous and more densely pubescent beneath, serrate, crenate or subentire, thin, becoming rigid; catkins numerous, leafy-bracted at base, appearing with the leaves, the staminate 2–4 cm. long, narrowly cylindrical, very hairy, the fertile loosely flowered, 2–6 cm. long; scales persistent, linear-oblong, pale, rose-tipped, thinly villous; capsule tapering to a very long, slender beak, pubescent, about 7 mm. long; pedicel thread-like, much exceeding the scales; style very short; stigmas entire or deeply parted. Flowers, April, May; fruit, June.

Ranges from Newfoundland to Alaska south to New Jersey, Pennsylvania, Illinois, eastern South Dakota, and in the western mountains to New Mexico and central California. Michigan, common throughout.

Unlike our other willows, which grow either in wet ground or in dry ground, the Beaked Willow is at home in both dry and wet habitats.

Salix candida Flügge. (Sage Willow, Hoary Willow). Fig. 21. A hoary shrub 0.5–2 m. tall, the young shoots white-woolly, the older, red; stipules lanceolate, about as long as the petioles; leaves oblong to linear-lanceolate, 4–12

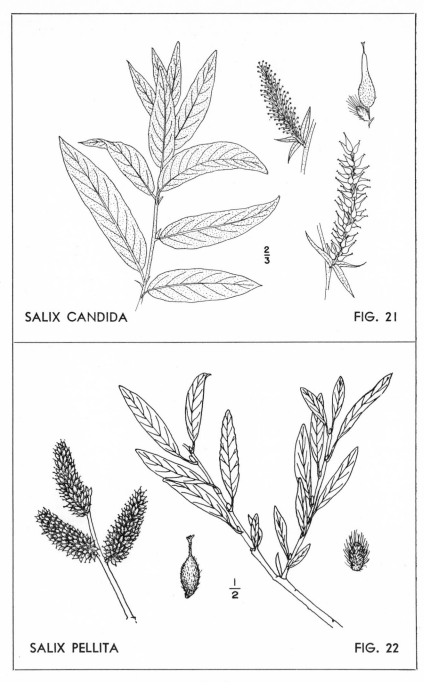

SALIX CANDIDA

$\frac{2}{3}$

FIG. 21

SALIX PELLITA

$\frac{1}{2}$

FIG. 22

cm. long, 5–17 mm. wide, narrowed at the base, acute at the apex, rather rigid, downy above, becoming glabrate, covered with dense white tomentum beneath, the margins revolute and subentire; catkins appearing with the leaves, subsessile, cylindrical, densely flowered, the pistillate 3–5

Salix candida

cm. long and 1–1.3 cm. wide in fruit; scales obovate, brown, thinly white-pilose; capsule densely white-woolly, lanceolate, short-pedicelled, 6-8 mm. long; style dark red; stigmas short, spreading. Flowers, May; fruit, June.

Cold bogs, in glaciated areas from Newfoundland, west to British Columbia, south to New England, New Jersey, the northern parts of Ohio, Indiana, Illinois, Iowa, North and South Dakota, and in the Rocky Mountains in Colorado, Wyoming and Montana. Michigan, common throughout.

The following variety has been described and is reported from Oakland and Kalamazoo counties by Bingham and Hanes respectively. No doubt it is present in other localities and should be looked for. *Salix candida* Flügge var. *denudata* Anders., leaves dark green and glabrate above, sparingly pubescent or glabrate beneath.

The Hoary Willow is always conspicuous whether growing in its native habitat or planted as an ornamental in our gardens. Its leaves and young shoots are densely covered with a white woolly pubescence which gives it this distinction. Its blossoms are also outstanding and it is entitled to a place in any garden.

Salix pellita Anders. (Satiny Willow). Fig. 22. Shrub 1–2 m. tall, or sometimes a small tree; twigs reddish to olive-brown; stipules minute; leaves lance-

Salix pellita

linear to oblanceolate, entire or obscurely crenulate, acute at both ends or bluntish at the apex, bright green and glabrous above, pale and satiny-pubescent or nearly glabrous beneath, 4–12 cm. long; petiole short; catkins on short leafy branches, the fertile 2–5 cm. long; capsule short-conic with rounded base, 4–5 mm. long, densely white-hairy; style yellowish, turning brown, longer than the stigmas. Flowers, April, May; fruit, June.

River banks and swamps, Gulf of St. Lawrence to Lake St. John, Quebec, and Lake Winnipeg south to Michigan, Maine, and Vermont. Michigan, so far recorded only from the Upper Peninsula. C. K. Dodge reported it as "abundant, low marshy banks of the Tahquamenon River." It is distinctly a northern species.

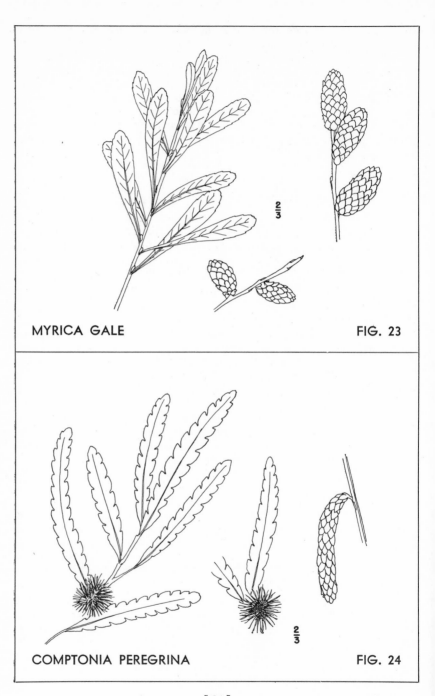

MYRICA GALE

$\frac{2}{3}$

FIG. 23

COMPTONIA PEREGRINA

$\frac{2}{3}$

FIG. 24

MYRICACEAE—Bayberry Family

Shrubs with simple, alternate, deciduous, resinous-dotted, aromatic leaves; flowers monoecious or dioecious in short scaly catkins, solitary in the axis of the bract; calyx and corolla none; stamens few to many with short, free or more or less united filaments; ovary 1-celled, ovule 1; style short; stigmas 2; fruit a drupe-like nut.

The family comprises 2 genera and about 40 species of wide geographic distribution, most abundant in the subtropics. Both of the genera are represented by shrubs growing in Michigan.

Leaves entire or slightly serrate, without stipules; ovary
subtended by 2–4 bractlets ....*Myrica,* p. 85

Leaves deeply pinnatifid or cut, stipules present; ovary
subtended by 8 linear, persistent bractlets...*Comptonia,* p. 85

Myrica L.—Sweet Gales

Myrica Gale L. (Sweet Gale). Fig. 23. A branching shrub 1–1.5 m. tall; leaves simple, alternate, deciduous, wedge-lanceolate, serrate toward the apex,

Myrica Gale

3–6 cm. long, 8–18 mm. wide, later than the flowers, resinous-dotted, fragrant; flowers mostly dioecious, individual flowers solitary under a scale-like bract, staminate in catkins 10–15 mm. long, pistillate catkins ovoid, about 5 mm. long; scales triangular; fruit small, globular or short-cylindric, dry, coated with resinous grains of wax, each nut 2-winged by thick persistent bractlets 2–3 mm. long. Flowers April; fruit ripe, July.

From Labrador to Alaska, through the New England and middle states, as far south as Virginia and along the Great Lakes to Minnesota, this shrub may be found growing along streams, borders of ponds and in swamps. Michigan, common throughout.

When crushed the leaves of the Sweet Gale feel somewhat resinous and exude a penetrating, rather fragrant odor. They are placed in clothing for the purpose of keeping out moths. The young buds were used for dyeing porcupine quills by the Indians.

Comptonia Banks—Sweet Fern

Comptonia peregrina (L.) Coult. (Sweet Fern). Fig. 24. (*Myrica aspleni-folia* L., Gray's Manual, 7th Edition, Shrubs of Michigan, 1st Edition.) A low, branching shrub, 3–6 dm. tall, sweet-scented; branches pubescent; leaves spiral, appearing alternate, simple, deciduous, fern-like, linear-lanceolate, 6–12 cm. long, 10–15 mm. wide, acute or rounded at the apex, narrowed at the base, cut into obtuse or pointed lobes their entire length, sinuses reaching nearly to the midrib, densely sprinkled with minute, yellow shining resinous dots; flowers in catkins,

[85]

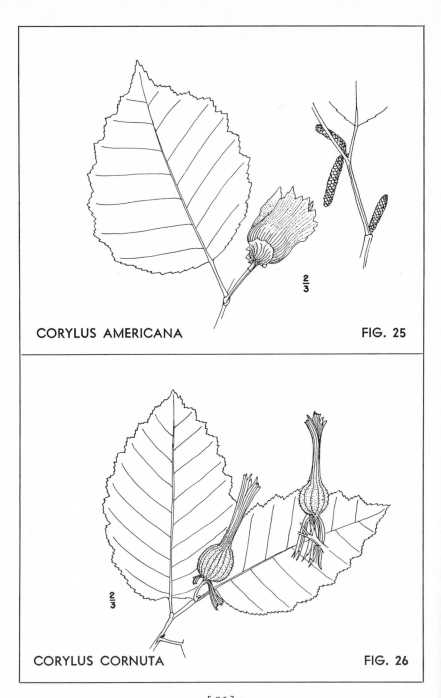

CORYLUS AMERICANA   FIG. 25

CORYLUS CORNUTA   FIG. 26

dioecious or monoecious, staminate about 2 cm. long, clustered at the ends of the branches, pistillate catkins ovoid or globose, at the ends of very short lateral branches, bur-like; ovary 1-celled, surrounded by 8 long awl-shaped persistent scales. Flowers, April, May; fruit ripe, July, August.

Ranges from New Brunswick to Saskatchewan, south to North Carolina, Indiana and Michigan. Michigan, common except in the southern counties.

Unlike the preceding species, which grows in water or very wet places, the Sweet Fern is found only in dry, sandy soil. In the pine country of Michigan it is one of the most common species. The whole plant gives out a pleasant, spicy odor. The leaves have been used as an ingredient in diet drinks and as a remedy for dysentery.

BETULACEAE—Birch Family

Monoecious or rarely dioecious trees or shrubs; leaves alternate, simple, deciduous, straight-veined; stipules deciduous; the sterile flowers in catkins, the fertile clustered, spiked or in scaly catkins; the staminate flowers 1-3 together in the axil of each bract, consisting of a membranous 2–4-parted perianth, or naked, 2–10 stamens, with distinct filaments, anthers 2-celled; pistillate flowers with or without a calyx attached to the 2-celled ovary; style 2-cleft or divided; fruit a one-seeded nut or nutlet, subglobose or ovoid, more or less flattened, and frequently with a membranous wing.

The following genera are represented by shrubs growing in Michigan.

1. Pistillate flowers with a calyx, clustered, not in catkins; nut not winged...*Corylus*, p. 87
1. Pistillate flowers without a calyx, in catkins; nut winged
    2. Stamens 2; fertile scales thin, 3-lobed, deciduous with or soon after the nuts..*Betula*, p. 89
    2. Stamens 4; fertile scales thick, becoming woody, long persistent...........*Alnus*, p. 90

Corylus [Tourn.] L.—Hazelnuts, Filberts

Twigs and petioles, glandular-bristly; involucre consisting of 2 broad, fringed bracts distinct nearly to the base....................................*C. americana*, p. 87
Twigs and petioles not glandular-bristly; involucre of united bracts, prolonged into a tubular beak...*C. cornuta*, p. 89

Corylus americana Walt. (American Hazelnut). Fig. 25. Shrubs 1–2.5 m. tall; bark gray and smooth; branchlets and petioles more or less densely glandular-bristly; leaves alternate, simple, deciduous, 6–16 cm. long, 4–12 cm. wide, roundish heart-shaped, serrate all around, nearly glabrous above, finely tomentose especially along the veins beneath; petioles 3–24 mm. long, pubescent and glandular; staminate catkins 4–8 cm. long in very early spring; pistillate flowers in bud-like clusters, inconspicuous; involucre of the nut consisting of two enlarged bracts, open above down to the nut, which is exposed at maturity, finely

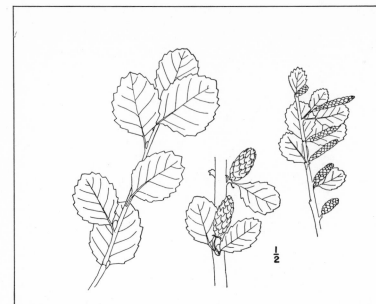

BETULA PUMILA   **FIG. 27**

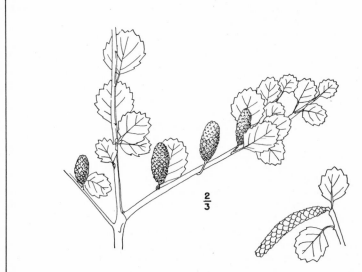

BETULA GLANDULOSA   **FIG. 28**

pubescent and glandular with stalked glands; nuts compressed-globose, 1–1.5 cm. long; seed edible. Flowers, March, April; nuts ripe, August, September.

The range of the American Hazelnut is from the New England states to Saskatchewan and southward, where it is found in thickets in both dry and moist soil and is very common. Michigan, throughout the Lower Peninsula.

The fruit of the American Hazelnut resembles the filbert of commerce (*C. avellana*) and is regarded as equal or superior to it. The squirrels and chipmunks are fully aware of this and it is rarely that the nuts are left long enough on the bushes to be gathered by humans.

Corylus cornuta Marsh. (Beaked Hazelnut). Fig. 26. (*Corylus rostrata* Ait., Gray's Manual, 7th Edition, Shrubs of Michigan, 1st Edition.) Shrubs 2–5 m. tall; bark gray; twigs glabrous or sometimes with a few long hairs; leaves simple,

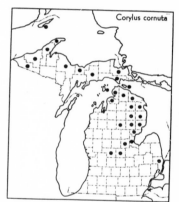

alternate, deciduous, ovate or ovate-oblong, 5-13 cm. long, 3.5-8 cm. wide, cordate or rounded at base, acuminate at the apex, sharply and irregularly serrate, or somewhat lobed, glabrous or with scattered hairs, pubescent on the veins beneath; petioles about 1 cm. long, puberulent; involucre of united bracts, much prolonged above the ovoid nut into a narrow tubular beak, densely bristly; seed edible. Flowers, April, May; fruit ripe, August, September.

The Beaked Hazel is distributed from Quebec to British Columbia, south to Delaware, Michigan, Missouri and westward. Michigan, common throughout the northern portion, rare in the southern.

Betula [Tourn.] L.—Birches

Young branchlets pubescent with long soft hairs, not glandular.................*B. pumila,* p. 89
Young branchlets glabrous or minutely puberulent, conspicuously
dotted with resinous wart-like glands...*B. glandulosa,* p. 90

Betula pumila L. (Low or Swamp Birch). Fig. 27. Stems 0.5–3 m. tall; bark dark gray to reddish-brown with numerous light-colored lenticels; young branches soft-downy; leaves alternate, simple, deciduous, obovate, orbicular or reniform, 1–3.5 cm. long, wedge-shaped at base and usually rounded at apex, coarsely serrate, hairy when young, becoming glabrate, veinlets on both sides finely reticulated; fruiting catkins 0.7–3 cm. long, 5–9 mm. thick; bracts variable;

[89]

wings narrower than or rarely as broad as the body of the fruit, or wanting; nut ovate to obovate. Flowers, May, June; fruit, August, September.

The Swamp Birch is found in bogs from Labrador and Newfoundland to Ontario, northern New Jersey, Ohio, Indiana, Illinois, Minnesota. Michigan, frequent throughout.

Betula pumila L. var. *glandulifera* Regel differs from the typical form in having its young branchlets and leaves resiniferous or glandular-dotted. Otherwise it is the same as the species. Its range is from Ontario and Michigan to Minnesota and Saskatchewan. In Michigan it appears to be more common northward than the species.

Betula glandulosa Michx. (Dwarf Birch). Fig. 28. Stems erect or depressed, 0.3–1 m. tall; twigs brown, glandular-dotted, not pubescent; leaves alternate, simple, deciduous, pinnately veined, 0.5–3 cm. long, wedge-obovate, green and glabrous both sides, irregularly denticulate-serrate, slightly reticulated; staminate catkins solitary, about 1 cm. long; fruiting catkins 0.5–2.5 cm. long, 5–9 mm. thick; nut very small, oblong, generally narrower than the wings. Flowers, June, July; fruit, August, September.

The Dwarf Birch ranges from the Arctic barrens south to the mountains of New Brunswick, Maine and New Hampshire, Lake Superior and Minnesota. Michigan, infrequent Upper and Lower Peninsula.

In alpine habitats the Dwarf Birch grows in a procumbent position, more like a creeping plant, to escape the force of the wind.

Alnus B. Ehrh.—ALDERS

In the first edition of this bulletin it was stated that the alders are exceedingly variable, leading to much confusion and overlapping in naming. For many years systematists have been aware that the common alder, which grows so abundantly as a shrub or small tree along our streams and around ponds, differed from the European species, *Alnus incana,* after which it had been named by the early botanists. However, it was not until 1945 that Fernald, after many years of preparation, published the results of his exhaustive study of the spring-flowering members of the genus. As a result of this publication (1945) the old name, *Alnus incana* (L.) Moench, has been abandoned for the American species and in its stead has been substituted the name entitled to be used under present-day rules of nomenclature. That Fernald realized the resistance which might develop over dropping the old-established name is evident when he says: "The name *Alnus incana* for the common Swamp Alder of the Labrador Peninsula, Newfoundland, eastern Canada and the more northeastern United States has been so thoroughly established . . . that to those who are more influenced by long-established usages than by precision its abandonment might seem mere iconoclasm. At the beginning, however, the name belonged strictly to a European tree and, of course, it must be retained for that variable but morphologically definite species."

Fernald has covered the extremely variable character of this shrub by recognizing and naming one variety and three forms, which will be referred to under the proper heading. As this revision of *Alnus* by Fernald is the latest and the one most likely to stand, it is here used.

Flowering as the leaves develop; leaves finely serrate;
samara with a conspicuous wing..*A. crispa*, p. 91
Flowering before the leaves develop; leaves coarsely serrate; samara wingless
or with a narrow coriaceous margin..*A. rugosa* var. *typica*, p. 91

Alnus crispa (Ait.) Pursh. (Green or Mountain Alder). Fig. 29. Shrubs 0.6–3 m. tall; bark gray or brownish; young branches and peduncles sparingly

puberulent or glabrate; leaves alternate, simple, deciduous, round-oval, ovate or slightly heart-shaped, in maturity 3–6 cm. long, glutinous and smooth, or slightly pubescent on the principal veins beneath, irregularly serrate, the margins often puckered; petioles 8–25 mm. long; staminate catkins 2–3 together, slender, 6–10 cm. long, the fertile slender-stalked, loosely racemose, in maturity 1–1.5 cm. long, 7–9 mm. thick, scales firm, woody, persistent, about 4 mm. long, 3–5 lobed; samara 2–2.5 mm. wide with a conspicuous wing, nutlet ovoid. Flowers, June; fruit, August, September.

Cool shores and mountains, Labrador to New Brunswick, Alaska, south to Massachusetts, New York, Michigan and British Columbia, and in the mountains to Virginia and North Carolina. Michigan, Upper Peninsula.

This species has variously been called in part *Alnus Alnobetula* and *Alnus viridis*. Also, what is possibly an extreme variation has been named *Alnus mollis* Fern. The leaves of this shrub are permanently covered beneath with dense soft hairs, and the young branches and peduncles are permanently soft-pubescent. It has been collected in Alger and Houghton counties.

Alnus rugosa (DuRoi) Spreng. var. *typica* H. Winkl. (Speckled Alder, Hoary Alder). Fig. 30. (*Alnus incana* (L.) Moench, Gray's Manual, 7th Edition, Shrubs of Michigan, 1st Edition.) A tall shrub, or sometimes a small tree, 2–8 m. tall, with erect or ascending stems; bark dark brown; young twigs reddish-brown, all speckled with abundant, conspicuous, linear-transverse, whitish lenticels up to 7 mm. or more long; leaves alternate, simple, deciduous, ovate, oval, subelliptic or rounded, broadest below or near the middle, with rounded to subcordate bases, often doubly-serrate or -dentate, often repand-undulate,

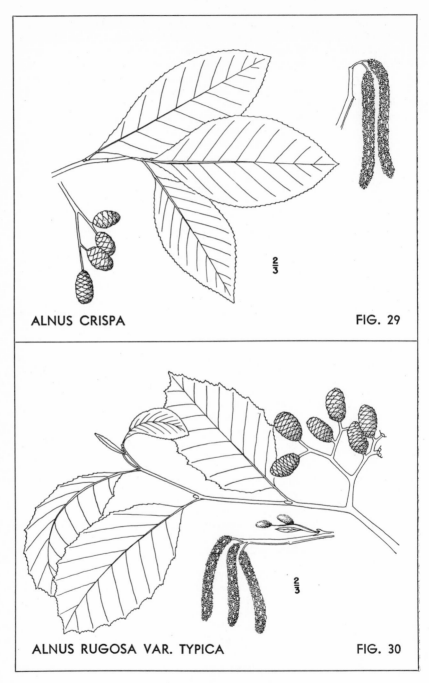

ALNUS CRISPA   FIG. 29

ALNUS RUGOSA VAR. TYPICA   FIG. 30

not at all or slightly glutinous, the mature blades with cross-veins beneath prominent and forming ladder-like reticulation between the main lateral veins, green or fulvous, not glaucous beneath, glabrous or promptly glabrate, only the principal veins or their axils sometimes permanently pilose; petiole 1.5–2 cm. long; staminate catkins 3–4 in a short raceme, 6–10 cm. long, formed during the previous autumn and expanding before the leaves in early spring, when a cloud of pollen issues from the anthers; the pistillate catkins are also formed during the previous autumn, 3–4 together below the staminate, and expand before the leaves, the fruiting 1–1.5 cm. long, 6–10 mm. thick; scales woody and 5-toothed, about 4 mm. long; samara orbicular or ovoid, wingless, 1-celled and 1-seeded. Flowers, March, April, before the leaves; fruit, September, October.

Low grounds, western Nova Scotia to northern Michigan, south to southern New England, locally to northern and eastern Pennsylvania and northern Indiana. Michigan, common throughout.

The following forms and varieties have essentially the same range as the type and may be sought for in our state: *Alnus rugosa* DuRoi var. *typica*, forma *Emersoniana* Fern., lower surface of leaves permanently soft-pilose or subvelutinous to touch; *Alnus rugosa* DuRoi var. *americana* (Regel) Fern., leaves ovate or oval to rounded-elliptic, with low toothing, lower surfaces glaucous or whitened, glabrous or promptly glabrate; *Alnus rugosa* DuRoi var. *americana*, forma *hypomalaca* Fern., lower surfaces of leaves densely soft-pilose or subvelutinous to touch.

The Speckled Alder grows as near the edge of our streams, lakes and ponds as possible and then leans over seemingly to get even nearer to the water. It fringes our northern trout streams, providing shade and protection for the fish and hurdles for the fishermen. The common name of this alder is derived from the lenticels, or spongy places, which are scattered over the external surface of the bark and serve to admit air to the interior of the stem. It is a valuable agent in holding stream banks and preventing erosion.

FAGACEAE—Beech Family

Trees or shrubs; leaves alternate, simple, deciduous, straight-veined; stipules deciduous; flowers monoecious, the sterile in pendulous or erect catkins, the fertile, solitary or several together; nut 1-celled and 1-seeded, fully or partly inclosed in a cup consisting of an involucre of united bracts; ovary 3–7-celled, with 1–2 ovules in each cell; styles 3.

Only one shrub in this family occurs in Michigan.

Quercus [Tourn.] L.—Oaks

Quercus prinoides Willd. (Scrub Oak, Dwarf Chestnut Oak). Fig. 31. Shrub or a very small tree; bark pale, often scaly; leaves alternate, simple, deciduous, oblanceolate, usually acute or pointed, 6–13 cm. long, 2–5 cm. broad,

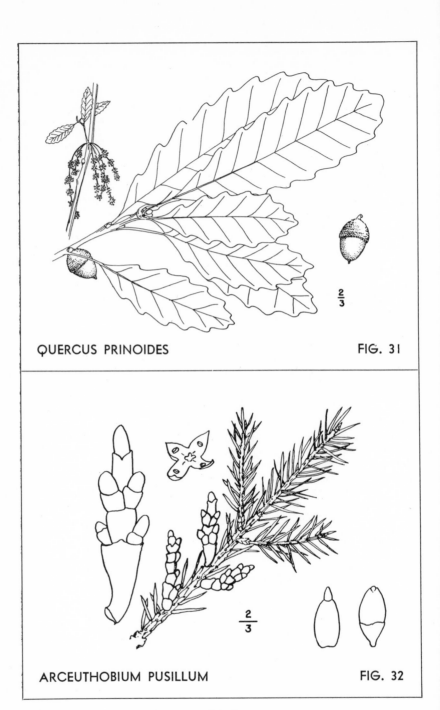

QUERCUS PRINOIDES

$\frac{2}{3}$

FIG. 31

ARCEUTHOBIUM PUSILLUM

$\frac{2}{3}$

FIG. 32

base wedge-shaped, undulate-toothed, upper side light green and glossy, a few scattered hairs, lower side pale, densely hairy; petioles 0.5–1.5 cm. long;

Quercus prinoides

staminate catkins about 4 cm. long; pistillate flowers sessile or short-stalked; acorns globose or obovoid, 1.5–2 cm. long, 1–1.5 cm. broad, light brown; cups pubescent, covering about one-third of the acorn. Flowers, April, May; fruit ripe, September, October.

Dry soil, New Hampshire to Minnesota, southward to North Carolina and Texas. Michigan, infrequent in lower portion of southern peninsula.

We are so accustomed to think of the oaks only as large trees that it is rather a novelty to find acorns growing on bushy shrubs. No doubt the squirrels bury the acorns for food the same as they do those from the tree species of oaks. No doubt, too, some proportion of the acorns thus stored are never found again and remain in the ground to sprout and grow another season, thus aiding in the distribution of the species.

LORANTHACEAE—Mistletoe Family

Parasitic green shrubs or herbs containing chlorophyll, growing on woody plants and absorbing food from their sap through specialized roots. In our genera the leaves are reduced to opposite scales; the flowers are regular and dioecious; the fruit a berry.

There are about 21 genera and 500 species widely distributed, mostly in the tropics. Only one genus, with one species, is represented in Michigan.

Arceuthobium Bieb.—Dwarf Mistletoes

Arceuthobium pusillum Peck. (Dwarf Mistletoe). Fig. 32. Small or minute fleshy, glabrous plants, parasitic on the branches of coniferous trees;

Arceuthobium pusillum

stems 6–20 mm. high, usually simple, olive-green to chestnut-colored, nearly round when fresh, 4-angled when dry; leaves reduced to connate suborbicular appressed scales about 1 mm. wide; flowers solitary in most of the axils, regular, dioecious; perianth simple; calyx mostly compressed, the staminate usually 3-parted, the pistillate 2-toothed; anthers a single orbicular cell; berry ovoid-oblong, acute, about 2 mm. long, borne on a short recurved pedicel; seeds enclosed in a viscid mucus. Flowers, April, June; berry ripe, June, September.

Growing on spruce and tamarack, New-foundland and eastern Quebec to Pennsyl-

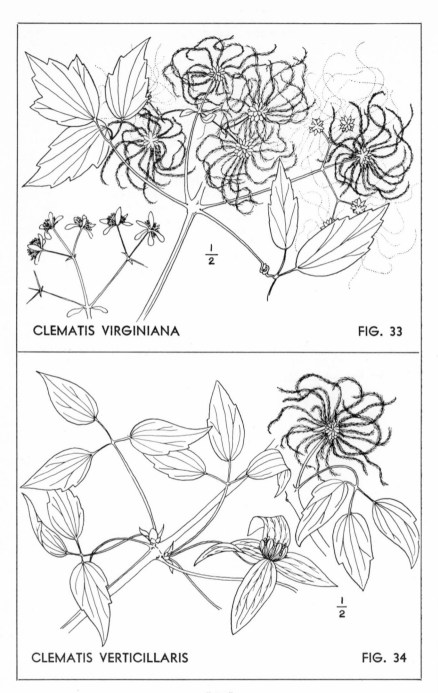

CLEMATIS VIRGINIANA   FIG. 33

CLEMATIS VERTICILLARIS   FIG. 34

vania and northern Michigan. Michigan, confined to the Upper Peninsula and the northern counties of the Lower Peninsula.

The Dwarf Mistletoe is distributed by the birds, which carry the seeds from tree to tree. It often causes the growth known as "Witch's Brooms" on the host tree.

To include such a little, inconspicuous plant among the shrubs may be stretching things too far. But it is a shrub, and to discover it may provide the discoverer with a greater thrill than locating many of the larger and more conspicuous plants.

This little parasite belongs to the same family as the famous mistletoe which, tradition has it, if hung on a chandelier or other suitable support at holiday time, will result in the person standing under it receiving a kiss. That plant does not grow in Michigan, and I cannot say whether or not our mistletoe will produce the same results, but it might be worth a trial.

RANUNCULACEAE—Crowfoot Family

Herbs or sometimes woody plants, with a colorless and usually acrid juice; leaves simple or compound, alternate, except *Clematis,* which has opposite leaves; flowers regular or irregular, with or without petals; sepals 3–15, often colored like petals; stamens many, rarely few; pistils 1-celled, many, rarely solitary; ovules 1 to numerous, anatropous; fruits either dry pods, achenes, or berries.

A family of some thirty-odd genera and over a thousand species, mostly in the temperate and frigid zones. Only the following genus is woody.

Clematis L.—Virgin's Bowers

Flowers white, borne in leafy panicles...*C. virginiana,* p. 97

Flowers purplish, borne on long slender peduncles, solitary
in the axils or at the ends of branches...*C. verticillaris,* p. 98

Clematis virginiana L. (Virginia Virgin's Bower). Fig. 33. A long, some-

Clematis virginiana

what woody vine, climbing freely over bushes and fences; stems shallow-grooved; leaves deciduous, opposite, trifoliate; petioles bent and acting as tendrils, or straight and deflexed; leaflets ovate, rounded or cordate at the base, acute or acuminate at the apex, coarsely toothed or lobed, bright green and glabrous above, paler and silky-villous beneath when young, becoming more or less completely glabrous in age, 4–9 cm. long, 2–6 cm. broad; flowers white, borne in leafy panicles, 1.5–2 cm. broad, polygamo-dioecious; sepals thin, petal-like, spreading; petals none; anthers short, blunt, styles persistent, plumose, 4–5 cm. long in fruit, attached to the achenes and forming showy, downy clusters. Flowers, June, July; fruits, August, September.

Stream banks, dry woods etc., Georgia to Tennessee, northward to Nova Scotia and Manitoba. Michigan, frequent throughout.

A very ornamental vine, particularly in the fall when furnished with the plume-like tufted fruits.

The staminate and pistillate flowers grow on separate plants, but the latter have the curious habit of producing sterile stamens along with the pistils, which may indicate a tendency or an aspiration on the part of the plant to produce perfect flowers.

This vine accomplishes its climbing by the bending or clasping of the leaf-stalks. The stalks are sensitive and when they come in contact with an available object clasp it and thus support the vine. Darwin found by rubbing a leaf-stalk of a young leaf a few times on any side the leaf would bend to that side in the course of a few hours, but that it would return to the original position if it did not find an object upon which it could hook.

The seeds with their plumose attachments are well suited to wide distribution by the autumn winds.

Clematis verticillaris DC. (Purple Virgin's Bower). Fig. 34. Perennial climbing vine; stems woody, nearly glabrous; leaves deciduous, opposite, tri-

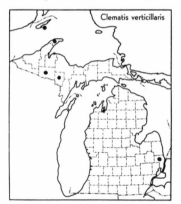

foliate with slender common and partial petioles; leaflets ovate or slightly heart-shaped, pointed, thin, toothed or entire, 3–8 cm. long, lower leaves sometimes entire or pinnately cleft, smaller than the upper; flowers solitary, terminal or axillary, long-peduncled, 5–7.5 cm. across, pinkish-purple, or purplish-blue; petals 12–18 mm. long, spatulate; sepals 4, very large, ovate-lanceolate, petaloid, widely spreading, silky along the margins and veins; stamens very numerous, the outer generally with broadened filaments resembling petals; styles about 5 cm. long, persistent, forming plumose tails on the fruit. Flowers, May, June; fruits, August, September.

Rocky woodlands and thickets chiefly in calcareous districts, Hudson Bay to Manitoba, Quebec, Lake Winnipeg, locally south to Delaware, Virginia, West Virginia, Michigan, and Minnesota. Michigan, rare in both peninsulas.

Not more than a half dozen or so collections of this vine are in the large state herbaria. Michigan is definitely within its geographic range, and the vine should be looked for and reported whenever found.

ANONACEAE—Custard Apple Family

Trees or shrubs; leaves deciduous, alternate, entire and feather-veined; stipules none; flowers axillary, nodding; calyx of 3 sepals; petals mostly 6, arranged in 2 series; stamens many; filaments very short; pistils many, separate or coherent; fruit large and fleshy; seeds large.

About 46 genera and 550 species, mostly in the tropics. Only the following in Michigan.

Asimina Adans.—North American Papaws

Asimina triloba Dunal. (Common Papaw). Fig. 35. Shrub or small tree, 1–12 m. tall; bark smooth, or ridged on the older plants; twigs reddish-brown, pubescent, becoming glabrous; leaves deciduous, alternate, entire, thin, obovate, wedge-shaped at base, acute, 1.5–3 dm. long; petioles 8–12 mm. long; flowers dark purple, axillary, appearing with the leaves on shoots of the preceding season, 2–4 cm. in diameter; sepals 3, ovate, 8–12 mm. long, densely dark-pubescent; petals 6, the outer spreading, nearly round, somewhat longer than the ovate inner ones; stamens many, very short; fruit a fleshy berry, pendulous with several on a thick peduncle, 7–13 cm. long, 2–7 cm. thick, green, turning dark brown when ripe, the pulp sweet and edible. Flowers, March, April; fruit ripe in October.

Asimina triloba

Banks of streams in rich soil, Ontario, New York, New Jersey to Michigan, Nebraska, Florida and Texas. Michigan, confined to about the southern one-third of the Lower Peninsula.

The Papaw has interesting foliage and is desirable for ornamental planting. I have tried many times to establish it, but found it difficult to transplant, perhaps because the attempt was made near the northern limits of its range. In some districts the Papaw is called the Wild Banana Tree. Where it grows in woods it makes an important under-story shrub.

MENISPERMACEAE—Moonseed Family

Climbing or twining woody or herbaceous vines with palmate or peltate, alternate leaves, without stipules; flowers small, dioecious, borne in panicles, racemes or cymes; sepals 4–12; petals 6, imbricated in 2 rows of 3 each, sometimes less or wanting; stamens about the same number as the petals; carpels 3 or more, generally 6; styles commonly incurved; fruit a 1-seeded berry; ovary nearly straight, with the stigma at the apex, mostly incurving at maturity, thus bending the seed and embryo into a crescent or a ring.

A family of about 55 genera and some 250 species, mostly tropical, but with a few extending northward into the temperate zone. It is represented in Michigan by the following genus only.

Menispermum [Tourn.] L.—Moonseeds

Menispermum canadense L. (Canada Moonseed). Fig. 36. Stems climbing over shrubs or fences, 2–4 m. long, somewhat pubescent or entirely glabrous,

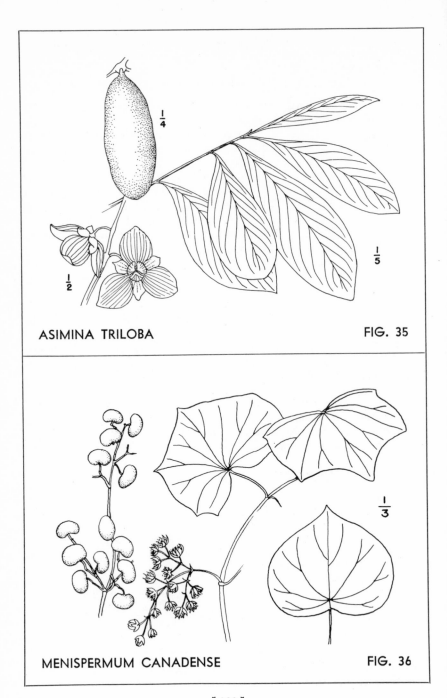

ASIMINA TRILOBA   FIG. 35

MENISPERMUM CANADENSE   FIG. 36

twining; petioles long, slender, attached peltately to the margin, although sometimes so near that this character is hardly apparent; leaves broadly ovate, 7–29 cm. in width, 6–17 cm. in depth, cor-

Menispermum canadense

date or sometimes nearly truncate at the base, acuminate, acute or obtuse at the apex, entire or with 3–7 lobes, smooth above, pubescent below; flowers small, dioecious, greenish-white, borne in loose panicles; sepals 4–8 in 2 whorls; petals 6–8, shorter than the sepals; stamens 12–24; pistils in fertile flowers, 2–4, inserted on a slightly raised receptacle; fruit a drupe, globose-oblong, 6–8 mm. in diameter, bluish-black; seed bent into a crescent. Flowers June, July; berries ripe in autumn.

In woods and along hillsides and streams, western Quebec to Manitoba, south to Georgia, Nebraska, and Arkansas. Michigan, frequent.

The crescent shape of its seeds furnishes the reason for calling this plant Moonseed. It is an appropriate name. With its bunches of bluish-black fruit it is rather attractive in the fall, but apparently is not entirely satisfactory as a cultivated plant. The root, which is yellow and bitter, was formerly used in medicine, but has now largely been supplanted.

BERBERIDACEAE—Barberry Family

Shrubs or herbs, with alternate or basal, simple or compound leaves, with or without stipules; flowers mostly terminal, solitary or in racemes; sepals and petals imbricated in the bud in two or several series; stamens as many as the petals and opposite them, or more numerous, situated on the receptacle beneath the ovary and free from it; anthers mostly opening by two valves; pistil single; style short or wanting; seeds few or many; fruit a berry or a pod.

A family of about 10 genera and over 200 species widely distributed, principally in the north temperate zone.

The following is the only woody genus in Michigan, which is here represented by one species.

Berberis [Tourn.] L.—Barberries

Berberis vulgaris L. (Common Barberry). Fig. 37. Thorny shrub, 1–2 m. in height, the branches arched and drooping at the ends; twigs gray; glabrous throughout; wood and inner bark yellow; leaves alternate or fascicled, obovate or spatulate, obtuse at the apex, cuneate at the base, closely bristly-serrate, prominently pinnately veined, 1.5–6 cm. long, 0.5–2.5 cm. wide, many of those on shoots reduced to 3-pronged spines; flowers perfect, yellow, about 8 mm. broad, numerous in drooping racemes, 4–8 cm. long, terminating lateral branches; sepals 6–9, petaloid, bracted; petals 6, entire, imbricated in two series; stamens 6; fruit an oblong or ellipsoid berry with 1 seed, scarlet when ripe, acid. Flowers April, May; fruit ripe in the autumn.

The Common Barberry is a native of Europe and formerly was much used in ornamental planting. From this source it spread and flourished as a wild

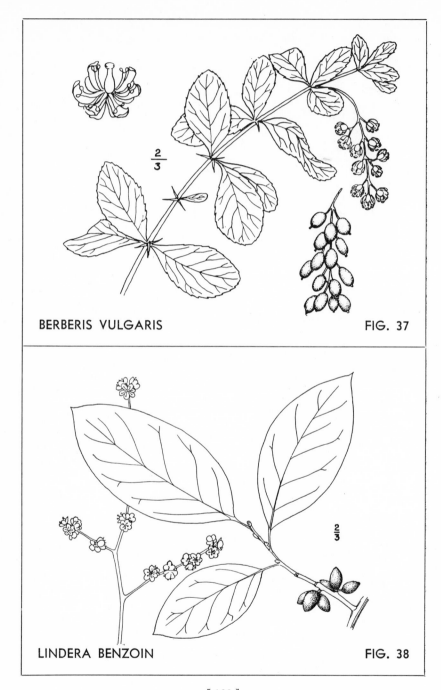

$\frac{2}{3}$

BERBERIS VULGARIS　　　　FIG. 37

$\frac{2}{3}$

LINDERA BENZOIN　　　　FIG. 38

shrub, becoming naturalized in many parts of Michigan. However, it is the alternate host of the fungus which causes black stem rust of wheat, and for this reason it has been outlawed. On the

Berberis vulgaris

assumption that it had been exterminated, the shrub was omitted from the first edition of 'Shrubs of Michigan,' but it no doubt still persists in some localities in spite of the efforts to get rid of it. It is included in the second edition with the hope that anyone finding the shrub will either destroy it or will report it to the proper authorities. In the Cranbrook herbarium is a specimen of this shrub, collected some years ago on a farm in Oakland County, showing the rust growth on the leaves.

It is unfortunate that it has been necessary to outlaw the Common Barberry, as it is a most interesting plant. It is perfectly hardy in our climate and becomes a graceful bush, bearing in the spring drooping racemes of attractive yellow flowers. Although not large and showy, the flowers are especially interesting because of the irritability of the stamens. When a filament is touched on the inside with a hard object, such as the point of a pin, the stamen bends forward toward the pistil, touches the stigma with the anther, and remains curved for a short time before partially recovering its original position.

Certain aspects of the leaves are also interesting. On the fresh shoots of the season they are mostly reduced to sharp, triple or branched slender spines. These spines, which are really reduced leaves, are responsible for the thorny reputation of the shrub. The next season from the axils of the thorns grow the rosettes or fascicles of regular leaves.

Berberis Thunbergii DC., Japanese Barberry, with reddish foliage, and *Berberis aquifolium* Pursh, Mahonia or Oregon Grapes, with holly-like green leaves, two frequently cultivated shrubs, have been reported by Hanes from Kalamazoo County as infrequent but persisting escapes.

LAURACEAE—Laurel Family

Aromatic trees or shrubs; leaves alternate, simple, deciduous, mostly with minute pellucid dots; flowers regular; calyx of 4-6 colored sepals, imbricated in two rows in the bud, free from the ovary, which is 1-celled and 1-ovuled; style single; fruit a 1-seeded drupe.

The genus *Lindera* is the only one in this family in Michigan having plants classed as shrubs. The Sassafras is a member of the Laurel family but it is rated as a tree and therefore not included.

Lindera Thunb.—Spice Bush

Lindera Benzoin Blume. (Spice Bush). Fig. 38. (*Benzoin aestivale* (L.) Nees, Gray's Manual, 7th Edition, Shrubs of Michigan, 1st Edition.) Aromatic shrubs 1–3 m. in height, well-shaped; branchlets at first green, smooth, later olive-green, at times gray, finally grayish-brown, roughened; leaves alternate, simple, deciduous, oblong-ovate to oval, 4–15 cm. long, 2–6.5 cm. wide, acute or short-acuminate at the apex, or the lower leaves blunt or rounded, nearly smooth, pale underneath, margin entire; petioles 0.5–2 cm. long, or shorter on the lower leaves; the honey-yellow flowers appearing before the leaves in small sessile clusters or umbels of 4–6, surrounded by an involucre of 4 deciduous scales; fruit a fleshy, obovoid drupe, bright red, about 1 cm. long. Flowers, March, April; fruit ripe, August, September.

Lindera Benzoin

The range of the Spice Bush is from Maine to Michigan, eastern Kansas and southward to Georgia and Mississippi. Michigan, frequent in central and southern portions.

Although generally found in damp rich woods it is easily transplanted and is worthy of a place in any cultivated border. The bush is aromatic in bark, fruit and leaf, and it is from this quality that it derives it generic name, *Benzoin,* the name of an Oriental gum. A concoction made from the bark has been used in intermittent fevers, and the berries are said to have been sometimes used in place of allspice.

The shrub is well supplied with common names: Wild Allspice, Fever Bush, Benjamin Bush, Snap-wood.

SAXIFRAGACEAE—Saxifrage Family

Shrubs or herbs; leaves deciduous, alternate or rarely opposite; true stipules, none, but often with stipule-like sheaths; flowers mostly perfect and regular; inflorescence of several kinds, or the flowers solitary; calyx either free or adherent, mostly persistent, or withering; petals 4–5, rarely wanting; stamens 4–10, or numerous; ovary 1- or 2-celled, rarely more; seeds small, numerous.

Of the Saxifrage family only one genus with shrubby plants is found in Michigan.

Ribes L.—Currants, Gooseberries

1. Peduncles 1–4 flowered; pedicels not jointed below the ovary; stems more or less prickly (The species in this group are often treated as the genus *Grossularia.*)
   2. Ovary bristly; fruit prickly; styles united to the top;
      leaves densely soft-pubescent both sides.................. ....*R. Cynosbati,* p. 105
   2. Ovary glabrous, pubescent or with stalked glands, not prickly;
      styles not united until above the middle
      3. Flowers white; stamens and styles long exserted........................*R. gracile,* p. 105
      3. Flowers greenish or purplish; stamens and styles
         little or not at all exserted
         4. Stamens about equalling the petals
            5. Calyx-tube tubular...*R. setosum,* p. 107
            5. Calyx-tube campanulate..................................*R. oxyacanthoides,* p. 107
         4. Stamens twice as long as the petals or longer;
            ovary glabrous or with some stalked glands;
            calyx-lobes about as long as the tube...........................*R. hirtellum,* p. 109
1. Peduncles 5- to several-flowered; pedicels jointed beneath the ovary; stems
   without prickles (except *R. lacustre*)
   6. Leaves with resinous dots beneath; calyx campanulate; fruit black

Ribes Cynosbati L. (Prickly Gooseberry, Dogberry). Fig. 39. Shrub, 0.5–1.5 m. tall, erect or spreading; nodal spines slender, solitary or sometimes 2–3

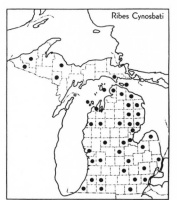

Ribes Cynosbati

together, 0.5 cm. long; leaves alternate, simple, deciduous, thin, round-ovate, rounded or subcordate at base, soft pubescent both sides, 3–5 cm. long, 3.5–5.5 cm. wide, 3–5-lobed, irregularly and finely dentate; petioles slender, generally pubescent; peduncles and pedicels slender, pubescent; flowers, 1–3, greenish-white, campanulate to urn-shaped; calyx-lobes oblong, shorter than the ovoid tube; petals shorter than the sepals; stamens and undivided style not exserted; berry armed with long prickles, 8–15 mm. in diameter, reddish-purple when ripe. Flowers, April, June; fruit ripe, July August.

Rocky woods, thickets and hillsides, western Maine to the mountains of North Carolina, west to Manitoba and Missouri. Michigan, common throughout.

This is our commonest wild gooseberry. The berries when ripe are sweet and pleasant, but the spines are very sharp and uncomfortable to handle. It is a common undershrub in our upland woods.

Ribes gracile

Ribes gracile Michx. (Missouri Gooseberry). Fig. 40. Erect shrub, 1–1.5 m. tall; young twigs greenish-yellow; nodal spines 1–3, 7–17 mm. long, stout and red; leaves slender-petioled, alternate, simple, deciduous, somewhat pubescent when young, nearly orbicular in outline, 2–4 cm. long and wide, rather bluntly 3–5-lobed, dentate, truncate slightly cordate, or sometimes obtuse at base; peduncles long and slender, more or less pubescent, 1–3-flowered; flowers white or whitish, drooping, pedicels about 1 cm. long in fruit; bractlets 2 mm. long, glandular; calyx-tube narrow, shorter than the linear lobes; petals small, spatulate, erect; filaments capillary, 1–1.5 cm. long,

[105]

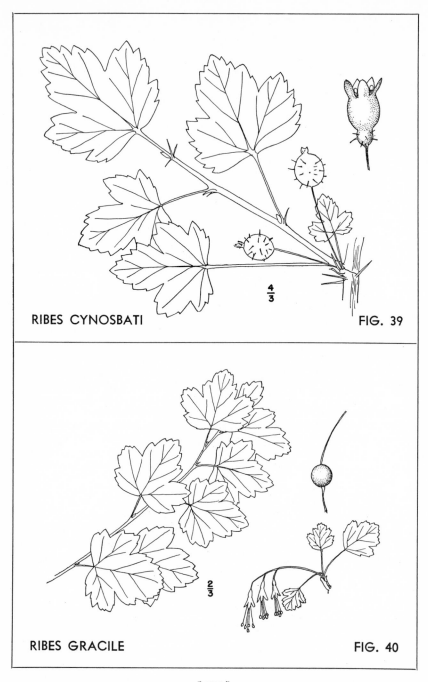

RIBES CYNOSBATI

$\frac{4}{3}$

FIG. 39

RIBES GRACILE

$\frac{2}{3}$

FIG. 40

connivent or parallel, conspicuously exserted; berry smooth, globose, 8–15 mm. in diameter, dark purple when ripe. Flowers, May; fruit, July, August.

In dry or rocky soil, Connecticut to South Dakota and southward. Michigan, recorded from upper counties of the Lower Peninsula only.

This species appears to be much less common than the preceding, which may be occasioned by the confusion of names. The following are synonyms: *Ribes missouriense* Nutt.; *Grossularia missouriensis* Cov. & Britt.

Ribes setosum Lindl. (Bristly Gooseberry). Fig. 41. Medium shrub, erect or spreading; nodal spines about 2 cm. long or less, slender, sometimes none;

bristles unusually numerous, scattered; leaves slender-petioled, alternate, simple, deciduous, more or less pubescent, at least when young, broadly ovate or orbicular, 3–5-lobed, the lobes incised-dentate; peduncles 1–4-flowered; flowers greenish-white, 6–10 mm. long; calyx-tube cylindric, longer than the lobes; stamens 5, not exserted; fruit red or black, sparingly bristly, or often glabrous. Flowers, May; fruit, July, August.

On lake shores and in thickets, western Ontario and Manitoba to Saskatchewan, Nebraska, and Wyoming. Michigan, so far recorded from Upper Peninsula only.

Ribes oxyacanthoides L. (Northern Gooseberry). Fig. 42. Low shrub 0.5–1 m. tall, branches slender, reddish-brown, usually smooth, but sometimes with scattered prickles; nodal spines 1–3, light-

colored; leaves alternate, simple, deciduous, suborbicular, 2–4 cm. long and about as wide, the lobes acute or obtuse, irregularly crenate-dentate, commonly pubescent above and beneath; petioles generally shorter than the blades, pubescent; peduncles very short, 1–2-flowered; flowers small, perfect, greenish-white to dull purplish; calyx-lobes mostly glabrous, oblong or obovate, recurved when mature; petals 5, broadly ovate or spatulate, alternate with the sepals; stamens 5, short, not exserted; pistil slightly longer than the stamens; berry globose, smooth, about 1 cm. in diameter, reddish-purple when ripe. Flowers, May, July; fruit ripe, July, August.

In woods and low grounds, Newfoundland to Hudson Bay, British Columbia, Michigan, North Dakota and Montana. Michigan, both Upper and Lower Peninsulas.

This is the common smooth-fruited gooseberry of the north. Its fruit is edible and has a very agreeable flavor. The following varieties, both found in Michigan, have been separated and named: *Ribes oxyacanthoides* L. var. *calcicola* Fern.,

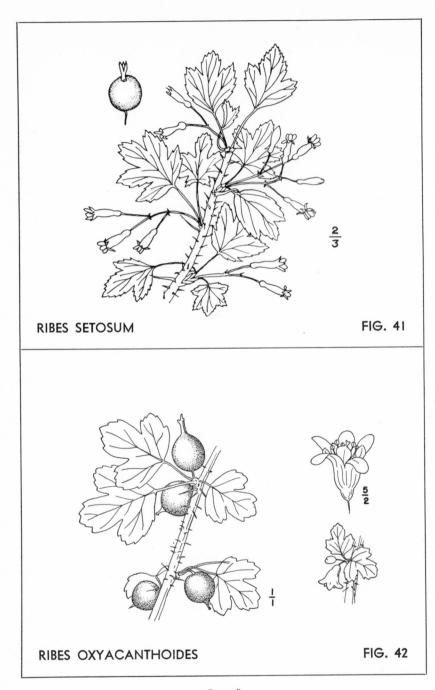

RIBES SETOSUM

$\frac{2}{3}$

FIG. 41

$\frac{5}{2}$

$\frac{1}{1}$

RIBES OXYACANTHOIDES

FIG. 42

with densely soft-pubescent leaves and pubescent calyx; *Ribes oxyacanthoides* L. var. *saxosum* (Hook.) Cov., with the calyx and subcordate leaves essentially glabrous.

Ribes hirtellum Michx. (Low Wild Gooseberry). Fig. 43. Shrub 1 m. tall or less; branches usually without spines, sometimes bristly, dark brown in age; nodal spines rarely present; leaves alternate, simple, deciduous, suborbicular or ovate-orbicular in outline, incisely 3–5-lobed and dentate, mostly cuneate at base, about 1–3 cm. in width, glabrous or sparingly pubescent; peduncles short, 1–3-flowered; bracts much shorter than the pedicels; sepals green or purplish; petals obovate; calyx-tube narrowly campanulate; ovary glabrous or rarely pubescent with stalked glands; berry globose, black or purple, 8–10 mm. in diameter. Flowers, late May or June; fruit ripe, late July or August.

Ribes hirtellum

Swamps and moist woods, Newfoundland to Manitoba, West Virginia and South Dakota. Michigan, infrequent throughout.

Ribes americanum Mill. (American Black Currant). Fig. 44. (*Ribes floridum* L'Hér., Gray's Manual, 7th Edition, Shrubs of Michigan, 1st Edition.)

Ribes americanum

Shrubs with erect, unarmed branches; bark becoming dark brown; leaves alternate, simple, deciduous, thin, nearly orbicular in outline, glabrous above, more or less pubescent and resinous-dotted beneath, 4–7 cm. in length and width, cordate or truncate at base, sharply 3–5-lobed, doubly serrate; petioles pubescent, 2–4 cm. long; racemes drooping, downy, 5–16-flowered; bracts linear-lanceolate, longer than the pedicels, persistent; flowers 8–10 mm. in diameter, yellow and whitish; calyx tubular bell-shaped, smooth, its lobes short, broad, obtuse; petals oblong, erect, more than half as long as the sepals; stamens not exserted; styles 6–7 mm. long, united nearly to the summit; berry black, 6–10 mm. in diameter, smooth, edible. Flowers, April, May; fruit ripe, July, August.

The Wild Black Currant ranges from Nova Scotia to Manitoba, southward to Kentucky, Iowa and Nebraska. Michigan, common throughout.

This species resembles the black currant of the garden, but is rarely cultivated. The foliage is luxuriant and it forms a graceful spreading bush, attractive both in flower and fruit.

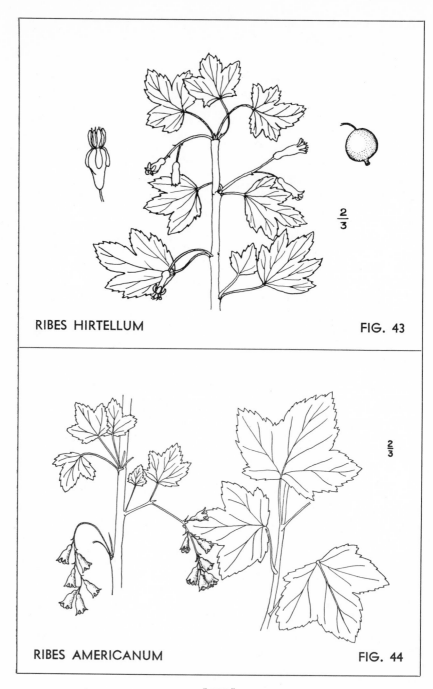

RIBES HIRTELLUM

$\frac{2}{3}$

FIG. 43

RIBES AMERICANUM

$\frac{2}{3}$

FIG. 44

Ribes ringens Michx. (Northern Black Currant). Fig. 45. (*Ribes hudson-ianum* Richards., Gray's Manual, 7th Edition.) Shrub, 5–10 cm. high, branches

Ribes ringens

erect, unarmed; old stems exfoliating and becoming reddish-black; foliage ill-scented; petioles slender, nearly as long as the blades, densely pubescent and bearing resinous glands; leaves alternate, simple, deciduous, suborbicular to reniform in outline, 4–7 cm. long, 5–9 cm. wide, nearly glabrate above, densely pubescent and resinous-dotted beneath, ciliate on the margins, 3–5-lobed, the lobes obtuse or acutish, coarsely dentate, deeply cordate at the base; racemes 2–4 cm. long, several-flowered, pedicels and peduncles puberulent; bracts bristle-like, usually equalling or shorter than the pedicels; flowers white, about 5 mm. in diameter; calyx broadly campanulate, the sepals oblong-lanceolate, slightly spreading and densely pubescent; petals about half as long as the sepals, narrowly cuneate; stamens short, not exserted; styles conical, united more than half their length; berry black, glabrous, 5–10 mm. in diameter. Flowers, May, June; fruit ripe, July, August.

Hudson Bay and western Ontario to Alaska, Minnesota and British Columbia. Michigan, both Lower and Upper Peninsulas.

Ribes lacustre (Pers.) Poir. (Swamp Black Currant). Fig. 46. Low shrub; young stems clothed with bristly prickles and with weak thorns; leaves simple,

Ribes lacustre

alternate, deciduous, nearly orbicular, thin, glabrous or nearly so, deeply 5–7-lobed, 2.5–7 cm. long and about the same width, the lobes obtuse or acutish, incised-dentate, cordate at base, without resinous dots; petioles slender, more or less pubescent; racemes loosely spreading or drooping, 2–5 cm. long, comparatively few-flowered, the peduncle and pedicels puberulent and glandular-bristly; flowers greenish or purplish, 7–8 mm. in diameter; calyx-tube short, sepals blunt, longer than the petals; stamens very short, not exserted; styles short, partly united; berry bristly, purplish-black, about 6–10 mm. in diameter. Flowers, May, June; fruit, July, August.

Cold woods and swamps, Newfoundland to British Columbia, south to northern New England, Michigan, Minnesota, Colorado and northern California and in the mountains to Pennsylvania. Michigan, mostly northern part of Lower Peninsula and the Upper Peninsula.

The fruit of the Swamp Black Currant is unpleasant to the taste.

[111]

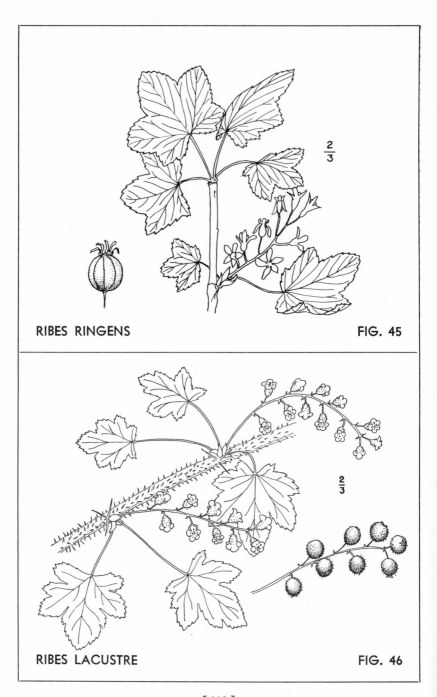

$\frac{2}{3}$

RIBES RINGENS   **FIG. 45**

$\frac{2}{3}$

RIBES LACUSTRE   **FIG. 46**

Ribes glandulosum Grauer. (Skunk Currant, Fetid Currant). Fig. 47. (*Ribes prostratum* L'Hér., Gray's Manual, 7th Edition, Shrubs of Michigan, 1st Edition.) Low shrub with reclining and spreading branches, thornless and without prickles; bark blackish on older branches; leaves simple, alternate, deciduous, thin, deeply heart-shaped, 5–7-lobed, smooth or somewhat pubescent on the veins beneath, the lobes ovate, acute, doubly serrate, 3.5–6 cm. long, 5–8 cm. wide; petioles about as long as the blades; racemes erect or ascending, 3–6 cm. long, loosely several-flowered, peduncles and pedicels puberulent, bracts glandular, shorter than the pedicels; flowers yellowish or purplish, about 4 mm. broad; calyx broadly campanulate, its lobes short and broad; stamens 5, short, not exserted; style 2-cleft; berry red, glandular-bristly, 6–7

Ribes glandulosum

mm. in diameter, disagreeable flavor. Flowers May, June; fruit, July, August.

In cold wet places, Newfoundland to Athabasca, British Columbia, south to northern New England, Michigan, Minnesota, and along the mountains to North Carolina. Michigan, upper part of Lower Peninsula and the Upper Peninsula.

Both plant and fruit emit a disagreeable odor when bruised, hence its common name, Skunk Currant. Its habitat is the cold, damp woods and it does not take kindly to cultivation or the warmth of sunshine.

Ribes sativum (Reichenb.) Syme. (Common Red Currant, Red Garden Currant). Fig. 48. (*Ribes vulgare* Lam., Gray's Manual, 7th Edition.) Erect shrub 1–2 m. tall, unarmed; petioles slender, about the length of the blades, glabrous or slightly pubescent; leaves simple, alternate, deciduous, rather firm, glabrate or somewhat pubescent beneath, glabrous above or with a few scattered hairs, orbicular or broader, cordate at base, 3–5-lobed, the lobes short-ovate, sharply dentate; racemes borne mostly among the leafy shoots, pendulous, 3–10 cm. long, loosely flowered; peduncles puberulent and somewhat glandular; pedicels mostly glandless, longer than the bracts; flowers greenish, about 5 mm. in diameter; calyx yellowish, flat-campanulate, the sepals oval and abruptly narrowed below the middle; petals narrowly cuneate, about 1/3 as long

Ribes sativum

as the sepals; stamens short; styles united at the base, separating at the top; ovary glabrous; fruit bright red, plump and juicy, 8–12 mm. in diameter. Flowers, May; fruit ripe, late June and July.

Commonly cultivated. Escaped to fence-rows, thickets, open woods and swamps, Massachusetts to Ontario, Virginia, Wisconsin, Oregon and British Columbia. Native of Europe. Michigan, both Upper and Lower Peninsulas.

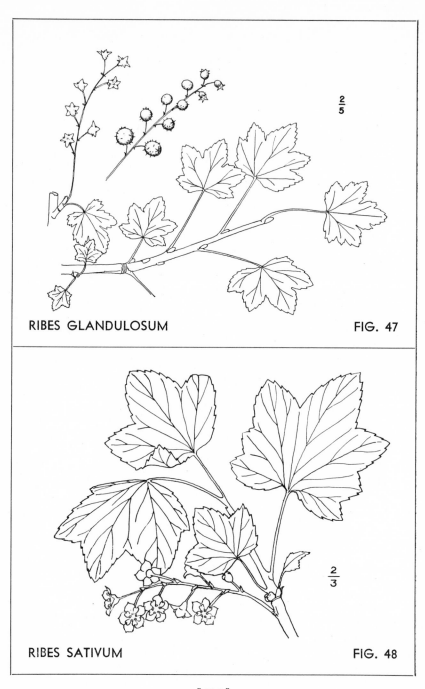

$\frac{2}{5}$

RIBES GLANDULOSUM   FIG. 47

$\frac{2}{3}$

RIBES SATIVUM   FIG. 48

[114]

Ribes triste Pall. (Swamp Red Currant). Fig. 49. Low, straggling or reclining shrub, the branches often rooting freely, unarmed, the bark becoming grayish-black; leaves simple, alternate, deciduous,

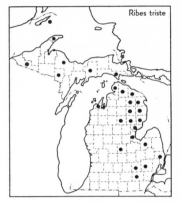

glabrous above, pale and more or less pubescent beneath, somewhat heart-shaped, the sides nearly parallel, 5–10 cm. long and broad, the lobes mostly broad-deltoid, doubly crenate-serrate; petioles more or less pubescent and generally shorter than the blades; racemes borne on the old wood and mostly below the tufted leaves, several-flowered, drooping, 3–9 cm. long; peduncles and pedicels puberulent and glandular, pedicels longer than the ovate bractlets; flowers 4–5 mm. in diameter, purplish; calyx saucer-shaped, its segments broadly cuneate, very obtuse; petals shorter than the sepals, broadly cuneate; styles deeply cleft; anther-sacs contiguous, nearly parallel; ovary glabrous; berry bright red, glabrous, 4–7 mm. in diameter, hard and acid. Flowers, June, July; fruit ripe, August, September.

Cold woods and bogs, Newfoundland to Alaska, New Jersey, Michigan, South Dakota and Oregon. Michigan, well distributed in both peninsulas.

Ribes triste Pall. var. *albinervium* (Michx.) Fern., with leaves glabrous or glabrate beneath, has the same general range as the species. In Michigan it has been recorded from Alger, Keweenaw, Oakland, Mackinac and Marquette counties. It is no doubt to be found throughout the state and should be looked for and reported when found. In addition to the foregoing, the three following cultivated currants have sparingly escaped in the state. Their abundance as evidenced by collections in the state herbaria, however, does not seem to warrant including them as permanent additions to our shrub population. *Ribes odoratum* Wendl. (*Ribes aureum* Pursh, Gray's Manual, 7th Edition), Washtenaw County; *Ribes Grossularia* L., Washtenaw County; *Ribes nigrum* L., Washtenaw and St. Clair counties.

HAMAMELIDACEAE—WITCH-HAZEL FAMILY

Shrubs or trees; leaves alternate, simple, deciduous; stipules deciduous; flowers in heads or spikes, often polygamous or monoecious; calyx adhering to the base of the ovary, which consists of two pistils united below, forming a 2-beaked and 2-celled woody capsule, opening at the summit, with one or more bony seeds in each cell; petals 4 to many or none, long and narrow; stamens twice as many as the petals.

Only the following genus occurs in Michigan.

Hamamelis L.—WITCH-HAZELS

Hamamelis virginiana L. (Common Witch-hazel). Fig. 50. Tall shrub with smooth bark, becoming broken on old specimens; twigs with a more or less rusty pubescence; leaves simple, alternate, deciduous short-petioled, obovate or oval, 6–15 cm. long, 4–10 cm. wide, wavy-toothed, with stellate pubescence

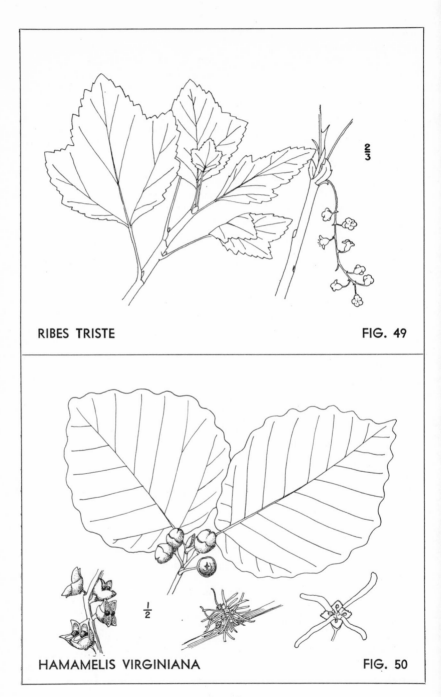

RIBES TRISTE   FIG. 49

$\frac{2}{3}$

HAMAMELIS VIRGINIANA   FIG. 50

$\frac{1}{2}$

when young; flowers in small axillary clusters appearing in the early autumn when the leaves are falling and while the fruit of the previous year remains;

calyx 4-parted, persistent, adnate to the base of the ovary; petals 4, narrow, strap-shaped, crinkly, bright yellow; fruit a woody 2-celled capsule, opening by 2 valves at the top of each cell containing 1 black, oblong, bony seed. Flowers, October; fruit mature the following summer.

The Common Witch-hazel is found from Nova Scotia to Minnesota, south to Florida and Texas. Michigan, common throughout.

The late flowering of this shrub puts it in a class by itself. In appearance it is no more beautiful than many of our spring flowering shrubs, but coming into bloom as its leaves are falling in autumn, it attracts more than ordinary attention and its fame has been sung in prose and poetry. It is quite widely distributed throughout the state and may be looked for on the sides of ravines and at the edges of damp woodlands. The leaves, bark and twigs enter into the preparation of fluid extracts, liniments and salves and the branches are said to have been used as divining rods to locate underground water when a well was to be dug.

As an aid in its distribution, the Witch-hazel 'shoots' its seeds a considerable distance. The shooting is accomplished by a constriction of the lining of the capsule upon the smooth, hard-polished seeds. This contraction continues until the enclosed seeds are explosively discharged, as one might shoot a slippery apple- or melon-seed between the thumb and finger. The usual distance seeds are thrown is about 4 meters, but under carefully controlled conditions they have been found to travel 9 meters, and there is a record in one case of a little over 11 meters.

ROSACEAE—Rose Family

Trees, shrubs, or herbs; branches unarmed, prickly or thorny; leaves deciduous, alternate, simple or compound, mostly with stipules which sometimes fall off early; flowers regular, perfect or polygamo-dioecious; calyx free from or attached to the ovary, generally 5-lobed; petals the same number as the sepals, or rarely lacking; stamens generally numerous, distinct, inserted on the calyx; anthers small; pistils 1 to many, distinct, or united with the calyx; ovary 1-celled or sometimes imperfectly 2-celled; style terminal or lateral; fruit various, follicles, achenes, pomes, drupes, hips, or a number of drupelets.

The Rose family is of wide distribution. Botanists differ greatly in their conception of the genera and species to be included within its limits. Some split it into a number of families, others consider the divisions as subfamilies. Using the broader interpretation the family embraces about 90 genera and some 2000 species. As here treated the Rose family embraces some of the most important of our ornamental and economic herbaceous plants, shrubs and trees. Under the heading of ornamentals may be listed the following: rose, spiraea, nine-bark, flowering almond, hawthorn, pearl bush, shad-bush, cotoneaster, shrub-

[117]

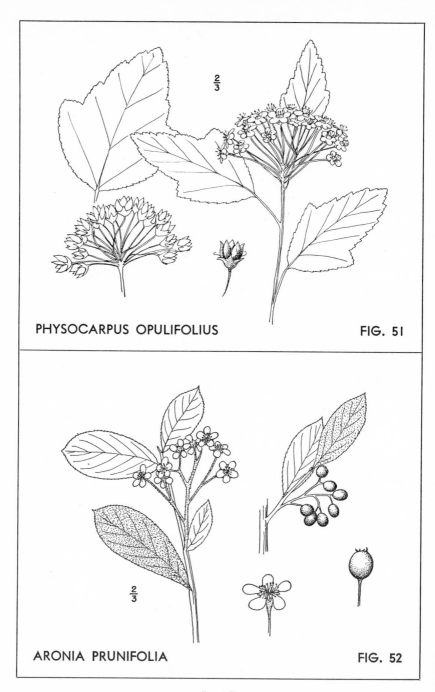

PHYSOCARPUS OPULIFOLIUS   FIG. 51

ARONIA PRUNIFOLIA   FIG. 52

by cinquefoil, Japanese quince, and many others, both shrubby and herbaceous. Under the heading of economic species may be listed such important items as apples, plums, cherries, raspberries, blackberries, strawberries, etc.

The following genera with shrubby plants are found in Michigan.

1. Leaves simple, serrate to entire, doubly-serrate and/or variously lobed
  2. Fruit a dry follicle
    3. Follicles inflated, opening both sides; seeds shining...............*Physocarpus*, p. 119
    3. Follicles not inflated, opening on one side only; seeds dull.........*Spiraea*, p. 121
  2. Fruit a fleshy pome, drupe or an aggregation of small drupelets
    4. Fruit a fleshy pome with several small 1-seeded nutlets
      5. Shrubs without spines or thorns
        6. Midrib of leaves glandular; flowers in corymbed or umbel-like
          cymes; fruit small, berry-like, sweetish, rather dry.........*Aronia*, p. 122
        6. Midrib of leaves not glandular and otherwise not as above
          7. Leaves 3–5-lobed or angled; flowers corymbose;
            fruit an aggregation of small drupelets, each
            enclosing 1 bony achene.............................*Rubus*, in part, p. 151
          7. Leaves not 3–5-lobed, merely serrate; flowers
            racemose; fruit small, berry-like, sweet,
            with a thin pulp..*Amelanchier*, p. 123
      5. Shrubs with spines or thorns; leaves more or less lobed and
        doubly serrate; flowers in corymbs; fruit a pome with 1 to
        several bony 1-seeded nutlets.....................................*Crataegus*, p. 134
    4. Fruit a fleshy drupe with one bony stone; leaves simple, serrate;
      flowers racemose or umbellate...*Prunus*, p. 180
1. Leaves compound
  8. Flowers yellow; fruit a dry achene; spineless shrubs........................*Potentilla*, p. 149
  8. Flowers white or pink; fruit not as above; spiny or prickly shrubs
    9. Fruit a collection of many small drupelets,
      each enclosing 1 bony achene...*Rubus*, in part, p. 151
    9. Fruit a globose or urn-shaped fleshy hip
      enclosing several bony achenes...*Rosa*, p. 169

Physocarpus Maxim.—NINE-BARKS

About five species and several varieties comprise this genus, one of which occurs in Michigan.

Physocarpus opulifolius (L.) Maxim. (Common Nine-Bark). Fig. 51. Shrub 1–3 m. tall, spreading with many branches; old bark loose and separating in numerous layers; twigs more or less

pubescent; stipules falling early; leaves deciduous, alternate, simple, ovate-orbicular, somewhat 3-lobed, 3–7 cm. long, wedge-shaped or heart-shaped at the base, mostly acute at the apex, crenate-dentate, dark green above, pale beneath, glabrous above, somewhat pubescent beneath in the axils of the nerves; petioles slender, 1–2 cm. long; flowers white, numerous in umbel-like terminal corymbs, about 1 cm. broad; peduncle and pedicels more or less pubescent; calyx 5-lobed, bell-shaped, pubescent; petals 5, rounded, inserted on the throat of the calyx; stamens 30–40, inserted with the petals; filaments white; pistils

[119]

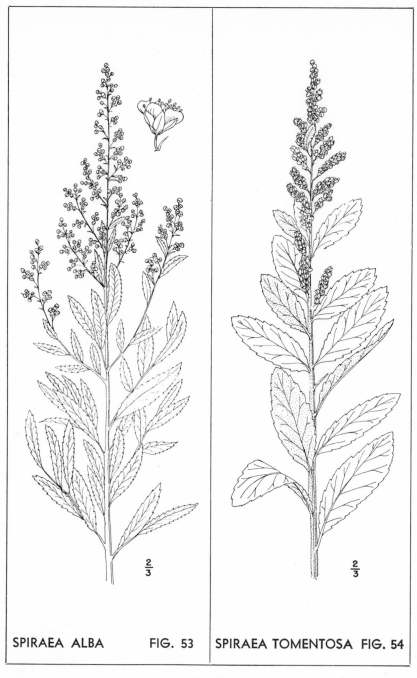

SPIRAEA ALBA   FIG. 53 | SPIRAEA TOMENTOSA FIG. 54

[120]

5, short-stalked, alternate with the calyx-lobes; stigma terminal, capitate; pods 1–5, inflated, acute, with an oblique awl-shaped tip, glabrous or somewhat pubescent, very conspicuous when ripe; seeds 2–4 in each pod, ovoid or globose, shining, light brown. Flowers, June; fruit, August, September.

River banks and rocky places, Quebec to Georgia, west to Manitoba and Kansas. Michigan, throughout.

The Common Nine-Bark is very generally planted in shrubbery borders and is a most satisfactory plant in cultivation. It is attractive both in flower and fruit. Its common name is derived from the numerous exfoliating strips of bark on the older branches. Var. *intermedius* (Rydb.) Rob., with pods permanently pubescent has been separated. Its range includes Michigan, and it should be looked for with the species.

Spiraea [Tourn.] L.—Spiraeas, Meadow-sweet

A genus of about 60 species, only 2 of which are native to Michigan.

Flowers white; leaves glabrous or sparingly pubescent beneath;
sepals erect or spreading...*S. alba*, p. 121
Flowers rose-color; leaves tomentose beneath; sepals reflexed................*S. tomentosa*, p. 121

Spiraea alba DuRoi. (Meadow-sweet). Fig. 53. (*Spiraea salicifolia* L., Gray's Manual, 7th Edition, Shrubs of Michigan, 1st Edition.) An erect shrub, 3–12 dm. tall, simple or branched; stems brownish-yellow, more or less pubescent; leaves deciduous, alternate, simple, lance-oblong, obovate or oblanceolate, 5–7 cm. long, 1–2 cm. wide, acute at the apex, wedge-shaped at the base, sharply fine-serrate, glabrous, or sparingly pubescent both sides; petioles short; in-

Spiraea alba

florescence a dense terminal panicle with axis, peduncles and pedicels tomentulose; flowers white, perfect, 6–8 mm. in diameter; calyx short-campanulate, 5-lobed, persistent; petals 5, suborbicular, short-clawed, inserted on the calyx; stamens numerous, exserted; filaments thread-like; stigma capitate; follicles usually 5, not inflated, few- to several-seeded; seeds about 2 mm. long. Flowers, July, August; fruit, September.

Found chiefly in low ground from New York and Ontario to Saskatchewan, south to North Carolina, Missouri and Mississippi. Michigan, throughout.

The Meadow-sweet is a common habitant of our low, open ground and swamps. Several varieties of it are in cultivation. It is also known as Queen-of-the-Meadow, Quaker Lady, and Willowleaf Spiraea.

A form with narrow leaves, separated as var. *lanceolata* T.&G. under the previous name, is now consolidated with the foregoing. It is reported from Oakland County by Bingham.

Spiraea tomentosa L. (Hardhack, Steeple Bush). Fig. 54. Erect shrub about 1 m. tall; stems usually simple; twigs covered with a floccose pubescence; leaves deciduous, alternate, simple, ovate to oblong or ovate-lanceolate,

3–7 cm. long, 1–3 cm. wide, rounded or wedge-shaped at the base, acute or blunt at the apex, margin unequally serrate, dark green above, covered with brown tomentum beneath when full grown; petioles short; inflorescence of short racemes crowded in a dense terminal panicle, tomentose; flowers rose or pale purple, very rarely white, about 4 mm. across; calyx tomentose, campanulate, 5-lobed, the lobes triangular, reflexed; petals 5, short-clawed, obovate, about 1.5 mm. long; stamens numerous, exserted; filaments threadlike; stigma capitate;

pods 5, about 2.5 mm. long, tomentose becoming glabrate; seeds 1.5 mm. long. Flowers, July to September; fruit, September, October.

Low grounds, Nova Scotia to Manitoba, south to Georgia, west to Kansas. Michigan, infrequent throughout.

The Steeple Bush no doubt received its common name from the shape of the panicle, which is terminal and pointed. One does not have to stretch the imagination much to see in it a marked resemblance to a steeple. The panicle begins flowering at the summit. When the upper flowers are open the lower are only in the bud. This spiraea is a desirable shrub for ornamental planting because of its late flowering period.

Aronia Medic.—CHOKEBERRIES

Pedicels and calyx canescent-tomentose; leaves persistently gray-tomentose beneath;
fruit red, claret-colored to purplish..*A. prunifolia*, p. 122
Pedicels and calyx nearly or quite smooth; leaves glabrous from the first,
or pubescent when very young; fruit black............... ....*A. melanocarpa*, p. 123

Aronia prunifolia (Marsh.) Rehd. (Red or Purple Chokeberry). Fig. 52. (*Pyrus arbutifolia* (L.) L.f., var. *atropurpurea* (Britt.) Rob., Gray's Manual,

7th Edition, Shrubs of Michigan, 1st Edition, *Aronia atropurpurea* Britt., Britton & Brown, Illustrated, 1913.) Shrub 1–2.5 m. tall; bark smooth or more or less roughened; twigs tomentose when young, becoming glabrous, reddish-brown to gray; leaves deciduous, alternate, simple, oblong-oblanceolate, or oval, 4–8 cm. long, 1.5–4 cm. wide, rounded or wedge-shaped at base, acute or abruptly short-acuminate at the apex, finely glandular-serrate, green and glabrous or glabrate above, paler and permanently canescent-tomentose below; petioles 2–10 mm. long; flowers borne in terminal, compound, pubescent cymes, perfect, white or purplish, 8–12 mm. in diameter; calyx urn-shaped, 5-lobed, tomentose, attached to the ovary; petals 5, spreading, obovate, 5–8 mm. long; stamens numerous; styles 3–5, united at base; pome globose or somewhat depressed, 8–10 mm.

in diameter, red, claret-colored to purplish. Flowers, May, June; fruit, September, October, remaining on the bush until early winter.

Swamps and low woods, New York to Ontario, south to Florida and Arkansas. Michigan, throughout.

The Chokeberries make desirable cultivated shrubs. Their foliage is attractive, as well as their flowers and fruit. The leaves turn red in the autumn.

Aronia melanocarpa (Michx.) Ell. (Black Chokeberry). Fig. 55. (*Pyrus melanocarpa* (Michx.) Willd., Gray's Manual, 7th Edition, Shrubs of Michigan, 1st Edition.) Shrub 1–2 m. tall; bark grayish-brown, smooth; leaves deciduous, simple, alternate, obovate, oblanceolate or oval, acute or scarcely pointed at the apex, narrowed at the base, glabrous, or soon glabrate on both sides, 2–8 cm. long, 1–2.5 cm. wide, dark green above, paler beneath, crenulate, the teeth incurved; petiole 2–5 mm. long; flowers white, 8–12 mm. in diameter, borne in compound cymes of which the peduncle and pedicels are nearly or quite smooth; calyx urn-shaped, glabrous, 5-lobed, the lobes triangular or ovate; petals rounded or ovate, 4–5 mm. long; stamens numerous; styles 3–5, united at the base; pome globose, 6–8 mm. in diameter, nearly black. Flowers, June; fruit, September, October.

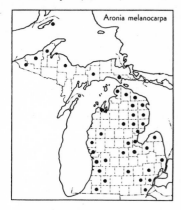

In swamps and low grounds, or at times in dryer situations, Nova Scotia to western Ontario and Minnesota, south to Florida. Michigan, throughout.

In common with other members of the Rose family, the aronias are extremely variable and, while this has been treated as a separate species, some regard it as only a variety. Individual plants occur which cannot be assigned either to the foregoing species or to this one, indicating that if a complete series could be assembled it would be found that they fully intergrade.

Amelanchier Medic.—JUNEBERRIES, SERVICEBERRIES, etc.

In the first edition of this bulletin the nomenclature followed Gray's Manual. The result was that only three species of *Amelanchier*, coming within the specifications established for shrubs, were listed from Michigan. As was stated in that edition the juneberries are highly variable; the species are closely related and difficult of definite determination, and the nomenclature is more or less confused. This situation has led a number of taxonomists to study the genus intensely, and several publications have been issued since 1908. These intensive studies have resulted in establishing several new species, and they have also attempted to straighten out the confused synonymy of the amelanchiers. Nevertheless, there is still considerable difference of opinion, and no two authorities agree as to the identity and range of all of the species.

Referring to the discouragement usually met with in identifying the forms of *Amelanchier*, Nielson in his paper on the subject (1939) says: "This is not surprising in view of the inherent variability and complexity of the genus . . . ."

To quote Jones (1946) on the same topic: "The species of Amelanchier are closely related and are sometimes somewhat difficult to distinguish." Wiegand (1912) began his publication on the genus as follows: "It is with some hesitation that the writer attempts a treatment of a genus which in the past has been subject to so much difference of opinion as has *Amelanchier.*"

From the foregoing quotations, all by professional taxonomists, it is apparent that we are dealing with a very difficult subject taxonomically, and the amateur need not be surprised if he finds it quite impossible to make book descriptions entirely fit the plants. In collecting *Amelanchier* material for study, care should be exercised to have ample specimens, and it is always to be remembered that by far the most useful taxonomic characters are found in the flowers and fruits. In the past probably too much emphasis has been placed on the leaves for differentiation of species. Most of the species do have a characteristic type of leaf serration, but the range of variation is frequently greater within the species than between different species. Also the habitat has a marked effect upon the growth of a plant so that too much reliance should not be placed upon a plant's stature and habit. For instance, the arborescent *Amelanchier canadensis* (L.) Medic. under favorable conditions becomes a small or moderate-sized tree, but under adverse conditions remains essentially a shrub. However, a truly shrubby species will not become a tree no matter how favorable its habitat.

In the first edition of this bulletin I stated that I believed the amelanchiers hybridize so freely that there are hardly two alike. In the past the idea of hybridity was advanced with more or less authority to account for the peculiar variations within the genus, but more recently cytological investigations have tended to refute this, and to show that the instability may be attributable to difference in chromosome numbers, as a change in chromosome balance is usually accompanied by a change in morphological characters. In a work of this sort it is not feasible to enter into a discussion of chromosomes and their effect upon the species of plants, but it seems entirely possible that they may have played a more important part in the differentiation of species and varieties than has heretofore been realized. Heaven help the ordinary amateur field botanist who wants to get a little fun from the out-of-doors when it becomes necessary to delve into the chromosomes to determine species and varieties. That is getting it down too fine.

After a review of the literature dealing with the species and nomenclature of *Amelanchier* and checking the material in the principal state herbaria, the following species, coming within our classification of shrubs and recorded from Michigan, have been selected for inclusion in the second edition.

1. Flowers in racemes, several to numerous; leaves cordate to rounded or subacute
   at base, conduplicate in the bud; petioles slender, generally more than
   1 cm. in length
   2. Teeth of the leaves coarse; main veins conspicuous, usually straight
      and parallel, without intermediate veins
      3. Leaves broadly acute or subobtuse at the apex
         4. Hypanthium flattish saucer-shaped; tall straggling shrubs, not colonial
            5. Principal veins running straight to the apex
               of coarse spreading teeth; petals linear or
               narrowly spatulate..................................*A. sanguinea*, p. 125
            5. Principal veins curving upward and generally forking
               near the margin, the branches running into
               the teeth; petals obovate...............................*A. huronensis*, p. 125.

Amelanchier sanguinea (Pursh) DC. (Round-leaved Juneberry). Fig. 56.
A slender arching or straggling shrub 1–2.5 m. tall, stems solitary or few in a

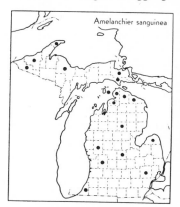

clump, not stoloniferous and not colonial; leaves deciduous, simple, alternate, oval to oval-oblong, sometimes nearly orbicular, rounded or subcordate at the base, mostly acutely or obtusely pointed at the apex, 2–6 cm. long, 2.5–4 cm. wide, margin coarsely dentate-serrate nearly or quite to the base, with broad, sharp, spreading teeth, 4–6 to the cm., green above when young, expanding before the flowers, at first yellowish tomentose below, the tomentum generally soon peeling off, at length pale green, slightly glaucous, and usually glabrous, or sometimes retaining traces of the tomentum; veins in average leaves 13–15 pairs rather close together, straight, conspicuous, all of the upper veins running straight to the margin and ending in the teeth; petiole 1.2–2.2 cm. long, persistently tomentose; flowers white, large and showy, borne in loose, many-flowered, usually drooping racemes, 4–7 cm. long, appearing when the leaves are nearly full grown; petals linear to narrowly spatulate, 11–15 mm. long, 3–4 mm. wide; hypanthium flattish, open, saucer-shaped, 4–5 mm. in diameter, sepals ovate-lanceolate or lanceolate, acute, about 2–4 mm. long, glabrous outside, tomentose within, at first spreading, becoming revolute with age; lowest pedicels 1–4 cm. long; pome when mature almost black, globose, glaucous, 6–8 mm. in diameter, very juicy and sweet; seeds brown, somewhat flattened, about 5 mm. long. Flowers, May or early June; fruit, August, September.

Dry rocky or gravelly soil, Quebec to Ontario and Minnesota, south to Massachusetts, New York, and along the mountains to northern Alabama. Michigan, infrequent in both peninsulas.

Amelanchier huronensis Wieg. (Lake Huron Juneberry). Fig. 57. A shrub or small tree 3–7 m. tall; leaves simple, deciduous, alternate, oblong, sub-

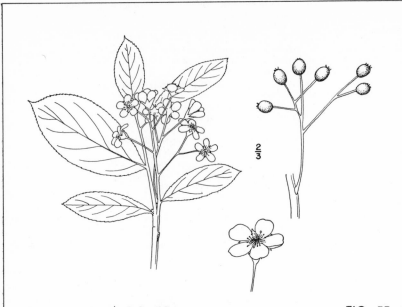

ARONIA MELANOCARPA   FIG. 55

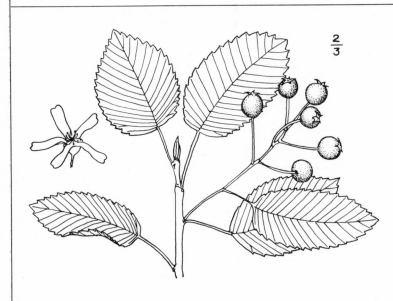

AMELANCHIER SANGUINEA   FIG. 56

[126]

orbicular, occasionally obovate, 3.5–5.5 cm. wide, 4–7 cm. long, rounded or subacute at the apex, rounded to subcordate at the base, margin coarsely serrate-dentate to near the base, rarely less than below the middle, 3–4 teeth per cm.;

veins about 12 lateral pairs, prominent especially near the base, curving upward and often forking near the margin, the branchlets running into the teeth; petiole slender, 1.5–3 cm. long; flowers white, racemes many-flowered, loose, 4–7.5 cm. long, axis tomentose when young, glabrate or with a few hairs at maturity; lowest pedicel 1.2–3 cm. long at anthesis; petals obovate to broad-oblanceolate, 1.2–1.8 cm. long; sepals acute, 3–5 mm. long, 2–3 mm. wide, at anthesis woolly above, soon glabrate, becoming reflexed as the petals fall; hypanthium 5–7 mm. in diameter, broadly saucer-shaped; ovary summit woolly; pome glabrous or slightly elongate, 5–8 mm. in diameter, dark purple, very sweet when ripe. Flowers, May, early June; fruit mature, August, September.

Along the Great Lakes from Ontario and Michigan to Wisconsin and Minnesota. Michigan, middle to northern part of Lower Peninsula and the Upper Peninsula.

This species was described and published by Wiegand (1920). He says: "The plant grows on sand dunes in Michigan, but on limestone rocky banks in other portions of its range." It appears to be a true citizen of the Great Lakes country.

Amelanchier humilis Wieg. (Low Juneberry). Fig. 58. A rather stiff upright stoloniferous shrub, 3–12 dm. tall, forming colonies with the individual

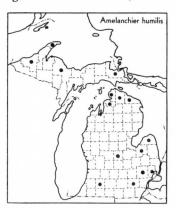

stems scattered; leaves simple, deciduous, alternate, commonly oval-oblong, sometimes oval, rarely obovate-cuneate, 2.5 cm. long, 2–4 cm. broad, subcordate, rarely rounded at the base, apex mostly broadly subacute, or subtruncate, sometimes rounded, margin coarsely dentate-serrate to below the middle, teeth 4–5 per cm., sinuses of teeth acute, unfolded or unfolding at anthesis, at first densely yellowish-white to grayish-green tomentose beneath, in age pale green and glabrate or with some tomentum persistent on the petiole; main veins in average leaves 9–13 pairs, conspicuous, ascending, forking and becoming indistinct before reaching the margin; petioles 8–20 mm. long when mature; flowers white, small and numerous in the rather dense terminal and lateral upright racemes, about 4–5 cm. long, pedicels and axis silky-tomentose, in flower 8–17 mm. long, in fruit 10–25 mm. long; petals obovate-oblong, 7–10 mm. long,

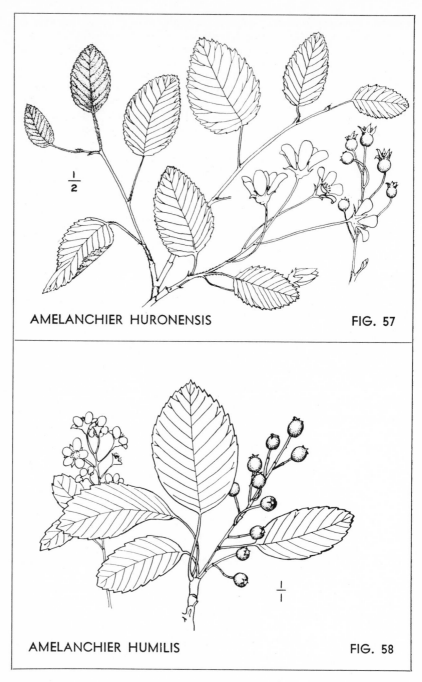

AMELANCHIER HURONENSIS   FIG. 57

AMELANCHIER HUMILIS   FIG. 58

4–5 mm. broad; hypanthium deeply saucer-shaped, or shallowly cup-shaped, about 4 mm. in diameter, tomentose outside, or glabrate toward the summit; sepals 2–4 mm. long, short triangular-lanceolate or ovate, reflexed from the middle after the petals fall, usually pubescent both sides; ovary densely woolly at the summit; pome globose, or slightly elongated, black, glaucous, sweet and juicy when ripe. Flowers, May; fruit ripe, July, August.

Dry, open rocky or gravelly soil in calcareous districts, Vermont and Ontario to New York, Ohio, Nebraska and Minnesota. Michigan, recorded from both peninsulas, apparently infrequent.

This species is always low and because of its stoloniferous character always grows in patches, somewhat after the habit of raspberries. The stolons just at or slightly below the surface of the ground extend horizontally a short distance in an irregular fashion and then send up strictly erect branched aerial shoots.

Amelanchier gaspensis (Wieg.) Fern. & Weath. (Northern Juneberry). Fig. 59. Low, much-branched shrubs 30–90 cm. tall, usually forming dense

Amelanchier gaspensis

thickets; bark grayish or brownish; leaves commonly oval varying to suborbicular, conduplicate in bud, unfolding before the flowers, nearly or quite full-grown at anthesis, glabrous or quickly glabrate, mature leaves relatively thin, 3–6 cm. long, 1.5–4 cm. wide, the apex usually rounded or subtruncate, or sometimes acutish, the base cordate or subcordate, or sometimes rounded, pale green beneath, glabrous on both surfaces, margins dentate-serrate to below the middle, varying and sometimes subentire, teeth broad and sharp, ascending, usually 3–6 per cm.; main lateral veins distant, curved upward, the upper ones usually extending to the margin and ending in the teeth, the others branching at their tips; petioles slender, 1–3 cm. long, glabrous or quickly glabrate; flowers white, small, borne in erect or ascending 5–15-flowered racemes; 3–6 cm. long, the lower pedicels 1–2 cm. long, rachis and pedicels glabrous or barely pilose; petals 5, oblanceolate, glabrous throughout, 6–9 mm. long, 2–3.5 mm. wide; hypanthium saucer-shaped, 3–4 mm. in diameter, essentially glabrous outside; sepals lanceolate, acutish or acuminate, 1.5–3 mm. long, usually recurved after anthesis, permanently glabrous on both sides, or with small tufts of tomentum near the tip; top of ovary tomentose; mature pome globose or subglobose, purplish-black, glaucous, glabrous, 8–10 mm. in diameter; seeds brown, smooth, 4–5 mm. long. Flowers, July, August; fruit, August, September.

On cliffs, ledges, gravelly beaches or in alluvial woods, Gaspé Peninsula and neighboring counties of Quebec, northward and westward to James Bay, and in the region about Lake Superior. Michigan, recorded from Isle Royal, the Upper Peninsula, and the northern portion of the Lower Peninsula.

This species is related to *Amelanchier sanguinea* (Pursh) DC. and in 1912 was described as a variety of that species by Wiegand. At that time its range was thought to be confined to the Gaspé Peninsula. However, additional collec-

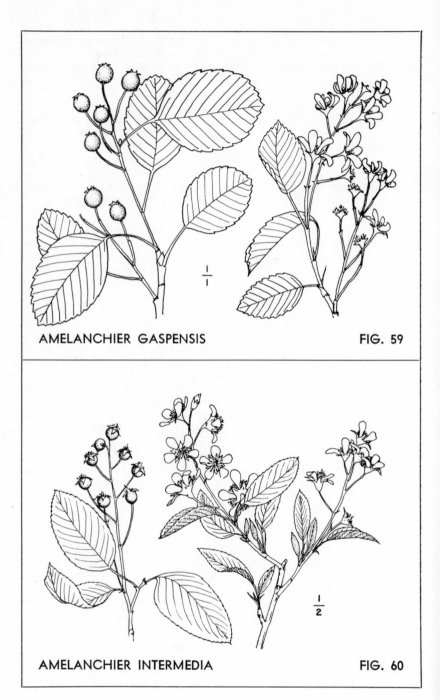

AMELANCHIER GASPENSIS $\frac{1}{1}$ FIG. 59

AMELANCHIER INTERMEDIA $\frac{1}{2}$ FIG. 60

tions and field studies have made possible a considerable extension of its geographical range, which is now known to extend westward to the region around Lake Superior. In 1931 it was elevated to specific rank by Fernald and Weatherby and has since been generally so accepted.

Amelanchier intermedia Spach. (Swamp Sugar Pear). Fig. 60. A tall shrub widely branching near the ground, or rarely a small tree; leaves simple,

deciduous, alternate, unfolding at flowering time, elliptic-oblong or elliptic-obovate, 3–4 cm. long, 1.5–2 cm. wide, rounded or sometimes subcordate at base, acute or shortly acuminate at the apex, margin finely but somewhat distantly serrate, veins 7–12 pairs, irregular, often with short intermediate veins branching and forming a network near the margin, surface often reddish or bronze-color when young, moderately tomentose, glabrate in age or slightly tomentose on the veins beneath and on the petiole; petiole 1–1.5 cm. long; racemes 2–5 cm. long, erect, rather compact, few-flowered, axis silky-pubescent in flower, glabrate with age, lower pedicels 8–14 mm. long; petals oblong-cuneate, 7–11 mm. long; sepals 2–3 mm. long, woolly above at flowering time, later glabrate and irregularly revolute; hypanthium about 3 mm. in diameter, cup-shaped; top of ovary glabrous or somewhat woolly; pome globose, dark purple when ripe, juicy and sweet. Flowers, May; fruit ripe in August.

In swamps and moist soil, Nova Scotia, Prince Edward Island, New England, south to the mountains of North Carolina, westward through central New York, Michigan and Minnesota. Michigan, infrequent in both peninsulas.

This species was not reported from Michigan until 1935, when Fernald collected it on the Keweenaw Peninsula. Like many of the more recently described species, it has not yet been widely collected in Michigan, and there is an excellent opportunity to supply specimens to the several state herbaria.

Amelanchier stolonifera Wieg. (Serviceberry). Fig. 61. Upright shrubs 3–12 dm. tall, stoloniferous and forming patches; leaves simple, deciduous, alternate, usually oval, rarely oblong-oval or orbicular, 2.5–5 cm. long, 2–3.5 cm. wide, base rounded, rarely subcordate with a small narrow sinus, apex rounded or subacute, mucronate, margin finely and sharply serrate along the upper two-thirds of the leaf, the lower one-third nearly entire, teeth obliquely mucronate, 5–8 per cm., sinuses open, acute or rounded, green and glabrous above when young, densely white-tomentose beneath, soon glabrous throughout, or the petioles and midrib remaining somewhat pubescent, about half-grown and unfolding at flowering time; primary veins in average leaves 7–11 pairs, usually curved upward, becoming very indistinct and irregular toward the margin; fully grown petioles slender, 10–18 mm. long, glabrous or somewhat pubescent; racemes short, dense, erect, 1.5–4 cm. long, appearing when the leaves are half grown and unfolding, lower pedicels 7–15 mm. long in flower, 12–22 mm. long

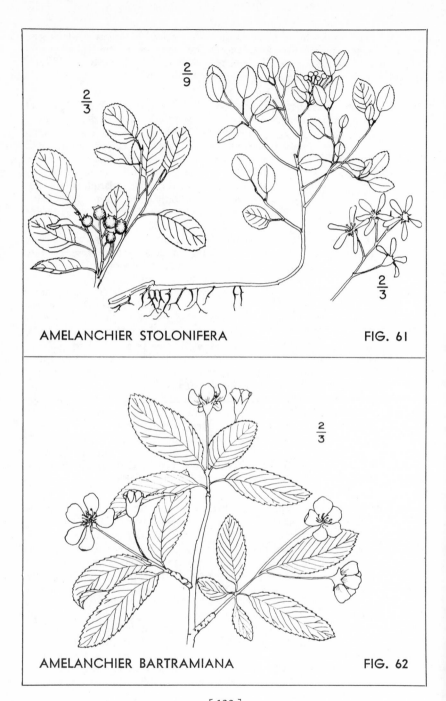

$\frac{2}{9}$

$\frac{2}{3}$

$\frac{2}{3}$

AMELANCHIER STOLONIFERA   FIG. 61

$\frac{2}{3}$

AMELANCHIER BARTRAMIANA   FIG. 62

in fruit, pedicels and axis silky-tomentose or at times nearly glabrous; flowers small, petals obovate-oblong, 7–9 mm. long; hypanthium open saucer-shaped, about 3–4 mm. in diameter, tomentose at the base or nearly glabrous; sepals

triangular-lanceolate, 2.5–3 mm. long, soon reflexed, inner surface tomentose; ovary densely woolly at the top; pome purplish-black when ripe, sweet, juicy and of good flavor. Flowers, late April, May; fruit maturing in July.

On dry rocks, gravel, or rarely in sand in non-calcareous districts, Newfoundland, coastal plain from Maine to Virginia, and on the shores of the Great Lakes. Michigan, apparently well distributed in the counties bordering the lakes in both peninsulas.

Amelanchier Bartramiana (Tausch) Roem. (Oblong-fruited Juneberry). Fig. 62. (*Amelanchier oligocarpa* (Michx.) Roem. Gray's Manual, 7th Edition, Shrubs of Michigan, 1st Edition.) Shrub 0.5–2.5 m. tall; stems erect and several growing close together; leaves simple, deciduous, alternate, elliptical or oblong-elliptical to somewhat obovate, 3–5 cm. long, 1.5–3

cm. wide, narrowed at the base, acute, apex acute or rarely somewhat rounded, margins sharply and often doubly serrate to below the middle or nearly to the base, teeth fine and very variable, 6–12 per cm., their sinuses usually sharp, but sometimes rounded, not conduplicate, flat from the beginning, glabrous when young, except at the base; older leaves bright green above, paler and glaucous beneath; veins 12–17 pairs, indistinct, very irregular, not equally spaced and with shorter ones between, forming a net-work in the outer portion of the leaf; petioles stout, 2–7 mm. long; flowers small, white, 1–2, rarely 3 together, appearing when the leaves are about half grown; petals elliptical or obovate, broad,

6–9 mm. in length; pedicels glabrous, 10–30 mm. long in both flower and fruit; hypanthium 3–6 mm. in diameter broadly campanulate; sepals narrowly triangular, with wide sinuses 3–4 mm. long, glabrous outside, tomentose within, later more or less reflexed; ovary densely woolly at the top; pome about 1 cm. in diameter, large for the amelanchiers, ovoid or somewhat pear-shaped, dark purple, edible. Flowers, May; fruit late July or August.

Damp uplands and borders of bogs, Labrador to the mountains of New England, New York and Pennsylvania, westward through Canada to northern Michigan and Minnesota. Michigan, infrequent Upper and Lower Peninsulas.

In this country and Canada the amelanchiers have been given many vernacular names. As a matter of personal interest I compiled as complete a list of them as I could discover. In addition to those given with the foregoing species the list contained 80 names and is far too voluminous to include here. A mimeographed copy will be sent to anyone requesting it, however.

It is doubtful if any group of plants ever had a greater number or variety of common names than the amelanchier. The affection in which the shrub is held by the people is easily understandable. Certain of the species are early-blooming, and after the long winter their white flowers are a welcome sight on the landscape. It is interesting to speculate upon the reason for some of the vernacular names. To mention only a few. The appellation "shad" in various combinations is perhaps used more often than any other. This apparently originated in the eastern part of the United States, where the early inhabitants applied the name to the amelanchiers because some of them bloom at the time the shad is ascending the tidal rivers to spawn. The Middle West does not have tidal rivers, but the people continued to apply the name to the familiar shrub or tree as they migrated westward. As a result, all over the country to the great majority of the people the name shadbush or some variant of it is still used to identify this beautiful plant.

Some of the names are plainly geographic, as Northwestern Juneberry. Leaf characters and habit furnish a reason for some of the names, as Round-leaved Juneberry and Swamp Serviceberry. Time of blooming or ripening of the fruit and its quality are also recognized in the following examples: Juneberry, May Pear and Sugar Pear. Others come from the use made of the fruits by the Indians; Saskatoon is one of these. Pemican was composed of dried and pulverized deer or buffalo meat to which was added "Saskatoon" berries. Indian-pear and Indian-cherry may also be mentioned here.

The fruit of the juneberries has a delicate flavor and is very palatable. When available it is used for domestic purposes. But the birds are fully aware of its fine quality, too, and for ages have been preempting it to their own uses. It is therefore sometimes difficult for the human to get his share.

The history of the Northwest contains many references to the uses made of the fruit by the early explorers and prospectors, who found it a welcome addition to their food supply. Lewis and Clark speak of the fine quality of the berries and it is recorded that they were used by members of the expedition when they ran short of food. Today the shrubs provide an important article of food among the northwestern Indians, who gather the fruit in large quantities, often drying it for future use.

The wood is heavy, very hard, close-grained, tough and strong, and it was used for tool handles and other purposes requiring such a material. Under the name of lancewood it was used for fishing rods, umbrella handles and canes.

In the West the foliage of some of the species is an acceptable forage for grazing animals. Some of the eastern species provide satisfactory stock upon which to graft horticultural varieties of pear and other fruits. Certain of the amelanchiers are widely used in landscape planting and taking it all in all, the members of this genus stand high in the scale of human usefulness.

Crataegus L.—HAWTHORNS

This genus offers great taxonomic difficulties, and the closely related species are subject to widely different interpretations by specialists. Otis in his work on Michigan trees says: "Owing to the complexity of the various forms in this group, the present state of uncertainty as to the value of certain characters and the questionable validity of many of the assigned names, it is thought to be beyond the scope of this bulletin to give more than a general description of the group as a whole, recommending the more ambitious student to the various manuals and botanical journals and papers for more detailed information." With the general reputation the hawthorns have for being difficult to name and with such an eminent authority as Professor Otis setting the example, it would have been very easy to omit the species of the genus from this compilation which is intended primarily for the beginner. However, it would seem inadvisable to omit entirely such a prominent group of plants. In the first edition I merely made a token-listing of four species which are commonly distributed in the state and regarding which there was the least uncertainty as to nomenclature. This was not entirely satisfactory. The thorns are numerous in woods and pastures, and in any field trip there would be encountered thorns belonging to some group other than the four listed.

The genus *Crataegus* is subdivided into a number of groups; acting upon the suggestion of Dr. Rogers McVaugh, of the University of Michigan Herbarium, I have decided, in order to make this bulletin of greater use, to include in the second edition those found in Michigan and to describe and illustrate, as a sample, one species under each group head. It should be understood that there is no unanimity of opinion regarding the identity of these groups, or the species which should be included under them. Both the groups and species differ somewhat from the presentation in established manuals, but have been compiled from recent publications and constitute as up-to-the-minute treatment as seems possible at this time. Any thorn collected should fit into one or another of the groups, if it does not actually match the species given.

Even with the expanded list of this edition the beginner should not be disappointed if he finds many thorns which he cannot classify. The specialists themselves have great difficulty in classifying them. Some time ago a story was current in botanical circles to the effect that two specimens from the same shrub were sent for identification to a noted specialist who pronounced them distinct species and supplied the names. I cannot vouch for the accuracy of this story, but it at least indicates the difficulty attendant upon the classification of the members of this genus. The student who desires to attempt a classification of the thorns should be particular to have specimens from the same plant in flower and with mature fruit. The color of the anthers and the color of the fruit should also be noted. To this end it is necessary that the shrub be marked in a way to absolutely identify it. I employed brass number tags which were fastened on the shrub with copper wire when the flower specimens were taken. The specimens were numbered the same as the brass tags and later when the fruit specimens were taken they were given the same number. The brass tags were inconspicuous and nearly indestructible and were pretty sure to remain on the shrub as long as required.

While the botanists may have a difficult time with this genus, the horticulturists have no such trouble. They are not so concerned with scientific names as they are with the ornamental value of the shrubs and several species of this genus are regularly used in landscape planting. The flowers and foliage are beautiful and their scarlet fruits, which remain on into the winter, give them an additional charm. The fruits, or haws, are also valuable as food for the birds.

The thorns graft readily, which is another useful quality in their favor. Not only thorns, but pears and other fruits may be made to grow upon them. I have seen one interesting example of this sort of grafting. On some wild native thorns down back of the barns on the farm of Mr. J. C. Townsend, in Addison Township, Oakland County, Mr. Townsend has grafted several Bartlett pear scions. They are growing luxuriantly and producing fruit, or were at the time of my last visit a few years ago. Some roving botanist might think he was "seeing things" if he happened upon them without previous knowledge of their existence. It is most interesting and unusual to see the large pears growing side by side with the small haws of the thorns.

The thorn has one disadvantage as an ornamental. It is the alternate host plant for the juniper rust, and it is difficult, if not impossible, to grow the Red Cedar and thorns in close proximity. If one or the other becomes infected it is practically impossible to obliterate the rust without getting rid of one of the host plants. Chocolate-brown "cedar-apples" are the response of the cedar to the irritation caused by the fungus in the leaf tissues. Beginning in the spring and during the warm rains, for several months gelatinous orange-yellow horns, made up of hundreds of spores, grow out from depressed areas on the surface of the "apples." When the rain stops and the weather clears the spores are liberated and carried by the wind to the leaves and twigs of the thorns, causing light yellow spots on the upper surface of the leaves. Later, swellings on the under surface of the leaves discharge spores which are blown back to the cedars, where they live over the winter, forming a small rounded enlargement the next spring, which increases in size during the summer, and the second spring matures as a gall or "cedar-apple." The fungus causes early defoliation of the thorns and the galls are very unsightly on the cedars. Heavy spraying is supposed to kill the spores, but complete elimination of one or the other of the host plants is the surer remedy.

The hawthorns can be grown from seeds very easily, but it takes two years for some of the species to sprout. The fully ripened seeds should be removed from the haws and placed in seed beds in November or December. The young plants should be transplanted at the end of their first year of growth, either to nursery rows or to where they are to remain if the small plants can be properly protected there.

With this rather discouraging introduction from the standpoint of the systematist we may proceed to a description of the groups and species selected for treatment here.

Something over a thousand species have been proposed from time to time throughout the country for the genus. Beal's 'Michigan Flora' lists 41 species for the state, most of which have been individually reported from one location only.

Key to the Groups of the Genus *Crataegus*.

1. Nutlets not pitted on the ventral surfaces; flowers usually opening before the middle of May.
   2. Leaves of flowering branches all narrowed or acuminate at the base, mostly of an obovate, oblong, or spatulate type, broadest at or above middle, margins merely serrate or with shallow or obscure lobes toward the apex
      3. Leaves of flowering branches usually $1\frac{1}{2}$ to 2 times as long as wide
         4. Leaves thick and usually glossy above, unlobed except rarely on shoots, veins not conspicuously impressed; styles and nutlets usually 1–3; fruit remaining hard and dry......................I CRUS-GALLI

  4. Leaves thin to firm, dull above, mostly obovate, symmetrical, with
   5–7 pairs of slightly ascending, deeply impressed veins, often
   slightly lobed on the flowering branches; fruit 9–16 mm. in
   diameter; nutlets usually 2–5..II PUNCTATAE
 3. Leaves of flowering branches usually 1 to 1½ times as long
   as wide...III ROTUNDIFOLIAE
2. Leaves of flowering branches abruptly narrowed, rounded, truncate, or
 subcordate at the base, mostly ovate, oblong or elliptic, broadest at or
 below the middle, usually lobed or incised.
  5. Leaves of flowering branches usually slightly narrowed or abruptly
   acuminate at the base; petioles and inflorescence conspicuously
   glandular; usually shrubs...IV INTRICATAE
  5. Leaves of flowering branches usually rounded to subcordate at base;
   petioles and inflorescence glandular or slightly glandular; large
   shrubs or small trees
    6. Leaves thin; fruit 10–18 mm. in diameter, with small sessile
     calyx; flowers 15–20 mm. in diameter................ ....V TENUIFOLIAE
    6. Leaves firm to subcoriaceous; fruit usually 10–20 mm. in
     diameter; flowers 16–25 mm. in diameter
      7. Fruit with the flesh and relatively large nutlets remaining
       hard and dry; fruiting calyx large and elevated...........VI PRUINOSAE
      7. Fruit becoming mellow or succulent, usually edible; fruiting
       calyx smaller, sessile or nearly so
        8. Leaves barely firm; petioles and primary veins slender;
         fruit glabrous; styles and nutlets usually 3–5......VII COCCINEAE
        8. Leaves firm to subcoriaceous; petioles and primary
         veins stout; fruit pubescent at least toward the base;
         styles and nutlets usually 5...................................VIII MOLLES
1. Nutlets pitted on the ventral surfaces; flowers usually
 opening after the middle of May
  9. Fruit scarlet or orange; stones 2–3; stamens usually 10–20; anthers pink or
   yellow; leaves pubescent on the veins beneath.............................IX MACRACANTHAE
  9. Fruit black; stones 3–5; stamens 20; anthers light yellow; leaves
   glabrous below.. ....X DOUGLASIANAE

GROUP I. CRUS-GALLI Loud.

Crataegus Crus-galli L. (Cock-spur Thorn). Fig. 63. Shrub or small tree;
bark dark gray, scaly; spines many, strong, straight, 3–18 cm. long; stipules

deciduous; leaves simple, alternate, deciduous, obovate to elliptical, leathery, dark
green and shining above, glabrous or occasionally slightly pubescent beneath, glandless,
acute or rounded at the apex, wedge-shaped
at the base, sharply serrate toward the base,
2–10 cm. long, 1–4 cm. wide; petiole slightly
winged above, glandless, 1–2 cm. long;
corymbs many-flowered, usually glabrous;
flowers white, about 1.5 cm. wide; calyx-tube
campanulate, 5-lobed, the lobes lanceolate-
acuminate, glabrous or somewhat pubescent;
petals 5, roundish; stamens 10–20; anthers
generally pink; styles 1–3; fruit ellipsoidal-
ovoid to subglobose, about 1 cm. thick,
greenish to red, flesh hard and dry; nutlets
generally 2, 8–9 mm. long, strongly ridged on the back. Flowers, May, June;
fruit, October.

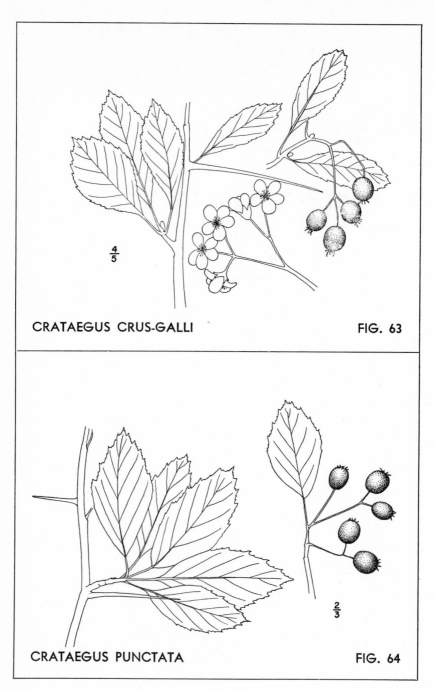

$\frac{4}{5}$

CRATAEGUS CRUS-GALLI   FIG. 63

$\frac{2}{3}$

CRATAEGUS PUNCTATA   FIG. 64

Generally in sandy or gravelly soil, New York to Ontario, Michigan, eastern Kansas, south to Georgia. Michigan, common throughout.

This species is extremely variable in leaves and fruit, and many varieties have been proposed. Two of these, *Crataegus Crus-galli* L. var. *pyracanthifolia* Ait., having more acute leaves and small bright red fruit, and *Crataegus Crus-galli* L. var. *oblongata* Sarg., with bright red ellipsoidal fruit, have been reported from Oakland County by Bingham.

The Cock-spur Thorn is extensively used in ornamental planting and is a very satisfactory shrub in any suitable location.

GROUP II. PUNCTATAE Loud.

Crataegus punctata Jacq. (Large-fruited Thorn, Dotted Haw). Fig. 64. Small flat-topped tree or shrub; bark grayish-brown; spines 2–7 cm. long, straight,

usually few; stipules deciduous; leaves simple, alternate, deciduous, obovate to oblong, impressed-veined above, dull gray-green, 2–8 cm. long, 1–5 cm. broad, mostly pubescent beneath, especially along the veins, acute or acuminate at the apex, sharply wedge-shaped at the base, sharply and doubly serrate above the middle, or slightly lobed; petioles 1–2 cm. long, slightly winged above, pubescent; corymbs tomentose, many-flowered; flowers white, about 2 cm. wide; calyx-tube pubescent, its 5 lobes linear-lanceolate and less pubescent, mostly entire; petals, 5, spreading, rounded; stamens about 20; anthers white to pink; styles 3–4; fruit short-ellipsoid, yellow or red, 1.2–2.5 cm. thick; nutlets 3–4, slightly ridged on the back, 6–7 mm. long. Flowers, May, June; fruit, October.

Quebec to Pennsylvania, Minnesota, Iowa, Illinois, south to Georgia and Kentucky. Michigan, throughout, common in the southern portion.

This is also an inconstant species and several varieties have been proposed.

GROUP III. INTRICATAE Sarg.

Crataegus intricata J. Lange. (Scarlet Thorn). Fig. 65. (*Crataegus coccinea* L., Gray's Manual, 7th Edition, Shrubs of Michigan, 1st Edition.) Irregularly topped shrubs or small trees; bark gray or brownish; spines occasional, stout, 3–5 cm. long; stipules deciduous; leaves simple, alternate, deciduous, broadly ovate, acute or acuminate at the apex, broadly wedge-shaped to truncate at the base, 2–7 cm. long, 1.5–5 cm. wide, rough-pubescent, becoming scabrous above and nearly glabrous beneath, doubly serrate or lobed; petioles 1–3 cm. long,

[139]

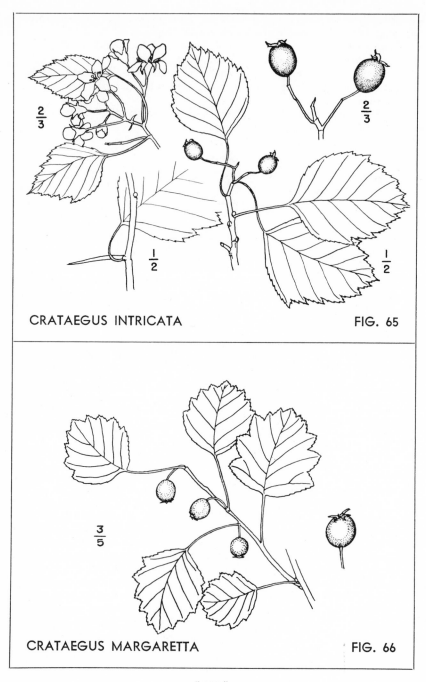

CRATAEGUS INTRICATA   FIG. 65

CRATAEGUS MARGARETTA   FIG. 66

glandular, slightly winged above; corymbs few-flowered, villous; flowers white, about 2.5 cm. broad; calyx-tube villous, 5-lobed, the lobes lance-acuminate or acute, strongly toothed at the apex; petals 5, spreading, rounded; stamens about 10; anthers light-yellow; styles 3–5; fruit subglobose to ellipsoidal, 8–12 mm. in diameter, red, pubescent or becoming nearly glabrous; nutlets 3–4, 5–7 mm. long, strongly ridged on the back. Flowers, May, June; fruit, October.

Rocky woods and thickets, Newfoundland to Manitoba, south to Florida and Texas. Michigan, common throughout.

The Scarlet Thorn excels in decorative value and is extensively used in ornamental planting.

GROUP IV. ROTUNDIFOLIAE Eggl.

Crataegus Margaretta Ashe. (Brown's Thorn, Mrs. Ashe's Thorn). Fig. 66. A shrub or small tree with ascending branches forming a rounded open

crown; spines 2–4 cm. long; leaves simple, alternate, deciduous, oblong-oval to oval, sometimes broadly so, 2–6 cm. long, 2–4 cm. wide, obtuse or acute at the apex, cuneate or rounded at the base, serrate or doubly serrate or lobed, dark green, shining and glabrous above, paler and somewhat pubescent along the veins beneath, usually membranaceous; petioles 1–3 cm. long, slightly winged, corymbs few- to many-flowered, becoming glabrous; flowers 1.5–2 cm. wide; stamens about 20; anthers yellow; styles usually 2; calyx-lobes lanceolate-acuminate, slightly pubescent inside; pome compressed-globose to short-ellipsoid, 8–25 mm. thick, dull rusty-green, yellow or red, flesh yellow, mealy, hard, thick; nutlets usually 2, about 6 mm. long and 3 mm. thick, ridged on the back. Flowers, May; fruit, October.

Woods and banks of streams, southern Ontario to central Iowa, south to central Pennsylvania, western Virginia and Missouri. Michigan, Lower Peninsula.

Regarding this hawthorn, Deam says (1940): "*Crataegus Margaretta* is difficult to describe because of the great variability in the shape and size of the leaves and fruit, but it is a well marked species, and it is easily recognized when once known in the field. There has been considerable difference of opinion as to the relationship of the species, some botanists placing it in the Punctatae group, or regarding it as the type of a distinct group, but it seems most related to such species as *Crataegus Dodgei, Crataegus chrysocarpa* and *Crataegus rotundifolia*, and it is therefore retained in the Rotundifoliae group in this treatment." It is a pleasure to follow Dr. Deam in this bulletin.

Crataegus Margaretta Ashe var. *angustifolia* Palmer, with the leaves oblong-lanceolate or lance-elliptic, 1–3 cm. long, 0.8–2 cm. wide, acute or acuminate at the apex, abruptly narrowed or acuminate at the base and decurrent on the slender petioles, which are one-half to two-thirds as long as the blades, is reported by Hanes from three stations in Kalamazoo County. It should be sought in other locations.

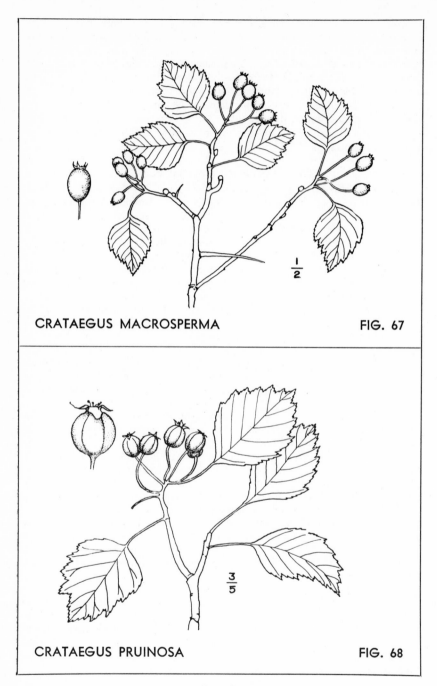

CRATAEGUS MACROSPERMA   FIG. 67

CRATAEGUS PRUINOSA   FIG. 68

GROUP V. TENUIFOLIAE Sarg.

Crataegus macrosperma Ashe. (Variable Thorn). Fig. 67. A shrub or small tree, with ascending branches; bark brown and scaly; spines numerous, stout, curved, 2–7 cm. long; leaves simple, alternate, deciduous, broadly elliptical-ovate to broadly ovate, rounded to truncate or rarely cordate at the base, 2.5–7 cm. long, 2–7 cm. wide, acute at the apex, serrate or doubly serrate, slightly villous, becoming glabrate, dark yellow-green above, membranaceous; petioles slender, 2–3 cm. long, slightly winged above; corymbs glabrous or slightly villous, many-flowered; flowers 1.5–2 cm. broad; stamens 5–20, usually 5–10; styles usually 3 or 4, calyx-lobes lanceolate-acuminate, entire; pome ellipsoidal or pyriform, 1–1.8 cm. thick, scarlet to crimson, often glaucous, flesh succulent, edible; nutlets usually 3–4, 6–8 mm. long. Flowers, May; fruit ripe, August, September.

Nova Scotia and Maine to southeastern Minnesota, North Carolina and Tennessee. Michigan, so far recorded from the Lower Peninsula only.

GROUP VI. PRUINOSAE Sarg.

Crataegus pruinosa (Wendl.) K. Koch. (Waxy-fruited Thorn). Fig. 68. A shrub or small tree with ascending branches and an irregular crown; bark dark brown; spines numerous, slender, 3–6 cm. long; leaves simple, alternate, deciduous, elliptic-ovate to broadly ovate, 2.5–6 cm. long and wide, membranaceous, acute or acuminate at the apex, abruptly cuneate, rounded or occasionally cordate at the base, serrate or doubly serrate with 3 or 4 pairs of broad, acute lobes toward the apex, blue-green, glabrous; petioles 2–3 cm. long, glabrous; corymbs glabrous, many-flowered; flowers about 2 cm. broad; stamens 10–20; anthers pink, rarely yellow; styles 4 or 5; calyx-lobes lanceolate-acuminate, entire or slightly serrate at the base; pome depressed-globose to short-ellipsoid, strongly angled, waxy, apple-green, becoming scarlet or purple, 1.2–1.5 cm. thick, firm, yellow, sweet; nutlets 6–8 mm. long. Flowers, May; fruit ripe, October.

Rocky open woods, western New England to Michigan, North Carolina and Missouri. Michigan, recorded from both peninsulas.

In common with other members of the Rose family this hawthorn has a number of named varieties of which the following have the same range as the species: var. *latisepala* (Ashe) Eggl., with leaves more nearly entire and the fruit reddish-brown; var. *conjuncta* (Sarg.) Eggl., fruit less angular and not

[143]

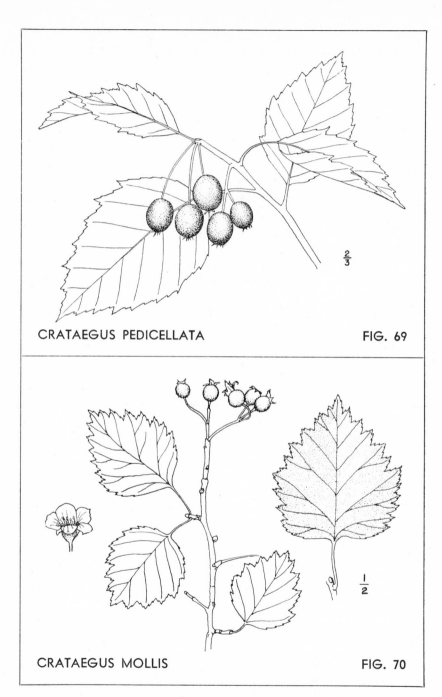

CRATAEGUS PEDICELLATA $\frac{2}{3}$ FIG. 69

CRATAEGUS MOLLIS $\frac{1}{2}$ FIG. 70

highly colored, anthers light yellow; var. *philadelphica* (Sarg.) Eggl., leaves with more acuminate lobes, those on the vegetative shoots usually cordate. These varieties should be looked for whenever the plant is found.

GROUP VII. COCCINEAE Loud.

Crataegus pedicellata Sarg. (Red Haw). Fig. 69. A large shrub or small tree with round symmetrical head; branches rather slender; spines 3–5 cm.

long, straight or slightly curved; leaves simple, alternate, deciduous, broadly ovate, simply or doubly serrate or lobed, 3–10 cm. long, 3–9 cm. wide, acute or acuminate at the apex, broadly cuneate to truncate at the base, slightly pubescent, becoming scabrous above, nearly glabrous beneath, membranaceous; corymbs many-flowered, glabrous or slightly villous; flowers 1.5–2 cm. wide; calyx-lobes lanceolate, acuminate, glandular-serrate, glabrous or the lobes slightly villous on the upper side; stamens 10–20; anthers red; styles 3–5; pome pyriform to short-ellipsoidal, scarlet, glabrous, 1.5–2 cm. thick, with rather persistent erect or spreading calyx-lobes, flesh dry, mealy; nutlets usually 4–5, 7–8 mm. long. Flowers, May; fruit, September.

Frequent, southern Connecticut to southern Ontario and northern Illinois, south to Pennsylvania and Delaware. Michigan, Lower Peninsula.

Crataegus pedicellata Sarg. var. *albicans* (Ashe) Palmer, differing from the species in its glabrous corymbs and petioles and in its generally broader leaves, is reported by Hanes from Kalamazoo County and should be sought in other localities.

GROUP VIII. MOLLES Sarg.

Crataegus mollis (T. & G.) Scheele. (Red-fruited Thorn, Downy Thorn). Fig. 70. A shrub or small tree with spreading branches; spines somewhat curved,

3–5 cm. long, blackish-brown; stipules deciduous; leaves simple, alternate, deciduous, yellow-green when young, broadly ovate, 4–13 cm. long, 4–10 cm. wide, cordate to truncate at the base, incised and sharply serrate with gland-tipped teeth, roughish above, densely tomentose beneath; petioles 2–5 cm. long, pubescent or tomentose; corymbs many-flowered and densely tomentose; flowers white, about 2.5 cm. wide; calyx ring 5-lobed, the lobes with glandular-serrate acuminate tips; petals 5, spreading, rounded; stamens about 20; anthers yellow; styles 4–5; fruit short-ellipsoid to subglobose, scarlet, 1.5–2.5 cm. thick, the calyx-lobes usually

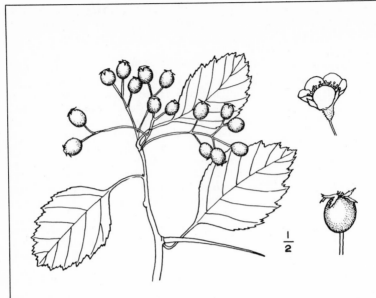

CRATAEGUS SUCCULENTA

FIG. 71

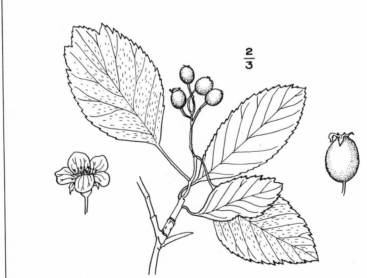

CRATAEGUS DOUGLASII

FIG. 72

deciduous, flesh yellow; nutlets mostly 5, 7–8 mm. long, obscurely ridged on the back. Flowers, May; fruit, August, September.

Southern Ontario to South Dakota, south to Tennessee and Arkansas. Michigan, throughout, common in the central portion.

The following variety has been reported (Bingham) from Oakland County: *Crataegus mollis* (T. & G.) Scheele var. *sera* (Sarg.) Eggl., leaves oblong-ovate, fruit pyriform-ellipsoidal, dull dark-red.

This is one of the best of the native thorns for horticultural use and development.

GROUP IX. MACRACANTHAE Loud.

Crataegus succulenta Schrad. (Soft-fruited Thorn). Fig. 71. A large shrub or small tree with ascending branches; bark reddish-brown, scaly; twigs gla-

Crataegus succulenta

brous when young, yellowish-green, becoming orange-brown and lustrous, turning dark gray in age; spines numerous, straight or slightly curved, 4–8 cm. long; leaves simple, alternate, deciduous, broadly rhombic-ovate to obovate, 4–8 cm. long, 3–7 cm. wide, rather coarsely and doubly serrate, the teeth spreading and with 4–6 short, acute or obtuse, often obscure lobes above the middle, the lower half of the leaf unlobed, simply serrate to entire, gradually narrowed from about the middle, acute at the apex, coriaceous, dark shining green above, veins strongly impressed, sparsely pubescent or glabrate, much paler beneath and pubescent, especially along the veins; petiole stout, 1–2 cm. long, winged above; corymbs sparingly villous, many-flowered; flowers about 16–20 mm. in diameter; sepals lanceolate, acuminate, glandular-laciniate, villous; stamens 10–20; anthers pink or sometimes yellow; disk prominent; styles 2–3; pome subglobose, 7–15 mm. in diameter, dark red, sparsely villous and pale-dotted, pulp soft; nutlets 2–3, prominently ridged on the back, deeply pitted on the ventral surfaces, 6–8 mm. long. Flowers, May; fruit, September, October.

Crataegus Douglasii

Southeastern Canada, westward to Iowa, southward to North Carolina and Missouri. Michigan, reported from both peninsulas.

GROUP X. DOUGLASIANAE (Loud.) Sarg.

Crataegus Douglasii Lindl. (Black-fruited Thorn, Douglas' Thorn). Fig. 72. A shrub or small tree 3–13 m. tall, with ascending branches; bark dark brown, scaly; twigs reddish; spines usually 1–2 cm. long, stipules deciduous; leaves simple, alternate, deciduous, ovate to obovate, 3–8 cm. long, 1.5–7 cm. wide, acute or obtuse at the apex, cuneate at the base, doubly serrate and lobed, except near the base, dark green and appressed-pubescent above, glabrous below, subcoriaceous; petioles slightly winged, pubescent and glandular, about 1 cm. long; corymbs many-flowered, glabrous or nearly so; flowers about 1.5 cm. wide; calyx-lobes acute or acuminate, entire, villous above, tinged with red; stamens 10–20; anthers light yellow; styles 3–5; fruit short-ellipsoid, dark purple to black, 8–10 mm. thick, sweet; nutlets 3–5, ear-shaped, roughly pitted on the inner face. Flowers, May, June; fruit ripe, August, September.

Ontario, shores of Lake Superior, Thunder Bay Island, Lake Huron, Upper Peninsula of Michigan, Michipicoten Island, Lake Superior and far westward and northwestward. Michigan, Upper Peninsula and northern part of Lower Peninsula.

This is another famous plant, of which we have several in Michigan, presenting something of a problem as to its distribution. It is found around the upper Great Lakes region and then skips to western Montana and Wyoming, from there extending westward across Idaho, and is known as a typical shrub or small tree of the Pacific slope from California to southern British Columbia.

The foregoing does not even scratch the surface of the species of thorns which may be found in Michigan. C. S. Sargent, Director of the Arnold Arboretum, wrote a monograph on 'Crataegus in Southern Michigan' which was published by the State Board of Geological Survey in its report for 1906. In this work he lists 55 species from the southern part of Michigan, of which 23 are proposed new species. Only 18 of the 41 species of Crataegus given in Beal's 'Michigan Flora' are included in Sargent's list. Therefore 37 new species were added by his work, making a total of 78 for the state. And he says: "Judging from the material which I have seen from other parts of the Lower Peninsula and which is too incomplete for critical study, it seems probable that there are still in the southern part of the state a large number of unnamed species, and when these are known it will not be surprising if the flora of Michigan is found to contain a much larger number of species than are now described." Professor Sargent in the above refers only to the southern portion of the state. The Upper Peninsula has many hawthorns among which a critical study would no doubt reveal many new species in addition to those already known from there.

Oliver A. Farwell (1930), sums up his experience with Crataegus in Michigan in part as follows: "This genus is well distributed through southern Michigan. No systematic study of the species of the whole state has ever been made; it would be mere guess work to suggest the number of the named and described species of North America that might be found in Michigan." He follows this statement with a list of 52 species and varieties which he has found in Michigan, in both Upper and Lower Peninsulas.

W. W. Ashe also worked extensively with Michigan Crataegi having named 18 of the 41 species listed in Beal's 'Michigan Flora.' Some of these were described in Ashe's 'New East American Thorns' (1902).

More recently Mr. C. A. Bazuin, of Grand Rapids, Michigan, has collected Crataegi extensively in western Michigan, concentrating largely on the territory contiguous to his home city. The Grand River moraine is particularly rich in hawthorns, and he has an impressive listing. Mr. Ernest J. Palmer, of the Arnold Arboretum, Harvard University, has cooperated with him in determining the more controversial collections.

Mr. Bazuin has prepared a check-list of the flora of western Michigan. This list contains a total of 54 species, varieties and forms of Crataegi, 13 of which are included in the foregoing treatment. The list has not yet been published, but it no doubt will be within a reasonable time. It will be seen that the number of species listed by Mr. Bazuin for the western side of the state does not vary greatly from that of the other Michigan lists.

Technical descriptions of these hawthorns referred to in the foregoing paragraphs are scattered through the literature, and it is not practical to give them here. Upon request of any user of this volume the Institute will, so far as possible, furnish the lists of species cited, together with references to the literature concerning them.

Although the various workers have covered a great deal of territory it will be seen from the above that there is still abundant opportunity in Michigan for original systematic work in this field, and it is hoped that some ambitious amateur will accept the challenge.

Potentilla L.—CINQUEFOILS

A genus of about 150 species, nearly all native to the north temperate zone. Eight species are listed in Beal's 'Michigan Flora' as native to Michigan, all of which are herbaceous except the following.

Potentilla fruticosa L. (Shrubby Cinquefoil). Fig. 73. Shrubs with numerous more or less erect branches, 3–10 dm. tall; bark reddish-brown and shreddy;

Potentilla fruticosa

leaves alternate, pinnate, deciduous, 1–3 cm. long; leaflets 5–7, mostly 5, crowded, oblong-lanceolate, entire, 1–2 cm. long, acute or acutish at each end, silky-pubescent, the margins revolute; flowers terminal, closely cymose, or solitary, about 2 cm. across; calyx-tube flat, deeply 5-cleft, with a bractlet in each sinus, appearing 10-cleft; petals yellow, orbicular; stamens 15–20; style lateral, filiform; stigma four-lobed; achenes numerous, collected in heads densely covered with long straight hairs. Flowers, June to September; fruits the same period.

In swamps or moist rocky places, Greenland and Labrador to Alaska, south to New Jersey, Pennsylvania, the Great Lakes region, Iowa, Arizona and California. Michigan, common throughout.

The late flowering period of the Shrubby Cinquefoil makes it a desirable shrub for ornamental planting, and it is frequently used when a suitable habitat is available. While we think of this species as one favoring low, wet ground it practically always edges out onto the higher ground surrounding a swamp where it grows in profusion.

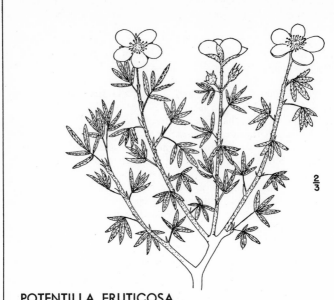

POTENTILLA FRUTICOSA   FIG. 73

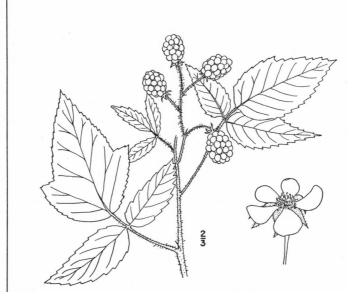

RUBUS IDAEUS VAR. ACULEATISSIMUS   FIG. 74

[150]

Rubus [Tourn.] L.—Brambles, Blackberries, Raspberries

A genus of many species, having a wide distribution, mostly in the temperate zone. The plants are extremely variable, and there is much confusion in their naming. They are reputed to be one of the most difficult groups to classify, and the author of a recent publication similar to this disposed of at least a part of the genus in the following manner: "The species of blackberries and dewberries are too difficult for the beginner to attempt." This is not entirely subscribed to here, but in selecting the following for treatment out of the sixty-odd species attributed to Michigan, an effort has been made to include only the better differentiated species which may be more or less readily recognized by the amateur. The stems of the brambles are woody, but they do not live on from year to year, bearing fruit as do those of the huckleberry or other such shrubs. The stems live about a year and a half and die after bearing fruit, while the roots live on indefinitely. The new growth develops rapidly until normal size has been reached, then growth stops. These stems are simple the first year. Branches are developed the second year upon which the fruit is borne.

1. Leaves simple, 3–5-lobed; flowers large and showy
  2. Flowers purple rose-color; petals rounded..................................*R. odoratus*, p. 155
  2. Flowers white; petals oval..*R. parviflorus*, p. 155
1. Leaves pinnately 3–7-foliate
  3. Fruit falling off whole from the dry receptacle (not separating easily in *R. pubescens*)
    4. Stems only slightly woody, 1–3-flowered; leaves not white beneath; flowers white......................*R. pubescens*, in part, p. 159
    4. Stems shrubby, many-flowered; leaves white-pubescent beneath
      5. Stems upright, beset with stiff, straight bristles, not glaucous; fruit red..............................*R. idaeus* var. *aculeatissimus*, p. 152
      5. Stems recurved, often rooting at the tips; prickles hooked; glaucous all over
        6. Fruit black; pedicels and calyx without stalked glands..*R. occidentalis*, p. 153
        6. Fruit dark red or purple; pedicels and calyx with stalked glands..*R. neglectus*, p. 153
  3. Fruit separating from the receptacle (except in *R. pubescens*, which does not separate easily)
    7. Stems erect or arch-ascending
      8. Pedicels unarmed, often pubescent or glandular-hispid
        9. Pedicels copiously glandular-hispid ....*R. allegheniensis*, p. 159
        9. Pedicels glandless, or, occasionally, with gland-tipped hairs
          10. Lower surface of leaflets downy to the touch, even at maturity
            11. Inflorescence conspicuously bracted throughout with unifoliate leaflets........................*R. frondosus*, p. 161
            11. Inflorescence with but one or two unifoliate leaflets................................*R. pergratus*, p. 161
          10. Lower surface of leaflets glabrous, glabrate or nearly so...*R. canadensis*, p. 163
      8. Pedicels armed with stoutish or slender sharp-pointed bristle-formed prickles
        12. Leaflets laciniate-cleft, pubescent beneath.............*R. laciniatus*, p. 163
        12. Leaflets not laciniate-cleft, glabrous both sides......*R. nigricans*, p. 165
    7. Stems trailing or decumbent
      13. Stems bristly or weakly prickly
        14. Fruit red or reddish, drupelets small....................*R. hispidus*, p. 165
        14. Fruit black; drupelets large and juicy.................*R. flagellaris*, p. 166
      13. Stems not bristly or prickly; fruit red.............*R. pubescens*, in part, p. 159

Rubus idaeus L. var. *aculeatissimus* [C. A. Mey.] Regel & Tiling. (Wild Red Raspberry). Fig. 74. Stems shrubby, biennial, branched, 5–20 dm. tall, new growth more or less bristly, red with a bloom, the older stems with small hooked prickles, dull reddish-brown; stipules narrow, deciduous; leaves deciduous, alternate, 3–5-foliate, leaflets ovate or ovate-oblong, acuminate, sharply and irregularly serrate, or slightly lobed, rounded at the base, 3–7 cm. long, the lateral sessile, when mature bright yellow-green above, whitish-pubescent beneath; petiole bearing very small bristles and prickles, 4–7 cm. long; inflorescence racemose or paniculate, loose, pubescent and more or less bristly; pedicels slender, curved in fruit; flowers perfect, white, about 1 cm. in diameter; calyx deeply 5-parted, the segments lanceolate-acuminate, bristly hispid; petals 5, about

Rubus idaeus var. aculeatissimus

as long as the sepals; stamens numerous; fruit elongate-hemispheric, light red, separating easily from the white receptacle when ripe; drupelets numerous, tomentose, edible. Flowers, May, July; fruit, July, September.

Thickets, hillsides and rocky situations, Labrador to Manitoba, British Columbia, New Jersey, Pennsylvania, region of the Great Lakes and south to Virginia, North Carolina and to New Mexico. Michigan, common throughout.

This is the common red raspberry of our waste lands and fence corners. It is exceedingly persistent and in some situations might be classed as a pestiferous weed. It is the progenitor of several cultivated raspberries, including the Cuthbert and Hansall varieties.

Also it is the subject of violent disagreement among the taxonomists. *Rubus idaeus* L. is supposed to be the European red raspberry. It is free of glands in the inflorescence. Some claim that it does not occur in North America and that our native red raspberry is an entirely different plant. This group has given it the name, *Rubus strigosus* Michx. Others as positively claim that *Rubus idaeus* L. is indigenous in certain sections of this continent, that the plant varies greatly and that the form with glandular inflorescence is merely a variety, which has been known as *aculeatissimus* for many years. From the evidence revealed by the herbarium material it appears that this is the plant most often met with in Michigan. Some herbarium specimens from Michigan bearing the name *Rubus idaeus* L. proved to have the inflorescence very glandular and had obviously been misidentified.

Occasionally it will be found with white fruit. This has been named: forma *albus* (Fuller) Fern. A colony with white fruit persisted for a long time in a real estate subdivison in Bloomfield Township, Oakland County.

Two other varieties have been named, the range of which includes Michigan: *Rubus idaeus* L. var. *strigosus* (Michx.) Maxim., having bristleform prickles, not much thickened at the base and with new canes bristly, has been collected in Menominee and Keweenaw counties. *Rubus idaeus* L. var. *canadensis* Richards., with bark of the new canes cinereous-tomentose beneath the prickles, which are all bristleform. It seems unfortunate that *"canadensis"* should have been chosen as a varietal name in this case. It offers the opportunity, at least, for confusion with the species *Rubus canadensis* L. The variety was not represented in the herbaria examined; it should be looked for and reported if found.

Rubus neglectus Peck. (Purple Wild Raspberry). Fig. 75. Canes usually elongated, recurved and rooting at the tip, glaucous; prickles slender, straightish;

leaves 3-foliate; leaflets ovate-acuminate to almost lance-ovate, the terminal leaflets on new canes often somewhat lobed, doubly serrate, green on upper surface, white-tomentose below, the lateral leaflets closely sessile; inflorescence corymbose, terminal and sometimes axillary; pedicels erect or ascending, closely covered with slender prickles and stiff glandular hairs; flowers 8–10 mm. broad, petals white; calyx hispid and glandular; fruit dark-red with a whitish bloom, having the flavor of the red raspberry. Flowers, June, July; fruit, July, August.

In dry or rocky soil, Vermont to Ontario, Pennsylvania, Ohio, Michigan, Minnesota. Michigan, reported only from the Lower Peninsula and apparently not widely distributed.

This bramble is intermediate between *Rubus idaeus* var. *aculeatissimus* and *Rubus occidentalis* and by some is considered to be a self-perpetuating hybrid between the two species. Bailey says, however (1945), that "this raspberry is not yet understood." Perhaps future cytological investigation may be necessary to determine correctly its true position.

Rubus occidentalis L. (Black Raspberry). Fig. 76. Stems biennial, slender, recurved and under favorable conditions rooting at the tips, glaucous all over,

sometimes reaching a length of 3–4 m., armed with hooked prickles, not bristly; stipules deciduous; leaves deciduous, alternate, 3-foliate, or very rarely 5-foliate; leaflets ovate, pointed, coarsely cut and irregularly serrate, whitened-downy below, glabrous or nearly so above, the lateral somewhat stalked; petioles with small prickles; inflorescence corymbose, compact, mostly terminal; pedicels short, ascending or erect in fruit; flowers perfect, white, about 1 cm. broad; calyx 5-parted, the lobes acute and reflexed, tomentose, persistent; petals 5, shorter than the sepals, deciduous; stamens numerous; fruit black, hemispheric, variable in size, separating easily from the receptacle when ripe, edible. Flowers, May, June; fruit, July.

Copses, fence rows and waste ground, New Brunswick to Quebec, Ontario, Georgia and Missouri. Michigan, common throughout.

[153]

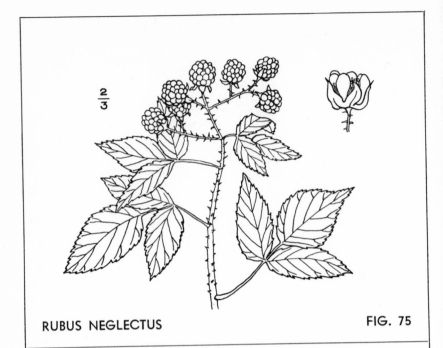

$\frac{2}{3}$

RUBUS NEGLECTUS   FIG. 75

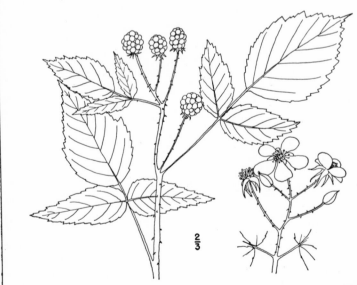

$\frac{2}{3}$

RUBUS OCCIDENTALIS   FIG. 76

The Black Raspberry is one of our best wild fruits, and few concoctions can equal wild black raspberry jam. It has a delicious flavor all its own. Like the Wild Red Raspberry, this is the progenitor of several cultivated raspberries, including the well-known Gregg and Hilborn varieties. Occasionally it will be found with yellow or amber fruit. Thus we have the strange combination of a yellow black raspberry. This has been named: forma *pallidus* (Bailey) Rob.

Rubus odoratus L. (Purple-flowering Raspberry). Fig. 77. Branched shrubs, erect, 1–1.6 m. tall; bark becoming loose and stringy; young shoots, flower

Rubus odoratus

branches and petioles thickly covered with glandular pubescence; leaves deciduous, alternate, simple, 12–17 cm. long and broad, 3–5-lobed, cordate at the base, lobes serrate, pointed, the middle one longer than the others, pubescent both surfaces; petiole long, very pubescent; inflorescence a loose, terminal corymbose or paniculate cluster; flowers perfect, rose-purple, 3–5 cm. broad; bracts membranous; calyx deeply 5-parted, densely covered with red, glandular hairs, the lobes tipped with a long, slender appendage; petals 5, rounded, inserted on the disk of the calyx; stamens many; filaments purple; style purplish; fruit red when ripe, depressed hemispheric, acid, dry and unpalatable. Flowers, May, September; fruit, July, September.

In rocky woods, Nova Scotia to Ontario and Michigan, south to Georgia and Tennessee. While Beal in his 'Michigan Flora' stated that it is common in the Upper Peninsula, this does not seem to be borne out by the records. Hermann (1935) says: "If it occurs as far north as Houghton and Keweenaw Counties it must be a rarity there since the writer during several years of botanizing in these counties has never detected it." Michigan distribution therefore is now stated as being confined to the Lower Peninsula. If any user of this bulletin is able to submit evidence that the species is found above the straits the information will be appreciated.

The Purple-flowering Raspberry makes a desirable cultivated shrub, but should always be given a shady place. Its rose-like blossoms are very attractive among its ample maple-shaped leaves. Like the other raspberries it spreads by underground stems which send up shoots in abundance.

Rubus parviflorus Nutt. (Salmon Berry, Thimbleberry). Fig. 78. Erect, branched shrubs, 1–2 m. tall; young shoots moderately glandular, scarcely bristly, older stems with gray shreddy bark; leaves deciduous, alternate, simple, cordate at base, 3–5 lobed, 7–20 cm. long and about as broad, lobes acute or obtusish, rarely acuminate, all approximately the same length, coarsely and unequally serrate, sparsely pubescent both sides; petiole glandular-hispid; inflorescence corymbose, few-flowered; flowers perfect, white, 3–5 cm. in diameter; calyx 5-lobed, the lobes tipped with a long, slender appendage; petals oval, 15–30 mm. long; stamens numerous; fruit depressed-hemispheric, red when ripe, separating

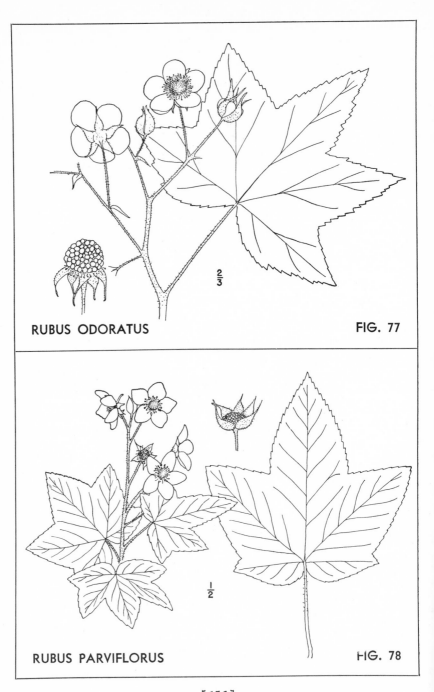

RUBUS ODORATUS

$\frac{2}{3}$

FIG. 77

RUBUS PARVIFLORUS

$\frac{1}{2}$

FIG. 78

from the receptacle, very tart. Flowers, June, July; fruit, August, September.

Rocky woods, shores, etc., western Ontario, northern Michigan, Minnesota and westward to Alaska and California. Michigan, upper part of Lower Peninsula and the Upper Peninsula.

The specific name of the Salmon Berry, *parviflorus*, means small-flowered, a name most unfitted to this plant, which has comparatively large flowers. In the north where the berries are abundant they are used for jam.

Rubus parviflorus

Like other members of the Rose family, *Rubus parviflorus* Nutt. is extremely variable. This has led to a great deal of "splitting," and there are something like three dozen varieties and forms now described and published. The following are to be found in Michigan, and a limited number of specimens are in the herbaria examined. Bailey (1945), in his monumental work on the genus *Rubus*, has reduced to synonymy a large number of the proposed varieties and forms of this thimbleberry and calls it simply *Rubus parviflorus* Nutt. In stating his reason for this procedure he says: "It will be inferred from my citation of synonymy in *R. parviflorus* that I do not accept these described categories as taxonomic descriptional varieties. I am not able to make them work." When such a noted authority as Dr. Bailey is "not able to make them work" the amateur should not be surprised if he also is not able to make them work and finds difficulty in recognizing the varieties listed.

Rubus parviflorus Nutt. var. *hypomalacus* Fern. Glands of pedicels and peduncles unequal, dark-colored, often 1–2 mm. long; lower surface of leaves with abundant divergent pubescence obviously soft to the touch. Recorded from Mackinac, Alger, Marquette, Houghton and Keweenaw counties.

Rubus parviflorus Nutt. var. *heteradenius* Fern. Lower surfaces of leaves glabrate to glabrous, not obviously soft to touch. Recorded from Mackinac, Marquette, Keweenaw and Delta counties.

Rubus parviflorus Nutt. var. *bifarius* Fern. Glands of pedicels and peduncles subequal and short, rarely more than 0.5 mm. long; lower surfaces of leaves with abundant soft divergent pubescence. Recorded from Mackinac, Houghton, Baraga, Keweenaw, Ontonagon, Menominee and Presque Isle counties.

Rubus parviflorus Nutt. var. *grandiflorus* Farw. Glands same as preceding; lower surfaces of leaves glabrous or soon glabrate. Recorded from Mackinac, Baraga, Keweenaw and Antrim counties.

Rubus parviflorus Nutt. forma *pedatifidus* Hermann. Leaves palmately-compound, leaflets deeply lobed and incised. Recorded from near Agate Harbor, Keweenaw County. Hermann discovered this mutation in a colony of typical *R. parviflorus* plants and published the description in 1935. The type specimen

[157]

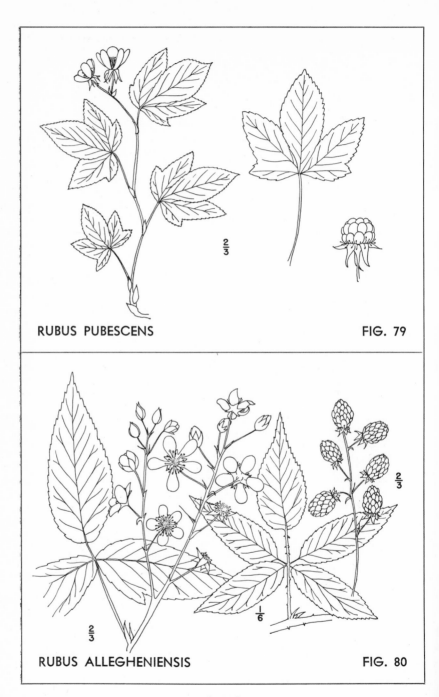

RUBUS PUBESCENS — FIG. 79

$\frac{2}{3}$

RUBUS ALLEGHENIENSIS — FIG. 80

$\frac{2}{3}$

$\frac{1}{6}$

$\frac{2}{3}$

is deposited in the herbarium of the University of Michigan. Others will find it interesting to look for similar mutations of this or other brambles.

Rubus pubescens Raf. (Dwarf Raspberry). Fig 79. (*Rubus triflorus* Richards., Gray's Manual, 7th Edition, Shrubs of Michigan, 1st Edition.) Stems

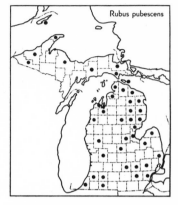
Rubus pubescens

trailing or ascending, unarmed, herbaceous or somewhat woody, those with flowers erect, 1–4 dm. tall, sterile more elongated, sparsely pubescent; stipules oval, entire or few-toothed, prominent; leaves deciduous, alternate 3- or rarely 5-foliate; leaflets rhombic-ovate, glabrous or nearly so, the terminal wedge-shaped, acute, the lateral mostly rounded at the base, coarsely and doubly serrate, thin; inflorescence slender, 1–3 flowered, glandular-pubescent; flowers white, 8–12 mm. broad; calyx lobes 5–7, acuminate, reflexed; petals 5–7, erect, spatulate-oblong, somewhat exceeding the sepals; stamens numerous; fruit red-purple, about 12 mm. long, the rather large drupelets not separating easily from the receptacle. Flowers, May, July; fruit, July, August.

In swamps Newfoundland to Alaska, south to New Jersey, Iowa and Nebraska. Michigan, frequent throughout.

This little creeping raspberry is found in swamps and low wet woods. Its fruit does not separate easily from the receptacle and yet it is not like the blackberries, the fruit of which does not separate from its receptacle at all. It is therefore intermediate between the blackberries and the raspberries. The fruit is edible, although not particularly attractive.

Rubus allegheniensis Porter. (High-bush Blackberry). Fig. 80. Shrubby, 1–2 m. tall, the stems somewhat arching, old canes purplish with stout straight-

Rubus allegheniensis

ish prickles, pubescent or becoming glabrous toward the base; leaves alternate, deciduous, 3–7-foliate, the leaflets ovate to ovate-lance-olate, all subcordate or rounded at the base, acute or acuminate, coarsely and unequally serrate, the terminal somewhat larger than the lateral, villous above, velvety beneath; petiole 5–12 cm. long, with stout prickles; inflorescence glandular-pubescent, racemose, leafy-bracted below; flowers white, 2.5–3.5 cm. broad; calyx persistent, its 5 lobes 6–8 mm. long, more or less pubescent; petals obovate, much exceeding the calyx-lobes; stamens numerous, inserted on the calyx; fruit, black, thimble-shaped, 1.2–2.5 cm. long, the drupelets not separating from the receptacle, but falling from the calyx together, of good flavor and edible. Flowers, May, June; fruit, July, August.

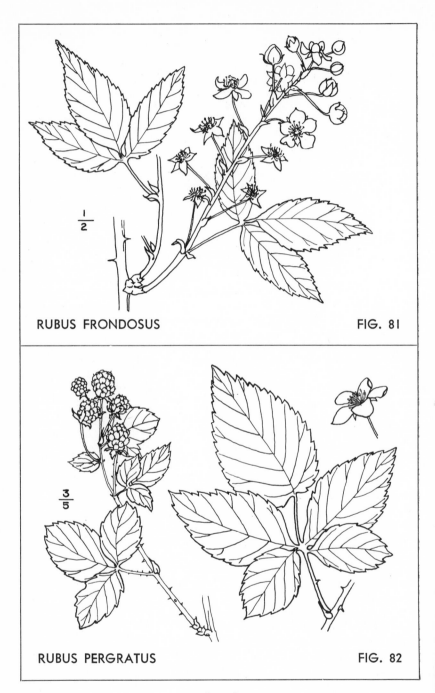

RUBUS FRONDOSUS   FIG. 81

RUBUS PERGRATUS   FIG. 82

Dry, open thickets and recent clearings, Nova Scotia to Ontario, Minnesota south to North Carolina and Arkansas. Michigan, common, Lower Peninsula, rare, Upper Peninsula.

This is the common blackberry of our fence rows, roadsides and clearings. It is very abundant and persistent, and from it have originated some of the cultivated blackberries of our gardens. Its fruit is delicious and blackberry jam is an old favorite.

The blackberry group is very confusing to the beginner; to distinguish among the varying forms is a task for the experts, and very often they do not agree. Speaking of *Rubus allegheniensis*, Bailey says: "Perhaps none of our highbush blackberries has so many disguises." In his work on the blackberries (1945) he lists one variety within our range and has since proposed another from Kalamazoo County: *Rubus allegheniensis* Porter var. *albinus* Bailey, with amber-colored fruit. This is the so-called "white blackberry" and may be looked for wherever the species is found. *Rubus allegheniensis* Porter var. *plausus* Bailey. This variety was described from material sent to Bailey by Clarence R. and Florence N. Hanes, Kalamazoo County, Michigan.

Rubus frondosus Bigel. (Leafy-flowered Blackberry). Fig. 81. Canes ascending or somewhat arching, 1–2.5 m. tall, more or less prominently angled,

glabrous; prickles scattered, stout, straightish; leaves 3–5-foliate, velvety-pubescent beneath, sparingly pubescent or glabrous above; leaflets sharply and irregularly serrate, ovate to ovate-oblong, the terminal on 5-foliate leaves with petiolule 3–5 cm. long, abruptly pointed at apex, rounded to cordate or semicordate at base, outer leaflets subsessile; flowers 6–10, white, about 2.5–3 cm. broad, borne in more or less elongated racemes, bearing, for more than half their length, nearly uniform unifoliate ovate-oblong petiolate persistent bracts; pedicels hairy-pubescent, glandless and unarmed; sepals broadly ovate, villous outside, tomentose inside; petals broadly obovate, about 1 cm. long; fruit black, subglobose, drupelets few and large, glabrous. Flowers, May, June; fruit, July, August.

In dry soil, Massachusetts to New York, Ohio, Michigan, Minnesota and Iowa. Michigan, sparingly distributed, Upper and Lower Peninsulas.

Rubus pergratus Blanch. Fig. 82. Large, erect plants, 1–2 m. tall, more or less pubescent, nearly or quite glandless; new canes red, glabrous, angled and furrowed, with a few short prickles; old canes purplish, strongly furrowed, prickles straightish, stout, broad-based, subremote; leaves long-stalked, 3–5-foliate; leaflets at first sparingly villous above, later for the most part glabrate, velvety beneath, oval, broad-oval, ovate or nearly orbicular, base semicordate or broadly wedge-shaped, taper-pointed, finely and sometimes doubly serrate;

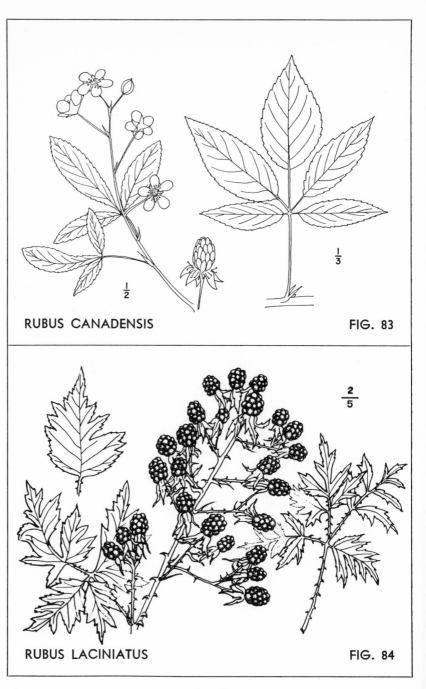

RUBUS CANADENSIS

$\frac{1}{2}$

$\frac{1}{3}$

FIG. 83

$\frac{2}{5}$

RUBUS LACINIATUS

FIG. 84

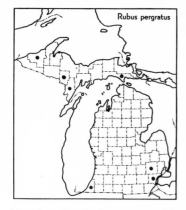

petiole stout, grooved above, nearly or quite glandless, with a few stout, hooked prickles; racemes short-cylindric, broadest at the top, rachis and pedicels villous, essentially glandless with but 1–2 unifoliate bracts; flowers large and showy, 2–3.5 cm. broad; petals broadly obovate; fruit black, short-cylindric, the numerous drupelets large and pulpy, sweet. Flowers June, fruit ripe, early August.

When the species was originally described the range was given simply as Vermont. The plant has since been collected from New Brunswick to Vermont and Massachusetts, New York, Pennsylvania, Ontario and Michigan. Michigan, apparently sparingly distributed in both Upper and Lower Peninsulas.

This species is very productive and resembles some cultivated blackberries.

Rubus canadensis L. (Millspaugh's Blackberry, Thornless Blackberry). Fig. 83. Stems erect or recurving 1.5–3 m. tall, wand-like, entirely unarmed or with a few weak prickles, glabrous or the

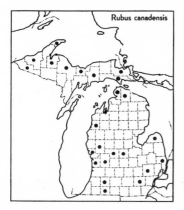

younger shoots scurfy-pubescent; leaves alternate, deciduous, palmately 3–5-foliate, leaflets glabrous both sides, thin, oval, long acuminate or acute, rounded or narrowed at the base, up to 15 cm. long and 5 cm. wide, sparsely but not deeply serrate, petiolule of the terminal leaflet 4–10 cm. long; petiole long; inflorescence loosely racemose, long-cylindric, leafy-bracted at the base; pedicels slender, ascending, fine pubescent; flowers white, 2.5–4 cm. broad; calyx-lobes lanceolate, acuminate; petals obovate; stamens numerous; fruit subglobose to short-cylindric, black, very pulpy, 1.5–2.5 cm. long, the drupelets not separating from the receptacle, edible. Flowers, June, August; fruit, August, September.

In thickets and woods Newfoundland to Michigan and in the uplands to North Carolina. Michigan, frequent throughout.

Rubus laciniatus Willd. (Cut-leaved Blackberry). Fig. 84. Canes measuring up to 3 m. in length, strong-growing, glandless; prickles 5–6 mm. long, woody, hooked, broad-based and curved; leaves on new canes 5-foliate, leaflets ovate in outline, variously laciniate-cleft, some of the margins serrate-dentate, upper surface glabrous, lower more or less soft pubescent; petioles, leaflet stalks and generally the midribs bearing hooked prickles; flowering cane leaves mostly 3-foliate, or unifoliate toward the upper part of the inflorescence, laciniate or divided; inflorescence terminal, irregular; pedicels strongly prickly and fre-

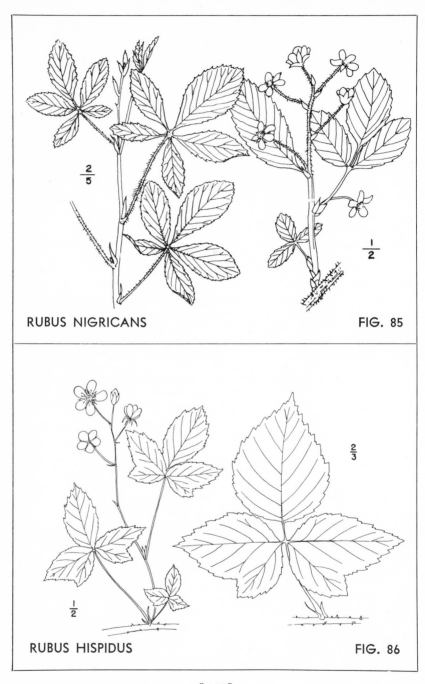

$\frac{2}{5}$

$\frac{1}{2}$

RUBUS NIGRICANS

FIG. 85

$\frac{2}{3}$

$\frac{1}{2}$

RUBUS HISPIDUS

FIG. 86

quently branched; flowers about 2 cm. broad, pinkish or rose-color, petals notched; calyx-lobes soon fully reflexed; fruit globular, about 1.5 cm. thick, edible. Flowers, June; fruit, August.

Escaped from cultivation and reported from Rhode Island, New York, New Jersey, District of Columbia, Virginia, West Virginia, South Carolina, Michigan, California, Oregon, Washington. Michigan, reported only from the Upper Peninsula.

The original habitat of this species is unknown, but it is now widely used in all parts of the world in ornamental planting. In milder climates it is evergreen. As a wild naturalized plant it is established across the United States. In Michigan it does not appear to be widely distributed. In his volume on North American blackberries Bailey states that he has a specimen from Michigan, but does not give the location. As far as available local records are concerned, Marjorie T. Bingham made the first collection in 1946 on the property of the Huron Mountain Club in Marquette County. The species should be looked for throughout the state.

Rubus nigricans Rydb. (Bristly Blackberry). Fig. 85. Canes erect or ascending, 5–10 dm. tall; new canes slender, covered with thin hair-like deflexed

prickles; leaves 3–5-foliate small, upper surfaces dark-colored and glabrous, lighter-colored, strongly ribbed and slightly pubescent beneath; leaflets nearly or quite sessile, mostly narrow-ovate to elliptic and definitely pointed, finely and sharply serrate; petiole slender, setose and somewhat glandular; flowering canes leafy, the leaves 3-foliate, leaflets elliptic-pointed, occasionally obovate, short-stalked or sessile, green and glabrous on both sides; flowers white, about 2 cm. across, 5–10 in racemose clusters; pedicels strongly prickly, mostly obscurely or not at all glandular; petals narrow, separate; calyx small, usually glandular-hairy; fruit black, globular, about 1 cm. across, sour, drupelets large. Flowers, June, July; fruit, August.

In dry open places or marshy soil, Quebec and northern New York to Michigan and eastern Pennsylvania. Michigan, apparently sparsely distributed, both peninsulas.

Rubus hispidus L. (Hispid or Running Swamp Blackberry). Fig. 86. Stems slender, prostrate and trailing, more or less beset with retrorse prickles; branchlets erect or ascending, 1–3 dm. high; leaves deciduous, although sometimes persisting through the winter, 3- or rarely 5-foliate; leaflets glabrous on both surfaces, somewhat shining above, firm, obovate, obtuse at the apex, narrowed or sometimes rounded at the base, 1–4 cm. long, sharply serrate above the middle; petiole glabrous or nearly so; inflorescence terminal or axillary, racemose-corymbose, few-flowered, nearly or entirely leafless, the pedicels and rachis pubescent and often bristly; flowers white, 1.5–2 cm. broad; calyx-lobes 3–4 mm. long, reflexed, pubescent; broadly obovate, exceeding the calyx-lobes; stamens numerous; fruit small, reddish-purple; drupelets glabrous, sour, not separating from the receptacle. Flowers, June, July; fruit, August.

Low woods and swampy meadows, Nova Scotia to Georgia, west to Minnesota and Kansas. Michigan, throughout; very abundant in central portion.

This trailing blackberry is very common. Although the leaves are deciduous the foliage looks evergreen and sometimes persists through the winter. In the autumn the foliage takes on many brilliant and changing tints.

In common with other members of this genus, *Rubus hispidus* is extremely variable. Bailey says: "It is polymorphous, and any number of foliage varieties and ecological forms can be separated; perhaps it will be broken into a number of species when new workers enter the field, but in my time I prefer to keep the unusual specimens in covers of Hispidus guises." Three varieties are recognized by Bailey, one of which occurs in Michigan: *Rubus hispidus* L. var. *obovalis* Fern., a very slender plant, less extensively running, bearing few bristles or practically unarmed; leaves much smaller and mostly rounded; range as of the species.

Rubus flagellaris Willd. (Dewberry, Low Running Blackberry). Fig. 87. (*Rubus villosus* Ait., Gray's Manual, 7th Edition, Shrubs of Michigan, 1st Edition.) Stem trailing, shrubby, often 1–4 m. long, glabrous, armed more or less with reflexed straightish prickles; branchlets upright, 1–3 dm. tall, more or less pubescent and sometimes prickly and glandular; leaves deciduous, 3- or rarely 5-foliate; leaflets ovate, oval or ovate-lanceolate, thin, acute or somewhat obtuse at apex, rounded or narrowed at the base, mostly sparingly pubescent both sides, doubly dentate-serrate; petiole 3–6 cm. long, more or less prickly; inflorescence a leafy, few-flowered corymbiform raceme, 2–3 cm. broad or the flowers sometimes solitary; flowers white, about 2.5 cm. broad; calyx-lobes ovate, acute, shorter than or exceeding the petals, pubescent; petals obovate to elliptic, about 10–15 mm. long; stamens numerous, generally exceeded by the stigmas; fruit subglobose to short-cylindric, black, juicy and delicious, 1–1.5 cm. long; drupelets not separating from the receptacle. Flowers, May, June; fruit, July, August.

Dry, open soil, southern Maine to Minnesota, south to Virginia and Missouri. Michigan, throughout.

This is the common Dewberry of our dry, open fields, banks and roadsides. It grows usually in poor soils, particularly in fields which were formerly cultivated. Bailey states that it is probably the most widely distributed of any of our North American Eubati, or blackberries. It is extremely variable and many varieties and forms have been described, some of which are to be found in Michigan. However, there is so much difference of opinion among specialists as to the applicability of the names that I am following the precedent set by Deam who states (1940) : "In the present treatment I believe it is best to regard this prostrate *Rubus* as a complex under one name."

In addition to the foregoing the following are reported from one or more stations within the state:

Rubus abactus Bailey	*Rubus mediocris* Bailey
associus Hanes	*meracus* Bailey
attractus Bailey	*michiganensis* Bailey
avipes Bailey	*notatus* var. *boreus* Bailey
Baileyanus Britt.	*pauper* Bailey
bellobatus Bailey	*peracer* Bailey
cauliflorus Bailey	*perspicuus* Bailey
complex Bailey	*plus* Bailey
conabilis Bailey	*potis* Bailey
dissensus Bailey	*Rappii* Bailey
distinctus Bailey	*Rosa* Bailey
Florenceae Bailey	*Schoolcraftianus* Bailey
Hanesii Bailey	*superioris* Bailey
jejunus Bailey	*tantalus* Bailey
kalamazoensis Bailey	*tenuicaulis* Bailey
laetabilis Bailey	*uvidus* Bailey
licens Bailey	*vagus* Bailey
limulus Bailey	*variispinus* Bailey
localis Bailey	*Wheeleri* Bailey

There may be others included in publications which have not been available for examination; still others may have been overlooked. The list does not include species which, as here treated, are synonymous with those illustrated or mentioned in the text. Altogether 63 species, varieties and forms of *Rubus* are here reported from Michigan, amply substantiating the contention that the brambles as a whole are a tremendously variable group.

In this connection it should be remembered that taxonomists severely disagree as to the identity of species; one will construe a species broadly, and its range will be increased accordingly; another will sharply delimit a species, and its range will shrink perhaps to a single station. Accordingly, by some not all of the species enumerated would be credited to Michigan. Others might find in Michigan a still greater number of species. Some years ago Bentham reduced all British brambles to a single species, *Rubus fruticosus* L. This is an extreme treatment, and no doubt the truth lies somewhere between the ideas of the so-called "lumpers" and "splitters." In checking the several herbaria for distribution it was not an uncommon experience to find as many as five or six

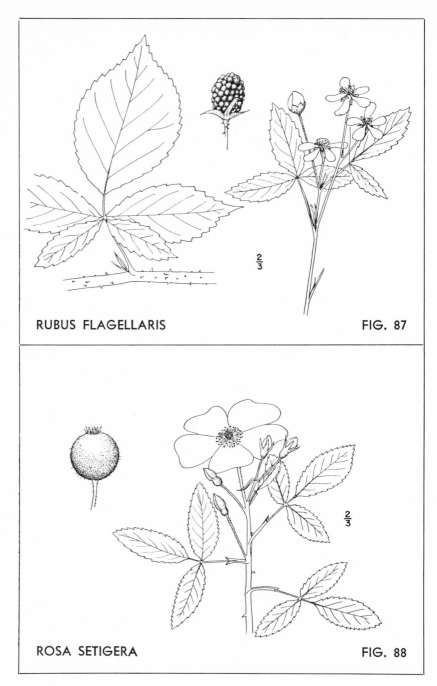

RUBUS FLAGELLARIS

$\frac{2}{3}$

FIG. 87

ROSA SETIGERA

$\frac{2}{3}$

FIG. 88

names given to the same plant, each worker as he studied the specimens having annexed his own version of its identity.

As to the reason for the great variability of the group and the abundance of intermediates, there seems to be as much difference of opinion as there is in relation to the nomenclature. In the past much of the blame has been placed upon hybridization. Later this idea has tended to be supplanted. Bailey (1945) says: "No longer do we assume that intermediateness is demonstration of hybridity." It is likely that edaphic conditions account for some of the confusion, particularly with less experienced collectors. Luxuriant and depauperate forms of the same species might appear quite different in the field and yet be taxonomically inseparable.

Those who may wish to pursue the study of the genus further are referred to the manuals, special monographs, and the various botanical periodicals. Articles on *Rubus* have appeared from time to time in the botanical literature, and it is not feasible to try to enumerate them here. The future will no doubt produce many such publications. The Institute will work with anyone interested in an endeavor to locate such publications on the subject as may be required.

Rosa [Tourn.] L.—ROSES

A very large genus, native of the northern hemisphere. Because of its beauty of form, color and fragrance the rose is undoubtedly the most universally admired and cultivated ornamental plant known to our gardens. It has been in cultivation from the earliest times of which we have record. The species of roses are extremely variable and freely hybridize whenever they occur together. These two characteristics have made it comparatively easy to develop varieties of the rose and literally thousands have been introduced and named. Many of these become obsolete and are superseded by better varieties. They go out of style much the same as suits and hats. The roses of my grandmother's garden could scarcely be compared to the beautiful varieties now in cultivation. Volumes have been written about the rose and devotees form societies to study and promote its development and cultivation.

When a plant is as popular with the people as the rose has always been, a wealth of romance is bound to attach to it. From the earliest times it has figured in the art, the poetry and the traditions of the people and has its place in the legends of the saints. *Sub rosa*, a phrase still in common, everyday use, had its origin in one of these legends. The rose was sacred to Venus, Goddess of Love, and was consecrated by Cupid to the god of silence to bribe him not to betray the amorous doings of the goddess. Hence the rose became the emblem of silence, i.e., "under the rose be it spoken," or *sub rosa*.

"The rose called by any other name would smell as sweet" is a phrase known to everyone, and "as sweet as a rose" has been invoked to sooth the wounded feelings of many an injured person. Roses have long been a favorite flower for weddings and equally so in honoring a departed friend.

From time immemorial the rose has been known as the Queen of Flowers. It has been the symbol of faction, the symbol of peace, the emblem of prospering nations. It has its place in religion and is a rosary by which piety numbers its prayers. The rose is carved in the stone ornamentation of cathedrals and blooms in decorative windows, tapestries, silks and canvasses.

The medicinal use of roses goes as far back as the known history of the plant. The proverbial bed of roses is not entirely a poetic fiction. In the ancient days luxurious persons slept on mattresses filled with roses. Now the phrase is mostly used to characterize the position of a person having rather rough going, i.e., "his is no bed of roses."

Over the centuries rose queens have been crowned at every favorable season, and now we have peach queens, apple queens, transportation queens and queens for almost every segment of human endeavor.

In the olden days the rose flower was served as a garnish, much as cress and parsley are used today. The leaves were sprinkled on meats and the juice used to savor certain dishes. They had rose water, rose ointment, rose conserve, sugar of roses, roses kept in wax, rose essence to burn on coals, rose sauce, rose cream, rose tinctures, pastes, syrups, lozenges and cordials.

The foregoing is only a hint of the wealth of material available to anyone desiring to go further into this phase of plant study.

The wild roses from which have been developed the myriads of horticultural varieties, although not as elaborate, are scarcely less beautiful. Our native roses vary greatly, and many have been separated and named as species and varieties, As these generally are based upon characters which, to say the least, are not plainly evident no attempt has been made to illustrate them here. Several are mentioned in the text, but for the most part they have been left to the specialists. Eileen Whitehead Erlanson, while a student at the University of Michigan, made a special study of the species of *Rosa*. In her paper (1928) she proposes two new species and one variety, as follows: *Rosa michiganensis, Rosa Schuetteana* and *Rosa blanda* Ait. var. *Hermanni*. All of these roses are found in Michigan, and the student desiring to go further than this with roses would do well to secure the publications by Mrs. Erlanson on this genus.

Rosa Lyoni Pursh, a *blanda* affiliate, may also be mentioned here. Three specimens in the University of Michigan Herbarium, identified by the collector as *Rosa blanda* Ait., have been renamed *Rosa Lyoni* Pursh. They are from Washtenaw, Oakland and Kent counties.

Beal's 'Michigan Flora' (1904) lists *Rosa Woodsii* Lindl. from one station. There are also collections from two other stations in the University of Michigan Herbarium. The general range of this plant is farther westward and northward. After examining and comparing the specimens, without further evidence than they provide for the purposes of this book, I do not feel warranted in listing it as a member of our flora.

1. Styles united in a protruding column; leaflets 3, very rarely 5; stems climbing..*R. setigera*, p. 171
1. Styles distinct, not exserted or very slightly so; leaflets 5–11, stems erect or spreading
   2. Sepals erect and connivent after flowering or spreading and reflexed, persistent on the fruit
      3. Sepals erect, connivent after flowering; leaflets 3–7 or 9–11
         4. Leaves more or less pubescent, 3–7-foliate
            5. Leaf-rachis glandular-puberulent or bristly; prickles very numerous ....*R. acicularis*, p. 171
            5. Leaf-rachis softly and finely villous or tomentose; prickles mostly few or none....................*R. blanda*, p. 175

4. Leaves glabrous or nearly so, 9–11-foliate; leaflets elliptic
or oval, dark green above, mostly rounded at apex..............*R. Lunellii,* p. 175

3. Sepals spreading or reflexed; leaflets 7–11, glabrous on both
sides, not resinous; flowers corymbose...*R. suffulta,* p. 173

2. Sepals reflexed after flowering and soon deciduous

6. Leaf-rachis very glandular; prickles numerous, strong and hooked;
leaflets rarely 2 cm. long, doubly serrate...................................*R. rubiginosa,* p. 177

6. Leaf-rachis puberulent or glabrous, scarcely if at
all glandular and otherwise not as above

7. Leaflets finely serrate, spines stout and recurved.................*R. palustris,* p. 177

7. Leaflets coarsely serrate; spines slender.................................*R. carolina,* p. 179

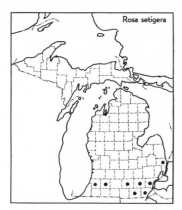
Rosa setigera

Rosa setigera Michx. (Michigan Rose, Prairie Rose, Climbing Rose). Fig. 88. Stems climbing or sprawling, up to several meters long, armed with scattered curving or straightish prickles, bristles none; twigs often glandular-pubescent; stipules very narrow; leaves alternate, deciduous, mostly 3-foliate, occasionally 5-foliate; leaflets mostly ovate, acute or obtusish at the apex, rounded at the base, 3–7 cm. long, sharply serrate, thick, smooth or downy beneath; petiole prickly, glandular - pubescent; inflorescence corymbose, with many flowers, pedicels covered with glandular hairs; flowers varying shades of pink to nearly white, about 6 cm. in diameter, not fragrant; calyx-lobes 5, ovate, acute, glandular, finally reflexed and deciduous; petals 5, obcordate, spreading; stamens many, inserted on the hollow ring which lines the calyx-tube; styles joined in a protruding column, as long as the stamens; fruit red, globose more or less glandular, 8–10 mm. in diameter. Flowers, June, July; hips ripe in autumn.

In thickets and on prairies, southern Ontario to Ohio, Wisconsin and Nebraska, West Virginia, Florida and Texas. Michigan, central and southern portion, rather rare.

Rosa setigera Michx. var. *tomentosa* T. & G., with tomentose leaves beneath, dull above, and with smaller and more numerous flowers, has been reported by Hanes from Kalamazoo County.

This is our only native climbing rose. It is the progenitor of several of our most valuable cultivated climbing roses. Michigan is highly honored in having such a beautiful and useful plant bear its name.

Rosa acicularis Lindl. (Prickly Wild Rose). Fig. 89. Shrubs 3–12 dm. tall, bushy, the stems and branches very prickly, greenish or reddish; stipules generally broad; leaves alternate, deciduous, 3–7-foliate, the rachis glandular; leaflets 2–4 cm. long, oval or oval-lanceolate, broadly elliptical to oblong-lanceolate, obtuse at the apex, rounded or subcordate at the base, usually pale and somewhat resinous-puberulent beneath, simply or doubly serrate; petiole glandular; flowers 5–7 cm. in diameter, solitary or rarely 2–3 in a cluster;

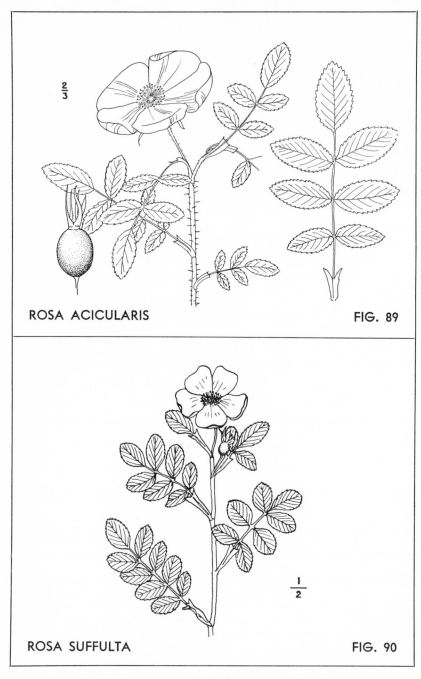

$\frac{2}{3}$

ROSA ACICULARIS   FIG. 89

ROSA SUFFULTA   FIG. 90

$\frac{1}{2}$

pedicel glabrous or rarely glandular; calyx-lobes lanceolate, acuminate or broadened at the tip, entire or few-toothed, persistent and erect upon the fruit; petals bright pink; stamens many; styles distinct; fruit globose or ellipsoid, about 1.5 cm. in diameter, red, generally glabrous. Flowers, May, June; hips ripe in autumn.

Rosa acicularis

Anticosti to Ontario, Alaska, northern Michigan, Minnesota, south in the Rocky Mountains to Colorado and Idaho. Michigan, Upper Peninsula and northern part of the Lower Peninsula.

The Prickly Wild Rose was first described from Siberia. It is a most variable species, differing in the form of the fruit and in the amount of pubescence. Several varieties have been separated, the following of which are found in Michigan: var. *Bourgeauiana* Crép., Presque Isle, Iron, Keweenaw and Mackinac counties; var. *Sayiana* Erlanson, Mackinac County; var. *rotunda* Erlanson, Emmett, Cheboygan, Gogebic and Keweenaw counties; var. *lacorum* Erlanson, Mackinac and Emmett counties.

Rosa suffulta Greene. (Arkansas Rose). Fig. 90. (*Rosa pratincola* Greene, Gray's Manual, 7th Edition.) Stems low, erect, 0.3–0.5 m. tall, densely prickly with very slender bristles; stipules narrow, more or less glandular-toothed or glandular-ciliate above; leaves alternate, deciduous; rachis softly and finely villous; leaflets 7–11, oval or obovate, sessile or nearly so, obtuse at the apex, subcuneate at base, the upper about 2.5 cm. long, the lower somewhat smaller, simply and sharply serrate, glabrous on both sides, rather firm and coarsely veined, not resinous; flowers pink, about 5 cm. in diameter, corymbose or rarely solitary; sepals lanceolate, acuminate, sparingly glandular-hispid or glabrous, or sometimes lobed, spreading or reflexed, persistent on the fruit; petals obovate or obcordate; stamens numerous; styles distinct; fruit globose or nearly so, 10–12 mm. in diameter, either bristly or smooth. Flowers, June, July; hips ripe in autumn.

Rosa suffulta

Prairies and waste places, Michigan, Indiana, Minnesota, Iowa, westward and southward to Colorado, New Mexico and Texas. Michigan, infrequent; so far recorded from the Lower Peninsula only.

The range of the Arkansas Rose has been found to extend eastward farther than its original specified limits, which were given as the prairie states and southward. It is now recorded from a number of stations in Indiana and Michigan.

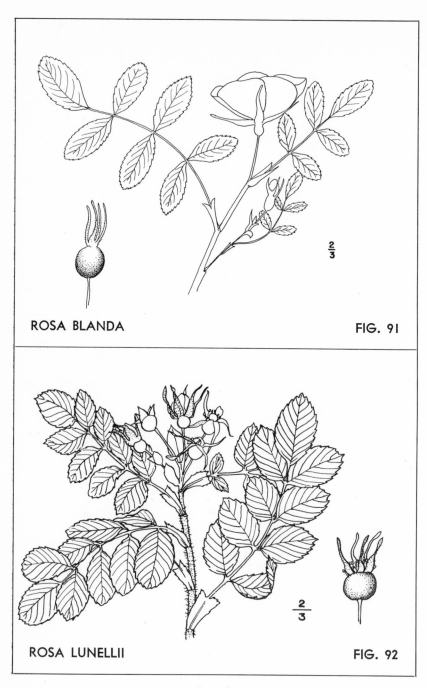

ROSA BLANDA

$\frac{2}{3}$

FIG. 91

ROSA LUNELLII

$\frac{2}{3}$

FIG. 92

Rosa blanda Ait. (Smooth Rose, Meadow Rose). Fig. 91. Shrub with erect branched stems, 3–15 dm. tall, entirely unarmed or with a few straight slender prickles; stipules broadened, naked and entire or slightly glandular-toothed; leaves alternate, deciduous, 5–7-foliate, rachis with fine woolly pubescence; leaflets oval or obovate, mostly pale beneath, thin, wedge-shaped at the base and short stalked, rounded at the apex, simply serrate, not resinous, the upper 2–4 cm. long, 1–2 cm. wide, the lower smaller; petiole with woolly pubescence, rarely glandular; flowers pink, few in a cluster or solitary, about 7 cm. broad; calyx-lobes acuminate, entire, hispid-pubescent, persistent and erect upon the fruit; petals obovate or obcordate, erose; stamens many; styles distinct; fruit about 1 cm. in diameter, red, subglobose, oval or somewhat pear-shaped, glabrous. Flowers, June, July; hips ripe in autumn.

In moist rocky places, Newfoundland through the New England States to central New York, west to Illinois and Missouri. Michigan throughout.

As indicated by its specific name one of the characteristics of this rose is its unarmed stems. Like the other roses, it shows great differentiation and several varieties have been named.

Rosa Lunellii Greene. Fig. 92. Shrub with erect simple stems, 1–3 dm. tall, densely bristly; stipules glabrous or nearly so, sometimes glandular, entire or gland-toothed on the margins; leaves alternate, deciduous, 9–11-foliate; petiole and rachis glabrous or sparingly puberulent, sometimes glandular, leaflets elliptic or oval, serrate, 1–2.5 cm. long, glabrous on both sides or sparingly pubescent on the veins beneath; flowers usually solitary or 2–3 together; petals obcordate, rarely 2 cm. long; sepals glandular on the back, connivent and long-persistent on the fruit; hip globose, glabrous, orange-red when ripe, 10–12 mm. thick. Flowers, June, July; hips ripe in autumn.

Plains and hills, Manitoba, North Dakota, South Dakota and Michigan.

Oliver A. Farwell, "while taking a constitutional on Sunday morning July 15, 1934," found this rose on the shores of Torch Lake at Hubbell, Keweenaw County. It therefore takes its place among the growing list of plants with such disjunct distribution that they have attracted the attention of botanists and geologists generally. Various theories have been advanced, no one of which meets with universal acceptance. For a very full and interesting discussion of this subject see Fernald (1935).

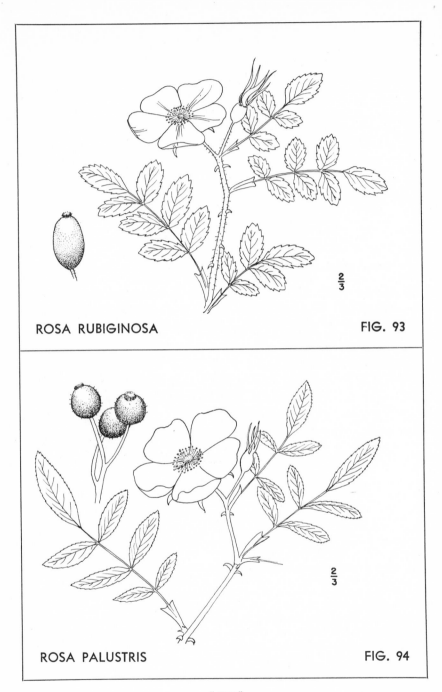

ROSA RUBIGINOSA $\frac{2}{3}$ FIG. 93

ROSA PALUSTRIS $\frac{2}{3}$ FIG. 94

Rosa rubiginosa L. (Sweetbrier, Eglantine Rose). Fig. 93. Shrubs with slender stems 1-2 m. tall or sometimes taller, greenish-brown, armed with

Rosa rubiginosa

stout hooked spines; stipules rather broad; leaves deciduous, alternate, 5-7-foliate, rachis glandular, very fragrant; leaflets broadly elliptical or obovate, rounded at the base, obtuse at the apex, doubly serrate, green and smoothish above, densely glandular-pubescent and resinous beneath; petiole prickly; flowers pink varying to white, 2-3.5 cm. in diameter, few in a cluster or solitary; pedicel prickly and glandular; calyx glandular, 5-lobed, the lobes lanceolate and usually with lateral lobes, spreading, deciduous; petals obcordate or obovate; stamens numerous; styles distinct; fruit scarlet, oval or ovoid, 1-2 cm. long, glandular. Flowers, May, June; hips ripe in the autumn.

In waste places, Nova Scotia to Ontario, Kansas, Tennessee and Virginia. Michigan, frequent in central and southern portion; occurs throughout.

The Sweetbrier Rose is a native of Europe but has been widely naturalized throughout the eastern portion of the United States and on the Pacific Coast. It appears to be thoroughly at home in its adopted country and the botanist is liable to find it by the side of the road, in a thin, upland woods or in almost any waste place. It has been a particular favorite in England for hundreds of years and as the Eglantine it has been used in the poetry of Shakespeare, Spenser and Chaucer.

The branches are fiercely armed and it is a wicked thing to deal with. It will seize hold of the clothing and flesh of the passer-by and scratch and claw. But in spite of these characteristics it has a charm all its own. Its aromatic fragrance comes from resinous glands which thickly cover the under surface of the leaves.

Rosa palustris Marsh. (Swamp Rose). Fig. 94. (*Rosa carolina* L. Gray's Manual, 7th Edition, Shrubs of Michigan, 1st Edition.) Stems erect, 3-25 dm.

Rosa palustris

tall with rather distant, stout, straight or recurved prickles, dull purple in age; stipules very narrow and long; leaves alternate, deciduous, 5-9-foliate, usually 7; leaflets very variable in outline, oval, ovate, oval-lanceolate, or obovate, 1.5-3.5 cm. long, wedge-shape or rounded at the base, ovate or obtuse at the apex, finely and simply serrate, mostly short-stalked, often pale or pubescent beneath; petiole often prickly; inflorescence a corymbose cluster or the flowers rarely solitary; pedicel glandular-hispid or smoothish, 1-2 cm. long; flowers bright pink, 5-7 cm. broad; calyx-lobes 5, lanceolate, acuminate or dilated above, sometimes more or less

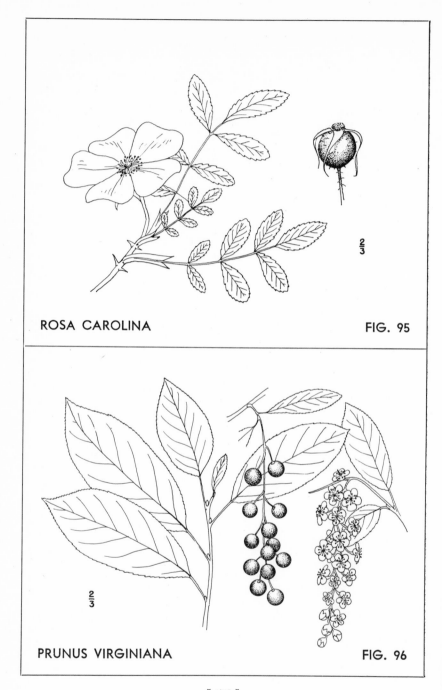

ROSA CAROLINA

$\frac{2}{3}$

FIG. 95

PRUNUS VIRGINIANA

$\frac{2}{3}$

FIG. 96

lobed, hispid-pubescent or reflexed, tardily deciduous after flowering; petals obcordate; stamens many; styles distinct; fruit scarlet, globose or depressed-globose, about 8–10 mm. high, glandular-hispid. Flowers, June, August; hips ripe in the autumn.

In swamps and low grounds, Nova Scotia to Ontario, Minnesota, south to Florida, Mississippi and Texas. Michigan, common throughout.

The Swamp Rose is one of our most abundant native roses and there is hardly a swamp or piece of low ground that does not have its quota. Its flowering season is long and as the hips cling to the stems all winter it is attractive throughout the year. It also takes kindly to cultivation and will thrive in almost any good soil.

Rosa carolina L. (Pasture Rose). Fig. 95. (*Rosa humilis* Marsh. Gray's Manual, 7th Edition, Shrubs of Michigan, 1st Edition.) Bushy shrub 1–10 dm. tall, slender, stems greenish, usually armed with slender, straight or curved spines

just below the stipules, also more or less prickly; stipules narrow, entire; leaves deciduous, alternate, 5–7-foliate, rachis glabrate or glabrous; leaflets thin, ovate, oval or obovate, rounded or pointed at the base, coarsely and sharply serrate, acute at apex, short-stalked or sessile, glabrous or pubescent beneath, upper surface glabrous, 1.2–2.5 cm. long; petiole glabrous or sparingly pubescent; flowers pink, usually few in a cluster or solitary, 5–7 cm. broad; pedicel usually glandular; calyx-lobes lanceolate, acuminate or dilated at apex, usually lobed, spreading and deciduous; petals obovate or obcordate; stamens many; styles distinct; fruit red, globose or depressed-globose, glandular-hispid, about 8–15 mm. in diameter. Flowers, May, July; hips ripe in the autumn.

In dry or rocky soil, Newfoundland to Ontario, Wisconsin, Missouri, Georgia, Louisiana and Texas. Michigan, throughout; more abundant in Lower Peninsula.

This is perhaps our commonest wild rose and it may be found in dry places generally. Its delicate pink blossoms are delightfully fragrant and the hips stay on the stems all through the winter thus prolonging its decorative qualities most of the year. In common with other roses it is extremely variable and several varieties have been separated and named.

The following varieties have been found in Michigan: *Rosa carolina* L. var. *villosa* (Best) Rehd. (*R. Lyoni* Pursh), under surface of leaflets slightly to densely pubescent; *Rosa carolina* L. var. *glandulosa* (Crép.) Farw., leaflets glabrate, often doubly serrate with some of the teeth having stipitate glands.

The following cultivated roses have been reported as infrequently persisting escapes: *Rosa gallica* L. var. *versicolor* L., French Rose, petals striped white and red; *Rosa gallica* L. var. *officinalis* Thory, with double flowers; *Rosa centifolia* L., Cabbage Rose; *Rosa cinnamomea* L., Cinnamon Rose; *Rosa spinosissima* L., Burnet Rose or Scotch Rose; *Rosa multiflora* Thunb., Japanese Rose; *Rosa canina* L., Dog Rose. It is possible that some or all of these roses might in time become well enough distributed and established to be regarded as part of our native flora. For the present, however, based on the evidence presented by our state herbaria, it seems sufficient to simply report them as infrequent escapes.

Prunus [Tourn.] L.—PLUMS, CHERRIES, etc.

Shrubs or trees, mostly with edible fruits. There are about 150 species in this genus, some 30 of which are found in North America. Of these the following, coming within our classification of shrubs, are found in Michigan.

1. Flowers in racemes, appearing after the leaves; leaves mostly obovate, thin,
   sharply serrate with spreading teeth...*P. virginiana*, p. 180
1. Flowers in umbellate clusters, appearing before or
   with the leaves; otherwise not as above
     2. Flowers small; petals mostly 4–6 mm. long; low shrubs
       3. Leaves oval, oblong or slightly obovate;
        petioles 8–20 mm. long..*P. susquehanae*, p. 181
       3. Leaves oblanceolate or spatulate; petioles 5–10 mm. long........*P. pumila*, p. 181
     2. Flowers large; petals 8–16 mm. long; tall shrubs
       4. Teeth of leaves obtusish, mostly glandular;
        calyx-lobes glandular-serrate, glabrous within..............................*P. nigra*, p. 183
       4. Teeth of leaves acute or acuminate, bristle-tipped,
        not glandular; calyx-lobes entire, hairy within...................*P. americana*, p. 183

Prunus virginiana L. (Choke Cherry). Fig. 96. A shrub or small tree 1–4 m. tall; bark gray, with numerous light-colored lenticels, the inner layers with a strong, disagreeable odor; leaves deciduous, alternate, simple, oval, oblong or obovate, 4–8 cm. long, 2–4.5 cm. wide, acute or acuminate at the apex, rounded at the base, glabrous or slightly pubescent along the veins beneath, sharply and finely serrate, thin; petiole 1–1.5 cm. long; flowers white, 8–10 mm. broad, in mainly loosely-flowered racemes terminating leafy branches of the season; calyx 5-cleft, short bell-shaped, deciduous; petals 5, obovate, spreading; stamens 15–20; drupe red to nearly black, globose, 8–10 mm. in diameter, astringent; stone globose and smooth. Flowers, May; fruit ripe, July, August.

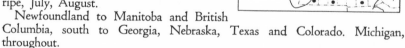

Newfoundland to Manitoba and British Columbia, south to Georgia, Nebraska, Texas and Colorado. Michigan, throughout.

Prunus virginiana L. forma *Deamii* G. N. Jones, is a form named for Charles C. Deam, the veteran botanist of Indiana; it is reported by Hanes from Kalamazoo County.

A fairly common shrub along fence lines and edges of woods. The fruit is attractive to birds.

The Choke Cherry acquired its common name from the fact that in trying to eat the fruit one is likely to choke. This is because the cherries are very puckery, harsh and bitter.

Prunus susquehanae Willd. (Appalachian Cherry). Fig. 97. (*Prunus cuneata* Raf., Gray's Manual, 7th Edition, Shrubs of Michigan, 1st Edition.)

Low erect shrub 3–12 dm. tall, sometimes branched and bushy, light-colored, glabrous or puberulent; leaves simple, alternate, deciduous, spatulate-oblong or oblanceolate, 3–6 cm. long, 0.8–2 cm. wide, obtuse or acute at the apex, wedge-shaped at the base, more or less serrate with appressed teeth above the middle, thin, glabrous above, pale beneath; petiole 8–20 mm. long; flowers white, 2–4 in umbels, appearing with the leaves, about 1 cm. broad; calyx 5-cleft, the lobes about 2 mm. long; petals 5, spreading; stamens 15–20; pedicels very slender, approximately 1 cm. long; drupe globose, nearly black, without bloom, about 1 cm. in diameter. Flowers, April, May; fruit ripe, August.

In thickets, wet soil, or among rocks, Maine and New Hampshire to Minnesota, North Carolina and Wisconsin. Michigan, throughout, more common in the northern portion of Lower Peninsula and in the Upper Peninsula. Similar to the Sand Cherry, but grows mostly in rocky situations.

Prunus pumila L. (Sand Cherry). Fig. 98. Depressed, trailing or sometimes with stems ascending to a height of 2 meters, young shoots angled, reddish,

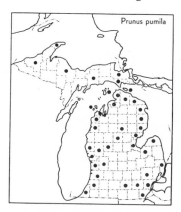

the older stems grayish, mostly glabrous; leaves deciduous, alternate, simple, linear-spatulate to oblanceolate, 3–7 cm. long, 1–2 cm. wide, acute or acutish at the apex, long wedge-shaped at the base, serrate or subentire above the middle, pale beneath, glabrous throughout; petiole 5–10 mm. long, generally with 1 or 2 glands; flowers white, 10–12 mm. broad, borne in lateral few-flowered sessile umbels, appearing with the leaves; calyx-lobes 5, rounded, about 2 mm. long, margins serrulate; petals 5, ovate to obovate; stamens many; pedicels 10–14 mm. long, slender; drupe globose, 8–12 mm. in diameter, dark red or dark purple, nearly black when ripe, without bloom, flesh thin, generally astringent. Flowers, May, June; fruit ripe, last of July and August.

On sandy and gravelly shores, New Brunswick to Manitoba, Maine, New Jersey, Indiana, Illinois, Michigan and westward. Michigan, chiefly bordering the Great Lakes, but also inland on the larger lakes and sandy plains.

The Sand Cherry, as might be expected from its common name, grows on beaches in almost pure sand. It is also found in dryer situations, but always in sandy soil and in the open.

[181]

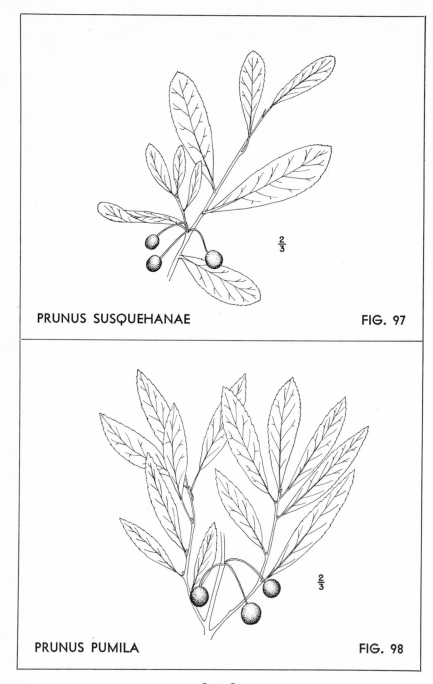

PRUNUS SUSQUEHANAE $\frac{2}{3}$ FIG. 97

PRUNUS PUMILA $\frac{2}{3}$ FIG. 98

Prunus nigra Ait. (Wild Plum, Canada Plum). Fig. 99. Shrub or small tree, 2–7 m. tall, armed with bluntish thorns; bark thin, brownish-gray; leaves

deciduous, alternate, simple, oval, ovate or broadly obovate, thin, 7–13 cm. long, 3–7 cm. wide, long-acuminate at the apex, rounded or somewhat heart-shaped at the base, doubly crenate-serrate, the teeth usually gland-tipped, pubescent when young; petiole stout, 1–2 cm. long, mostly with 1 or 2 red glands near the blade; flowers white, fragrant, turning pink in age, 2.5–3 cm. broad, borne in lateral umbels, expanding before the leaves; calyx-lobes 5, glandular-serrate, glabrous within; petals 5, broadly obovate, 1.2–1.4 cm. long; stamens many, tinged with pink; pedicels 1–2 cm. long, glabrous; drupe compressed-ovoid or sub-globose, orange-red or yellow, 2.5–3 cm.

long, bloom little or none; stone oval, compressed or flattened, sharply ridged on one edge and grooved on the other. Flowers, May; fruit, August.

River banks and roadside thickets, Newfoundland to Alberta, Massachusetts, Georgia, along the Great Lakes to Wisconsin and Iowa. Michigan throughout, but more abundant northward.

The fruit of this wild plum is of first class quality and it makes delicious jellies and preserves.

Prunus americana Marsh. (Wild Yellow Plum, Red Plum). Fig. 100. A shrub or small tree with a maximum height of about 7 or 8 m.; branches

more or less thorny; bark dark grayish-brown, thick and rough; leaves deciduous, alternate, simple, ovate or obovate, rounded at the base, long-acuminate at the apex, 4–10 cm. long, 2–5 cm. wide, sharply and doubly serrate, the teeth not glandular, pubescent on expanding, nearly or quite glabrous when mature; petiole about 1 cm. long, with or without glands; flowers white, fragrant 1.5–2.5 cm. broad, appearing in lateral sessile umbels before the leaves; calyx-lobes 5, entire, hairy on the inner surface; petals 5, narrowly obovate, about 1 cm. long; stamens many; pedicels 1–2 cm. long; drupe sub-globose, 1.8–2.5 cm. in diameter, red or yellow, the skin tough with little or no

bloom; stone somewhat flattened, one edge acute or margined, the other faintly grooved. Flowers, April, May; fruit, August, October.

River banks and borders of woods Connecticut to Manitoba, Florida, Texas and Colorado. Michigan, throughout.

This is our common wild plum. It prefers rich alluvial soil along streams, but also will be found in higher ground. It suckers freely, forming dense thickets,

[183]

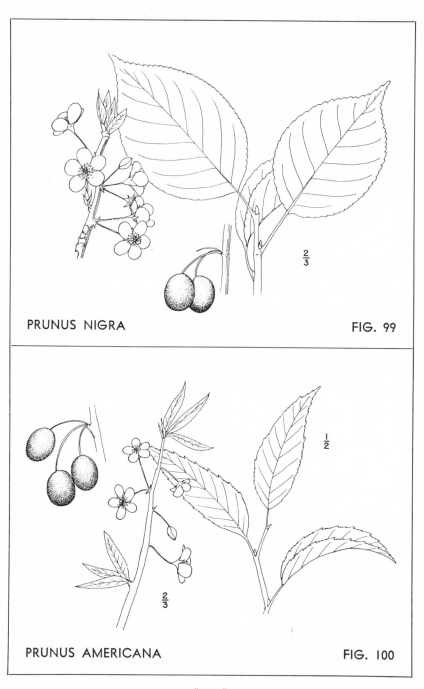

PRUNUS NIGRA $\frac{2}{3}$ FIG. 99

PRUNUS AMERICANA $\frac{1}{2}$ $\frac{2}{3}$ FIG. 100

and as "plum-brush" it is the bane of the farmer who wishes to keep his fence rows trim and neat. The fruit is pleasantly flavored and when eaten raw is very palatable. It is also much used for plum jelly and preserves.

The majority of our cultivated plums have been developed from this and the preceding species. Hedrick in 'The Plums of New York' says: *"Prunus americana* is the predominating native plum. It is the most widely distributed, is most abundant in individual specimens and has yielded the largest number of horticultural varieties of any of the native species. . . . The species was well named by Marshall *'americana'."*

LEGUMINOSAE—Pulse Family

The Pulse family consists of an immense number of species embracing herbs, shrubs, vines and trees. The family is divided into three subfamilies, and our Michigan shrubs and trees belong to the subfamily III, the general characters of which may be summarized as follows:

Subfamily—**Papilionoideae**

Trees, shrubs or herbs; leaves alternate, deciduous, mostly compound; flowers perfect; calyx of 5 sepals, more or less united, often unequally so; corolla inserted on the base of the calyx, of 5 irregular petals, the upper or odd petal larger than the others, called the standard, the two lateral spreading, called the wings, the two lower more or less united, called the keel, and enclosing the stamens and pistil; stamens 10, more or less united, or occasionally distinct; ovary 1–2-celled; pistil 1, simple, 1- to many-seeded, becoming a pod or legume in fruit.

Flowers small, in dense spikes, 1-petaled; pods less than 2 cm. long,
1–2-seeded; leaflets glandular-dotted..*Amorpha,* p. 185
Flowers large and showy, in drooping racemes, 5-petaled; pods over 2 cm. long,
several-seeded; leaflets not glandular-dotted....................................*Robinia,* p. 187

Amorpha L.—False Indigos, etc.

Leaflets 6–12 mm. long, crowded; low shrubs, 3–4 dm. high,
whitened with hoary down..*A. canescens,* p. 185
Leaflets 2–5 cm. long; tall shrubs, 1–3 m. high; pubescent or smoothish...*A. fruticosa,* p. 187

Amorpha canescens

Amorpha canescens Pursh. (Lead Plant). Fig. 101. An erect shrub, 3–14 dm. tall, whitened with hoary down all over; leaves alternate, deciduous, odd-pinnate, 5–10 cm. long; leaflets 21–51, short-stalked, oblong-elliptical, rounded at the base, obtuse or acutish and mucronate at the tip, 8–14 mm. long, 4–9 mm. wide, margin entire, woolly-pubescent beneath, becoming smoothish above; flowers small, purplish-blue, in dense terminal spikes; calyx 5-toothed, persistent; petals, only one, the standard, present; stamens orange-yellow; pods 1-seeded, about 4 mm. long, densely hairy. Flowers, July, August; fruit, September, October.

[185]

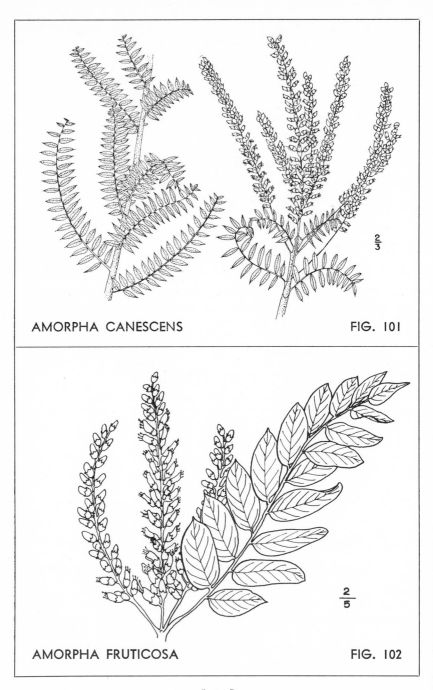

AMORPHA CANESCENS   FIG. 101

AMORPHA FRUTICOSA   FIG. 102

The Lead Plant is found on hills and prairies, Indiana to Manitoba, south to Louisiana, Texas and New Mexico. Michigan, rare, southern portion of Lower Peninsula.

In some sections of the west where the Lead Plant is found in abundance there has grown up the belief that it marks the existence of lead ore in the soil, probably for no other reason than that the plant is densely covered with silvery hairs and has a leaden color.

The Lead Plant continues in bloom for a long period. The deep purple spikes of flowers with their yellow stamens form a pleasing contrast with the gray foliage, and altogether it makes a valuable plant for landscape use.

Amorpha fruticosa L. (False Indigo). Fig. 102. A branching shrub, 1.5–3 m. tall; leaves alternate, deciduous, compound and odd-pinnate, petioled, 1.5–4 dm. long; leaflets 11–21, not crowded, short-stalked, oval or elliptic, entire, obtuse and mucronate at the tip, rounded or somewhat narrowed at the base, 2–5 cm. long, about 1.2 cm. wide, pubescent or glabrous; racemes terminal, dense, 7–15 cm. long, solitary or in clusters; flowers violet-purple, 6–9 mm. long; calyx teeth 5, nearly equal, persistent; only one petal, the standard, present, wings and keel absent; stamens 10, united at the base, exserted; anthers bright orange; ovary 2-celled; style curved; stigma terminal; pods glandular, thick-stalked, 5–10 mm. long; seeds usually 2. Flowers, May, July; pods ripe, August.

Amorpha fruticosa

Banks of rivers, streams and lakes, southern Pennsylvania and Ohio to Florida, westward to Texas, Minnesota, Manitoba, Saskatchewan, and in the Rocky Mountains. Escaped from cultivation in the middle and eastern states. Michigan, infrequent, Lower Peninsula.

The False Indigo is an effective ornamental infrequently used in landscape planting. The flowers are interesting. Only one petal, the standard, is present. This is wrapped around the stamens and pistil, simulating a complete corolla and protecting the vital parts of the flower.

Specimens are few in state herberia, and collections should be made and distributed whenever possible.

Robinia L.—LOCUSTS

Branchlets and petioles glandular; flowers pinkish...................................*R. viscosa*, p. 187
Branchlets and petioles bristly; flowers rose-color or purple.....................*R. hispida*, p. 189

Robinia viscosa Vent. (Clammy Locust). Fig. 103. A shrub or small tree; bark dark brown, smoothish; branchlets dark reddish-brown, covered with glandular hairs which at first exude a clammy, sticky substance, later becoming dry; stipules short, at times spiny when developed; petioles slightly enlarged at base; leaves alternate, deciduous, odd-pinnately compound; leaflets 11–25, stalked, entire, obtuse and mucronate at apex, wedge-shaped at base, ovate or oval, nearly glabrous, 2.5–5 cm. long, thickish; flowers 18–25 mm.

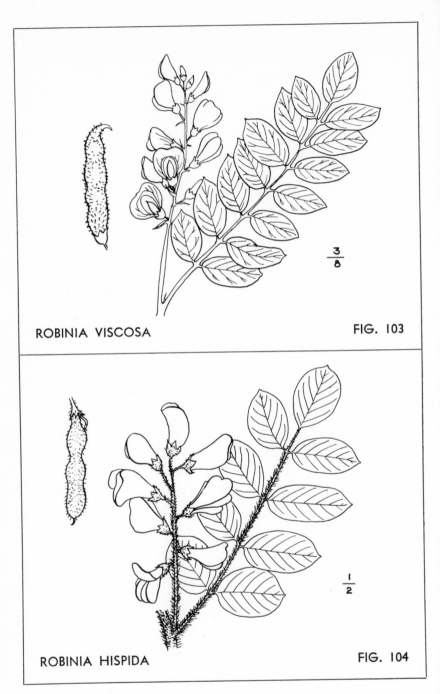

ROBINIA VISCOSA   FIG. 103

ROBINIA HISPIDA   FIG. 104

Robinia viscosa

long, pinkish, not fragrant, borne in crowded, oblong, clammy, hairy racemes; pedicels 4–9 cm. long; calyx 5-toothed, hairy; standard large, reflexed; wings oblong, curved; keel curved, obtuse; stamens 10, in 2 groups, 9, and 1 alone; ovary stalked, 1-celled; ovules several; style recurved; pod flat, linear, 5–10 cm. long, glandular hispid; seeds numerous. Flowers, June; pods ripe, September.

Southwestern Virginia to Georgia. Cultivated in the eastern and middle states, where it occasionally escapes and becomes naturalized. Michigan, reported from Lower Peninsula only.

The classification of the Clammy Locust as a shrub may be open to question. In cultivation it may attain a maximum height of 40 feet. In its natural habitat it has been found growing as a shrub only a few feet high. As an escape it may revert to this form. It has always been a popular cultivated plant because of its fine foliage and beautiful flowers.

Robinia hispida L. (Rose Acacia, Bristly Locust). Fig. 104. A much-branched shrub, 1–3 m. tall; branches, twigs and petioles bristly; stipules small,

Robinia hispida

often spiny; petioles slightly enlarged at base; leaves alternate, deciduous, odd-pinnate, 10–20 cm. long; leaflets 9–15, stalked, broadly ovate or oblong, entire, 2–5 cm. long, 2–3.5 cm. wide, mostly obtuse or rounded at each end, mucronate, glabrous above, pubescent on the veins beneath; racemes drooping, loose, 6–10 cm. long; flowers large, deep rose-color or purple, not fragrant, 2–3 cm. long; calyx 5-toothed; upper petal or standard rounded, large, reflexed; wings oblong, curved, blunt; keel obtuse, curved; stamens 10, in 2 groups, 9, and 1 alone; pistil stalked, 1-celled; ovules numerous; style recurved; pod brown, 4–6 cm. long, linear, bristly hispid, constricted between the seeds; seeds several. Flowers, June; fruit ripe in September.

Native of the mountains from Virginia to eastern Tennessee and Georgia, but often cultivated as an ornamental northward and escaping there. Michigan, reported from several counties in the Lower Peninsula.

The Rose Acacia, although a native of the south, is perfectly hardy in the north and is greatly prized for its beauty. The twigs, petioles and pods are so thickly beset with bristly hairs that they appear mossy. In June, sometimes extending into July, it produces beautiful rose-colored or purple pea-like blossoms in loose, lax racemes. The shrub suckers freely, however, and if permitted to do so will make dense thickets.

[189]

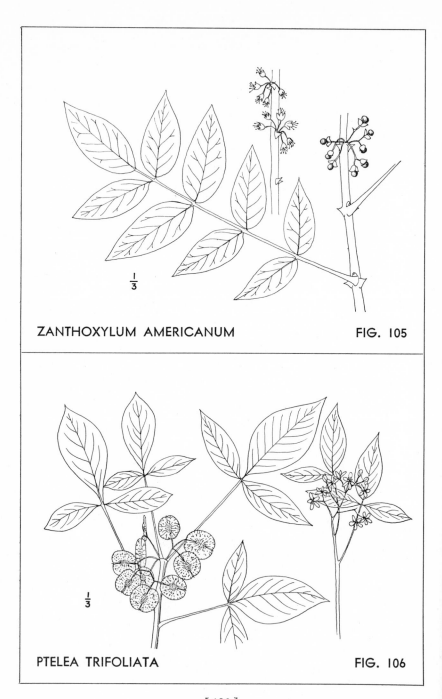

ZANTHOXYLUM AMERICANUM   FIG. 105

PTELEA TRIFOLIATA   FIG. 106

RUTACEAE—Rue Family

Trees or shrubs; foliage strong-scented, dotted with translucent oil glands; leaves deciduous, alternate or opposite, mainly compound; flowers polygamo-dioecious, generally borne in cymes; sepals 4–5, or none; petals 3–5, free or rarely united; stamens as many as the petals and alternate with them; carpels 1–5, free or more or less united into a compound pistil; fruit a capsule or samara; seeds oblong or reniform.

Two genera containing shrubs are represented in Michigan, as follows:

Shrubs with sharp spines; leaves compound, with more than 3 leaflets............*Zanthoxylum*
Shrubs without spines; leaves compound, with 3 leaflets...*Ptelea*

Zanthoxylum L.—Prickly Ashes

Zanthoxylum americanum Mill. (Prickly Ash, Northern Prickly Ash, Toothache Tree). Fig. 105. A prickly, branched shrub, sometimes forming dense thickets, 1.5–4 m. tall; bark smooth, gray or brownish; branches and branchlets smooth; spines persistent, flattened at the base; leaves alternate, deciduous, pinnate; leaflets 2–4 pairs and an odd one, ovate-oblong, downy when young; flowers dioecious, small, greenish, in cymose axillary clusters, appearing before or with the leaves; sepals obsolete; petals 4–5; stamens 4–5; pistils 2–5; styles slender; fruit short-stalked, reddish-brown when mature, strongly aromatic; seeds black, shining. Flowers, April, May; fruit, August, September.

The general range of the Prickly Ash is from western Quebec to Minnesota, south to Virginia, Kentucky, Missouri and eastern Kansas. Michigan, common throughout Lower Peninsula; recorded from one county in the Upper Peninsula.

The Prickly Ash is found in rocky woods, fence rows and along river banks. A dense thicket of this prickly shrub is very difficult to negotiate and makes an effective barrier. The foliage and fruit have a pleasantly aromatic oil, but are very disagreeable to the taste. When I was a boy it was a favorite trick to persuade some uninitiated comrade to eat the berries. The result was always amusing, not, however, to the victim.

Ptelea L.—Hop Trees

Ptelea trifoliata L. (Shrubby Trefoil, Common Hop Tree, Wafer Ash). Fig. 106. A shrub, 1.5–5 m. tall; bark smooth, gray or grayish-brown, roughened on older specimens; twigs glabrous, dark red-brown; leaves deciduous, opposite, trifoliate; leaflets nearly sessile, margins entire or serrulate, variable, obovate or lance-ovate, 5–15 cm. long, 2.5–9 cm. wide, the terminal leaflets generally somewhat larger and longer-stalked than the lateral, downy when young, becoming glabrous before they are full grown, dark green and glossy above, paler beneath, with black dots on both surfaces; petioles 6–10 cm. long;

flowers polygamous, small, greenish-white, in terminal compound clusters; sepals 3–5; petals 3–5; stamens 3–5; fruit a 2-celled and 2-seeded samara, winged all round, nearly orbicular, 1.5–3 cm. across. Flowers, June, July; fruit ripe, September, October.

The Wafer Ash is found from New York, Connecticut and southern Ontario to Wisconsin and Kansas; south to Florida and northern Mexico. Michigan, throughout, more frequent in the Lower Peninsula.

The Wafer Ash is by no means a common shrub in Michigan, but it is found in some abundance in the sand dunes along the Lake Michigan shore and occasionally in the interior. It may be used successfully as an ornamental shrub. Although its flowers are rather inconspicuous this is more than compensated for by the shining green leaves and large clusters of interesting fruits. In relation to the flowers Gray's Manual states: "Odor of flowers disagreeable." To me this odor is always very pleasant. The fruit is bitter and has been used as a substitute for hops; hence one of its common names.

EMPETRACEAE—Crowberry Family

Low, shrubby, branching evergreens, heath-like in aspect; leaves sessile, narrow, small, and channeled underneath by the revolute margins; flowers axillary or terminal, dioecious or monoecious, rarely perfect or polygamous; calyx of 3 sepals; petals 2–3 or none; fruit a berry-like drupe with 2 to several 1-seeded nutlets.

There are three known genera in this family, one of which is represented in Michigan by one species.

Empetrum [Tourn.] L.—Crowberries

Empetrum nigrum L. (Black Crowberry). Fig. 107. A procumbent, much-branched and diffused evergreen shrub, glabrous or the young shoots pubescent; leaves simple, scattered or whorled, dark green, thick, obtuse, 4–7 mm. long, about 1 mm. wide, the margins revolute and roughish; flowers solitary in the axils of the upper leaves, dioecious, small and inconspicuous, purplish; sepals and petals usually 3; staminate flowers with 3 exserted stamens, the anthers turned inward; pistillate flowers with a globose 6–9-celled ovary; styles 6–9-lobed, short and

[192]

thick; drupe berry-like, black or red, 4–6 mm. in diameter, containing 6–9 seed-like nutlets. Flowers, summer; fruit, fall.

In rocky places, Arctic America, south to the coast of Maine, in the mountains of northern New England and New York, northern Michigan and the coast of Oregon. Michigan, Upper Peninsula, Isle Royale.

The Black Crowberry is a subarctic plant and is found in Europe and Asia, as well as in America. It stands extremely low temperatures and will persist where other plants perish with the cold. The berries are not unpalatable and are eagerly eaten by the Arctic birds.

Two other species of *Empetrum* have been named, neither of which has so far been reported from Michigan: *Empetrum atropurpureum* Fern., with young branchlets white-tomentose and trailing; berries 5–9 mm. in diameter, red or purplish-black, opaque; and *Empetrum Eamesii* Fern., with closely prostrate branchlets, the young ones white-tomentose; berries 3–5 mm. in diameter, pink or light red, translucent skin and nearly colorless pulp. The range of these two species appears to be farther north and east, but it is not unlikely that they might be found in our state.

ANACARDIACEAE—Cashew Family

Shrubs or trees with resinous or milky, acrid juice; leaves deciduous, alternate; stipules none; flowers small, regular, perfect or polygamous, 5-parted; styles 3; fruit a small 1-seeded drupe; seed bony.

A family of about 60 genera, of which only the following is represented in Michigan.

Rhus L.—Sumacs, Poison Ivies

1. Leaflets regularly more than 3
   2. Twigs and petioles hairy
      3. Leaflets serrate to the base; rachis terete............................*R. typhina*, p. 193
      3. Leaflets mostly entire, or if with a few teeth never
         at the base; rachis winged................................*R. copallina* var. *latifolia*, p. 197
   2. Twigs and petioles glabrous
      4. Leaflets serrate; fruit red..*R. glabra*, p. 195
      4. Leaflets entire; fruit grayish-white...*R. Vernix*, p. 197
1. Leaflets regularly 3
   5. Terminal leaflets long-stalked; flowers greenish, loosely clustered,
      appearing after the leaves; fruit whitish, smooth........................*R. radicans*, p. 199
   5. Terminal leaflets short-stalked; flowers yellow, in dense clusters,
      appearing before the leaves; fruit red, densely hairy ....*R. aromatica*, p. 199

Rhus typhina Torner. (Staghorn Sumac). Fig. 108. (*Rhus typhina* L., Gray's Manual, 7th Edition, Shrubs of Michigan, 1st Edition.) Erect shrubs or small trees, 1–6 m. tall; bark gray; twigs densely velvety with long hairs; leaves alternate, deciduous, compound, 2–6 dm. long; petioles pubescent, 4–9 cm. long; leaflets 11–31, oblong to linear-oblong, 4–14 cm. long, 1–3 cm. broad, narrowed or rounded at base, acuminate at apex, sharply and sometimes coarsely serrate, dark green and nearly glabrous above, paler and pubescent

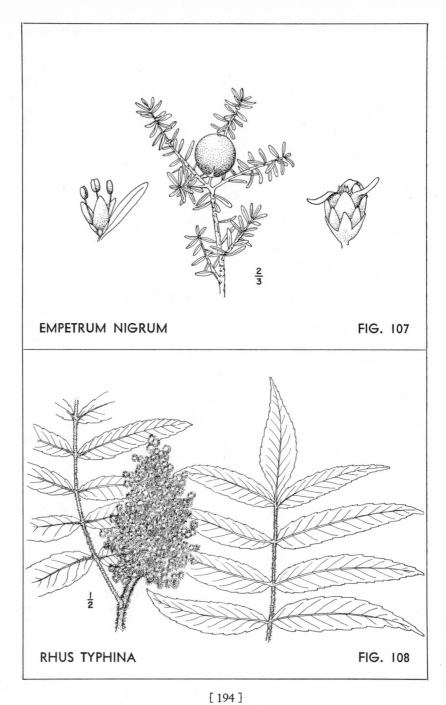

EMPETRUM NIGRUM

$\frac{2}{3}$

FIG. 107

RHUS TYPHINA

$\frac{1}{2}$

FIG. 108

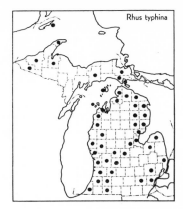

beneath, sessile; flowers in dense terminal panicles up to 30 cm. long, yellowish-green, polygamous, 5–6 mm. broad; fruit a globose drupe densely covered with long, red hairs; seed light brown, smooth. Flowers, June, July; fruit, autumn.

Dry or gravelly soil, eastern Quebec to Ontario, south to Georgia and Mississippi; Indiana, Iowa and North Dakota. Michigan, common throughout.

The Staghorn Sumac is one of our commonest shrubs. It is a rapid and vigorous grower frequently used for ornamental planting where mass effects are required. The sumac is noted for its brilliant autumn coloring and the pyramidal heads of velvety-red berries are an interesting feature of our landscape.

Rhus glabra L. (Smooth Sumac). Fig. 109. Upright shrubs, 1–4 m. tall; bark smooth and grayish; twigs smooth, glaucous; petioles 3–13 cm. long, some-

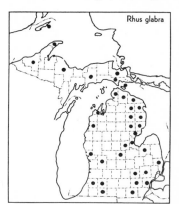

times purplish; leaves alternate, deciduous, compound; leaflets 11–31, whitened beneath, lanceolate-oblong, pointed, serrate, 6–13 cm. long, 1.5–3 cm. wide; flowers in large terminal panicles, greenish-yellow, about 5 mm. across; fruit globose, 3–4 mm. in diameter, covered with short, sticky crimson hairs, sour to the taste; seed light brown, smooth. Flowers, June, August; fruit, autumn.

The range of the Smooth Sumac is from central Maine westward and southward. Michigan, throughout.

In Michigan the Smooth Sumac seems to be less common than the Staghorn. Like the other sumacs, it is rich in tannic acid and is used for tanning leather. The leaves and berries have been used in medicine and the berries were used by the Indians as a dye.

Over the years a number of names have been given to sumacs apparently related to this species. They have varied from full specific rank to varieties and hybrids. One of them was *Rhus glabra* L. var. *borealis* Britt. Quite properly, the records of this plant are all from the northern part of the state, Cheboygan County and Isle Royale, which is a part of Keweenaw County. However, a later treatment by Little (1945) seems more fully to meet the requirements of the situation. He regards the several plants as hybrids between *R. typhina* and *R. glabra* and under Article 34 of the International Rules of Botanical Nomenclature has adopted *Rhus borealis* Greene as the name of the plant, reducing some 10 or 11 others, including var. *borealis* Britt. mentioned above, to synonymy.

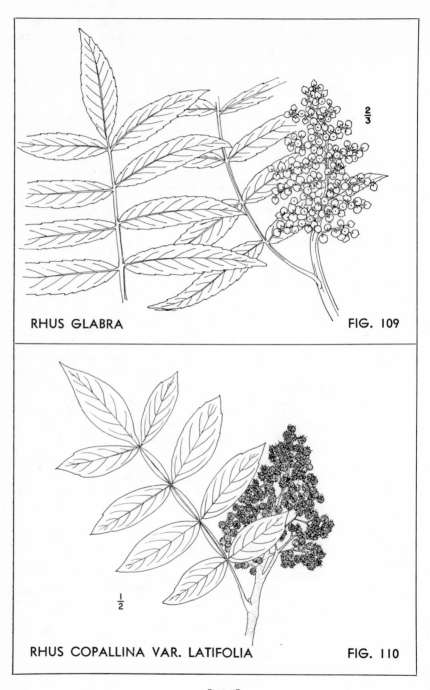

RHUS GLABRA   FIG. 109

$\frac{2}{3}$

RHUS COPALLINA VAR. LATIFOLIA   FIG. 110

$\frac{1}{2}$

Rhus copallina L. var. *latifolia* Engl. (Dwarf Sumac, Shining Sumac).
Fig. 110. (*Rhus copallina* L., Gray's Manual, 7th Edition, Shrubs of Michigan,

1st Edition.) Shrub 0.3–2 m. tall, or taller southward; branches and stalks downy; leaves alternate, deciduous, compound, 1–3 dm. long, rachis more or less winged between the 9–21 oblong or ovate-lanceolate, often entire, leaflets, which are oblique or unequal at the base, smooth and shining above, more or less pubescent beneath; inflorescence a terminal panicle, 1–2 dm. long; flowers greenish-yellow, about 4 mm. across; fruit about 4 mm. in diameter, red, densely covered with hairs and with short-stalked glands; seeds smooth, light brown. Flowers, July, August; fruit autumn.

Rocky or dry sandy soil, southern Maine to Michigan, southward into the upland of North Carolina, and to Oklahoma. Michigan, frequent in Lower Peninsula.

This is another case where the old established name is relegated to the side lines because of further detailed study of our flora. Fernald and Griscom (1935) state: "we are now able to identify *R. copallina* as the small tree of the southeastern United States (south into Florida) with the lance-oblong leaflets definitely attenuate at the base. This typical *R. copallina* extends locally along the coast to southeastern New York."

Like the others, the foliage of this sumac colors beautifully in the fall.

Rhus Vernix L. (Poison Sumac, Poison Oak, Poison Dogwood, Poison Elder, Swamp Sumac). Fig. 111. Shrub 2–5 m. tall; bark gray; twigs greenish,

smooth; leaves alternate, deciduous, petioled, pinnate, 15–36 cm. long; leaflets 7–13, obovate-oblong, 4–11 cm. long, 2–6 cm. wide, acute or acuminate at the apex, tapering at base, nearly sessile, terminal leaflet stalked, margins entire or wavy, dark green and glabrous, or slightly puberulent; flowers greenish-yellow, very small; panicles axillary, numerous, long-peduncled, drooping; fruit yellowish-green, smooth and shining, about 4 mm. in diameter. Flowers, June; fruit, ripe in the autumn.

Ranges from northern New England to Minnesota and south to Florida and Texas. Michigan, common in swamps of Lower Peninsula.

The Poison Sumac is our most poisonous woody plant and it is fortunate that it grows mostly in wet inaccessible swamps. It is found sometimes, however, in roadside ditches, where its branches overhang the roadway. Its juices are extremely poisonous to most people and although there are some who are

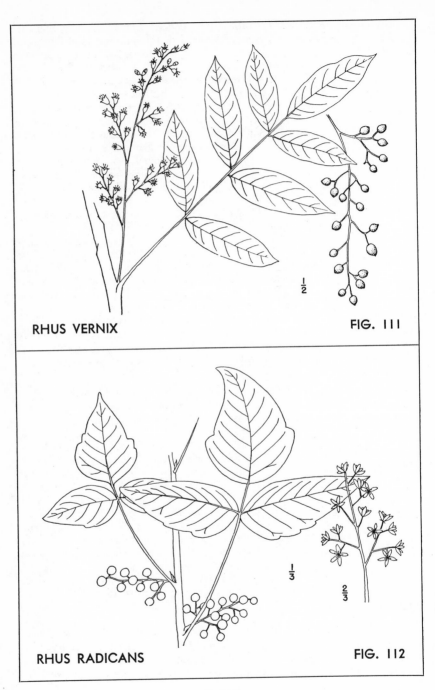

RHUS VERNIX

$\frac{1}{2}$

FIG. 111

RHUS RADICANS

$\frac{1}{3}$

$\frac{2}{3}$

FIG. 112

entirely immune it is unsafe to experiment. It will be noted that the common names with one exception all refer to the poisonous qualities of the shrub, and that refers to its habitat.

The foliage of the Poison Sumac colors beautifully and a swamp full of this shrub is a glorious sight after the first frost in the fall. This is amply demonstrated by the frontispiece, which is reproduced from a color photograph of a section of a swamp in Oakland County, Michigan.

Rhus radicans L. (Poison Ivy, Poison Oak, Three-leaved Ivy). Fig 112. (*Rhus Toxicodendron* L., Gray's Manual, 7th Edition, Shrubs of Michigan, 1st Edition.) A low, erect, suberect or climbing shrub with creeping rhizomes, scrambling over fences, walls or on trees, climbing by aerial rootlets to considerable heights; bark on older wood gray; twigs yellowish or brownish-green, sparingly pubescent or glabrate; leaves deciduous, alternate, pinnately 3-foliate, 1.5–3.5 dm. long; petioles 5–25 cm. long; leaflets ovate to rhombic, mostly acuminate, entire, crenate, or with a few irregular, coarse teeth, paler and with more or less pubescence beneath, the terminal leaflets much longer stalked than the lateral, very variable in size, shape, texture and pubescence; flowers polygamous, in loose, slender axillary panicles, greenish, about 4 mm. across; fruit globose, whitish or cream-colored, glabrous, shining, 5–6 mm. in diameter. Flowers, May, June; fruit, August, September.

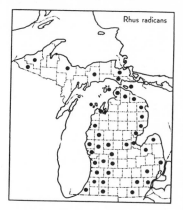

Ranges from Nova Scotia to British Columbia, south to Florida and Mexico. Michigan, common throughout.

Poison Ivy is too widely distributed and in too great abundance wherever it is growing. It will grow in almost any sort of soil, with the possible exception of peat bogs, where it gives way to its close relative, *Rhus Vernix*.

In the introduction to this bulletin I mentioned the fact that, although Poison Ivy is usually a climbing vine, when a support is lacking it assumes a shrubby upright growth. This form has been separated as *Rhus radicans* L. var. *Rydbergii* (Small) Rehd. It does not climb and does not have aerial roots. Hanes reports it from Kalamazoo County, and no doubt it is to be found in other localities.

The plant is very poisonous to the touch, producing an irritation known as ivy poisoning. While some are immune, or much less sensitive to the poison than others, no one should handle the plant because of supposed immunity. It should always be remembered that the compound leaves have three leaflets, rendering it easily distinguishable from the Virginia Creeper, which has five leaflets.

Rhus aromatica Ait. (Fragrant Sumac, Aromatic Sumac). Fig. 113. (*Rhus canadensis* Marsh., Gray's Manual, 7th Edition, Shrubs of Michigan, 1st Edition.) Shrubs with spreading branches, or sometimes ascending, 1–2.5 m. tall; branchlets smooth or pubescent, brown or reddish-brown; leaves alter-

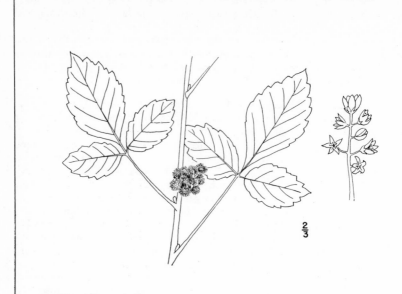

RHUS AROMATICA   **FIG. 113**

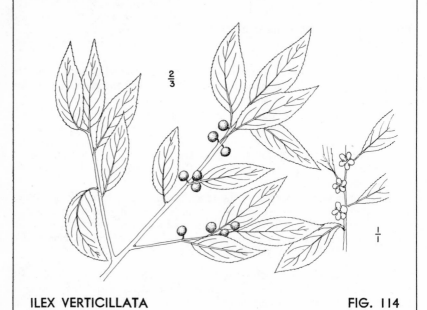

ILEX VERTICILLATA   **FIG. 114**

nate, deciduous, trifoliate, 5–12 cm. long; petioles 1–3 cm. long; leaflets soft pubescent both sides when young, becoming glabrate, rhombic-obovate or ovate, unequally cut-toothed, 2.5–7.5 cm. long, the terminal one cuneate at base and sometimes 3-cleft, slightly stalked, the lateral smaller, sessile, oblique and narrowed or rounded at the base, short-acute or rounded at the apex; flowers yellow, appearing before the leaves in small solitary or clustered spikes; petals elliptic or ovate 2–2.5 mm. long; fruit a red globose drupe, densely hairy, 6–8 mm. in diameter; seeds smooth, slightly flattened, about 4 mm. long. Flowers, March, April; fruit, July, August.

Rhus aromatica

The range of this sumac is from Vermont to Minnesota, south to Florida and Louisiana. Michigan, infrequent throughout; specimens were found only from Lower Peninsula. The Aromatic Sumac grows in dry, gravelly or rocky soil. Its common name derives from the scent of the crushed leaves, which is not unpleasant. It is a desirable shrub for ornamental planting and will thrive in almost any dry soil.

AQUIFOLIACEAE—HOLLY FAMILY

Trees or shrubs; leaves simple, deciduous, mostly alternate; flowers small, axillary, white or greenish, mostly polygamo-dioecious; calyx minute, free from 4–8-celled ovary; petals 4–8, separate or slightly united at the base; stamens as many as the divisions and alternate with them, attached to their base; stigmas 4–8, or united into 1, nearly sessile; fruit a small berry-like drupe enclosing 4–8 seeds.

The family contains 5 genera and about 170 species. Two of the genera are represented in Michigan.

Leaves serrate, veins prominent; flowers on very short pedicels; petals oval or obovate, united at base..*Ilex,* p. 201

Leaves entire, veins inconspicuous; flowers on elongated pedicels; petals linear, not united..*Nemopanthus,* p. 203

Ilex L.—HOLLIES

Ilex verticillata (L.) Gray. (Winterberry, Black Alder). Fig. 114. Shrub 1–5 m. tall; bark smooth, grayish; branches reddish-brown to gray; branchlets glabrous or sometimes slightly pubescent; leaves simple, alternate, deciduous, oval, obovate, or wedge-lanceolate, pointed, acute at base, serrate, downy chiefly on the veins beneath, 4–11 cm. long, 1.5–4 cm. wide; petioles 8–12 mm. long, channeled above, more or less pubescent; flowers mostly crowded, all on very short peduncles; calyx small, 4–6-toothed; sepals ciliate on the margins; petals 4–6, separate, or united only at base, oval or obovate, spreading or reflexed;

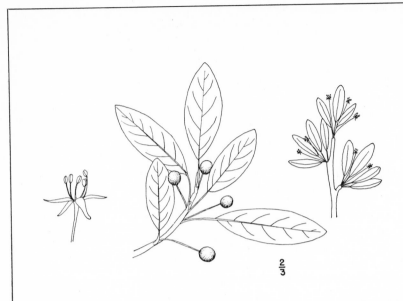

NEMOPANTHUS MUCRONATA   FIG. 115

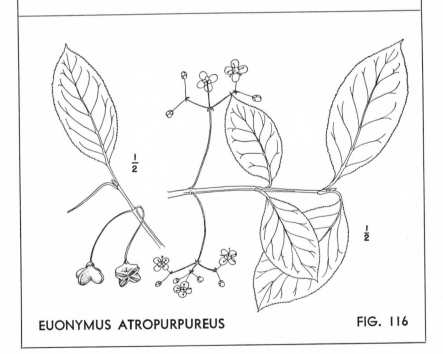

EUONYMUS ATROPURPUREUS   FIG. 116

fruit a bright red drupe, 6–7 mm. in diameter. Flowers, May, June; fruit ripe, September, October.

The range of this shrub is from Nova Scotia to Florida, west to Ontario, Wisconsin and Missouri; found in low grounds, moist woods and swamps. Michigan, frequent throughout.

Ilex verticillata

At blooming time the Winterberry has little to commend it. Its flowers are comparatively inconspicuous and unattractive, but when October comes and it is clothed in scarlet berries to the very tip of its slenderest branches it comes into its own. The berries remain on the branches until midwinter and a cluster of Winterberry shrubs in full fruit adds much gaiety and beauty to an otherwise drab landscape.

Ilex is very inconstant, and several varieties and forms have been named. Some are very local, but the following have been reported from one or more stations in Michigan: *Ilex verticillata* (L.) Gray var. *tenuifolia* (Torr.) Wats.; *Ilex verticillata* (L.) Gray var. *padifolia* (Willd.) T.&G. A careful examination of the species filed, however, seemed to indicate that it was hardly possible to separate them and that in reality we have but one extremely variable species.

Nemopanthus Raf.—Mountain Hollies

Nemopanthus mucronata (L.) Trel. (Mountain Holly). Fig. 115. Erect branching shrubs 1–4 m. tall; bark gray; branches smooth; leaves alternate, simple, deciduous, entire or very rarely with a few teeth, elliptic-oblong, thin, paler beneath, 2–5 cm. long, 1–2.5 cm. wide, rounded or narrowed at the base,

Nemopanthus mucronata

blunt and mucronate at the apex, or sometimes acute, smooth on both sides; petioles 6–12 mm. long; flowers solitary or sometimes 2–4 together in the axils of the leaves, on pedicels 1–3 cm. long, very slender; calyx of 4–5 minute, mostly deciduous sepals; petals 4–5, oblong-linear, spreading, distinct; stamens 4–5, filaments slender; fruit a subglobose drupe, crimson-red, usually with 4 slightly ridged nutlets. Flowers, May; fruit ripe, July, August.

Ranges from Newfoundland to Minnesota, south to Virginia and Indiana. Michigan, frequent throughout.

The habitat of the Mountain Holly is given as damp cool woods, but in Michigan, so far as I have observed, it is found only in deep cedar and tamarack bogs, where it is associated with poison sumac, high bush blueberries and other bog plants.

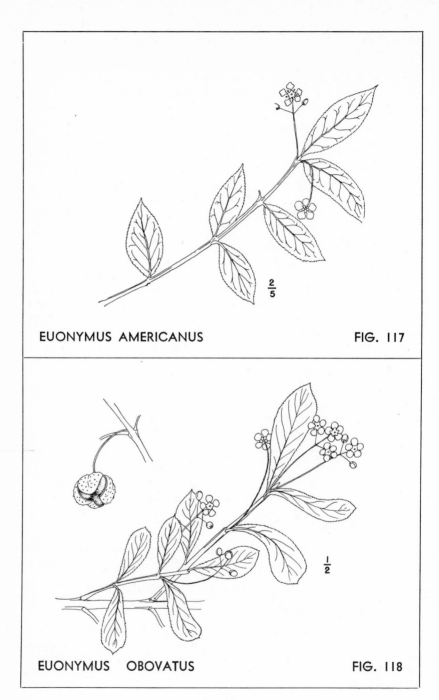

EUONYMUS AMERICANUS   FIG. 117

$\frac{2}{5}$

EUONYMUS   OBOVATUS   FIG. 118

$\frac{1}{2}$

CELASTRACEAE—Staff Tree Family

Shrubs or climbing vines; leaves simple, alternate or opposite, deciduous; flowers small, regular, in axillary cymes or racemes; sepals 4–5, more or less united; petals 4–5; stamens as many as the petals and alternate with them, borne on a fleshy disk, which fills the bottom of the calyx and sometimes covers the 3–5-celled ovary; fruit fleshy, dehiscent; seeds with arils.

The family comprises about 40 genera and 350 species. Following are the 2 genera found in Michigan.

Erect or decumbent shrubs; leaves opposite........................ ....*Euonymus*, p. 205
Shrubby climber; leaves alternate..*Celastrus*, p. 207

Euonymus [Tourn.] L.—Spindle Trees

1. Capsule smooth; tall shrub; leaves distinctly petioled.................*E. atropurpureus*, p. 205
1. Capsule tuberculate; low shrubs; leaves subsessile
    2. Erect or ascending shrubs; leaves ovate-lanceolate, acuminate....*E. americanus*, p. 205
    2. Decumbent shrubs; rooting at the nodes; leaves obovate, obtuse...*E. obovatus*, p. 207

Euonymus atropurpureus Jacq. (Burning Bush, Wahoo). Fig. 116. A tree-like shrub up to 4 m. tall; bark grayish-green; twigs four-sided, green,

glabrous; leaves opposite, simple, deciduous, thin, ovate-lanceolate, acuminate, 5–13 cm. long, 1–4 cm. wide, narrowed or rounded at the base, glabrous above, pubescent beneath, particularly along the nerves; petioles 5–18 mm. long; flowers perfect, dark purple, commonly in fours, 6–8 mm. in diameter, borne in branching cymes of 5–15 flowers; peduncles slender, 1.5–4 cm. long; petals broadly ovate, 2–2.5 mm. long, spreading; style short, conical; fruit a smooth, deeply-lobed capsule, pink when ripe in the fall; aril scarlet; seeds light brown, about 7 mm. long. Flowers, June; fruit, September.

Ranges from New York to Wisconsin, Nebraska southward to Florida and Texas; found principally along streams and in alluvial soil. Michigan, infrequent, central and southern portion of Lower Peninsula.

The Burning Bush is also cultivated extensively as an ornamental shrub and is entirely worthy of such treatment.

Euonymus americanus L. (Strawberry Bush). Fig. 117. Erect or ascending straggling shrub 1–2 m. tall; branches and branchlets greenish, four-sided, glabrous; leaves opposite, simple, deciduous, almost sessile, thickish, bright green, ovate to oblong-lanceolate, acute or pointed, 2.5–9 cm. long, 1.5–3.5 cm. wide, margin serrulate, glabrous both sides, midrib sometimes pubescent; flowers greenish-purple in cymes of

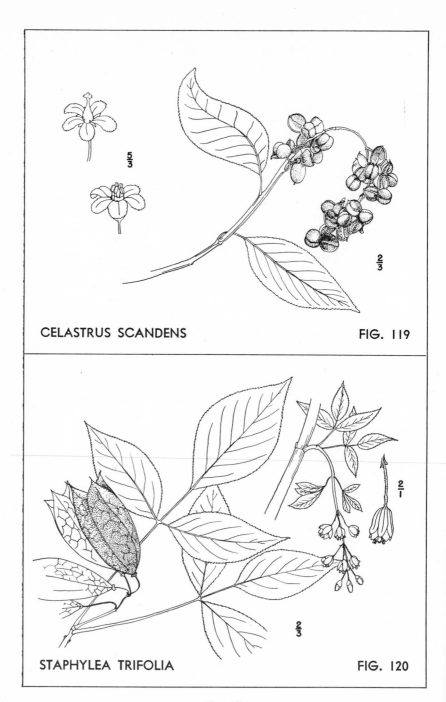

CELASTRUS SCANDENS   FIG. 119

STAPHYLEA TRIFOLIA   FIG. 120

1–3 flowers, about 10 mm. across; petals distinctly clawed, margin toothed; fruit a rough-warty pod, crimson when ripe, the aril scarlet; seeds 1–4 in each cell, about 5 mm. long. Flowers, June; fruit, September.

Wooded river banks and low woods from New York to Illinois, Florida and Texas. Michigan, common, central and southern portion of Lower Peninsula.

The Strawberry Bush is a very attractive shrub in fruit.

Euonymus obovatus Nutt. (Running Strawberry Bush). Fig. 118. Trailing shrub with rooting branches, usually not rising more than 2–3 dm. from the

ground; branches green, 4-sided, or somewhat winged, glabrous or rarely pubescent; leaves simple, opposite, deciduous, 3–9 cm. long and 1.5–4 cm. wide, obovate or oblong, wedge-shaped at base, obtuse at apex, crenulate-serrate, glabrous both sides, or sometimes pubescent on the veins, thin, dull green above, paler beneath; flowers perfect, 1–3 on a long-peduncled cyme, greenish-yellow, about 6–7 mm. across; petals 5, orbicular, without distinct claw; fruit a rough-warty capsule, orange-red, generally 3-celled; seeds, 1–2.5 mm. long; aril scarlet. Flowers, April, May; fruit, September.

Distributed from Ontario to Pennsylvania, Kentucky and Illinois; found in low or wet places. Michigan, frequent in southern portion of the Lower Peninsula.

The Running Strawberry Bush makes an attractive vine in cultivation for covering shaded ground.

Celastrus L.—SHRUBBY BITTERSWEET

Celastrus scandens L. (Waxwork, Climbing Bittersweet). Fig. 119. A

twining shrub, climbing trees to a height of 8–10 m. or more, and developing trunks up to 13 cm. in circumference, or growing on fences or trailing on the ground without support; bark gray or brownish, smooth; leaves simple, alternate, deciduous, ovate-oblong, finely serrate, pointed, narrowed or sometimes rounded at the base, 5–10 cm. long, 3–5 cm. wide, glabrous both sides; petioles 5–15 mm. long; flowers polygamo-dioecious, greenish-yellow, in terminal raceme-like clusters, 8–9 mm. broad; sepals short; petals crenulate, 3–4 mm. long; fruit a globuse capsule maturing in the fall, about 10–12 mm. in diameter, orange-colored, displaying the scarlet covering of the seeds, which are reddish-brown and about 5 mm. long. Flowers, June; fruit ripe, September, October.

Distributed from Maine to Manitoba and southward. Michigan, common throughout.

The natural habitat of the Climbing Bittersweet is along streams and in thickets, but it also seems to thrive in sandy situations. It is extensively planted as an ornamental vine and always gives a good accounting of itself. It is easily propagated by any of the well-known horticultural methods. The Bittersweet is probably our best-known and most-loved native shrub.

STAPHYLEACEAE—BLADDER NUT FAMILY

Shrubs or small trees with opposite, deciduous, odd-pinnate or 3-foliate stipulate leaves; flowers perfect, in terminal or axillary clusters; sepals, petals and stamens usually 5; carpels 3; stamens alternate with the petals, borne outside a large disk; fruit a bladdery capsule; seeds solitary or few in each cavity of the ovary.

The family contains about 5 genera and 22 species, of which the following is found in Michigan.

Staphylea L.—BLADDER NUTS

Staphylea trifolia L. (American Bladder Nut). Fig. 120. Erect shrubs, 1–4 m. tall; bark grayish; branches greenish-striped, glabrous; leaves opposite, deciduous, trifoliate; petioles 2.5–12 cm. long; leaflets ovate to obovate, 4–10 cm. long; 2–6 cm. wide, the terminal somewhat larger than the lateral, narrowed or rounded at the base, short-acuminate at the apex, margin closely serrate, smooth above, pubescent, at least along the veins beneath; flowers about 1 cm. long; in racemes 3–6 cm. long, corolla white; fruit an inflated 3-celled pod, 2–3 cm. in diameter and up to 8 cm. long; seeds 1–3, light brown, smooth, about 6 mm. long, 5 mm. wide. Flowers, April, May; fruit, September.

The American Bladder Nut grows in thickets in moist soil from Quebec south to South Carolina, west to Minnesota and Kansas. Michigan, throughout, more frequent in the Lower Peninsula.

The interesting fruits of the Bladder Nut make it a desirable shrub for ornamental planting.

Some years ago from the vicinity of Toledo, Ohio, J. Francis Macbride described (1918) a new species of Bladder Nut which he called *Staphylea Brighamii*, after the individual who discovered it. This new Bladder Nut has much smaller, pear-shaped pods, smooth and brightly tinted on one or more sides with pink, darkening sometimes to maroon. The leaves are not at all oblique at the base and are long-stalked; also it has more numerous seeds than the older species. Up to this time it has not been reported from Michigan. Its location is not far over the state line in Ohio, and it is mentioned here with the hope that it may sometime be discovered and recorded from Michigan.

ACERACEAE—Maple Family

Trees and shrubs with watery, sugary sap; leaves deciduous, opposite, simple and palmately lobed or more rarely palmately or pinnately divided; flowers regular, mostly polygamous or dioecious, sometimes apetalous; ovary 2-celled, 2-lobed; styles 2; fruit 2 long-winged samaras united at the base, each 1-seeded.

This family embraces two genera, one of which, the maples, is represented in Michigan.

Acer [Tourn.] L.—Maples

Racemes drooping; leaves finely serrate..*A. pennsylvanicum*

Racemes erect; leaves coarsely serrate..*A. spicatum*

Acer pennsylvanicum L. (Striped Maple, Moosewood). Fig. 121. A small tree or large shrub; bark light green, striped with dark lines; leaves opposite,

simple, deciduous, 1.5–2 dm. long, 3-lobed at the apex, finely and sharply double-serrate, the short lobes taper-pointed and serrate, rounded or cordate at the base, glabrous, yellowish-green above, paler beneath; flowers greenish-yellow in loose, drooping terminal racemes 7.5–10 cm. long, appearing after the leaves; calyx 5-parted; petals 5, obovate; stamens 6–8; fruit glabrous with large divergent wings. Flowers, May, June; fruit ripening late summer, autumn.

The Striped Maple is found in rich, cool woods from Quebec to western Ontario, south to New England, New York, the Great Lakes region and in the mountains to Georgia. Michigan, throughout, except the extreme southern tier of counties; more abundant northward.

This maple is on the border line between the trees and shrubs; Otis includes it in his list of the trees of Michigan. He says: "Habit—a small tree at best,

more often a large shrub." This furnishes the excuse for including it among the shrubs of Michigan.

The common name, Moosewood, which this species bears indicates that it is browsed by the moose. It is also a great favorite of the deer and where these animals range the undergrowth of Striped Maple is inevitably browsed.

Acer spicatum Lam. (Mountain Maple). Fig. 122. A shrub 2–4 m. tall, or rarely a bushy tree; bark greenish, smooth or somewhat furrowed; leaves simple, deciduous, opposite, 3-lobed, 6–12 cm. long, 5–10 cm.

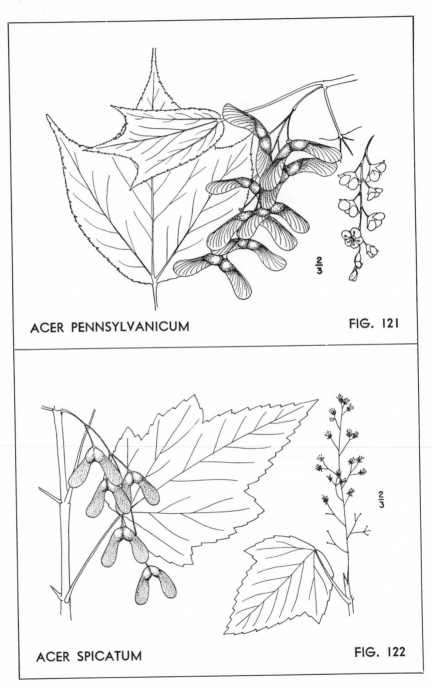

ACER PENNSYLVANICUM   FIG. 121

ACER SPICATUM   FIG. 122

wide, coarsely crenate-serrate with pointed teeth, cordate at base, lobes acute or taper-pointed, thin, glabrous, dark green above, whitish-pubescent beneath; petioles 3–10 cm. long; flowers, after the leaves are full grown, small, greenish-yellow, borne in erect terminal racemes, 7–10 cm. long; calyx 5-lobed; petals 5; stamens 7–8; samaras somewhat divergent, 1.8–2 cm. long, bright red, glabrous. Flowers, May, June; fruit, ripening in July.

Found in moist woods, Newfoundland and Labrador to Hudson Bay and Manitoba, south to New England, New York, the Great Lakes region, eastern Iowa and in the mountains to Georgia. Michigan, throughout both peninsulas.

The Mountain Maple always grows in the shade of other trees. Like various typically northern plants, it has found a congenial habitat in the deep bogs of our southern counties, where it grows in considerable abundance.

RHAMNACEAE—Buckthorn Family

Shrubs or small trees; leaves simple, deciduous, mostly alternate; flowers small and regular, in axillary or terminal cymes or racemes, perfect or polygamous; calyx 4–5-toothed; petals 4–5, inserted on the calyx, or wanting; stamens 4–5, inserted with the petals and opposite them; ovary 2–5-celled; fruit a drupe or capsule, mostly 3-celled; seeds 1 in each cell.

Two genera of this family are represented in Michigan.

Fruit a drupe; flowers greenish-yellow; calyx and disk free from the ovary....*Rhamnus,* p. 211
Fruit a dry capsule; flowers white; calyx and disk adherent
    to the base of the ovary..*Ceanothus,* p. 215

Rhamnus [Tourn.] L.—Buckthorns

1. Leaf margins serrate or serrulate; flowers dioecious or
    polygamous; nutlets grooved on the back
      2. Leaves and buds opposite or nearly so; veins 5–7 pairs; twigs mostly ending
        in sharp, black spines; calyx-lobes, petals and stamens 4............*R. cathartica,* p. 213
      2. Leaves and buds alternate; veins 3–4 pairs; twigs not ending in spines;
        calyx-lobes and stamens 5; petals absent......................................*R. alnifolia,* p. 211
1. Leaf margins entire or undulate; flowers perfect; nutlets not grooved....*R. Frangula,* p. 213

Rhamnus alnifolia L'Hér. (Alder Buckthorn, Dwarf Alder). Fig. 123.

A low shrub, up to 1 m. in height, without thorns; bark reddish-brown, smooth;

Rhamnus alnifolia

twigs puberulent; leaves simple, alternate, deciduous, ovate to obovate, 4–10 cm. long, 2–5 cm. wide, acute or acuminate at the apex, rounded or narrowed at the base, crenate-serrate, glabrous above, puberulent along the veins beneath; petioles 4–10 mm. long; flowers usually dioecious, from the axils of the lower leaves and appearing with them, green, small, about 3 mm. across; sepals 5; petals none; pedicels slender, 1–8 mm. long; fruit a black, ovoid or globose drupe, about 6 mm. in diameter; nutlets 3, deeply grooved on the back. Flowers, May, June; fruit, August, September.

Tamarack swamps, cedar bogs, from New-

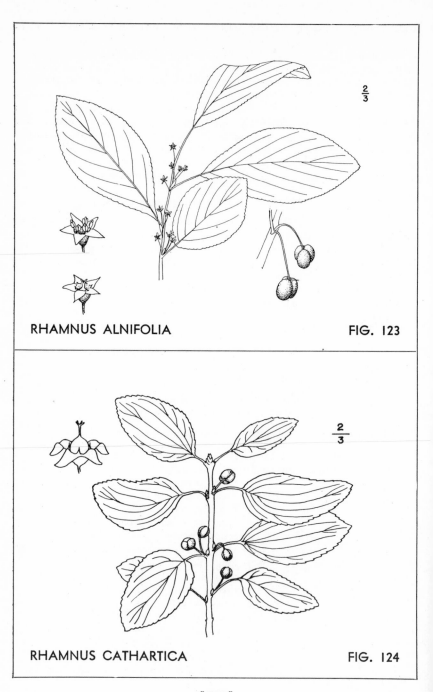

$\frac{2}{3}$

RHAMNUS ALNIFOLIA

FIG. 123

$\frac{2}{3}$

RHAMNUS CATHARTICA

FIG. 124

foundland to British Columbia, south to New Jersey, Pennsylvania, Illinois, Nebraska and Wyoming. Michigan, common throughout.

While this shrub is a native of the swamps, it takes kindly to cultivation and is sometimes used as a border shrub in landscaping. The small yellow flowers are inconspicuous, the black fruit is not attractive and altogether this is probably the least useful of our shrubs.

Rhamnus cathartica L. (Common Buckthorn). Fig. 124. A shrub, 2–6 m. tall; bark brownish; twigs often ending in stout thorns; leaves simple, opposite

Rhamnus cathartica

or nearly so, deciduous, 4–8 cm. long, about 2.5 cm. wide, regularly crenate or crenulate, with 3–4 pairs of veins, ovate to elliptic, rounded or narrowed at the base, acute or obtuse at the apex, glabrous above, puberulent along the veins beneath; petioles 1–2 cm. long; flowers clustered in the axils of the leaves, dioecious, greenish, about 4 mm. broad; sepals 4, about 2 mm. long, lanceolate, spreading or reflexed; petals 4, minute, erect, about the same length as the stamens; stamens 4; ovary 3–4-celled; style 3–4-cleft; pedicels 5–8 mm. long, slender; fruit a globose drupe, black, about 8 mm. in diameter; nutlets 3–4, grooved on the back. Flowers, May, June; fruit ripe, August, September.

Escaped from hedges and landscape plantings, in dry soil, New England, Ontario and the middle states. Introduced from Europe. Michigan, recorded only from the Lower Peninsula.

The Common Buckthorn is an excellent hedge plant. It is perfectly hardy in our zone and does not sucker. Also, it is free from insect attack and does not have to be sprayed continually. The seeds do germinate easily, however, and the seedlings create a green carpet under the bushes, calling for vigorous action with the hoe or spade.

The distribution map gives all the locations from which collections have been

Rhamnus Frangula

made and recorded in our state herbaria. Back in 1904 when the 'Flora of Michigan' was published by Beal, he stated in reference to this species: "Escaped from cultivation, Lansing, and very likely other portions of the state." Apparently it has not spread very rapidly. Those who find it are invited to record the location with the Institute.

Rhamnus Frangula L. (Alder Buckthorn). Fig. 125. A shrub or small tree sometimes up to 7 m. tall; young twigs grayish-brown, finely and sparsely puberulent;older twigs and branches with numerous light-colored lenticles; leaves thin, elliptic or

[213]

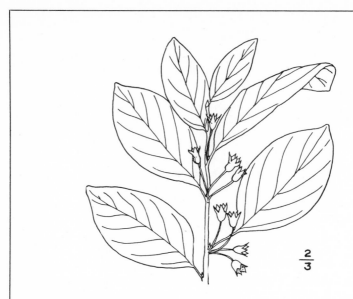

RHAMNUS FRANGULA

$\frac{2}{3}$

FIG. 125

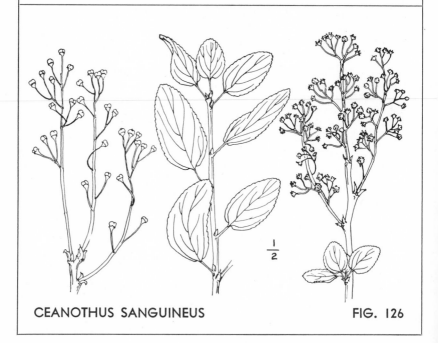

CEANOTHUS SANGUINEUS

$\frac{1}{2}$

FIG. 126

obovate, 4–7 cm. long, 2.5–4 cm. wide, with 5–8 pairs of veins, rounded or narrowed at the base, acute or short-acuminate at the apex, bright green and glabrous above, somewhat paler and finely pubescent along the veins beneath, becoming nearly or quite glabrous in age, margin entire or undulate; petioles 1–1.5 cm. long; flowers greenish, 1–6 in axillary umbels; sepals 5, narrow, ovate, acute, mostly erect; petals obovate, slightly indented at the apex; fruiting pedicels 5–10 mm. long; fruit a drupe, 6–8 mm. in diameter, purplish-black when ripe; nutlets 3, smooth. Flowers, May and June; fruit ripe, July, August.

Native of Europe and western Asia. Used in landscape planting from which source it has sparingly escaped and become naturalized in New York, New Jersey, Ontario, Michigan and no doubt other states. Michigan, so far recorded from the Lower Peninsula only.

The Alder Buckthorn apparently has not become established in Michigan to such an extent as has the previous species. It is, however, a very satisfactory shrub in landscape work. The flowers are inconspicuous, but the shining foliage and purple-black berries give the shrub an outstanding appearance.

Ceanothus L.—RED-ROOTS

1. Leaves rounded oval, frequently cordate at base, closely glandular-dentate or crenate, sparingly pubescent beneath, soon glabrate; peduncles from lateral buds, often without leaves...*C. sanguineus*, p. 215

1. Leaves oblong to elliptic or ovate, glandular-serrate to subentire; umbels panicled, mostly terminal

    2. Common peduncle elongate; leaves ovate, or ovate-oblong, pubescent; seeds smooth ....*C. americanus*, p. 217

    2. Common peduncle short; leaves oblong, narrowly oval or elliptic-lanceolate, glabrous or nearly so; seeds pitted.................................*C. ovatus*, p. 217

Ceanothus sanguineus Pursh. (Mountain Laurel, Deer Bush, Snow Bush). Fig. 126. Shrub 1–3 m. tall; young twigs greenish, those of the preceding

Ceanothus sanguineus

season red or purple; leaves alternate, simple, deciduous, oval, rounded at the apex, rounded or cordate at the base, glabrate, three-ribbed; petioles about 0.7–2 cm. long; flowers perfect, borne in panicles from lateral buds; sepals 5, deciduous; petals 5, white, spatulate; stamens 5, exserted; styles short, united below; stigmas 3; fruit dry, obovoid, 3-lobed above, about 4 mm. thick; nutlets 3, flattened. Flowers, April, July; fruit, September, October.

Hillsides and copses, Michigan, South Dakota to California and British Columbia. This is another of those rare plants which seems to be far from home in Michigan. According to present records the nearest station is in South Dakota, from which point it spreads westward in a normal distribution. It has been collected only in Keweenaw County.

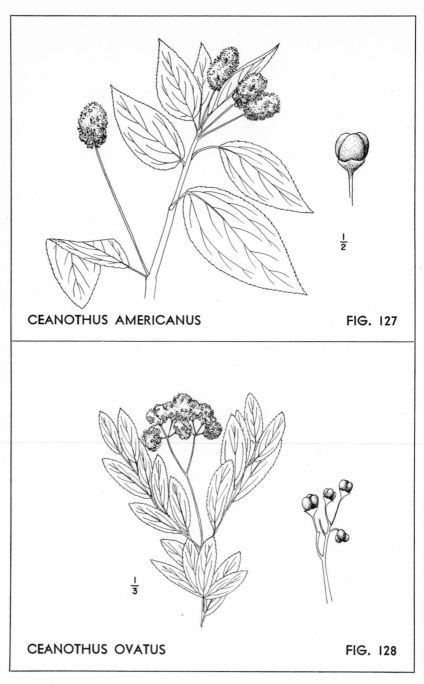

CEANOTHUS AMERICANUS   FIG. 127

$\frac{1}{2}$

CEANOTHUS OVATUS   FIG. 128

$\frac{1}{3}$

Ceanothus americanus L. (New Jersey Tea, Red-root). Fig. 127. Branching shrubs less than a meter tall, with several stems from the deep, reddish,

root stem; grayish or reddish-brown, somewhat downy-pubescent above, glabrous below; leaves alternate, simple, deciduous, ovate or ovate-oblong, 2.5–7.5 cm. long, 1–2.5 cm. broad, acutish to acuminate at the apex, obtuse or subcordate at the base, serrate, strongly 3-ribbed, more or less pubescent; petioles 6–12 mm. long; flowers in dense clusters at the ends of long axillary or terminal peduncles, white, small; calyx 5-lobed, incurved; petals 5, clawed, hooded, longer than the calyx-lobes, attached under the disk; stamens 5, filaments elongated; pedicels glabrous, 4–5 cm. long; fruit a 3-celled capsule, about 3 mm. long, one seed in each cell; nutlets 2.5–2 mm. long, light-brown, smooth. Flowers, July; fruit ripe, September, October.

In dry open woods, along roadsides and gravelly shores, Maine and Ontario to Manitoba, Kansas, Florida and Texas. Michigan, frequent throughout.

According to tradition the leaves of this shrub were used as a substitute for tea during the Revolutionary War. The clusters of delicate white flowers are very attractive.

Ceanothus ovatus Desf. (Smaller Red-root, Inland Jersey Tea). Fig. 128. Erect shrubs 3–6 dm. tall, much branched, nearly glabrous throughout; leaves simple, alternate, deciduous, oblong, narrowly oval or elliptic-lanceolate, 1.5–6

cm. long, 1.2–5 cm. wide, obtuse or rounded at the apex, narrowed at the base, finely and sharply glandular-serrate, glabrous beneath, or slightly pubescent along the veins; petioles about 5 mm. long; flowers on short peduncles, white, about 5 mm. broad; pedicels 10–15 mm. long; fruit globose, slightly flattened at the top; seeds dark brown, about 2 mm. in length, surface pitted. Flowers, June, July; fruit, September, October.

In dry rocky or sandy soil from Vermont and eastern Massachusetts to Manitoba, Minnesota, Illinois and southwestward. Michigan, upper portion of Lower Peninsula and the Upper Peninsula.

This species has a variety, *pubescens* T.&G., with permanently sordid-tomentose leaves which has a more western and southern range. It has been collected in Keweenaw County and might be looked for in other localities.

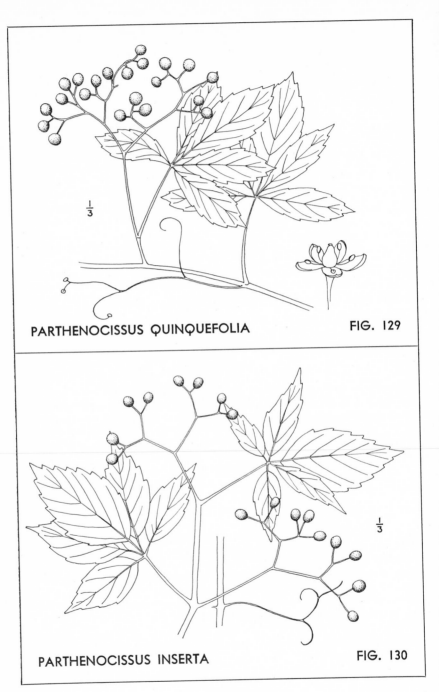

$\frac{1}{3}$

PARTHENOCISSUS QUINQUEFOLIA

FIG. 129

$\frac{1}{3}$

PARTHENOCISSUS INSERTA

FIG. 130

VITACEAE—Vine Family

Climbing or erect shrubs with watery, acid juice and nodose joints; leaves deciduous, alternate, simple, palmately veined or lobed, or compound; tendrils and flower-clusters opposite the leaves; stipules deciduous; flowers small, regular, greenish, commonly polygamous, borne in racemes, panicles or cymes; calyx entire or 4–5-lobed; petals 4–5, separate or coherent, valvate, very deciduous; stamens as many as the petals and opposite them; filaments slender; style short or none; stigma slightly 2-lobed; ovary 2-celled, generally immersed in the disk; ovules 1 or 2 in each cell; fruit a 2-celled berry; seeds usually 4, with a bony coat.

Two genera including shrubs belonging to this family are found in Michigan.

Leaves palmately compound; corolla expanding..................................*Parthenocissus*, p. 219
Leaves simple; corolla falling without expanding..*Vitis*, p. 220

Parthenocissus Planch.—Virginia Creepers

Leaflets with upper surface dull and much paler beneath; tendrils mostly
with adhesive disks, 5–12-branched..*P. quinquefolia*, p. 219
Leaflets with upper surface shining and not much paler beneath;
tendrils mostly without adhesive disks, 2–5 branched....................................*P. inserta*, p. 220

Parthenocissus quinquefolia (L.) Planch. (Virginia Creeper, Woodbine). Fig. 129. (*Psedera quinquefolia* (L.) Greene, Gray's Manual, 7th Edition, Shrubs of Michigan, 1st Edition.) High-climbing or trailing woody vines; stem sometimes reaching a diameter of 3–6 cm.; tendrils with 5–12 branches, mostly ending with adhesive disks; leaves deciduous, alternate, petioled, usually 5-foliate; leaflets stalked, ovate, oblong-ovate or obovate, 4–12 cm. long, 2–6 cm. wide, acute or acuminate, narrowed at base, coarsely serrate, dull green above, decidedly paler beneath, glabrous or pubescent; panicles with branches 6–12 cm. long, loose, erect or spreading in fruit; flowers small, greenish, about 6 mm. broad; petals 5, spreading; stamens 5; style short, thick; berry subglobose, blue-black, 5–8 mm. in diameter; pedicels about 5 mm. long, red; seeds 1–4, resembling those of the grape in size and color. Flowers, June, July; fruit ripe, September, October.

Parthenocissus quinquefolia

In woods and thickets, New England, westward to Missouri, south to Florida, Texas and Mexico; very common. Michigan, throughout.

This plant, often called the Five-fingered Ivy, is one of our most common vines. Its leaves are brilliantly colored in the fall, and it is used extensively in landscape work as a covering for fences, trellises, etc. Given the benefit of the right support and other favorable conditions, this vine will grow to unusual size and height. At the home of Dr. Howard Baker near Chelsea my attention

[219]

was directed to what must be a very old specimen. It is growing in low, rich ground and climbing the trunk of a large willow tree. The stem 1 m. from the ground measured approximately 10 cm. in diameter and grew as a solid trunk to a height of 7 or 8 m., at which point it branched out and continued up into the tree in a normal vine-like manner. The three-leaved poison ivy is often confused with this plant. The species is extremely variable in pubescence and size of leaves.

Although our description is drawn to include both glabrous and pubescent plants, the following form, which was described from those with pubescence, is mentioned for the benefit of anyone desiring to get down to the fine points of the matter: *Parthenocissus quinquefolia* (L.) Planch., forma *hirsuta* (Donn) Fern. It has been reported by Hanes from Kalamazoo County and is no doubt present in other localities.

The adhesive disks of this vine have a very tenacious quality. After extensive experimentation, Darwin concluded that a tendril with 5 disk-bearing branches would stand a strain of 10 pounds without separating from its support.

Parthenocissus inserta (Kern.) Fritsch. (False Grape). Fig. 130. (*Psedera vitacea* (Knerr) Greene, Gray's Manual, 7th Edition, Shrubs of Michigan, 1st Edition.) Woody climbing or trailing vines up to several meters in length; glabrous or sparingly pubescent; tendrils with 2–5 long-twining branches, these only very rarely ending in adhesive disks; aerial rootlets none; leaves deciduous, alternate, petioled, normally 5-foliate; leaflets stalked, ovate, oblong-ovate, 4–13 cm. long, 2–8 cm. wide, deep green, thin, somewhat shining above, not much paler beneath, glabrous or some-what hairy; petioles long, glabrous; inflorescence regularly dichotomous, the primary branches nearly equal; peduncles 4–8 cm. long; flowers about 5 mm. in diameter, greenish; calyx small, not divided; petals 5, spreading or reflexed; stamens 5; style short, thick; berry somewhat obovoid, 6–10 mm. in diameter, fleshy, blue-black; seeds 1–4, 4–5 mm. long and resembling those of the grape in size and color. Flowers, June, July; fruit ripe, September, October.

Moist woods, alluvial thickets, Quebec to Manitoba, south to Pennsylvania, Arizona and Texas. Michigan, throughout.

This is similar to the preceding species and grows in like situations. The more shining leaves and tendrils without adhesive disks are distinguishing marks which can be readily recognized. Its leaves are brilliantly colored in the fall.

Vitis [Tourn.] L.—GRAPES

1. Lower surface of leaves woolly
   2. Pubescence rusty-brown; berries few, about 12–14 mm. in diameter, brownish-purple or amber, pulp musky..*V. labrusca*, p. 221
   2. Pubescence becoming whitish; berries numerous, about 8–10 mm. in diameter, black, pulp not musky...*V. aestivalis*, p. 221

1. Leaves glabrate, sometimes slightly pubescent when young, or pubescent along the veins and in their axils beneath
    3. Leaves bluish-white glaucous beneath...................*V. aestivalis* var. *argentifolia*, p. 223
    3. Leaves not glaucous beneath
        4. Teeth of leaves broadly deltoid; inflorescence
        loose; berries black, shining...*V. vulpina*, p. 223
        4. Teeth of leaves narrowly deltoid; inflorescence
        compact; berries bluish-black, glaucous.................................*V. riparia*, p. 225

Vitis labrusca L. (Northern Fox Grape). Fig. 131. Long-climbing or trailing vines; bark loose and shreddy; branchlets very woolly; leaves deciduous, alternate, simple, entire or deeply lobed,

slightly dentate, with rounded sinuses, cordate, 4–12 cm. long, 5–14 cm. wide, very woolly and mostly red or rusty when young, becoming dark green and glabrous or nearly so above at maturity, continuing tawny or rusty-pubescent beneath; petioles 5–10 cm. long, rusty-pubescent; fertile panicles compact, the staminate looser; flowers yellowish-green, fragrant, polygamo-dioecious; calyx very short; petals deciduous without expanding; style short; berries few, large, brownish-purple or amber-color, with a tough musky pulp; seeds 3–6, about 8 mm. long. Flowers, May, June; fruit ripe, August, September.

Moist or dry thickets from New England States to Indiana and south to Georgia. Michigan, distribution confined to the southern portion of the Lower Peninusla.

The Northern Fox Grape is the species from which has been developed through cultivation several of our garden and vineyard grapes, among which the Concord is the most prominent.

Vitis aestivalis Michx. (Summer Grape, Pigeon Grape). Fig. 132. High-climbing vines; bark loose and shreddy; branches terete, more or less pubescent when young, becoming glabrate; pith interrupted at nodes; leaves simple, deciduous, alternate, large, unlobed or more or less deeply and obtusely 3–5-lobed, dentate, 5–17 cm. long and about as broad, very woolly with whitish or rusty pubescence, particularly when young, sometimes becoming nearly glabrous and bright green above in maturity, remaining more or less pubescent beneath; petioles pubescent, mostly shorter than the leaves, but sometimes longer; inflorescence generally long and loose; berries numerous, about 8–10 mm. in diameter, black with a bloom, edible; seeds 2–3, about 5–6 mm. long. Flowers, May, June; fruit ripe, September and October.

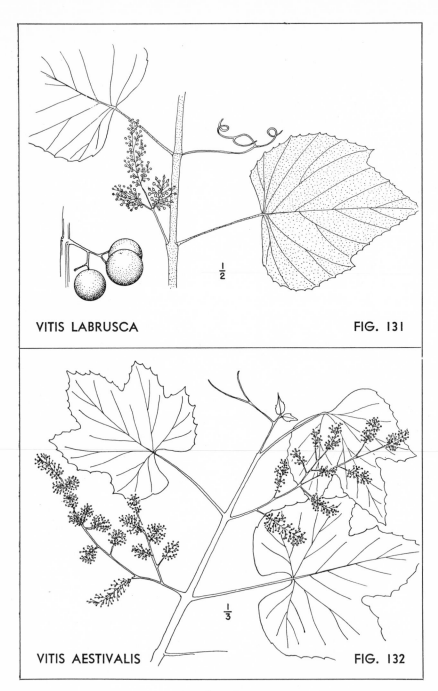

VITIS LABRUSCA   FIG. 131

VITIS AESTIVALIS   FIG. 132

In thickets, southern New Hampshire to Florida, west to Kansas and Texas. Michigan, distribution confined to the southern portion of the Lower Peninsula.

One or more varieties of this species have been named. By some they are regarded as geographical forms only and not entitled to varietal rank. They are omitted here.

Vitis aestivalis Michx. var. *argentifolia* (Munson) Fern. (Blue Grape, Winter Grape). Fig. 133. (*Vitis bicolor* LeConte, Gray's Manual, 7th Edition,

Vitis aestivalis var. argentifolia

Shrubs of Michigan, 1st Edition.) A long-trailing or high-climbing vine; bark cinnamon-colored; tendrils intermittent; branches terete; twigs and leaves glabrous or somewhat pubescent, bluish-glaucous or later without the bloom; leaves nearly orbicular in outline, up to 3 dm. long and as broad, deeply cordate at base, usually 3-lobed, the sinuses rounded, the lobes acute or acuminate, margin crenate-dentate, bright green and glabrous above, glaucous or whitened below, the bloom sometimes disappearing at the end of the season; petioles stout, 8–15 cm. long; inflorescence compact; berries 8–10 mm. in diameter, bluish black with a bloom, sour; seeds about 4 mm. long. Flowers, May, June; fruit ripe in September and October.

Ranges from New Hampshire to Michigan, North Carolina, Tennessee and Missouri. Michigan, infrequent, central and southern portion of Lower Peninsula.

In the first edition of this bulletin mention was made of the fact that *V. bicolor* resembled *V. aestivalis,* except in a few characters. Instead of a separate species it is now more generally regarded as a northern form of *V. aestivalis* and, although illustrated, is treated as a variety of that species in this edition. It is separated from the species by its less dense pubescence and by the pale and glaucous under surface of the leaves. Any series of specimens will no doubt be found to have all degrees of intermediates, however, and even a varietal name may not be entirely justified.

Vitis vulpina

Vitis vulpina L. (Frost Grape, Chicken Grape). Fig. 134. (*Vitis cordifolia* Michx., Gray's Manual, 7th Edition, Shrubs of Michigan, 1st Edition.) High-climbing, large vines; bark loose; twigs glabrous or slightly pubescent, terete or indistinctly angled; pith interrupted; tendrils intermittent, forked; leaves simple, deciduous, alternate, 7.5–10 cm. wide, slightly 3-lobed or unlobed, cordate with deep, acute sinuses, acuminate at the apex, sharply and coarsely dentate with acute teeth, thin, glabrous, or sparingly pubescent on the veins beneath; stipules

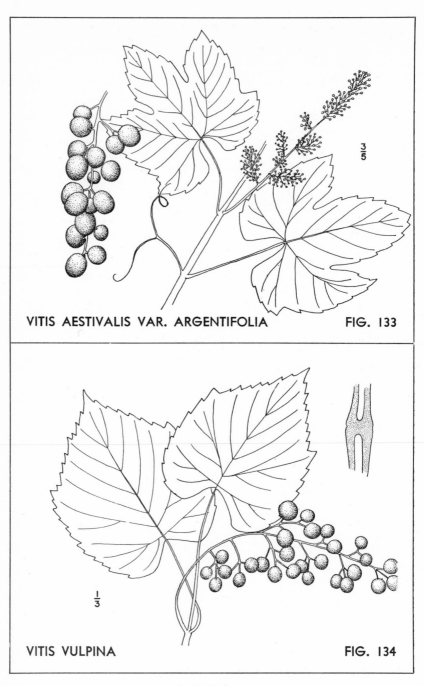

VITIS AESTIVALIS VAR. ARGENTIFOLIA   FIG. 133

$\frac{3}{5}$

VITIS VULPINA   FIG. 134

$\frac{1}{3}$

small; petioles pubescent, or glabrous at maturity, usually shorter than the leaf midrib; inflorescence medium to large, loose, with long peduncle; berries small, black and shining, 8–10 mm. in diameter, ripening after a frost; seeds 2–3, about 4 mm. long. Flowers, May, June; fruit ripe, October, November.

Thickets and stream banks, Pennsylvania, southern New York to central Illinois, Missouri, Nebraska and southward. Michigan, both peninsulas, more common southward.

The Chicken Grape has little horticultural value and is seldom cultivated.

In the process of clarifying the botanical nomenclature which is being continually carried on by systematists, *V. cordifolia* Michx. is relegated to synonomy and in its place is *V. vulpina* L., a name previously applied to an entirely different plant. The plant formerly bearing this name is now called *V. riparia* Michx.

Vitis riparia Michx. (River-bank Grape, Frost Grape). Fig. 135. (*Vitis vulpina* L., Gray's Manual, 7th Edition, Shrubs of Michigan, 1st Edition.)

Large climbing or trailing vines; bark shreddy; branches greenish, glabrous, terete or slightly angled; pith interrupted; tendrils intermittent; leaves deciduous, simple, alternate, thin, shining, 6–15 cm. long, mostly 3–7-lobed, the sinuses angular, the lobes acute or acuminate at the apex, teeth sharp; stipules 4–6 mm. long, sometimes persistent until the fruit is formed; petiole shorter than the midrib, more or less pubescent; inflorescence compact; berries 8–10 mm. in diameter, bluish-black with a bloom, acid and juicy; seeds 2–4, about 5 mm. long. Flowers, May, June; fruit ripening, July to fall.

Stream banks, near water, New Brunswick to West Virginia, North Dakota and Kansas. Michigan throughout, but infrequent in the pine region.

The grapes intergrade and are difficult of determination, but it is to this species that I have referred most of those found growing so plentifully around the many lakes of southeastern Michigan.

The shift of names previously referred to has resulted in this plant acquiring a title which fits it perfectly. *Riparia*, or riparian, signifies "living on the bank of a river or lake," and that is exactly where this grape is generally found.

Vitis riparia Michx. var. *syrticola* (Fern. & Weath.) Fern., a form with much more pubescent branches, petioles and leaves, is reported by Hanes from Kalamazoo County.

HYPERICACEAE—St. John's-wort Family

Herbs or shrubs; leaves deciduous, simple, mostly sessile, opposite, entire, dotted and without stipules; flowers regular; stamens many or few, sometimes collected in clusters; fruit a many-seeded capsule; plants usually smooth; flowers solitary or cymose.

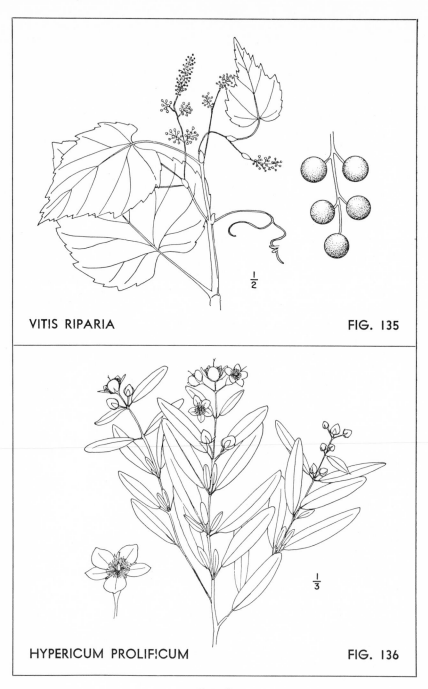

VITIS RIPARIA $\frac{1}{2}$ FIG. 135

HYPERICUM PROLIFICUM $\frac{1}{3}$ FIG. 136

The family consists of two genera, *Ascyrum* and *Hypericum*, of which only the latter is represented in Michigan.

Hypericum [Tourn.] L.—St. John's-worts

Pod completely 3-celled; styles 3; leaves petioled..................................*H. prolificum*, p. 227
Pod completely 5-celled; styles 5; leaves sessile..................................*H. Kalmianum*, p. 227

Hypericum prolificum L. (Shrubby St. John's-wort). Fig. 136. Erect bushy shrubs, 3–9 dm. tall; branchlets 2-edged; bark shreddy; leaves deciduous, opposite, simple, linear-oblong or oblanceolate, 2–10 cm. long, 3–15 mm. wide, pale beneath, narrowed at the base or tapering, obtuse or often mucronate at the apex, punctate with small translucent dots; petiole 1–5 mm. long; flowers numerous in simple or compound terminal or axillary cymes, about 2 cm. across, on pedicels 12 mm. long or shorter; sepals 5, subequal; petals 5, brilliant yellow, oblique; stamens numerous, distinct; capsule 3-celled, about 10 mm. long, many-seeded; seeds about 2 mm. long, pitted. Flowers, July, September; fruit, autumn.

Hypericum prolificum

Found in sandy or rocky soil from New Jersey to Georgia, west to Michigan and Minnesota. Michigan, frequent in lower half of the Southern Peninsula.

The flowers of Shrubby St. John's-wort are extremely showy, and as they are borne late in the season after most other shrubs are through blooming it makes a very desirable shrub for cultivation.

Hypericum Kalmianum L. (Kalm's St. John's-wort). Fig. 137. Low shrubs 3–7 dm. tall, leafy; branches 4-angled; twigs flattened and 2-edged; leaves simple, deciduous, opposite, sessile, oblanceolate or linear-oblong, obtuse, 2–6 cm. long, 3–11 mm. wide, obtuse, or acute at apex, narrowed at the base, glaucous beneath; cymes terminal, few-flowered; pedicels 4–20 mm. long; flowers 2–2.5 cm. across; sepals foliaceous, oblong, acute, 6–8 mm. long; petals 5, golden-yellow; stamens very numerous, distinct; styles 5, united below; capsule ovoid, 5-celled, about 7 mm. long; seeds numerous, about 1 mm. long. Flowers, August; fruit, autumn.

Hypericum Kalmianum

Rocky or sandy soil, Quebec, along the Great Lakes to Wisconsin, south to New York and Illinois. Michigan, throughout, more abundant northward.

Kalm's St. John's-wort is not as common as the preceding species. It was first discovered on the wet rocks at Niagara Falls and is most at home in the region of the Great Lakes.

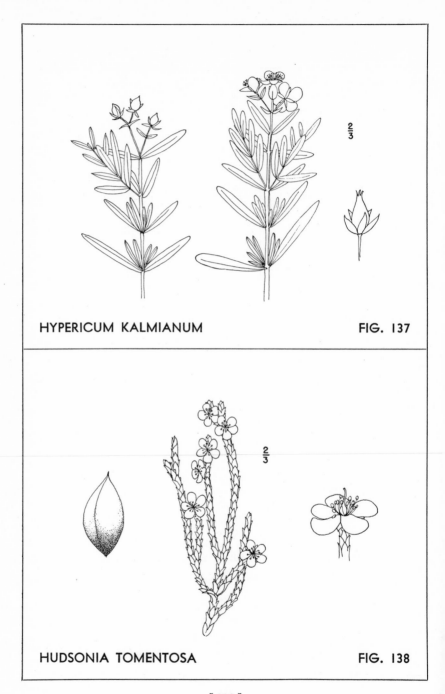

HYPERICUM KALMIANUM   FIG. 137

HUDSONIA TOMENTOSA   FIG. 138

CISTACEAE—ROCKROSE FAMILY

Low shrubs or herbs; leaves alternate or opposite, simple, sometimes scale-like; flowers regular, generally perfect; sepals 3–5, persistent, when 5, the 2 outer much smaller and bract-like; petals 3–5 or wanting, convolute in the bud; stamens many, free; filaments slender; style single or none; ovary 1-celled; fruit a capsule opening by valves; seeds several or numerous.

A family of three genera, one of which is represented in Michigan by a single species.

Hudsonia L.—HUDSONIAS

Hudsonia tomentosa Nutt. (Woolly Hudsonia). Fig. 138. Low, densely-tufted, bushy shrubs, 1–2 dm. tall, hoary-pubescent, pale; leaves persistent, alternate, simple, 2 mm. long, oval or oblong, imbricated and appressed; flowers numerous, sessile or on very short pedicels, bright yellow; sepals 3, obtuse and shorter than the obovate-oblong petals; stamens numerous; style long and slender; stigma minute; pod ovoid, inclosed in the calyx; seeds few. Flowers, May, June; fruit, summer.

Sandy shores, dunes, etc., New Brunswick to Virginia and along the Great Lakes to Minnesota. Michigan, frequent both peninsulas, except in the interior.

The species passes into a variety which has been named *intermedia* by Peck. Its leaves tend to be more awl-shaped and its flowers are obviously peduncled.

This little gray bush is fairly frequent on the sand dunes along the shores of the Great Lakes. Through its long, slender root fibers it holds its own and flourishes in spite of the shifting sands.

THYMELAEACEAE—MEZEREUM FAMILY

Shrubs or trees with tough bark; leaves deciduous, alternate, simple and entire; flowers perfect, borne singly or in racemes or capitate clusters; calyx-tube cylindric or urn-shaped, colored; petals none; stamens twice as many as the lobes of the calyx and free from the ovary which is 1-celled and 1-ovuled; stigma mostly capitate; fruit a berry-like drupe.

Only one genus of this family is represented in Michigan.

Dirca L.—LEATHERWOODS

Dirca palustris L. (Leatherwood, Wicopy). Fig. 139. Shrubs, 0.5–2 m. tall, widely branching; bark very tough, fibrous, grayish; branches jointed; leaves alternate, deciduous, simple, entire, mostly obovate or oval, obtuse, glabrous or nearly so, 5–8 cm. long, 1.5–5 cm. wide, rounded at base, obtuse at apex; petioles very short; bud scales 3 or 4, oval or oblong, pubescent with

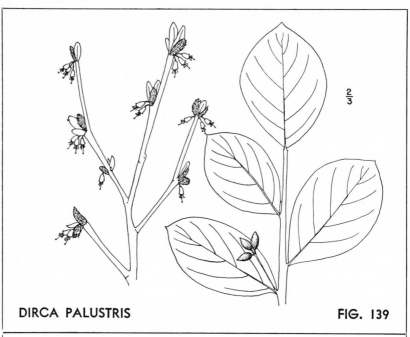

DIRCA PALUSTRIS   FIG. 139

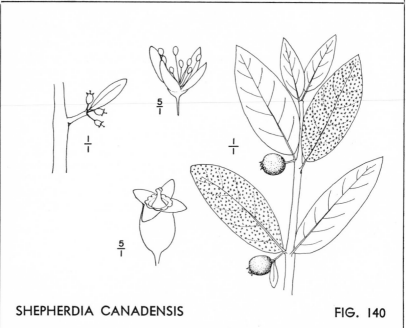

SHEPHERDIA CANADENSIS   FIG. 140

[230]

brown hairs; flowers light yellow, preceding the leaves, 3 or 4 in a cluster; petals none; calyx petal-like, campanulate, obscurely 4-toothed; stamens 8, inserted on the calyx above the middle, alternate ones longer; filaments very slender; ovary sessile; stigma small, capitate; fruit a red, oval-oblong drupe, about 12 mm. long; seed dark brown. Flowers, April, May; fruit, June, falling early.

Dirca palustris

Damp rich woods, New Brunswick to Minnesota, south to Florida and Mississippi. Michigan, frequent throughout.

The Leatherwood is one of our earliest flowering shrubs. It is conspicuous when it flowers, but its flowers fade and fall rapidly as the leaves expand. The bark is unusually tough and it has such strength that it is very difficult to break it by pulling. This accounts for its common name and for the fact that it was used by the Indians for cordage and in making baskets.

When taken internally the bark will produce vomiting and the berries are said to be narcotic.

ELAEAGNACEAE—Oleaster Family

Shrubs or small trees, mostly silvery-scaly or stellate-pubescent; leaves deciduous, simple, entire, alternate or opposite; flowers perfect, polygamous or dioecious, clustered in the axils or at the nodes of twigs of the preceding season; calyx of perfect or pistillate flowers, urn-shaped, 4-lobed or -cleft, upper part deciduous; stamens 4 or 8, those of the perfect flowers borne on the throat of the perianth; filaments mostly short; disk annular or lobed; ovary sessile, 1-celled; ovule 1, erect; style slender; fruit drupe-like, the perianth base becoming thickened and enclosing the achene.

There are three known genera in this family, of which the following is represented in Michigan by one species.

Shepherdia canadensis

Shepherdia Nutt.—Buffalo Berry

Shepherdia canadensis (L.) Nutt. (Canadian Buffalo Berry). Fig. 140. A thornless spreading shrub, 1–3 m. in height; bark gray, or brownish on the younger twigs; leaves simple, deciduous, opposite, ovate or oval, obtuse at the apex, rounded or narrowed at the base, 2–4 cm. long, 1–2.5 cm. wide, green and sparingly stellate-scurfy above, densely stellate-scurfy beneath; petioles 4–6 mm. long; flowers yellowish, small, dioecious, or sometimes polygamous, borne in short spikes at the nodes of the twigs; the pistillate flowers few or sometimes solitary, with a 4-lobed perianth bearing an 8-lobed disk at its mouth nearly closing it, the sterile with a 4-parted calyx and 8 stamens alternating with the lobes of the disk; style slender, somewhat exserted; fruit drupe-like, 1-seeded, red or yellowish, oval, about 8 mm. long. Flowers, April, May; fruit, July, August.

Growing on calcareous rocks and banks, Newfoundland to Alaska, south to Nova Scotia, Maine, Vermont, western New York, Michigan, Wisconsin and Minnesota. Michigan, throughout.

This is definitely a wildling species. It grows in different situations, but it is very hard to transplant and is seldom used in cultivation.

LYTHRACEAE Lindl.—LOOSESTRIFE FAMILY

Herbs, shrubs or often trees in the tropical regions, mostly with opposite leaves and perfect flowers; stipules usually wanting; calyx persistent, free from the ovary, the limb toothed; petals as many as the primary calyx-teeth, inserted on the calyx, or sometimes wanting; stamens inserted on the calyx; ovary 2–6-celled, or sometimes 1-celled; style 1; stigma capitate, or rarely 2-lobed; capsule 1- to several-celled; seeds without albumen.

This family comprises about 21 genera and 350 species of wide distribution. The following genus with a single species, variously treated as an herb and a semi-woody shrub, is found in Michigan.

Decodon J. F. Gmel.—SWAMP LOOSESTRIFES

Decodon verticillatus (L.) Ell. (Swamp Loosestrife, Willow-herb). Fig. 141. Aquatic perennial; stems somewhat woody, angular, recurved, glabrous

Decodon verticillatus

or slightly pubescent, 1–3 m. long, rooting at the tip upon reaching the mud or water; bark of submerged parts often spongy-thickened; leaves deciduous, opposite or verticillate, entire, lanceolate, 5–13 cm. long, glabrous above, somewhat pubescent beneath, acute at both ends; petioles 4–8 mm. long; flowers borne in nearly sessile axillary cymes, showy, purple, trimorphous, about 2–5 cm. broad; petals wedge-shaped at base; calyx broadly campanulate, or hemispheric, nerved, 5–7-toothed, with the same number of slender elongated accessory teeth in the sinuses; stamens 10, rarely 8, alternately longer and shorter, inserted on the calyx-tube, the longer ones very slender, exserted; style filiform; stigma small; capsule globose, about 5 mm. in diameter, 3–5-celled, included in the calyx. Flowers, July, September; fruit, autumn.

In swamps, shallow water, edges of streams, ponds and lakes, Maine to Florida, west to southern Ontario, Minnesota, Tennessee, Kentucky and Louisiana. Michigan, throughout, more plentiful in the Lower Peninsula.

Some authors separate the smooth form of this plant as var. *laevigatus* T. & G. Our description is written to include both the smooth and the pubescent forms, but many smooth plants will no doubt be found which may be given the varietal name if anyone cares to do so.

ARALIACEAE—Ginseng Family

Herbs, shrubs or trees; stems frequently prickly or spiny; leaves deciduous, alternate or rarely opposite, simple or pinnately compound; flowers perfect or polygamous, borne in umbels, heads, racemes or panicles, mostly small, greenish or whitish; calyx small, toothed or entire; petals mostly 5, sometimes united at the apex, inserted on the margin of the calyx; stamens as many as the petals and alternate with them; ovary inferior, 1- to several-celled; styles distinct or united; fruit a berry or a drupe; seeds flattened or partially 3-angled.

A family of about 50 genera and 450 species widely distributed in the temperate and tropical zones. The following genera are represented in Michigan.

Leaves compound; fruit black...*Aralia*, p. 233
Leaves simple, but palmately lobed; fruit red...*Oplopanax*, p. 235

Aralia [Tourn.] L.—Spikenards

Umbels numerous, panicled or racemose; tall erect
shrub or small tree; stout-spiny...*A. spinosa*, p. 233
Umbels mostly 2–7, terminal or corymbose; low
semi-woody shrub; weak prickles..*A. hispida*, p. 235

Aralia spinosa L. (Hercules' Club, Angelica-tree, Devil's Walking Stick). Fig. 142. Large, stout and erect shrub or a small tree; stem and branches spiny;

Aralia spinosa

leaves deciduous, alternate, bipinnate, leaflets ovate, thick, acute or acuminate at the apex, rounded or subcordate at the base, on short stalks or sessile, 3–9 cm. long, 2–5 cm. wide, margin serrate, dark green above, glaucous and sometimes more or less pubescent beneath or glabrous; petiole 2–5 dm. long, generally spiny; flowers perfect, white, 4 mm. wide, borne in umbels of from 10–30 flowers arranged in large terminal compound panicles; peduncles and pedicels pubescent; calyx 5-toothed; petals 5, spreading, obtuse; stamens 5; ovary 5-celled; styles 5, distinct; fruit ovoid, black, 5-lobed, about 6 mm. long. Flowers, June, August; fruit, September and October.

In low grounds and along streams, southern New York to Florida, west to Indiana, Missouri and Texas. Freely planted for ornament and sometimes escaping from cultivation farther north. Michigan: it is doubtful if this shrub is native to Michigan, but it is reported from several counties in the

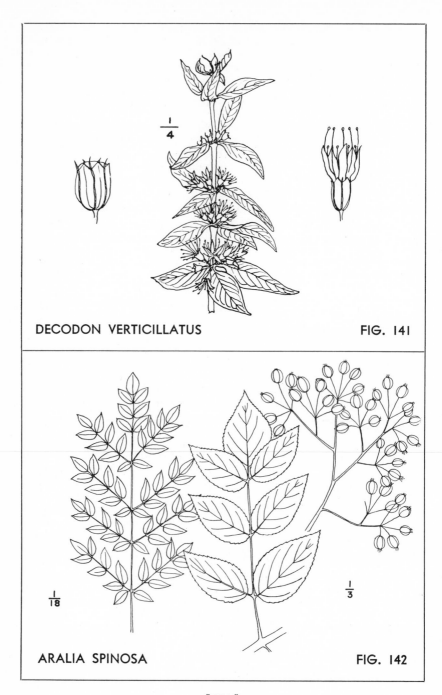

$\frac{1}{4}$

DECODON VERTICILLATUS

FIG. 141

$\frac{1}{18}$

$\frac{1}{3}$

ARALIA SPINOSA

FIG. 142

southern portion of the state, where it has doubtless escaped from cultivation.

The Hercules' Club is particularly attractive on account of its large leaves and enormous panicles of white flowers. Farther north it is not fully hardy and it is liable to freeze back.

In addition to its usual common name of Hercules' Club or Devil's Walking Stick it is known as Toothache Tree, indicating some medicinal properties.

Aralia hispida Vent. (Bristly Sarsaparilla, Wild Elder). Fig. 143. A semi-woody plant, 4–9 dm. tall; stems simple, rather slender, woody at the base and

Aralia hispida

sometimes higher; prickles numerous, bristle-like; leaves alternate, deciduous, twice-pin-nate, 1–3 dm. long; leaflets mostly sessile, lanceolate to lance-ovate, 2.5–5 cm. long, rounded or narrowed at the base, acute to acuminate at the apex, margin sharply and irregularly serrate, dark green above, pale beneath, glabrous or somewhat bristly on the veins beneath; petioles of lower leaves 4–10 cm. long, the upper leaves nearly sessile, the petiole and leaf-rachis more or less bristly; flowers polygamous, white, about 2 mm. in diameter, borne in umbels about 2 cm. in diameter, the lower solitary, long-peduncled, the upper ones forming a loose irregular cyme; calyx 5-toothed; petals 5, spreading, obtuse; stamens 5; ovary 5-celled; styles 5; fruit a purple-black drupe, 6–8 mm. in diameter, strongly 5-lobed when dry. Flowers, June, July; fruit, August, September.

In rocky or sandy woods and clearings, Newfoundland to North Carolina, Hudson Bay, Minnesota, Indiana and Michigan. Michigan, to quote from Beal's 'Michigan Flora': "Apparently not common south of the pine region." The records, however, indicate that it is fairly common throughout.

This plant is variously known as Rough Sarsaparilla, Dwarf Elder, Hyeble and Pigeon-berry. It belongs to that border-line group of semi-woody plants which were omitted from the first edition but which are now included with the idea of making the book of greater use to the reader.

Oplopanax (T.&G.) Miq.—Devil's Clubs

Oplopanax horridum (Sm.) Miq. (Devil's Club). Fig. 144. (*Fatsia horrida* (Sm.) B. & H., Gray's Manual, 7th Edition, Shrubs of Michigan, 1st Edition.) A coarse shrub, erect from a decumbent base, 2–3 m. in height; stems densely prickly, leafy above; leaves simple, alternate, deciduous, long-petioled, nearly round in outline, 1–3 dm. in diameter, palmately lobed, the 3–11 lobes acute, sharply and irregularly serrate, cordate at base with a narrow sinus, prickles scattered on the ribs beneath; flowers perfect or polygamous,

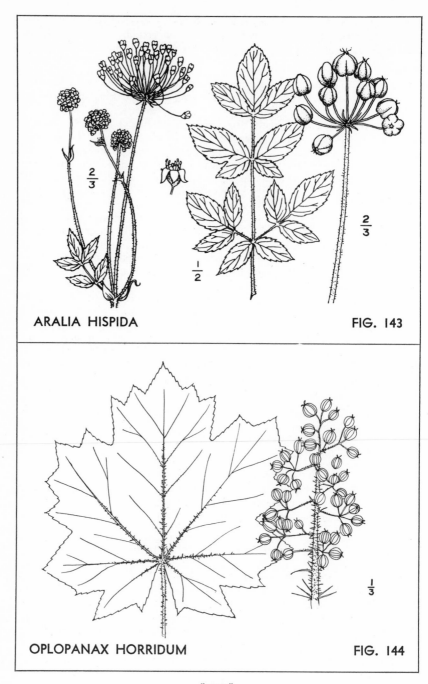

ARALIA HISPIDA   FIG. 143

OPLOPANAX HORRIDUM   FIG. 144

Oplopanax horridum

greenish-white, borne in terminal paniculate umbels 1–3 dm. in length, the branches woolly; calyx-teeth obsolete; petals 5, stamens 5; filaments thread-like; anthers oblong or ovate; ovary 2–3-celled; styles 2; stigma terminal; fruit laterally compressed, 4–6 mm. long, scarlet. Flowers, June; fruit, August, September.

In rocky places, Isle Royale, Lake Superior, Montana to Oregon and southern Alaska; also in Japan. Michigan, reported only from Isle Royale.

The Devil's Club is essentially a plant of the northwest. See remarks under the heading of Rare Species.

CORNACEAE—Dogwood Family

Shrubs or small trees, rarely herbs; leaves deciduous, simple, opposite or alternate, usually entire; flowers perfect, polygamous or dioecious, borne in cymes, heads or rarely solitary; calyx 4–5-dentate, adherent to the top of the 1–2-celled ovary; petals 4–5, or sometimes wanting, valvate or imbricate, inserted at the base of the epigynous disk; stamens as many as the petals and inserted with them; ovary inferior, 1–2-celled; style 1; ovules 1 in each cavity; fruit a drupe with 1–2 seeds.

This family includes two genera, one of which is represented in Michigan.

Cornus [Tourn.] L.—Dogwoods

1. Leaves opposite
   2. Pubescence more or less spreading, often woolly
      3. Fruit blue or bluish
         4. Leaves broadly ovate or orbicular, mostly white-woolly beneath; branches greenish, gray, or brownish; branchlets yellow-green, more or less streaked with dark purplish dots; pith white...C. rugosa, p. 239
         4. Leaves ovate or ovate-lanceolate, pubescent beneath with colorless hairs; branches light red to reddish-brown; branchlets greenish-gray, densely appressed pubescent, not streaked with purplish dots; pith brown...................C. obliqua, p. 239
      3. Fruit white
         5. Leaves oblong or ovate, rough above with harsh pubescence; branches brownish.....................................C. asperifolia, p. 241
         5. Leaves ovate to ovate-lanceolate, not rough above, branches red...C. stolonifera var. Baileyi, p. 242
   2. Pubescence closely appressed, straight and silky, or none
      6. Leaves ovate, short pointed, twigs purple; petals ovate-oblong...C. stolonifera, p. 242
      6. Leaves ovate-lanceolate, taper pointed; twigs gray; petals lanceolate..C. racemosa, p. 243
1. Leaves alternate, clustered near the ends of the twigs; fruit blue..C. alternifolia, p. 243

[237]

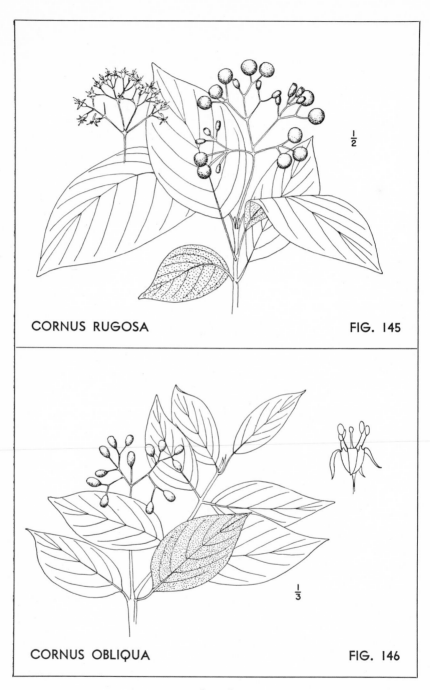

CORNUS RUGOSA

$\frac{1}{2}$

FIG. 145

CORNUS OBLIQUA

$\frac{1}{3}$

FIG. 146

Cornus rugosa Lam. (Round-leaved Dogwood). Fig. 145. (*Cornus cir-cinata* L'Hér., Gray's Manual, 7th Edition, Shrubs of Michigan, 1st Edi-

tion.) Shrubs 2–3 m. tall; branches greenish, more or less warty-dotted; young twigs greenish-yellow, sparsely to woolly-pubescent; pith white; leaves simple, opposite, deciduous, round-oval, 6–14 cm. long, 5–12 cm. broad, abruptly pointed, woolly beneath; mostly rounded at the base, finely appressed-pubescent above; petioles 1–2 cm. long; flowers perfect, white, in rather compact flat cymes, 3–7 cm. broad; peduncle and pedicels somewhat pubescent; sepals minute; petals ovate, 3–4 mm. long, becoming reflexed; stamens 4, exceeding the petals; ovary inferior, 2-celled; style slender; stigma capitate; fruit globose, pale blue, 5–6 mm. in diameter; stone subglobose, ridged. Flowers, May, June; fruit ripe, September.

Growing in rich or sandy soil, or on rocks, from Quebec to Manitoba, south to Virginia, Indiana, Illinois, Iowa and North Dakota. Michigan, throughout; more abundant northward.

This is one of the most attractive of the dogwoods. In cultivation it will do best in a rather shaded position. The flowers are somewhat larger than usual for the dogwoods, and the fruit, though not plentiful, is attractive.

Cornus obliqua Raf. (Pale Dogwood, Silky Cornel). Fig. 146. (*Cornus Amomum* Mill., Gray's Manual, 7th Edition, Shrubs of Michigan, 1st Edi-

tion.) A shrub 1–2.5 m. high; branches light red to reddish-brown; young twigs round, greenish-gray to yellowish, usually appressed-pubescent with colorless hairs; pith brown, small; petioles 1–2 cm. long, somewhat pubescent; leaves simple, opposite, deciduous, ovate, elliptic to lanceolate, 3–9 cm. long, 1–6 cm. wide, short-pointed at apex, narrowed or rounded and oblique at the base, yellow-green and more or less short appressed-pubescent above or sometimes nearly glabrous, finely appressed-pubescent and densely farinose beneath, hairs colorless; inflorescence pubescent; flowers perfect, cream-white, borne in convex cymes 3–5 cm. broad; calyx-teeth lanceolate; petals 4, narrowly oblong, acute, 4–5 mm. long; stamens 4, exserted; ovary inferior, 2-celled; style slender; stigma capitate; fruit globose, dull pale blue, about 8 mm. in diameter; stone broader than long, slightly flattened, oblique, ribbed, about 5 mm. broad. Flowers, May, July; fruit ripe, August, September.

In wet ground, Ontario southward and westward. Michigan, frequent throughout.

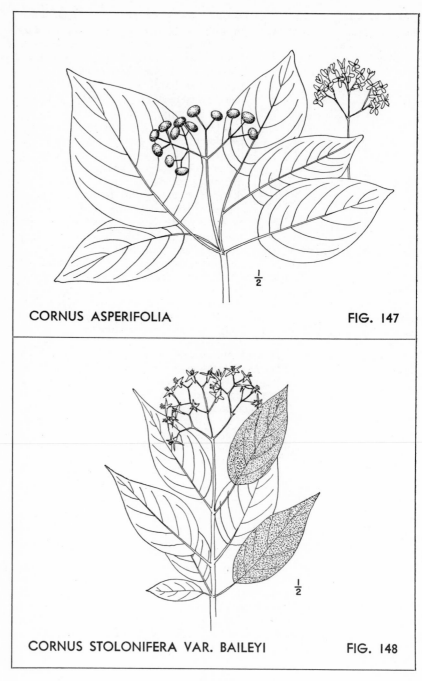

CORNUS ASPERIFOLIA   FIG. 147

$\frac{1}{2}$

CORNUS STOLONIFERA VAR. BAILEYI   FIG. 148

$\frac{1}{2}$

The Silky Cornel is the latest to bloom of any of the genus. This feature, together with its abundant pale blue fruit, gives it a decided ornamental value.

It was like parting with an old friend to give up the name *Amomum* for this dogwood. The name now adopted, *obliqua*, was not even mentioned in Gray's Manual, 7th Edition. It was included in the synonymy for *Amomum* in Britton and Brown's 'Illustrated Flora,' and to this species practically all of the records for the state have been referred. As far as the manuals covering the territory are concerned, there was no other place to which to refer them. In reference to *Cornus Amomum* Mill., Deam in his 'Shrubs of Indiana,' (1932) states: "This species has been reported for many counties by various authors, but, no doubt, all or practically all of these records should be referred to *C. obliqua*, which until recently has been confused with *Cornus Amomum,* Mill. The status of this species and that of *Cornus obliqua* is questionable. The range of the first appears to be along and east of the Allegheny Mountains, while the latter has a range west of these mountains. Since the principal difference between the species is the color of the pubescence, the latter species might be considered only a forma of the first or vice versa." This statement by Dr. Deam sums up the whole matter. The situation seems to be the same in Michigan as it is in Indiana. The species recorded meet the definition of *obliqua* better than they do that of *Amomum*, and it is therefore logical that the name which has now come into general usage should supplant the older and more familiar one.

In the Cranbrook Institute Herbarium there is one sheet which very closely meets the description of *Cornus Amomum* Mill., i.e. it has somewhat reddish hairs. It was collected in Oakland County. Dr. Deam has specimens from only two stations in southern Indiana. The shrub is clearly rare this far west, but should be looked for and reported whenever found.

Cornus asperifolia Michx. (Rough-leaved Dogwood). Fig. 147. An erect shrub, up to 3 or 4 m. in height; stems reddish-brown; branchlets rough-pubescent; leaves simple, opposite, deciduous, ovate-oval, or elliptic, acuminate at apex, rounded at base, entire, rough with a harsh pubescence above and downy beneath, 3–13 cm. long, about 6 cm. broad; petioles slender, rough-hairy; flowers, perfect, cream-white, borne in loose cymes 5–8 cm. broad, the branches and pedicels of which are rough-hairy; calyx-teeth minute; petals 4, about 3 mm. long, oblong-lanceolate; stamens 4, exserted; filament threadlike; stigma capitate; fruit globose, white, about 6 mm. in diameter; stone 5–6 mm. wide, 4–5 mm. high, variable in shape. Flowers, May, June; fruit ripe, September.

In wet soil or near streams, north shore of Lake Erie to Minnesota, Kansas and southward. Michigan, infrequent throughout.

This species resembles the Red-osier Dogwood, but its branches are brown instead of red.

Cornus stolonifera Michx. var. ***Baileyi*** (Coult. & Evans) Drescher. (Bailey's Dogwood). Fig. 148. (*Cornus Baileyi* Coult. & Evans, Gray's Manual, 7th Edition, Shrubs of Michigan, 1st Edition.) Erect shrubs, 1–3 m. tall, without stolons; stems purplish-red; branches brownish, somewhat spreading-pubescent, becoming glabrous and purplish or red, not rough; leaves simple, opposite, deciduous, ovate to ovate-lanceolate, not scabrous, appressed-pubescent above, woolly-pubescent beneath, 3–13 cm. long, 1.5–6 cm. wide, long- or short-acuminate at the apex, rounded or narrowed at the base; petioles 0.5–1.5 cm. long, pubescent; flowers white, about 6 mm. in diameter, in compact cymes, 2–5 cm. broad, the branches of which are pubescent; buds short ovoid; calyx-lobes narrowly triangular, short, very pubescent; petals ovate-oblong; stamens exserted; style cylindrical; fruit pure white, about 6 mm. in diameter; stone flattened, oblique. Flowers from May through October; fruit, July, October.

Cornus stolonifera var. Baileyi

Sandy shores, in swamps and moist rocky places, western Pennsylvania and southern Ontario to Minnesota and Manitoba. Michigan, throughout

In the first edition I called attention to the fact that *Cornus Baileyi* Coult. & Evans, which is confined principally to the Great Lakes region in its distribution, was originally considered a form of *Cornus stolonifera*, and that the white woolliness of the lower surface of the leaves seemed to be the most constant character by which to separate the two species. Instead of treating it as a separate species, recent usage has given it varietal status only, and it is so regarded here.

Bailey's Dogwood begins to bloom in May and it is not unusual to find it with flowers in October. Its fruit begins to ripen the first of July and likewise continues through the season to October. The berries are favorite food for several species of birds, which no doubt appreciate the long season.

Cornus stolonifera

Cornus stolonifera Michx. (Red-osier Dogwood). Fig. 149. An erect or spreading shrub, 1–3 m. tall, stoloniferous; bark purplish-red or bright red, becoming more vivid, especially toward spring, glabrous; young branchlets green, pubescent, becoming glabrous; leaves opposite, simple, deciduous, entire, ovate to ovate-lanceolate or oval, 5–10 cm. long, 2–4 cm. wide, narrowed or rounded at the base, abruptly short-pointed at the apex, green and short appressed-pubescent above, under side whitish and somewhat appressed-downy; petioles stoutish, 1–2 cm. long; flowers white, borne in pubescent flat cymes 2–4 cm. across; calyx with 4 minute teeth; petals 4, ovate-oblong, 3–5 mm. long; stamens 4, exserted; filaments very slender; stigma capitate; fruit globose, white or whitish, 6–7 mm. in diameter; stone variable in size and shape. Flowers, June, July; fruit, August, October.

Generally in wet places, Newfoundland to British Columbia, south to Virginia, the Great Lakes region, westward to Iowa, Nebraska, New Mexico and California. Michigan, very common throughout.

The Red-osier is a very common northern shrub. It will be found in abundance in swampy areas, where its glowing red-purple stems and branches are conspicuous, particularly in the winter against the snow.

Cornus racemosa Lam. (Panicled Dogwood). Fig. 150. (*Cornus paniculata* L'Hér., Gray's Manual, 7th Edition, Shrubs of Michigan, 1st Edition.)

Erect branching shrub 1–2.5 m. tall; stems, branches and twigs smooth and gray; leaves deciduous, opposite, simple, entire, ovate-lanceolate, wedge-shaped or obtuse at base, long-acuminate at the apex, 4–8 cm. long, 2–4 cm. wide, minutely appressed-pubescent on both sides, pale beneath; flowers perfect, cream-white, about 6 mm. in diameter, borne in loose convex cymes, the peduncle and branches more or less appressed-pubescent; calyx lobes triangular, minute; petals 4, lanceolate, spreading; stamens 4, exserted; filaments threadlike, inserted with the petals; ovary 2-celled, silvery-pubescent; stigma capitate; drupes on bright red pedicels, globose, white, 5–6 mm. in diameter; stone subglobose, slightly furrowed. Flowers, May, June; fruit, July, September.

In dry and wet places, Maine to Ontario, Minnesota and southward. Michigan, common in Lower Peninsula; occurs also in Upper Peninsula.

The Panicled Dogwood is one of our most common shrubs. It grows abundantly along the roadsides and in fence rows bordering our fields and woods. It grows on the banks of streams and on hillsides, and everywhere it makes a beautiful appearance when in flower. Its white fruit is set off to advantage by the bright red fruit-stalks, making it a doubly attractive shrub.

Cornus alternifolia L. f. (Alternate-leaved Dogwood). Fig. 151. A shrub or small tree, 2–6 m. tall; bark smooth, brownish on older stems; branches greenish, streaked with white; leaves simple, deciduous, alternate, entire, often clustered at the ends of the branches, ovate, obovate or oval, long-pointed, 5–9 cm. long, 3–6 cm. wide, mostly narrowed at the base, whitish and minutely pubescent beneath, yellow-green, at first pubescent, soon becoming glabrous above; petiole slender, 1–7 cm. long; flowers white, borne in a broad

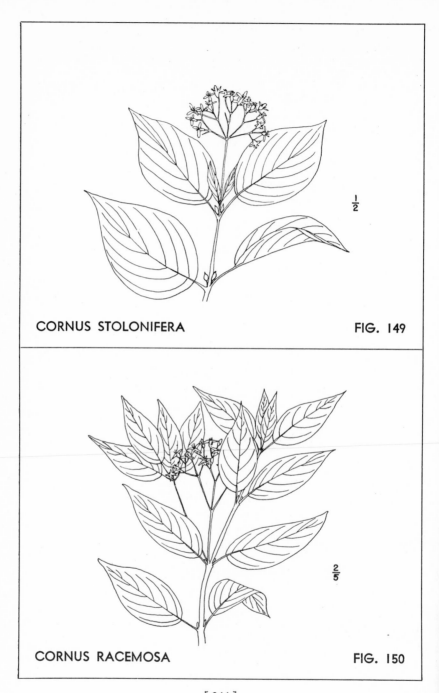

CORNUS STOLONIFERA

FIG. 149

$\frac{1}{2}$

CORNUS RACEMOSA

FIG. 150

$\frac{2}{5}$

Cornus alternifolia

open cymose panicle, the peduncle stout, glabrous, the branches pubescent; sepals minute or obsolete; petals ovate-oblong, 3–3.5 mm. long; stamens exserted; stigma capitate: ovary densely pubescent; drupe globose, 6–8 mm. in diameter, deep blue on reddish stalks; stone obovoid, shallowly channeled. Flowers, May, July; fruit, September.

In woods and copses, New Brunswick west to Minnesota and southward to Georgia, Alabama and Iowa. Michigan, frequent throughout.

Unlike all the other dogwoods, this species has alternate leaves. It is often used in landscape work and its green stems and twigs give excellent results when grouped with other dogwoods for winter color effects.

ERICACEAE—Heath Family

Shrubs or herbs, often evergreen; flowers regular or nearly so; calyx free from the ovary, 4–5-parted or cleft, generally persistent; petals 4–5, more or less completely united; stamens usually 8–10, or at times the same number as the petals; style 1; ovary 3–10-celled; fruit a capsule, berry or drupe; seeds small.

The Heath family is a very large one, comprising several well-marked subfamilies or tribes which by some authors are treated as families. Altogether there are about 90 genera and some 1400 species, the following of which, classifiable as shrubby plants, are found in Michigan.

1. Leaves evergreen
  2. Prostrate or creeping plants
    3. Leaves 1–4 cm. wide; fruit a capsule or berry-like
      4. Leaves narrowed to the base, margin serrate; stems puberulent;
        foliage with wintergreen-flavor; fruit red, berry-like........*Gaultheria,* p. 257
      4. Leaves cordate at base, margin entire; stems with bristly hairs;
        not wintergreen-flavored; fruit a capsule...............................*Epigaea,* p. 256
    3. Leaves 2–10 mm. wide; fruit a berry
      5. Stems covered with brown hairs; leaves with coarse, brown
        scale-like hairs on the lower surface, elliptical, thin;
        fruit a white berry..*Chiogenes,* p. 259
      5. Stems not covered with brown hairs or scales;
        fruit a red, purple or blue berry
        6. Leaves glaucous on the lower surface
          7. Leaves oblong or ovate, 3–8 mm. long, strongly revolute;
            bracts of pedicel mostly narrow, involute, borne near
            the middle; berry globose,
            6–8 mm. in diameter......................*Vaccinium Oxycoccos,* p. 273
          7. Leaves oblong, 6–17 mm. long, only slightly revolute;
            bracts of pedicel generally flat,
            borne above the middle...............*Vaccinium macrocarpon,* p. 275
        6. Leaves green on the lower surface

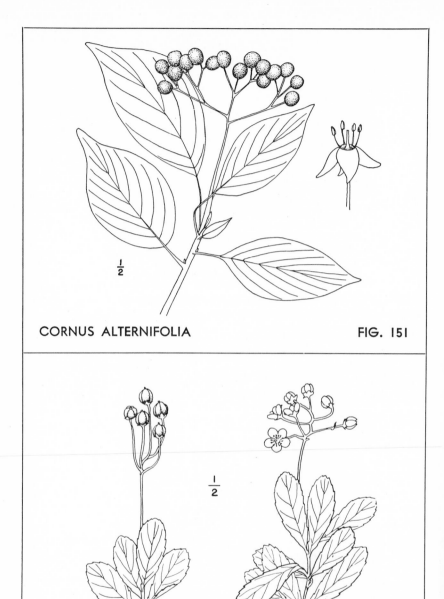

CORNUS ALTERNIFOLIA   FIG. 151

CHIMAPHILA UMBELLATA VAR. CISATLANTICA   FIG. 152

[246]

8. Leaves with black dots on the lower surface, mostly 15–30 mm.
long, oval or slightly obovate..............*Vaccinium Vitis-Idaea* var. *minus,* p. 273

8. Leaves without black dots on the lower surface,
mostly 6–15 mm. long, obovate-spatulate........................*Arctostaphylos,* p. 259

2. Erect plants

    9. Leaves with strongly revolute margins

        10. Leaves densely woolly beneath......................................*Ledum,* p. 249

        10. Leaves merely whitened beneath, not woolly

            11. Leaves opposite...*Kalmia polifolia,* p. 253

            11. Leaves alternate.............................. ....*Andromeda,* p. 253

    9. Leaf margins not revolute

        12. Leaves alternate or somewhat whorled or scattered

            13. Leaves alternate, oblong, obtuse, crenulate,
lower surface covered with yellow scurf;
flowers in 1-sided racemes...........................*Chamaedaphne,* p. 256

            13. Leaves somewhat whorled or scattered, wedge- or
ovate-lanceolate, sharply serrate, lower surface
not covered with yellow scurf;
flowers in few-flowered umbels...........................*Chimaphila,* p. 247

        12. Leaves opposite..*Kalmia angustifolia,* p. 251

1. Leaves deciduous (except in 3 species of *Vaccinium* keyed above)

    14. Lower surface of leaves covered with yellow resinous glands or
dots; branchlets gray or brown; fruit a capsule or berry

        15. Fruit a globose capsule...*Lyonia,* p. 255

        15. Fruit a berry with 10 seed-like nutlets..............................*Gaylussacia,* p. 261

    14. Lower surface of leaves not covered with yellow resinous glands or
dots (leaves persistent in 3 species keyed above), branchlets greenish
or reddish; fruit a many-seeded berry.......................................*Vaccinium,* p. 263

Chimaphila Pursh—PRINCE'S PINES, PIPSISSEWAS

Leaves wedge-lanceolate, not spotted with white.............*C. umbellata* var. *cisatlantica,* p. 247

Leaves ovate-lanceolate, spotted or lined with white..............................*C. maculata,* p. 249

Chimaphila umbellata (L.) Bart. var. ***cisatlantica*** Blake. (Prince's
Pine, Pipsissewa). Fig. 152. (*Chimaphila umbellata* L., Gray's Manual, 7th

: Chimaphila umbellata var. cisatlantica

Edition.) Low, semi-herbaceous plants, with
upright stems from long-running underground shoots; stems 1–4 dm. tall; leaves
evergreen, thick, leathery, shining, not
spotted or lined with white, more or less
crowded toward the summit of the stems,
wedge-lanceolate, sharply serrate, 2–6 cm.
long, 0.8–2 cm. wide; petioles 3–6 mm.
long; peduncles 6–10 cm. high, 2–8-flowered;
pedicels about 1 cm. long; sepals 5, very
small, persistent in fruit; petals 5, nearly
orbicular, separate, white, pinkish or roseate;
stamens 10; anthers violet; style very short,
obconic; stigma large, orbicular; capsule
erect, depressed-globose, splitting downward

[247]

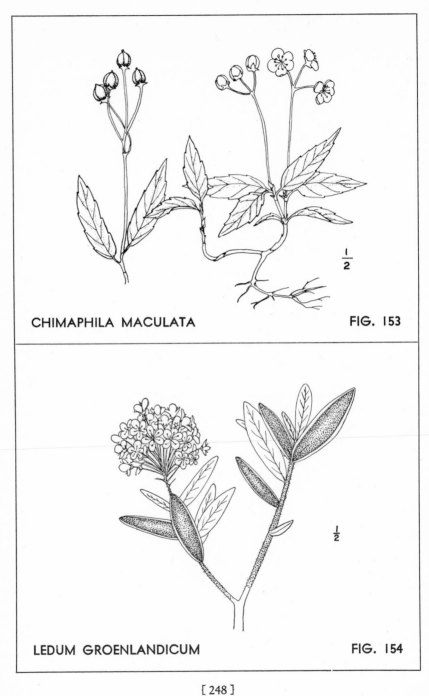

CHIMAPHILA MACULATA   FIG. 153

LEDUM GROENLANDICUM   FIG. 154

from the top; seeds numerous, minute. Flowers, June; capsules ripe in autumn.

In dry woods, Quebec, northern New Brunswick, Prince Edward Island and Nova Scotia to Virginia and Georgia. Michigan, common throughout.

With the change of names above indicated, another old familiar friend is benched, to use a highly unscientific American phrase. Genuine *Chimaphila umbellata* L. is now determined to be confined to Eurasia. Blake (1917), distinguishes four varieties, of which *cisatlantica* includes Michigan within its distributional range. His variety *occidentalis* is given a range from British Columbia to California, but in the University of Michigan Herbarium there is a specimen identified by Fernald as *occidentalis;* also one by Hermann from the same locality. It appears therefore that in this plant Michigan has still another with that greatly disjunct distribution which has attracted so much attention from systematists, geologists and biogeographers.

One colloquial name for this little plant is King's-cure, which seems to indicate that either a monarch or a family by the name of King used it successfully as a medicine.

Chimaphila maculata (L.) Pursh. (Spotted Wintergreen). Fig. 153. Similar to the preceding species, but commonly more slender, extensively trailing; stems 1–2.5 dm. tall; leaves lanceolate or ovate-lanceolate, obtuse at base, remotely sharp-toothed, dark green and variegated with white on the upper surface, 2.5–7.5 cm. long, 0.5–1.7 cm. wide below the middle; peduncles 1–5-flowered, puberulent; flowers white or pinkish; petals 5, roundish; sepals 5, persistent; stamens 10; style very short, obconic; capsule erect, depressed-globose, opening from the top; seeds very numerous, minute. Flowers, June; capsules ripe in autumn.

Chimaphila maculata

In dry woods, Maine and Ontario to Minnesota, south to Georgia and Mississippi. Michigan: in relation to the distribution of this species Beal (1904) says, "Rare or local." Recorded specimens are from the Lower Peninsula only.

Common names often reveal the uses which have been made of a plant or the manner in which it was regarded by the people at some time in the past. Judging by these names, Spotted Wintergreen seems to have been a very versatile plant. Rheumatism-root indicates that it was used as a medicine in treating rheumatism; Ratsbane, as a poison in combating these rodents; Dragon's-tongue, that it was not regarded very highly in some quarters—a rather awesome plant; and Wild Arsenic, that it was poisonous and no doubt to be avoided.

Ledum L.—Labrador Teas

Ledum groenlandicum Oeder. (Labrador Tea). Fig. 154. Erect evergreen shrub, 3–10 dm. tall; bark gray; twigs brown-woolly; leaves simple, alternate, persistent, entire, oblong or linear-oblong, 2–5 cm. long, very obtuse, margins revolute, upper surface green, midrib depressed, lower surface completely

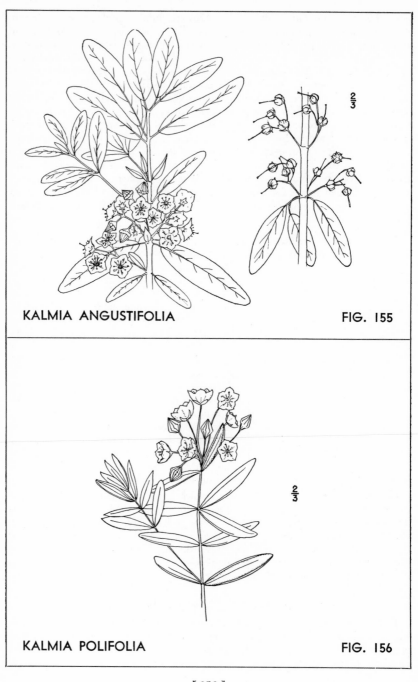

KALMIA ANGUSTIFOLIA

FIG. 155

KALMIA POLIFOLIA

FIG. 156

clothed with rusty wool; petiole about 2 mm. long; flowers in dense terminal clusters, white; sepals 5, united; petals 5, narrowly ovate, free; stamens 5–7, exserted; pistil 5-parted; ovary free from the calyx; fruit a slender capsule splitting from the base upward, many-seeded. Flowers, May, June; fruit, August, September.

Ledum groenlandicum

Ranges from Greenland to Alaska south to New Jersey, Pennsylvania, Michigan, Wisconsin, Minnesota, Washington. Its habitat is bogs, damp thickets and mountain slopes, where it is common northward. Michigan, common in Upper Peninsula and northern portion of the Lower Peninsula.

Labrador Tea is essentially a citizen of the northland and an interesting example of a plant fitted to hold its own in a subarctic climate. It carries a thick woolly coat over its stems and on the under surface of its leaves which tends to prevent the loss of water through evaporation in cold, drying weather. In Michigan it follows that it is more common northward, but like many of the northern plants, it is found in the bogs of our southern counties, where it grows in association with the Pale Laurel. They bloom at the same time and it is difficult to imagine a more beautiful combination than the pink and white flowers make as they mingle together among the green leaves with their reflections mirrored in a pool of dark bog-water.

Kalmia L.—LAURELS

Leaves pale and glabrate beneath, not strongly revolute; twigs terete; corymbs lateral; flowers crimson..*K. angustifolia*, p. 251
Leaves white-glaucous beneath, strongly revolute; 2-edged corymbs terminal; flowers rose-purple..*K. polifolia*, p. 253

Kalmia angustifolia L. (Sheep Laurel, Lambkill, Wicky). Fig. 155. Low, erect, evergreen shrub, rarely 1 m. tall; bark grayish-brown; branches terete, glabrous or nearly so; leaves simple, persistent, mostly opposite or verticillate in 3's, pale and glabrate underneath, dark green above, narrowly oblong, obtuse or sometimes acute, 2.5–6.5 cm. long, 6–22 mm. wide; petiole short; flowers in lateral compound or simple corymbs, slightly glandular, purple or crimson; corolla saucer-shaped, the limb with 10 pouches receiving 10 anthers; pedicels filiform, 12–24 mm. long, recurved in fruit; sepals 5, ovate, acute, glandular, persistent; fruit capsule depressed-globose, nearly smooth, 3–4 mm. in diameter; seeds small, subglobose. Flowers, June, July; fruit, September.

Kalmia angustifolia

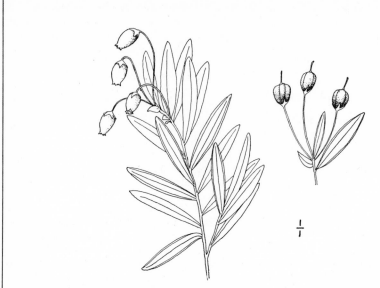

ANDROMEDA POLIFOLIA   FIG. 157

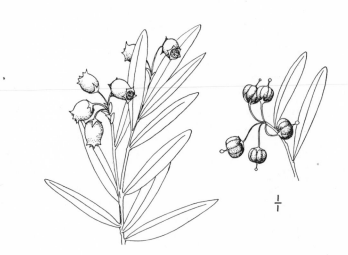

ANDROMEDA GLAUCOPHYLLA   FIG. 158

The Sheep Laurel is found on hillsides, in pastures and bogs from Labrador to Ontario and southward. Michigan, upper part of Lower Peninsula.

As indicated by one of its common names, Lambkill, this laurel is credited with killing lambs. It also kills young calves. It is said that the older cattle know enough to let the plants alone, but that in the early spring when the tender leaves appear, the calves and young cattle eager for green food eat them and, unless promptly treated, die.

Kalmia polifolia Wang. (Pale Laurel, Swamp Laurel). Fig. 156. Low, straggling, evergreen shrub, 1–6 dm. tall; twigs 2-edged; leaves simple, persistent, opposite or sometimes in 3's, sessile

or nearly so, oblong or linear-oblong, white-glaucous beneath, green above, 1–3 cm. long, 2–10 mm. wide, margins entire and revolute, tip blunt-pointed; flowers few, in terminal clusters or umbels, rose-purple, about 1.5 cm. across; corolla saucer-shaped, 5-lobed with 10 tiny sacs in the saucer into which the stamens are thrust; pedicels thread-like, 1–3.5 cm. long, erect even in fruit; sepals ovate, scarious-margined, persistent; capsule ovoid, smooth, about 5 mm. in diameter. Flowers, May, July; fruit, autumn.

In cold bogs and on the mountains, Labrador to Alaska, south to New Jersey, Pennsylvania, Michigan, Minnesota and California. Michigan, infrequent throughout.

This beautiful little shrub is found in our deepest bogs. The blossoms are similar to those of the well-known Mountain Laurel, but much smaller and a fewer number in each cluster. Where it occurs in great abundance, as it sometimes does in our northern swamps, it produces magnificent color effects.

Andromeda L.—Wild Rosemaries

Leaves white beneath with close, fine pubescence...............................*A. glaucophylla*, p. 255
Leaves whitened beneath with a varnish-like coat...*A. Polifolia*, p. 253

Andromeda Polifolia L. (Wild Rosemary). Fig. 157. Low, glabrous, evergreen shrub with elongate creeping base; stem simple with ascending branches; bark brownish to gray; leaves simple, alternate, persistent, linear-oblong or lanceolate-oblong, flat or revolute, glabrous, generally whitened beneath with a varnish-like coat, later often green, tip mucronulate, narrowed at base, 2.5–6.5 cm. long, 4–8 mm. wide; petioles about 2 mm. long; flowers white, small, drooping in terminal umbels; pedicels filiform, straightish, 2–4 times longer than the nodding flower and erect fruit; corolla urceolate, with 5 recurved teeth; stamens 10, included; calyx 5-parted, persistent; capsule subglobose, brown or reddish, as high as broad; seeds small, oval, shining. Flowers, May, June; fruit, autumn.

[253]

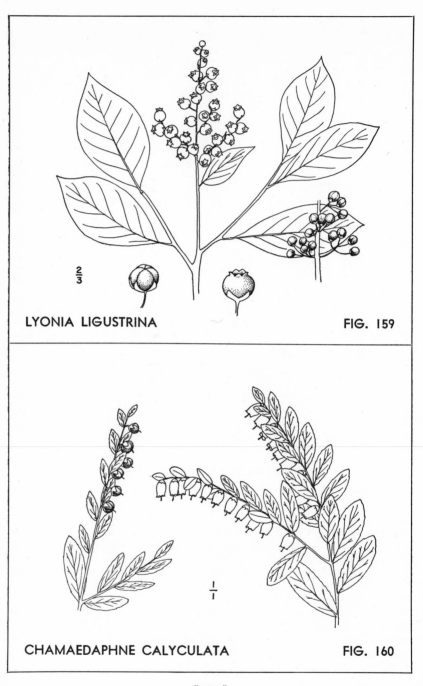

$\frac{2}{3}$

LYONIA LIGUSTRINA   FIG. 159

$\frac{1}{1}$

CHAMAEDAPHNE CALYCULATA   FIG. 160

Andromeda Polifolia

Found in the Arctic regions, but extending very locally south to the Adirondack Mountains, Great Lakes region. Michigan, infrequent throughout.

As with some of the other Arctic plants, this species grows only in our deep sphagnum bogs.

Andromeda glaucophylla Link. (Bog Rosemary). Fig. 158. Low, branching evergreen shrub, 5–30 cm. tall; bark brown to gray; branches glaucous; leaves simple, alternate, persistent, linear, 2–5 cm. long, 2–5 mm. wide, leathery, dark green above, white beneath with close, fine pubescence, margins revolute, acute and mucronate at apex, base wedge-shaped, midrib prominent; flowers in small terminal umbel-like clusters on thickish curved pedicels rarely twice the flower length; corolla 5-parted, white or pinkish, about 6 mm. long; calyx-lobes whitish, usually spreading; capsule depressed, turban-shaped, glaucous; seeds numerous, shining, light brown. Flowers, May, June; fruit, autumn.

Andromeda glaucophylla

Appropriate to its name the Bog Rosemary is found in bogs and on wet shores from Labrador to Manitoba, south to New Jersey, Pennsylvania and Minnesota. Michigan, frequent throughout.

This species has a much wider distribution in Michigan than the former. There is considerable confusion in the two species of *Andromeda* here given, some authors treating them as one species.

Lyonia Nutt.—PRIVET ANDROMEDAS

Lyonia ligustrina

Lyonia ligustrina (L.) DC. (Privet Andromeda). Fig. 159. A much branched shrub 0.5–3 m. tall; twigs minutely pubescent or glabrous; leaves simple, alternate, deciduous, obovate, oblong, oval or lanceolate-oblong, 2.5–6.5 cm. long, acute at each end, or abruptly acuminate at the apex, serrulate or entire, mostly glabrous above, more or less pubescent on the veins below, or older leaves entirely glabrous; petiole short; flowers small, white, borne in numerous terminal many-flowered mostly leafless panicles; bracts small, soon falling; pedicels pubescent, 2–6 mm. long; calyx 5-lobed, the lobes triangular-ovate, acute; corolla globular,

5-toothed, the teeth recurved, mostly 3–4 mm. wide; stamens 8–10, included; filaments flat, pubescent, incurved, not appendaged; ovary 4–5-celled; style columnar; stigma truncate; capsule depressed-globose, obtusely 5-angled; seeds numerous, elongated. Flowers, June, July; fruit, autumn.

Moist thickets, central Maine to central New York and southward. Michigan, rare. It will be noted that the Michigan stations are far west of the general range of this shrub.

Chamaedaphne Moench—LEATHERLEAF

Chamaedaphne calyculata (L.) Moench. (Leatherleaf, Cassandra). Fig. 160. An erect, branched, evergreen shrub 3–10 dm. tall; branches slender, with minute scurfy scales when young; leaves sim-
ple, alternate, evergreen, oblong, obtuse, flat, thick, coriaceous, scurfy beneath, 1–4 cm. long, 5–15 mm. wide, apex pointed, rounded at the base; petioles short; flowers in leafy racemes; calyx of 5 distinct, acute sepals; corolla cylindric, of 5 united petals, white, about 5 mm. long; stamens 10, included; fruit a 5-celled depressed capsule, about 4 mm. across; seeds small and very numerous. Flowers, April, June; fruit, autumn.

Chamaedaphne calyculata

The Leatherleaf has a range from Labrador to British Columbia south to Minne-
sota, Wisconsin, Illinois and Georgia; found in bogs, Michigan, common throughout.

This shrub forms large beds in swamps or boggy meadows, and a *Chamaedaphne* swamp is one of our best marked ecological associations.

The Heath family plants are not subject to as great variation as those of the Rosaceae, but some varieties have been proposed. *Chamaedaphne calyculata* (L.) Moench var. *angustifolia* (Ait.) Rehd., with the leaves linear-lanceolate and wavy on the margin, is recorded from Kalamazoo County by Hanes.

Epigaea L.—TRAILING ARBUTUS

Epigaea repens L. (Trailing Arbutus, Ground Laurel). Fig. 161. A prostrate or trailing semi-herbaceous plant, bristly with rusty hairs; leaves simple, alternate, evergreen, oval, oblong, ovate, reticulated, rough-hairy, rounded or heart-shaped at the base, rounded or acute at the apex, green both sides, 2–7 cm. long, 1.5–4 cm. wide; petioles pubescent, 1–3.5 cm. long; flowers pink or white in terminal clusters; sepals 5, oblong, persistent; corolla salver-form, with a 5-lobed limb; stamens 10, with slender filaments; style columnar; stigma 5-lobed; capsule depressed-globular, 5-lobed and 5-celled; seeds many, oval, dark brown. Flowers, April, May; fruit, summer.

In sandy or rocky woods from Newfoundland to Saskatchewan, Wisconsin, Michigan, Kentucky and Florida. Michigan, rare in the southern counties, frequent in the central portion and common northward.

Plants of Trailing Arbutus from the southern portion of the range apparently have a tendency toward rough leaf surfaces, while those of the northern extremes are more nearly smooth or glabrate. On the basis of this character it has been proposed to recognize two geographic varieties, in which case the

southern form would retain the original name, *Epigaea repens* L., the northern form being separated as *Epigaea repens* L. var. *glabrifolia* Fern.

To ascertain the exact nomenclatorial status of our plants, some seventy-odd herbarium sheets of *Epigaea* from Michigan and other locations were examined and compared. Michigan is near the middle of the geographical range, and plants from this state exhibit both the northern and the southern characteristics; on one plant, both hairy and smooth leaves are often present. This, no doubt, is to be expected. It was, therefore, concluded that the specific name, *repens*, used in the first edition, should be retained, particularly in a work intended primarily for amateur use.

The Trailing Arbutus blooms early in the spring, sometimes before the snow is entirely gone from the hollows of the woods, exhaling a rich, spicy fragrance, and is probably our best known wild flower. For that reason it has been gathered almost to the point of extermination. If it is picked at all it should be done with the greatest care.

Gaultheria [Kalm] L.—AROMATIC WINTERGREENS

Gaultheria procumbens L. (Teaberry, Checkerberry, Aromatic Wintergreen). Fig. 162. Low creeping, aromatic shrubs having underground stems,

with erect branches; leaves simple, alternate, evergreen, borne at the top of the branches, thick and leathery, smooth, dark glossy-green above, paler below, oval to nearly orbicular, 2–5 cm. long, 1–3 cm. wide, margin crenate with shallow teeth, bristle-tipped, mostly rounded or sometimes wedge-shaped at the tip, narrowed or rarely rounded at the base; petioles 2–5 mm. long, more or less pubescent; flowers white or pale pink, single in the axils of the leaves, on curved peduncles 4–8 mm. long, with 2 bracteoles close under the calyx; calyx 5-parted, persistent; corolla ovoid-urceolate, 4–6 mm. long, 5-toothed; fruit a depressed-globose berry formed of the calyx, slightly 5-lobed, bright red when ripe, 8–12 mm. in diameter, mealy, very spicy; seeds numerous, small. Flowers, June, September; fruit remaining on over the winter.

From Newfoundland to Manitoba, south to Georgia, Tennessee, Michigan and Minnesota, the Aromatic Wintergreen is found growing in thin, sandy woods. Michigan, common throughout.

[257]

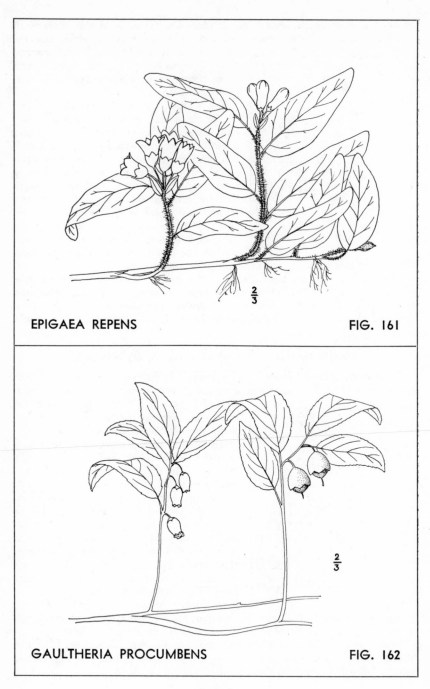

EPIGAEA REPENS

$\frac{2}{3}$

FIG. 161

GAULTHERIA PROCUMBENS

$\frac{2}{3}$

FIG. 162

The Wintergreen is one of our most interesting little plants. All parts of it, especially the fruit and leaves, contain the fragrant oil of wintergreen which is used in perfumery and in medicine. The commercial product, however, is generally made from the twigs and leaves of the black birch, which is lower in cost. A synthetic wintergreen oil is also made. The ripe fruit remains on the plant until May and June of the following season.

Arctostaphylos Adans.—BEARBERRIES

Arctostaphylos Uva-ursi (L.) Spreng. var. *coactilis* Fern. & Macbr. (Bearberry). Fig. 163 (*Arctostaphylos Uva-ursi* (L.) Spreng. Gray's Manual,

Arctostaphylos Uva-ursi var. coactilis

7th Edition, Shrubs of Michigan, 1st Edition.) Trailing shrub; branches often rooting at the nodes; bark gray and rough, becoming smooth and reddish-brown; branchlets canescent-tomentose, not viscid, the minute tomentum persistent; leaves simple, evergreen, alternate, spatulate, obtuse, entire, glabrous or minutely puberulent toward the base, 1–1.5 cm. long, 5–7 mm. wide, finely reticulate-veined; petioles about 2 mm. long; flowers few, in short terminal racemes, white to pale pink; pedicels 2–4 mm. long, recurved; sepals 4–5, short, rounded; corolla ovoid, throat constricted, about 6 mm. long; stamens 8–10, included; fruit a globose drupe, bright cherry-red, 5–10 mm. in diameter, dry and inedible; seed, 5 coalescent nutlets. Flowers, May, June; fruit ripe, July, September, remaining on all winter.

Dry, sandy or rocky soil, Labrador to Alaska, New Jersey, Pennsylvania, Illinois, Nebraska, Colorado and California. Michigan, throughout; common northward, but rare southward.

The Bearberry from America was given the same specific name as the European plant when first studied. Subsequent investigations have disclosed the fact, however, that it is varietally different over a large portion of its range. To quote from an article on the plant in Vol. 16 of *Rhodora* by Fernald and Macbride: "The commonest variety in North America is a shrub with the branches invested with a dense canescent almost felt-like minute tomentum, which is persistent at least for several years. This variety which is apparently restricted to North America, does not extend so far north as the typical form of the species, but is very general through the southern half of its range, especially in the east." Michigan is within the range of one of the varieties and, while it is possible the typical form may be found here, the herbarium material available clearly belongs under the heading of the variety *coactilis*, which means felt-like or closely pubescent.

The shrub has a number of common names, among which may be mentioned Foxberry, Mealberry, Bear's Grape, Barren Myrtle, Bilberry, Kinnikinnick.

Chiogenes Salisb.—CREEPING SNOWBERRIES

Chiogenes hispidula (L.) T.&G. (Creeping Snowberry, Moxie Plum,

[259]

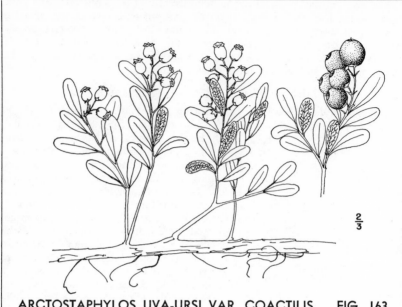

$\frac{2}{3}$

ARCTOSTAPHYLOS UVA-URSI VAR. COACTILIS   FIG. 163

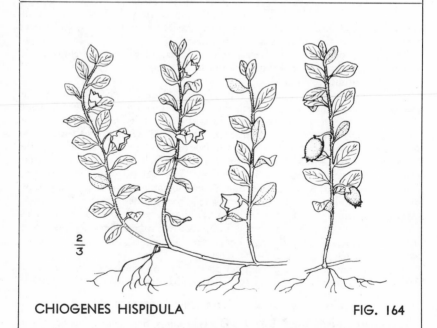

$\frac{2}{3}$

CHIOGENES HISPIDULA   FIG. 164

Capillaire). Fig. 164. Creeping, prostrate, evergreen branching shrub; branches strigose-pubescent, brown; leaves elliptical, 5–9 mm. long, 4–7 mm. wide, acute at the apex, rounded or narrowed at the base, entire, thin, margin revolute, dark green and glabrous above, sprinkled with appressed stiff, brownish hairs below; petiole about 1 mm. long; flowers few, axillary, solitary, about 4 mm.

long; calyx-limb 4-cleft, attached to the lower half of the ovary; corolla bell-shaped, 4-cleft, the lobes rounded; stamens 8, included; ovary 4-celled; style short; berry snow-white, globose, about 8 mm. in diameter; seeds numerous. Flowers, May, June; berries ripe, August, September.

In cold wet woods and bogs, Newfoundland to British Columbia, south to North Carolina and Michigan. Michigan, infrequent throughout.

This little aromatic plant has the flavor of Sweet Birch, and one of its common names is Running Birch. Another, indicating its delicate form, is Maidenhair-berry.

To the nature lover, few experiences can equal the discovery of a patch of Creeping Snowberry trailing on a rotting log in a deep tamarack bog.

Gaylussacia HBK—Huckleberries

Gaylussacia baccata (Wang.) K. Koch. (Black Huckleberry). Fig. 165. Much branched shrub, 3–15 dm. tall; twigs more or less pubescent; leaves

simple, alternate, deciduous, oval, oblong-ovate, or oblong, 2–4 cm. long, 1–2 cm. wide, acute, obtuse or rounded at the apex, base wedge-shaped, tough and leathery, thickly clothed beneath with shining resinous globules, margin entire, ciliate, green on both sides; petioles about 2 mm. long, pubescent; flowers in small lateral one-sided racemes; pedicels about the length of the flower, resinous-dotted as well as the peduncle, bracts and bractlets reddish; calyx-tube glabrous, covered with resinous scales, soon deciduous, tips of lobes broadly triangular; corolla ovoid-conical or oblong, reddish, 3–5 mm. long; stamens 10, included; fruit a black drupe, with bloom, about 7 mm. in diameter, edible; seeds about 10, more or less grown together. Flowers, May, June; fruit ripe, July.

Rocky woodlands, swamps and bogs, Newfoundland to Manitoba south to Georgia and Kentucky. Michigan, frequent throughout.

This huckleberry is exceedingly variable in leaves, flowers and fruit. Several

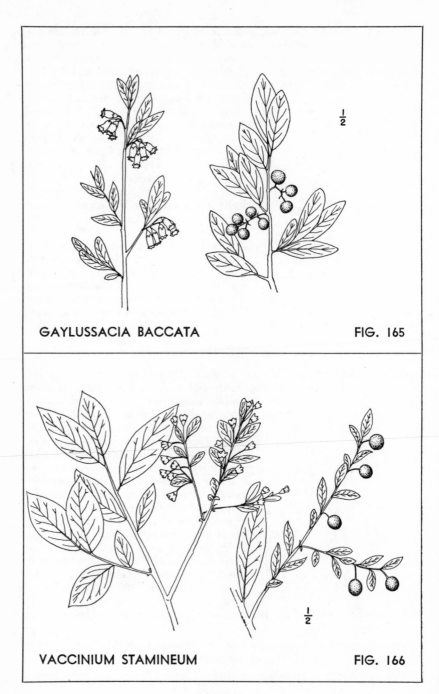

GAYLUSSACIA BACCATA   FIG. 165

VACCINIUM STAMINEUM   FIG. 166

forms have been separated and named. Forma *glaucocarpa* (Rob.) Mackenzie has blue fruit with a bloom, while forma *leucocarpa* (Porter) Fern. has its berries white to pinkish.

Vaccinium L.—BLUEBERRIES, CRANBERRIES

1. Leaves deciduous; shrubs with erect or ascending stems
  2. Low shrubs, 2–15 dm. high
    3. Leaves glaucous or very pale on the lower surface
      4. Berries greenish-yellow; branchlets recurved, spreading, hairy, not covered with speckles; leaves ovate or oval, pubescent; corolla open-campanulate, 5-lobed............*V. stamineum*, p. 263
      4. Berries blue and shrub otherwise not as above
        5. Leaves entire, elliptical, obtuse; corolla ellipsoid to globular, 4–5-toothed; filaments glabrous.....*V. ovalifolium*, p. 273
        5. Leaves entire or minutely ciliate-serrate, obovate or oval; corolla cylindraceous to campanulate, 5-toothed; filaments hairy.......................*V. vacillans*, p. 267
    3. Leaves bright green on the lower surface
      6. Margins of leaves entire
        7. Leaves oblong lanceolate, 2–4 cm. long, very pubescent; branches hairy and covered with speckles; berries blue................................*V. myrtilloides*, p. 266
        7. Leaves oblong-lanceolate, 2–4 cm. long, glabrous or nearly so; berries black...................*V. uliginosum*, p. 269
      6. Margins of leaves serrate or serrulate
        8. Berries black; leaves ovate, oval or oblong, acute or pointed, serrulate, 2–7 cm. long, nearly smooth; branchlets somewhat angled.........................*V. membranaceum*, p. 271
        8. Berries blue and shrub otherwise not as above
          9. Leaves lanceolate or oblong-lanceolate, serrulate, 1.5–3.5 cm. long; branches grooved or lined, warty......................*V. pennsylvanicum*, p. 265
          9. Leaves obovate or spatulate, 1–4 cm. long, serrate; branches round...................*V. caespitosum*, p. 271
  2. Tall shrubs, 1–4 m. high
    10. Leaves smooth or only slightly pubescent, half-grown at flowering time; berries blue-black with a bloom........*V. corymbosum*, p. 267
    10. Leaves downy or woolly underneath, expanded at flowering time; berries polished-black without bloom....*V. atrococcum*, p. 269
1. Leaves persistent, leathery; stems trailing or creeping
  11. Stems somewhat tufted, forming mats; leaves dotted with black bristle-points below; berry dark red.......................*V. Vitis-Idaea* var. *minus*, p. 273
  11. Stems very slender, creeping or trailing; leaves not black-dotted below; berry bright red
    12. Leaves oblong or ovate, 3–8 mm. long, strongly revolute; berry globose, 6–8 mm. in diameter; bracts of pedicels mostly narrow, involute, colored, borne near or below the middle............*V. Oxycoccos*, p. 273
    12. Leaves oblong elliptic, 6–17 mm. long, slightly revolute; berry not · globose, 1–2 cm. in diameter; bracts of the pedicel generally flat, green (foliaceous), borne above the middle................*V. macrocarpon*, p. 275

Vaccinium stamineum L. (Deerberry, Squaw Huckleberry). Fig. 166. A divergently branched shrub, 6–15 dm. tall; branches more or less pubescent; leaves simple, alternate, deciduous, ovate, oval or sometimes obovate, acute or acuminate at the apex, rounded or cordate at the base, entire, firm, green above,

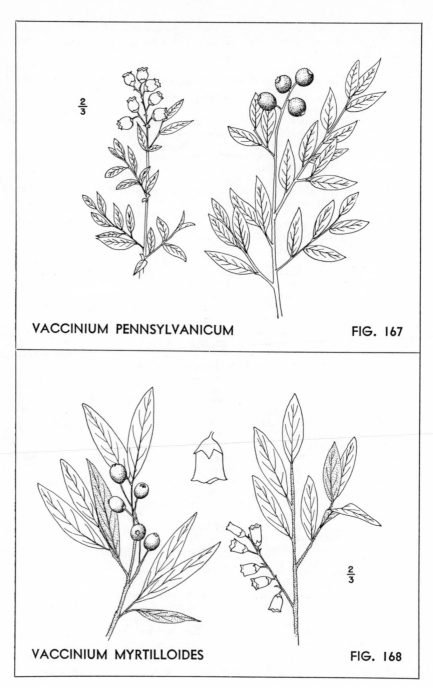

$\frac{2}{3}$

VACCINIUM PENNSYLVANICUM   FIG. 167

$\frac{2}{3}$

VACCINIUM MYRTILLOIDES   FIG. 168

Vaccinium stamineum

pale beneath and more or less pubescent, 2.5–10 cm. long, 1.2–3.5 cm. wide; petiole short, pubescent; flowers very numerous, borne in graceful, leafy-bracted racemes; calyx essentially glabrous, 5-toothed; corolla open-campanulate, 5-lobed, white or with a purplish tinge, greenish-white or yellowish-green, 4–6 mm. long, 6–10 mm. broad; stamens 10, exserted; anthers upwardly prolonged into tubes; style exserted; berries greenish-white, yellowish or dull red, globular or pear-shaped, 8–10 mm. in diameter, inedible; seeds few, pitted. Flowers, May, June; fruit, September.

Dry woods and thickets, Maine, Massachusetts to Ontario, Minnesota, Arkansas, Kentucky and Alabama. Michigan, recorded only from Washtenaw County.

The Deerberry is said to flourish in cultivation, where with proper handling it develops into a very fine shrub.

Vaccinium pennsylvanicum Lam. (Low Sweet Blueberry, Early Sweet Blueberry). Fig. 167. Dwarf, upright shrub, 2.5–5 dm. tall; stems yellow-green,

Vaccinium pennsylvanicum

warty with pubescent lines; leaves simple, alternate, deciduous, lanceolate or oblong-lanceolate, 1.5–3.5 cm. long, 0.5–1.5 cm. wide, acute at the apex, narrowed at the base, margin distinctly serrulate with bristle-pointed teeth, thin, bright green, smooth both sides, or sometimes with a few hairs on the midrib beneath; petioles short, ciliate; flowers borne in few-flowered racemes generally with the leaves; bracts reddish; calyx attached to the ovary, 5-toothed; corolla white or pinkish, 6–7 mm. long, cylindric-bell-shaped, 5-toothed, teeth acute, somewhat reflexed; stamens 10, included; filaments short, hairy; style straight, very slightly exserted; berry globular, 6–10 mm. in diameter, blue with a bloom. Flowers, May, June; fruit, July, August.

In dry, rocky or sandy soil, Newfoundland to southern New Jersey, westward to Illinois and Michigan. Michigan, throughout.

This is the earliest of the blueberries. Its typical habitat is thin sandy soil, covering the ground in many sections of our state and furnishing a considerable portion of the market blueberries.

Var. *nigrum* Wood has black berries without bloom, and forma *leucocarpum* Deane has dull white fruit. These may be looked for with the type. Another variety, *angustifolium* (Ait.) Gray, with narrow lanceolate leaves, a dwarf high-mountain or northern form, has been reported from the Upper Peninsula. A specimen of still another variety, *myrtilloides* (Michx.) Fern.,

[265]

with lower surfaces of leaves strongly pubescent along the midrib, and sometimes on the other veins as well, and with petioles and twigs more pubescent than the type, is in the Cranbrook Herbarium, from Oakland County.

Since the publication of the first edition of this bulletin Camp (1945) in a monograph on the blueberries of North America, proposed a new alignment for this group. Under his treatment, the species *Vaccinium pennsylvanicum* Lam. becomes *Vaccinium Lamarckii* Camp; var. *nigrum* Wood has been given specific rank and is *Vaccinium Brittonii* Porter ex Bickn.; while var. *angustifolium* (Ait.) Gray is again *Vaccinium angustifolium* Ait. In his paper, Camp disposes of occasional abnormalities (among which might be included forma *leucocarpum* Deane, mentioned above) in the following manner: "Nor has there been any attempt to treat certain abnormal forms. Those with non-pigmented or red (acid?) fruit on occasion have been noted in the literature of the group and given names, but since it is our experience that they are likely to be found in almost any species, there seemed no reason to make special mention of them in the present work."

Vaccinium myrtilloides Michx. (Sour-top, Velvet-leaf Blueberry, Canada Blueberry). Fig. 168. (*Vaccinium canadense* Kalm, Gray's Manual, 7th Edition, Shrubs of Michigan, 1st Edition.)

Low shrubs, erect or ascending, 2–5 dm. tall; branches and twigs pubescent, speckled, greenish-brown; leaves simple, alternate, deciduous, oblong-lanceolate or elliptic, entire, downy both sides, acute or rounded at the apex, base wedge-shaped or rounded, 2–4 cm. long, 0.5–1.5 cm. wide; petioles about 1 mm. long; flowers few in the clusters, opening with the leaves; pedicels generally shorter than the flowers; calyx 5-toothed, glabrous; corolla 5-toothed, oblong-campanulate, greenish-white, tinged with pink, about 4 mm. long and 3 mm. thick; stamens 10, not exserted; filaments hairy; style included; berry depressed-globose, blue, rarely white, with much bloom. Flowers, May, June; fruit, July, August.

Dry plains, swamps or moist woods, Labrador to Manitoba, south to Virginia and Illinois. Michigan, throughout.

The fruit of the Canada Blueberry is edible, but not as palatable as that of some of the other species. The rare form with white fruit has been separated as forma *chiococcum* Deane.

Camp (1945) says regarding the change in nomenclature: "It is perhaps unfortunate that a name so well fixed in literature as *V. canadense* must be changed, but the original description of the prior *V. myrtilloides* leaves no doubt of what kind of plant Michaux had." The quotation concerning abnormalities from Camp's monograph given under the preceding species is also applicable here concerning the forma *chiococcum* Deane. In other words he does not feel that it warrants recognition.

Vaccinium vacillans Kalm. (Late Low Blueberry, Dryland Blueberry, Blue Huckleberry). Fig. 169. A stiff, branching shrub 3–9 dm. tall; branches and

twigs yellowish-green, glabrous; leaves simple, alternate, deciduous, obovate or oval, 2.5–4.5 cm. long, 1.5–2.5 cm. broad when full grown, very pale or dull, glaucous beneath, acute or obtuse at the apex, narrowed at the base, entire or minutely ciliolate-serrulate; petioles 1–2 cm. long; flowers before the leaves are half grown, in racemose clusters; calyx 5-toothed, adnate to the ovary, usually reddish; corolla 5-toothed, 5–8 mm. long, greenish-yellow, tinged with red, oblong-cylindric, somewhat narrowed at the throat; stamens 10, included; filaments hairy; berries globular, blue with a bloom, about 8 mm. in diameter. Flowers, May, June; fruit, late July to September.

Dry places, New Hampshire, Ontario, Michigan; south to Georgia, Tennessee and Kansas. Michigan, throughout.

The fruit of this blueberry is of good size and is borne in large quantities. It is conveniently produced at the ends of the branches, where it is easily picked. As in the case of other species of *Vaccinium*, it is inconstant, and varieties with black fruits have been found.

Vaccinium vacillans Kalm var. *crinitum* Fern., a much taller shrub with larger leaves, has been collected on Isle Royale.

Vaccinium corymbosum L. (High-bush or Swamp Blueberry, Tall Blueberry). Fig. 170. Erect shrub 1–4 m. tall, stems and branches grayish or

mottled; twigs greenish-brown, warty, glabrous or puberulent in lines; leaves simple, alternate, deciduous, ovate to elliptic-lanceolate, entire or serrulate, sometimes ciliate, mostly acute at each end, green and glabrous above, paler, smooth or slightly pubescent beneath, 4–8 cm. long, 2–4 cm. broad; petioles 1–2 mm. long; flowers appearing when the leaves are about half grown, borne in short racemes, as long or longer than the pedicels; bracts deciduous; calyx 5-lobed, glaucous; corolla white or pinkish, 6–10 mm. long, varying cylindric-urn-shaped to ovoid, 5-toothed, the teeth reflexed; stamens 10; stigma small; berries blue-black with more or less bloom, 7–10 mm. in diameter. Flowers, May, June; fruit, July, August.

Swamps, thickets and woods, Maine to Virginia, Minnesota and south to Louisiana. Michigan, common throughout.

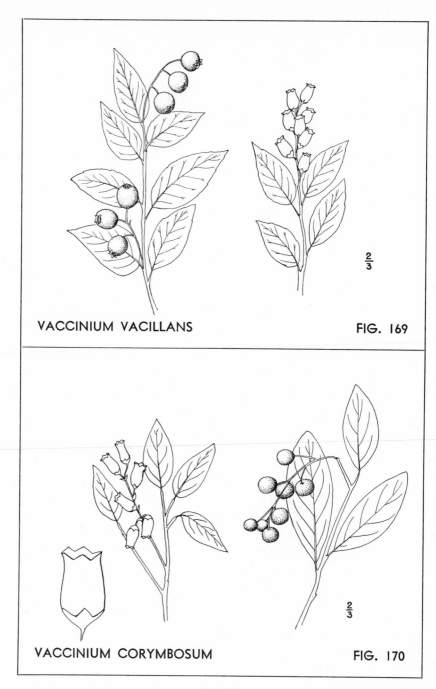

VACCINIUM VACILLANS

$\frac{2}{3}$

FIG. 169

VACCINIUM CORYMBOSUM

$\frac{2}{3}$

FIG. 170

In Michigan this is the common blueberry of our swamp areas, where it reaches its maximum height. I have never found it growing in pastures or upland woods here although it may do so. The fruit of this species is the latest to ripen and furnishes a major portion of the blueberries found in our markets.

Like the others, this species is exceedingly variable and several varieties have been named. Two of these varieties have been reported from Oakland County and, as they have the general range of the species, may be looked for whereever it is found: *Vaccinium corymbosum* L. var. *amoenum* (Ait.) Gray, leaves bright green both sides, ciliate-serrulate or bristly-ciliate; *Vaccinium corymbosum* L. var. *pallidum* (Ait.) Gray, glaucous, leaves ciliate-serrulate, whitened beneath.

Vaccinium atrococcum (Gray) Heller. (Black High Blueberry). Fig. 171. Shrub 2–4.5 m. tall; branches minutely warty; branchlets pubescent; leaves

simple, alternate, deciduous, entire, downy or woolly beneath, even when old, dark green above, light green beneath, mostly acute at both ends, mucronate, thick, 3.5–7.5 cm. long, 1.2–3.5 cm. wide; flowers in short racemes, appearing with leaves; pedicels about the length of the flowers; calyx 5-lobed; corolla ovoid to short-cylindric, yellowish- or greenish-red, 5–8 mm. long, about 3 mm. thick, 5-toothed, throat contracted; stamens 10, included; filaments pubescent; berries black and shining, without bloom, sweet and pleasant, 5–8 mm. in diameter. Flowers, May, June; fruit, July, August.

In swamps and low woods, New Brunswick and Ontario to New Jersey, North Carolina and Ontario. Michigan, infrequent in both peninsulas.

By some authors this blueberry is regarded only as a variety of *V. corymbosum* L., which it closely resembles. Be that as it may, there are many varieties,

differing in the size of the bush, which changes according to the soil in which it is growing, and also in the size, shape and color of the flowers. It flowers and fruits a week or 10 days earlier than *V. corymbosum* L.

Vaccinium uliginosum L. (Bog Bilberry). Fig. 172. Low and spreading, much-branched shrub, 1.5–6 dm. tall; stems stiff, round and smooth; leaves simple, alternate, deciduous, oval, obovate or oblong, wedge-shaped at base, apex rounded, thick, glabrous or nearly so, dull, pale or glaucous and somewhat pubescent beneath, entire,

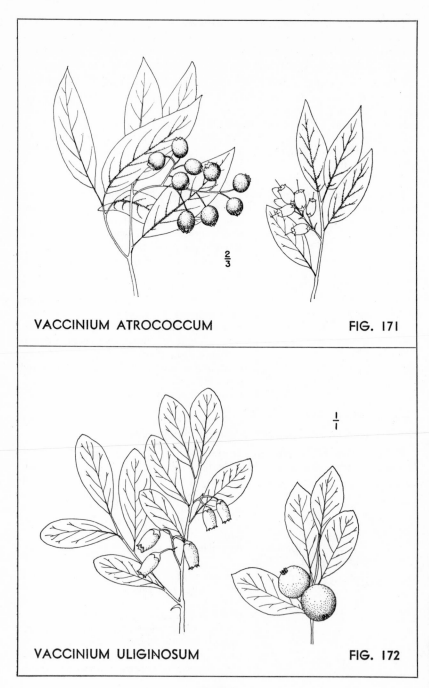

$\frac{2}{3}$

VACCINIUM ATROCOCCUM   FIG. 171

$\frac{1}{1}$

VACCINIUM ULIGINOSUM   FIG. 172

nearly sessile, 5–20 mm. long, 2.5–10 mm. wide, finely reticulate-veined; flowers solitary, or in clusters of 2–4 with a scaly bud, mostly shorter than the pedicels; calyx 4-, rarely 5-lobed; corolla short urn-shaped, pink, 4-toothed; stamens 8, included, 2-awned on the back; filaments smooth; style shorter than the corolla; berries globular, about 6 mm. in diameter, bluish-black with a bloom, sweet and edible. Flowers, June, July; fruit, July, August.

The Bog Bilberry is found throughout Arctic America, Europe and Asia. Also on the summits of the higher mountains of New England and New York, mostly above timber line, along the shores of Lake Superior and northward to Alaska. Michigan, recorded from the Upper Peninsula and the northern part of the Lower Peninsula.

Vaccinium caespitosum Michx. (Dwarf Bilberry). Fig. 173. A dwarf, much-branched shrub, nearly glabrous throughout, 5–30 cm. tall; branches

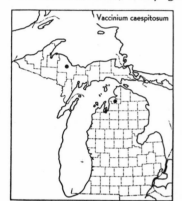

rounded; leaves simple, alternate, deciduous, thin, obovate, wedge-shaped at base, obtuse or acute at the apex, 1–4 cm. long, 4–20 mm. wide, smooth and shining, serrate with small, blunt teeth, nearly sessile; flowers drooping, mostly solitary in the axils of the leaves; pedicels 2–3 mm. long; calyx slightly 5-toothed, or rarely 4-toothed; corolla obovoid or oblong-obovoid, pink or white, about 5 mm. long; stamens 10, included; filaments smooth, style straight, about equalling the corolla; berries, globular, blue with a bloom, about 6 mm. in diameter, sweet and edible. Flowers, June, July; fruit, August.

Gravelly or rocky woods and shores, Labrador to Alaska, south to southern Maine, Vermont, northern Michigan, Wisconsin, Colorado and California. Michigan, rare, Upper Peninsula and northern part of Lower Peninsula. See comments in section on Rare Species.

Vaccinium membranaceum Dougl. (Thin-leaved Bilberry). Fig. 174.

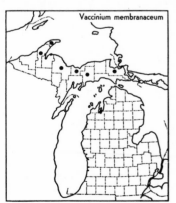

Erect, branching, nearly glabrous shrub, 3–15 dm. tall, twigs somewhat angled; leaves simple, alternate, deciduous, thin, dull, oval, oblong or ovate, green both sides and nearly smooth, acutish to acuminate, sharply and finely serrate, 2–7 cm. long, 1.5–3 cm. broad when full grown; flowers nodding, solitary on short axillary peduncles; calyx border almost entire; corolla depressed-globular, greenish or purplish, usually 5-toothed; stamens 10, included; anthers 2-awned on the back; berries large, dark purple to black, rather acid. Flowers, June, July; fruit ripe, July, August.

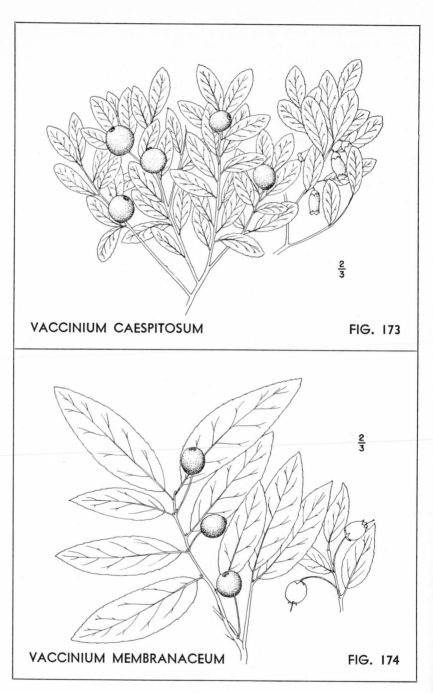

VACCINIUM CAESPITOSUM $\frac{2}{3}$ FIG. 173

VACCINIUM MEMBRANACEUM $\frac{2}{3}$ FIG. 174

In moist woods, northern Michigan, Oregon and British Columbia. Michigan, Upper Peninsula.

This is a western shrub which has its recorded eastern limit in our state.

Vaccinium ovalifolium Sm. (Tall or Oval-leaved Bilberry). Fig. 175. A straggling shrub, 9–15 dm. tall; branchlets sharply angled, glabrous; leaves

simple, alternate, deciduous, glabrous, elliptical, obtuse, nearly entire, 2.5–5 cm. long, green above, pale and glaucous beneath, thin, occasionally with a small abrupt tip; petiole short; flowers solitary on short recurved pedicels; calyx 5-toothed; corolla globose-ovoid; stamens 10, included; filaments glabrous; berries blue, 8–10 mm. in diameter. Flowers, June, July; fruit, September, October.

Woods and mountain slopes, Quebec to northern Michigan, Oregon and Alaska. Michigan, Upper Peninsula and northern portion of Lower Peninsula.

Vaccinium Vitis-Idaea L. var. *minus* Lodd. (Mountain Cranberry, Rock Cranberry). Fig. 176. A low evergreen shrub, 2–15 cm. tall; stems creeping

and forming mats, branches erect; leaves simple, alternate, evergreen, crowded on the branches, obovate or oval, margins revolute, entire or sparingly serrate, thick and leathery, green and shining above, paler and black-dotted beneath, glabrous or minutely pubescent toward the base, 5–18 mm. long, 4–9 mm. broad; petiole short; flowers white or pinkish, borne in short terminal 1-sided racemes, nodding; pedicels shorter than the corollas; bracts reddish, short-oblong; calyx 4-toothed; corolla open bell-shaped, 4-lobed; stamens 8; ovary 4-celled, inferior; fruit a dark red berry, globular, 8–10 mm. in diameter, bitter acid, edible when cooked. Flowers, June, July; fruit, August, September.

Arctic America south to the mountains of Maine, New Hampshire and Vermont, Lake Superior, British Columbia and Alaska. Michigan, Isle Royale, and on the mainland of Keweenaw County.

In the far north the fruit of the Mountain Cranberry is gathered in large quantities for household use. It is also eaten extensively by the larger migratory birds, in some instances being their only food.

Vaccinium Oxycoccos L. (Small Cranberry). Fig. 177. Creeping or trailing prostrate shrub; stems very slender, rooting at the nodes; branches

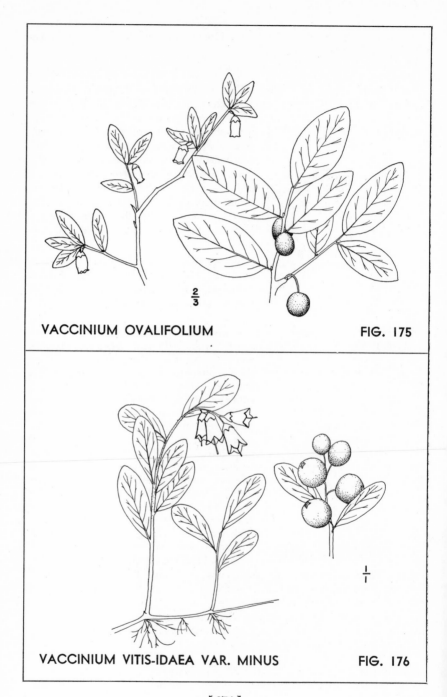

VACCINIUM OVALIFOLIUM   FIG. 175

$\frac{2}{3}$

VACCINIUM VITIS-IDAEA VAR. MINUS   FIG. 176

$\frac{1}{1}$

nearly capillary, erect or ascending, more or less pubescent; leaves simple, alternate, evergreen, oblong or ovate, 3–8 mm. long, 1–3 mm. wide, strongly

Vaccinium Oxycoccos

revolute, acute or obtuse at the apex, rounded or cordate at the base, entire, dark green and glabrous above, white beneath; petioles very short; flowers 1–6 in slightly racemose clusters, nodding; pedicels slender, erect, 1.5–5 cm. long with 2 bracts below or at the middle; calyx 4-parted; corolla pink or rose colored, 4-parted, the segments 5–6 mm. long, reflexed; filaments puberulent, $\frac{1}{2}$ as long as the anthers; berries 6–8 mm. in diameter, reddish, acid. Flowers, May, July; fruit, August, September.

In cold sphagnum bogs, Newfoundland to Alaska, New Jersey, North Carolina, Michigan and British Columbia. Michigan, infrequent throughout.

The Small Cranberry has a wide distribution in Michigan. It may be found growing with the Large Cranberry in many of our bogs. Var. *intermedium* Gray, coarser in all respects and generally with more flowers, might be looked for in the same locations as the species.

Camp (1945) in a publication on the cranberries says: "The cranberries are a compact group of the Vacciniaceae, with a circumboreal distribution. Any decision whether they should be treated as a separate genus, *Oxycoccus*, or as a section, or subgenus of *Vaccinium*, must await a more thorough investigation of the phylogeny of the entire group than is now available. Certainly if this group is to be recognized as a genus, then a number of genera should be segregated from within what is now the widespread and polymorphic genus *Vaccinium*."

To me the cranberries are more entitled to separate generic treatment than some other plants which are accorded that distinction. They bear little outward resemblance to the other vacciniums in any particular. However, as the taxonomists have not arrived at a definite conclusion concerning the status of the group I feel it is better for the purposes of this bulletin to lean to the conservative side and not disturb the nomenclature of the first edition.

Vaccinium macrocarpon Ait. (Large or American Cranberry). Fig.178. Creeping prostrate shrub, rooting at the nodes, comparatively stout, often up to 1 m. long; branches erect or ascending, more or less pubescent; leaves evergreen, alternate, simple, oblong-elliptic, 0.6–1.7 cm. long, 0.2–0.5 cm. wide, blunt or rounded at the tip, rounded at the base, pale or somewhat whitened beneath, glabrous, upper side dark green, glossy, flat or slightly revolute, margin entire; petioles about 1 mm. long, slender; flowers 1–8, in slightly racemose clusters, the elongated rachis of which is terminated by a long, leafy shoot, nodding on erect, pubescent pedicels, 2–4 cm. long, bearing toward the tip 2 flat leaf-like bractlets; calyx 4-parted, the lobes ciliate; corolla pink, its 4 segments 6–10 mm. long, reflexed; stamens 8, exserted; filaments puberulent, about one-third the length of the anthers; style straight; berry globose, red, 1–2 cm. in

[275]

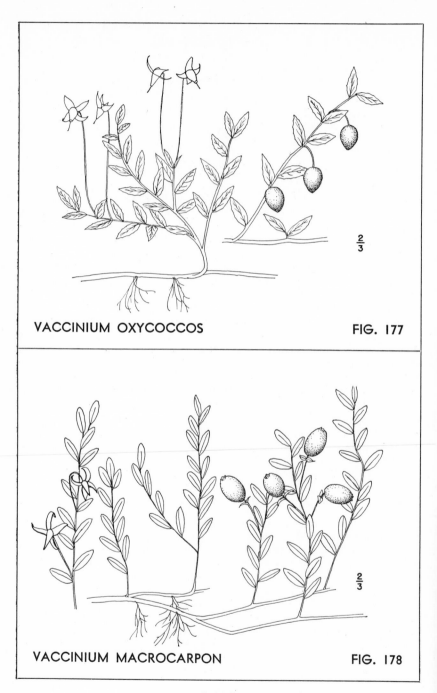

VACCINIUM OXYCOCCOS   FIG. 177

VACCINIUM MACROCARPON   FIG. 178

Vaccinium macrocarpon

diameter, acid. Flowers, June, July; fruit, September, October.

Open bogs, swamps and wet shores, Newfoundland to western Ontario, Virginia, Michigan and Arkansas. Michigan, common throughout.

This is the common cranberry of commerce. It is cultivated extensively on Cape Cod, in New Jersey and Wisconsin. It has not been grown commercially in Michigan, although many bushels are picked and disposed of from the native bogs in good fruiting years. It is frequent in our sphagnum bogs throughout the state. The fruit often remains on the vines until the following season and it is not uncommon to find flowers and mature berries on the same plant.

A market berry called the Cape Cod Bell may be grown with some success in cultivation by using a soil combination of muck and sand.

Solanum [Tourn.] L.—NIGHTSHADES

Herbs, shrubs, vines, or trees in some tropical species, with colorless juice; leaves entire, dentate, lobed or dissected; flowers perfect, regular or nearly regular; calyx inferior, united, mostly 5-lobed; corolla rotate, campanulate, funnel-form, salver-form or tubular, mostly 5-lobed; stamens as many as the corolla lobes and alternate with them, inserted on the tube; style and stigma single; fruit generally a 2-celled, many-seeded capsule or berry.

A family of about 75 genera and nearly 2000 species, widely distributed, mostly in tropical regions. The genus *Solanum* of this family has one species growing in Michigan with stems sufficiently woody to be included among those treated here.

The Nightshade family contains a number of important food and flowering plants. Among the food plants may be mentioned the potato, tomato and egg-plant. The petunia is perhaps the best known and most widely used flowering plant; others are equally attractive although not as well known.

The fruits of most of the species are narcotic and often very poisonous, although some are edible.

Solanum [Tourn.] L.—NIGHTSHADES

Solanum Dulcamara L. (Climbing Nightshade, Bittersweet). Fig. 179. Stems climbing or trailing, somewhat woody below, 0.5–2 m. long, more or less pubescent with simple hairs; leaves petioled, simple, alternate, with a rank odor when crushed, about 5–10 cm. long, 2.5–6 cm. wide, ovate or hastate in outline, acute or acuminate at the apex, generally slightly cordate at the base, some entire, others with a lobe on one side near the base, and some 3-lobed or divided, the terminal segment much the largest; flowers blue, purple or white, 10–15 mm. broad, borne in compound lateral cymes; pedicels slender,

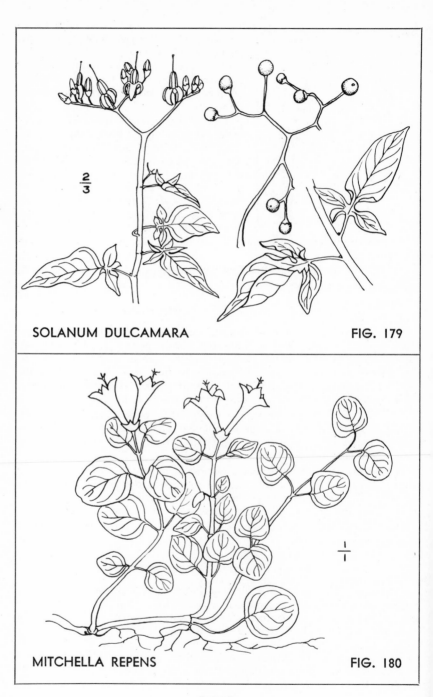

$\frac{2}{3}$

SOLANUM DULCAMARA   FIG. 179

$\frac{1}{1}$

MITCHELLA REPENS   FIG. 180

articulated at base, spreading or drooping; calyx-lobes short, oblong, obtuse, persistent at the base of the fruit; corolla deeply 5-cleft, the lobes triangular-lanceolate, acuminate; stamens exserted; berries bright red, oval or globose, 2-celled; seeds numerous. Flowers, May, September; fruit, June, Autumn.

Solanum Dulcamara

In waste places, moist thickets and around buildings, Nova Scotia to Minnesota, Washington, New Jersey, Pennsylvania and Kansas. Michigan, throughout, common in the Lower Peninsula.

The berries of this plant have rather conflicting reputations. Some claim they are poisonous when eaten and others that they are perfectly harmless. No doubt the safest course would be not to experiment. This nightshade was formerly extensively used in medicine, but like many other plants it has somewhat lost its reputation for high medicinal qualities. Although one of its common names is Bittersweet it should not be confused with *Celastrus scandens* L., also called Bittersweet, and which is, no doubt, the best known and most popular of our native Michigan vines.

RUBIACEAE—MADDER FAMILY

Herbaceous or woody plants; leaves deciduous, simple, opposite, entire, connected by interposed stipules, or in whorls without apparent stipules; flowers perfect, but often appearing in two forms, regular; calyx-tube adherent to the ovary which is 2–4-celled; stamens 4–5, inserted on the tube of the regular corolla, equal in number to and alternate with its lobes; ovary 1–10-celled, inferior; style short or elongated; fruit various.

A very large family, of which only two genera with woody plants occur in Michigan.

Tall, deciduous, erect shrubs or small trees; leaves 7–14 cm. long; flowers in a dense globular head............................*Cephalanthus*, p. 280

Low, evergreen, trailing semi-herbaceous plants; leaves 6–20 mm. long; flowers 2 together, their ovaries united................................*Mitchella*, p. 279

Mitchella L.—PARTRIDGE-BERRIES

Mitchella repens L. (Partridge-berry, Twin Berry). Fig. 180. Stems slender, semi-herbaceous, creeping or trailing, rooting at the nodes, 1.5–3 dm. long, branching, glabrous, or slightly pubescent; leaves opposite, evergreen, ovate-orbicular, obtuse at the apex, rounded or somewhat cordate at the base, 6–20 mm. long, dark green, shining, often with white veins; petioles commonly 2–10 mm. long, occasionally as long as 15 mm.; peduncles shorter than the leaves, bearing 2 sessile white flowers at the summit; corolla 10–12 mm. long, funnel-form, generally 4-lobed, the lobes recurved, bearded on the inner side;

stamens as many as the corolla lobes, inserted on its throat; filaments short and style exserted, or vice versa; ovary 4-celled; stigmas 4; ovules 1 in each cavity; fruit composed of 2 united drupes, red, rarely white, 4–8 mm. in diameter, generally with 8 rounded nutlets, edible, persistent through the winter. Flowers, April, June and occasionally in the autumn; fruit generally present continuously.

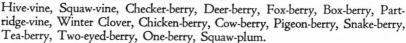

Dry woods, creeping about the base of trees, Nova Scotia to Florida, Ontario, Minnesota, Arkansas and Texas. Michigan, frequent throughout.

The Partridge-berry was named after Dr. John Mitchell, botanist and correspondent of Linnaeus in Virginia. For such a very modest little plant it has an unusual number of colloquial names, the applicableness of some of which it is difficult to understand: Hive-vine, Squaw-vine, Checker-berry, Deer-berry, Fox-berry, Box-berry, Partridge-vine, Winter Clover, Chicken-berry, Cow-berry, Pigeon-berry, Snake-berry, Tea-berry, Two-eyed-berry, One-berry, Squaw-plum.

By experimentation it has been proven that when only one of the pair of blossoms has been fertilized fruit is rarely set.

Cephalanthus L.—BUTTONBUSHES

Cephalanthus occidentalis L. (Common Buttonbush, Honey Balls). Fig. 181. A large spreading shrub, 1–3 m. tall; bark dark gray, mostly furrowed; branches glabrous; leaves simple, deciduous, entire, opposite or in whorls of 3, ovate, oval or lanceolate, mostly narrowed at the base, acuminate at the apex, glabrous both sides, or sometimes sparingly pubescent beneath, 7–14 cm. long, 4–6 cm. wide; petiole 1–2 cm. long; inflorescence axillary and terminal; peduncles 2–8 cm. long; heads globose, 2–4 cm. in diameter; flowers white, sessile and closely crowded, the receptacle pubescent; calyx-tube inversely pyramidal, 4-toothed, longer than the ovary, persistent; corolla tubular-funnel-form with 4 short lobes; stamens 4, inserted on the throat of the corolla; style slender and about twice as long as the ovary; fruit small, dry, 1–2-seeded. Flowers, July, August; fruit, September, October.

The Buttonbush grows in swamps and along streams. It is found from New Brunswick to western Ontario and California, south to Florida, Texas and Arizona. Michigan, Lower Peninsula; more abundant southward.

[280]

The Buttonbush is found growing in many low places no matter how small their area, where it can have water about its roots at least a part of the season. The flowers form a perfect globe with the thread-like styles protruding from every side and are the shrub's chief attraction. There are about 200 in each head, every one full of nectar and so attractive to bees that one of the shrub's common names is Honey Balls.

CAPRIFOLIACEAE—Honeysuckle Family

Shrubs, trees, vines or perennial herbs; leaves deciduous, opposite, simple or pinnately compound; stipules none, or sometimes present; flowers perfect and mostly cymose; calyx-tube adherent to the 2–5-celled ovary, its limb 3–5-toothed or -lobed; corolla with the petals more or less united, the limb 5-lobed, or 2-lipped; stamens 5 (rarely 4), inserted on the tube of the corolla and alternate with its lobes; ovary inferior, 1–6-celled; style slender; stigma capitate, or 2–5-lobed; fruit a 1–6-celled berry, drupe or capsule; seeds oblong, globose or angular.

A family of about 10 genera and 300 species, mostly found in the northern hemisphere. The following genera include shrubs or vines which are found in Michigan.

1. Leaves simple
   2. Stems climbing, creeping or prostrate
      3. Stems trailing, semi-herbaceous evergreens; flowers generally in pairs on long, slender upright peduncles; leaves rounded-oval or nearly orbicular; fruit a capsule......................*Linnaea*, p. 296
      3. Stems woody, twining and climbing, leaves entire, deciduous, the upper usually connate-perfoliate; flowers in whorled clusters; fruit a berry.................................*Lonicera*, p. 283
   2. Upright, bushy shrubs
      4. Flowers in pairs or few-flowered racemes; fruit a berry or capsule
         5. Leaves serrate; fruit a capsule...*Diervilla*, p. 281
         5. Leaves not serrate, sometimes lobed; fruit a berry
            6. Corolla short-campanulate or short funnel-form, regular..*Symphoricarpos*, p. 293
            6. Corolla tubular or long-campanulate, more or less irregular..*Lonicera*, p. 283
      4. Flowers in compound cymes; corolla rotate, small; fruit a 1-seeded drupe...*Viburnum*, p. 297
1. Leaves compound; flowers white in compound cymes.............................*Sambucus*, p. 309

Diervilla [Tourn.] Mill.—Bush Honeysuckles

Diervilla Lonicera Mill. (Bush Honeysuckle). Fig. 182. Low, upright shrubs, mostly less than 1 m. tall; bark grayish-brown, shreddy when old; twigs glabrous or hispid in 2 lines; leaves deciduous, opposite, simple, ovate or ovate-lanceolate, glabrous except on the veins, finely serrate and ciliate 6–13 cm. long, 2–5 cm. wide, long-acuminate at the apex, wedge-shaped to

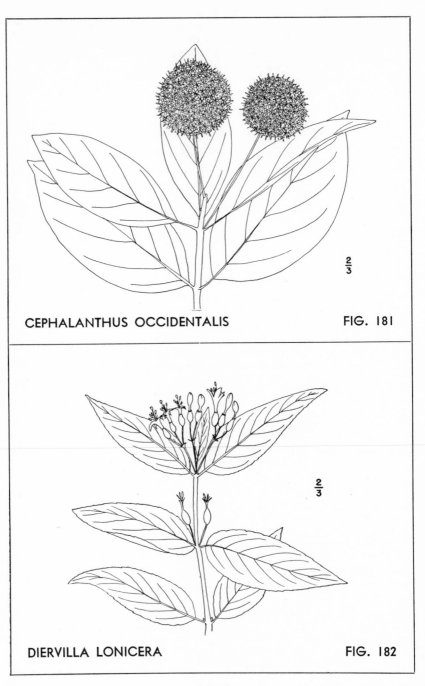

CEPHALANTHUS OCCIDENTALIS $\frac{2}{3}$ FIG. 181

DIERVILLA LONICERA $\frac{2}{3}$ FIG. 182

rounded at the base; petiole 5–10 mm. long, ciliate; flowers terminal or axillary in clusters of 2–6; calyx-tube slender; sepals bristle-like, about 5 mm. long; corolla light yellow, turning reddish, 10–15 mm. long, tubular or funnel-shaped, slightly gibbous at the base, 5-lobed; stamens 5, borne on the corolla-tube; ovary inferior, 2-celled; style long and slender; stigma capitate; fruit a slender, pointed pod, 7–10 mm. long with a beak half as long terminated with 5 persistent linear sepals; seeds numerous, small. Flowers, June, August; fruit, September, October.

Diervilla Lonicera

Dry woods and rocky places, Newfoundland to Manitoba, south to North Carolina, and in the Great Lakes region. Michigan, common throughout.

Lonicera L.—HONEYSUCKLES

1. Upright bushy shrubs; leaves all distinct; flowers in pairs on axillary branches; calyx-teeth not persistent on the fruit
    2. Bracts of the peduncles subulate, linear, minute, or wanting
        3. Corolla-lobes subequal
            4. Peduncle short, 2–7 mm. in length; leaves elliptical, pilose beneath, strigose to glabrate above; young branchlets puberulent and more or less pilose-hirsute; limb of calyx glabrous, rarely pilose; tube gibbous on one side at base..................*L. villosa* var. *Solonis*, p. 285
            4. Peduncle long and slender, 1.4–3 cm. in length
                5. Leaves rarely cordate, ovate or oval, downy beneath when young, margin strongly ciliate...................*L. canadensis*, p. 287
                5. Leaves cordate, ovate, glabrous, margin not ciliate....*L. tatarica*, p. 285
        3. Corolla-lobes strongly 2-lipped; leaves tapering at the base, glabrous or nearly so; fruit red or purplish...................................*L. oblongifolia*, p.287
    2. Bracts of the peduncle broad, foliaceous; leaves ovate-oblong, 0.5–1.5 dm. long; fruit dark purple...*L. involucrata*, p. 289
1. Trailing or twining shrubs; leaves often connate-perfoliate; flowers in sessile whorled clusters or interrupted spikes; calyx-teeth persistent on the fruit
    6. Corolla tubular, long trumpet-shaped, narrow and nearly regular, scarlet or yellow; stamens and style little exserted...............................*L. sempervirens*, p. 289
    6. Corolla broader, the lower lip narrow, the upper wider and 4-lobed, orange or pale yellow; stamens and styles conspicuously exserted
        7. Leaves pubescent, at least beneath; corolla yellow
            8. Branches glandular-villous; leaves pubescent on both sides, ciliate; corolla slightly gibbous at base............................*L. hirsuta*, p. 291
            8. Branches glabrous; leaves glabrous above, decidedly pubescent beneath, not ciliate; corolla strongly gibbous at base............................*L. dioica* var. *glaucescens*, p. 291
        7. Leaves glabrous on both sides, 3–8 cm. long, very glaucous beneath; corolla greenish-yellow, the tube somewhat gibbous...................*L. dioica*, p. 293

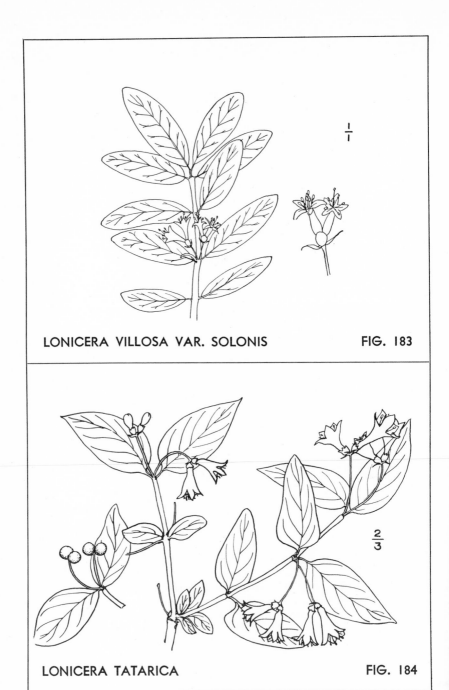

$\frac{1}{1}$

LONICERA VILLOSA VAR. SOLONIS   FIG. 183

$\frac{2}{3}$

LONICERA TATARICA   FIG. 184

Lonicera villosa (Michx.) R.&S. var. *Solonis* (Eat.) Fern. (Mountain Fly Honeysuckle). Fig. 183. (*Lonicera caerulea* L. var. *villosa* (Michx.) T.&G., Gray's Manual, 7th Edition, Shrubs of Michigan, 1st Edition.) Low erect shrub, up to 1 m. in height; bark shreddy, brown; young branchlets puberulent and more or less pilose-hirsute; leaves simple, deciduous, opposite, elliptical, narrow, oblong or obovate, 2–4 cm. long, 8–16 mm. wide, rounded or obtusely angled at the apex, mostly mucronate, base rounded, pilose beneath, strigose to glabrate above, veins prominent and reticulate, margin ciliate; petioles very short, villous; flowers 2 together in the axils of the lower leaves; bracts at the base of the ovaries small, lance-oblong; peduncles 2–7 mm. long, villous; calyx-lobes glabrous, border slightly 5-toothed; corolla pale-yellow, narrowly bell-shaped, glabrous, rarely pilose, tube gibbous at the base on one side, 7–8 mm. long, lobes nearly equal; stamens exserted; fruit a bluish-black, edible, oval berry formed by the uniting of the ovaries of the two flowers, the scars of which are borne at the summit; seeds several. Flowers, May, June; fruit ripe, July, August.

Lonicera villosa var. Solonis

Low woods and bogs, southern Newfoundland to southeastern Manitoba, south to Massachusetts, northern Rhode Island, Connecticut, Michigan, Wisconsin and Minnesota. Michigan, infrequent in both the Lower and the Upper Peninsulas.

The Mountain Fly Honeysuckle has the rather unusual characteristic that it produces two perfect flowers in order to make one berry. After the flowers have fallen the two ovaries enlarge and begin to grow toward each other, finally uniting into a single berry, which shows its double origin by the two so-called "eyes," each of which is the remnant of a flower calyx. It is a satisfactory shrub in cultivation.

This plant has generally been considered a variety of the Old World honeysuckle, *Lonicera caerulea* L. In 1925 a comprehensive study of the species was made by Fernald and the nomenclature clarified. The plant is variable in the extreme, and in addition to the variety *Solonis,* four others, having somewhat different geographic limits, were separated by Fernald. Michigan is not within the range of any of these varieties.

Lonicera tatarica L. (Tartarian Honeysuckle). Fig. 184. A smooth, upright shrub 1.5–3 m. tall; light gray bark and green or reddish twigs; leaves simple, deciduous, opposite, ovate, entire, glabrous, rather thin, not conspicuously reticulate-veined, 3–7 cm. long, 1.7–4 cm. wide, acute or obtuse at apex, cordate at the base, not ciliate on margin; petiole short; flowers in pairs from the axils of the upper leaves; peduncles slender, 1–2 cm. in length; bracts at base of the ovaries linear, sometimes equalling the corolla-tube; corolla showy, pink or whitish, the lobes subequal, widely spreading, nearly as long as the tube,

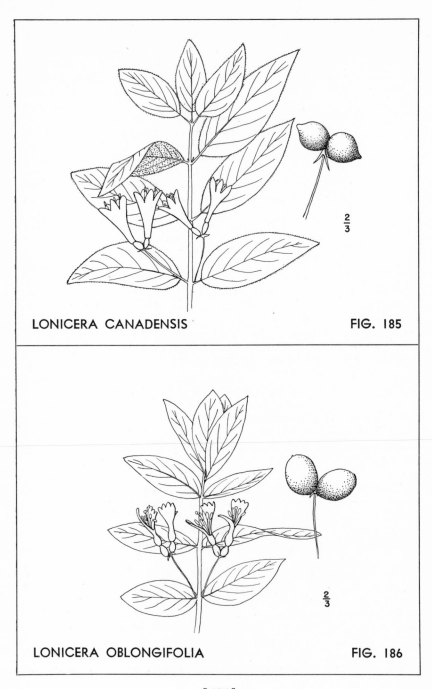

LONICERA CANADENSIS   FIG. 185

LONICERA OBLONGIFOLIA   FIG. 186

Lonicera tatarica

which is gibbous at the base; stamens and style scarcely exserted; berries slightly united at the base, red or orange. Flowers, May, June; fruit ripe, late July, August.

Escaped from cultivation and established on rocky shores and sheltered banks, Maine to Ontario, Michigan, New Jersey, Vermont, southern New York and Kentucky. Michigan, infrequent in both peninsulas.

This hardy ornamental shrub is a native of southeastern Russia and central Asia. It is extensively cultivated in Michigan, having escaped and become naturalized to the extent that it can fairly be included as a permanent member of our flora.

Lonicera canadensis Marsh. (American Fly Honeysuckle). Fig. 185. A shrub with straggling branches, 1–1.5 m. in height; branchlets glabrous; leaves

Lonicera canadensis

simple, opposite, deciduous, ovate-oblong, sometimes heart-shaped at the base, acute or acutish at the apex, villous-pubescent beneath when young, glabrous or nearly so when mature, 2–9 cm. long, 1.5–4 cm. wide, margins ciliate; petioles 4–6 mm. long, very slender; flowers in pairs on long filiform peduncles from the axils of the lower leaves; bracts very small; calyx margin obscurely lobed; corolla funnel-form, about 2 cm. long, greenish-yellow, the lobes much shorter than the tube, which is gibbous at the base, glabrous without, slightly hairy within; stamens included; berries separate, reddish; seeds usually 3–4. Flowers, April, June; fruit, July, September.

In moist woods from New Brunswick to Manitoba, south to Connecticut and west to Pennsylvania and Michigan. Michigan, frequent throughout.

Lonicera oblongifolia

Lonicera oblongifolia (Goldie) Hook. (Swamp Fly Honeysuckle). Fig. 186. Shrub 5–15 dm. tall; branches upright; bark grayish; leaves simple, opposite, deciduous, 2–7 cm. long, 1–3.5 cm. wide, oblong, downy when young, glabrous in maturity, dark green above, pale beneath, apex acute or obtuse, base tapering; petioles very short; flowers in pairs on slender peduncles, 1–3 cm. long, from the axils of the lower leaves;

[287]

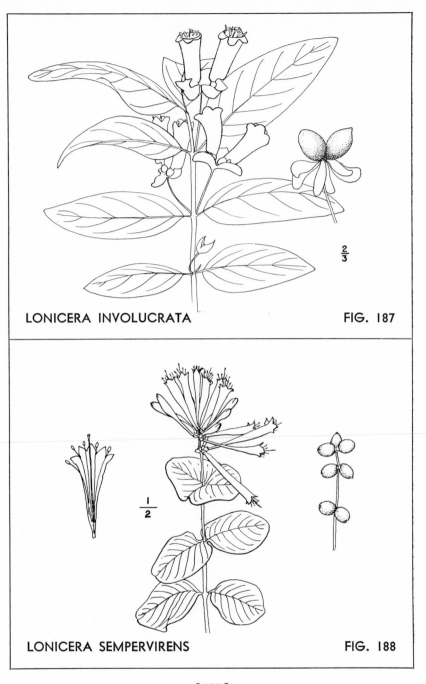

LONICERA INVOLUCRATA

$\frac{2}{3}$

FIG. 187

LONICERA SEMPERVIRENS

$\frac{1}{2}$

FIG. 188

bracts very small, or wanting; calyx obscurely 5-lobed; corolla deeply 2-lipped, 1–1.5 cm. long, yellowish-white, often purplish within, more or less hairy, gibbous at base; stamens exserted; filaments hairy; fruit red or purplish, the berries united or nearly distinct. Flowers, May, July; fruit August, September.

Tamarack and arbor vitae swamps, Quebec to Manitoba, Vermont, New York, Pennsylvania, Michigan and Minnesota. Michigan, frequent except in the extreme southern counties.

Lonicera involucrata (Richards.) Banks. (Involucred Fly Honeysuckle). Fig. 187. Shrub, 1–3 m. tall, pubescent or becoming glabrous; branches 4-

Lonicera involucrata

angled; leaves simple, opposite, deciduous, ovate, oval or obovate, 5–15 cm. long, acute or acuminate at the apex, narrowed or rounded at the base, more or less pubescent when young, midrib prominent; petioles short; flowers borne on axillary peduncles, 2–5 cm. long, 2–3-flowered; bracts foliaceous, ovate or oval, often cordate; bractlets also large and at length surrounding the fruit; flowers yellow; calyx-teeth very short; corolla funnel-form, 1–1.5 cm. long, viscid-pubescent, the border with 5 short, nearly equal little-spreading lobes; stamens 5, slightly exserted; style slender, as long as the stamens; berries distinct, globose or oval, nearly black, about 8 mm. in diameter. Flowers June, July; fruit ripe, August, September.

In woodlands, banks of streams, New Brunswick and Quebec to western Ontario and Michigan, west to British Columbia and Alaska, south to Utah and California. Michigan, reported from Washtenaw, Macomb and Keweenaw counties.

See remarks regarding this honeysuckle in section on Rare Species.

Lonicera sempervirens L. (Trumpet Honeysuckle). Fig. 188. Tall, twin-

Lonicera sempervirens

ing, shrubby vine; bark pale brown, somewhat shreddy; twigs glabrous; leaves simple, opposite, deciduous except in the south, where they are evergreen, elliptic, or oblong, 4–8 cm. long, 2–5 cm. wide, sometimes much larger on sterile shoots, the lower short-petioled, the upper pairs connate-perfoliate, rounded at the apex, rounded or narrowed at the base, dark green and glabrous above, pale, glaucous and finely appressed-puberulent below; flowers in somewhat distant whorls, nearly 5 cm. long, scarlet or yellow, glabrous or somewhat pubescent, the tube narrow, slightly expanded above, the limb short and nearly regular,

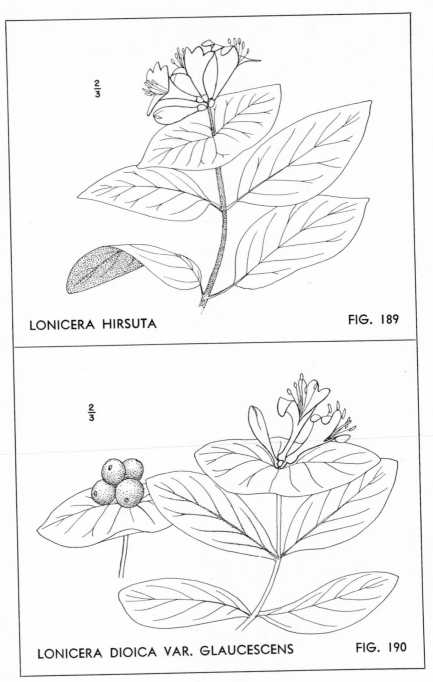

$\frac{2}{3}$

LONICERA HIRSUTA   FIG. 189

$\frac{2}{3}$

LONICERA DIOICA VAR. GLAUCESCENS   FIG. 190

about 6 mm. wide at the throat; stamens and style barely exserted; berries scarlet. Flowers in June and at intervals until frost in the fall; fruit, July and through the season.

Copses, Maine to Nebraska and southward. Michigan, infrequent in both peninsulas.

Lonicera hirsuta Eat. (Hairy Honeysuckle). Fig. 189. Twining and rather high-climbing vine; branches glandular, hirsute-pubescent; leaves simple, opposite,

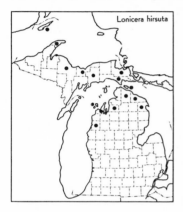

Lonicera hirsuta

deciduous, broadly oval, the uppermost united forming a rhombic or nearly orbicular disk, the lower short-petioled, 5–11 cm. long, 3.5–8 cm. wide, upper surface dark green and appressed-pubescent, pale, and downy-pubescent below, margin ciliate; flowers in approximate whorls in short terminal interrupted spikes; peduncles hirsute and glandular; calyx-teeth minute, persistent on the fruit; corolla 2–2.5 cm. long, orange-yellow, clammy-pubescent within and without, slender, somewhat gibbous at base, the limb 2-lipped, about as long as the tube; stamens and style strongly exserted, somewhat hairy below; fruit a red berry. Flowers, July; fruit, September.

Woodlands, Vermont and Ontario to Manitoba, Pennsylvania, Ohio and Michigan. Michigan, frequent in upper part of Lower Peninsula and in the Upper Peninsula.

This honeysuckle appears to prefer coniferous woods.

Lonicera dioica L. var. **glaucescens** (Rydb.) Butters. (Douglas' Honeysuckle). Fig. 190. (*Lonicera glaucescens* Rydb., Gray's Manual, 7th Edition,

Lonicera dioica var. glaucescens

Shrubs of Michigan, 1st Edition.) Twining, climbing vine, in habit similar to the preceding; branches glabrous; leaves simple, opposite, deciduous, 3–9 cm. long, glabrous above, decidedly pubescent beneath, at least on the veins, margin not ciliate, usually only the upper pair connate-perfoliate; flowers verticillate in a short terminal interrupted spike; corolla pale yellow, changing to reddish, 1.2–2 cm. long, pubescent or puberulent without, pubescent within, the 2-lipped limb shorter than the tube, which is gibbous at the base; stamens somewhat pubescent or nearly glabrous; style hirsute; both exserted; ovary glabrous or nearly so; berry salmon-color; seeds about 3. Flowers, May, June; fruit, August, September.

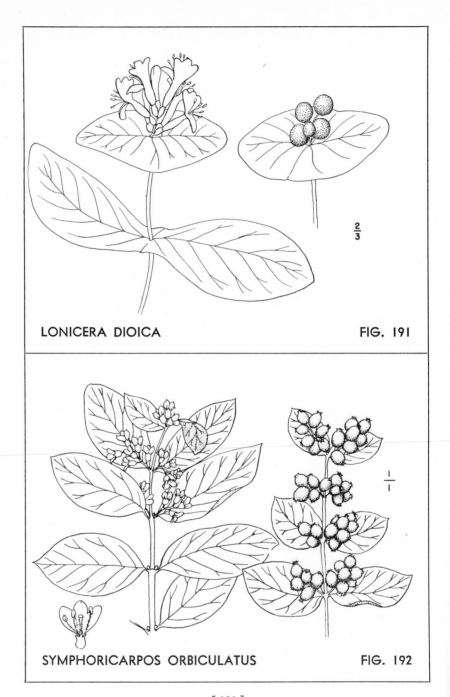

LONICERA DIOICA   FIG. 191

$\frac{2}{3}$

SYMPHORICARPOS ORBICULATUS   FIG. 192

$\frac{1}{1}$

Ranges from Ontario and Manitoba south to Virginia, Ohio and Nebraska. Michigan, infrequent throughout.

The twining honeysuckles are exceedingly variable, and the nomenclature is correspondingly confused. While this plant was treated as a separate species in the first edition, attention was directed to the fact that some authors regard it as only a variety of *L. dioica* L. and that others separate a variety which still others call a form of the variety. The latest usage seems to favor classifying the plant as a variety of *L. dioica* L., and this treatment is adopted for the second edition.

Lonicera dioica L. (Smooth-leaved Honeysuckle, Glaucous Honeysuckle). Fig. 191. Twining shrubs, 1–3 m. long; branches glabrous; leaves simple, oppo-

site, deciduous, glaucous and glabrous beneath, 3–8 cm. long, up to 4 cm. wide, the upper 1–4 pairs connate into disks, of which even the upper are oblong or rhombic, more or less pointed at each end, the lower sessile or short-petioled and narrower, margin entire; flowers several in a cluster at the end of the branchlets; peduncle up to 2 cm. long; corolla with a 2-lipped limb, greenish-yellow or purplish, the tube barely 1 cm. long, pubescent within, gibbous at base; stamens and style hairy, exserted; fruit salmon-color; seeds usually 3. Flowers, May, June; fruit, July, September.

Rocky grounds and dry situations, Quebec to Manitoba, south to North Carolina, Ohio and Missouri. Michigan, common throughout.

The following cultivated honeysuckles have escaped only sparingly and do not appear to be well enough established to warrant inclusion as permanent members of our state flora:

Lonicera caprifolium L. (American Woodbine). Gratiot, Oakland and Marquette counties.

Lonicera Morrowi Gray. Introduced from Japan. Washtenaw County.

Lonicera Xylosteum L. (European Fly Honeysuckle). Introduced from Europe. Oakland County.

Symphoricarpos [Dill.] Ludwig—SNOWBERRIES

1. Style bearded; fruit red; flowers all in dense axillary clusters............*S. orbiculatus*, p. 295
1. Style glabrous; fruit white; flowers not as above
    2. Flowers sessile in several-flowered axillary and
       terminal spikes; stamens and styles exserted................................*S. occidentalis*, p. 295
    2. Flowers short-pedicelled, spikes few-flowered; stamens and styles not exserted
       3. Under surface of leaves pilose
          4. Under surface of leaves pale green; 2–10 dm. tall...............*S. albus*, p. 295
          4. Under surface of leaves strongly whitened;
             1.5–2.5 dm. tall..*S. albus* var. *pauciflorus*, p. 296
       3. Under surface of leaves glabrous;
          up to 2 m. tall..*S. albus* var. *laevigatus*, p. 296

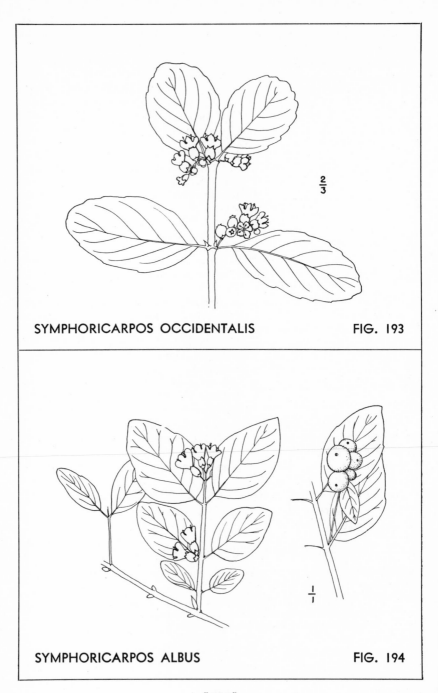

SYMPHORICARPOS OCCIDENTALIS

$\frac{2}{3}$

FIG. 193

SYMPHORICARPOS ALBUS

$\frac{1}{1}$

FIG. 194

Symphoricarpos orbiculatus Moench. (Indian Currant, Coral-berry).
Fig. 192. Shrub 6–15 dm. tall; branches erect or somewhat recurved; twigs

purplish-brown, generally pubescent; leaves simple, opposite, deciduous, oval or ovate, entire or undulate, mostly obtuse at each end, glabrous or nearly so above, soft pubescent beneath, 2.5–4 dm. long; petioles about 2–4 mm. long; flowers borne in dense clusters in the axils of the leaves; calyx 5-toothed, teeth short, persistent; corolla pinkish, campanulate, sparingly pubescent inside, about 5 mm. long; style bearded; stamens included; berry purplish-red, ovoid-globose, about 5 mm. long. Flowers, July; fruit, autumn.

Rocky banks, New York to North Dakota, south to Georgia and Texas. Michigan, infrequent, Upper and Lower Peninsulas. Not many stations are recorded, and the species should be collected and reported whenever possible.

The Indian Currant is a satisfactory cultivated shrub and is frequently used in landscape plantings. It bears an abundance of fruit, which is very persistent.

Symphoricarpos occidentalis Hook. (Wolfberry). Fig. 193. An erect free-branching shrub, glabrous or nearly so, 3–10 dm. tall; twigs puberulent,

reddish-brown, slender; leaves simple, opposite, deciduous, thickish, ovate, entire or wavy-toothed, 2–10 cm. long, 1.5–7 cm. wide, more or less pubescent beneath, rounded or narrowed at the base, apex acute or rounded, mucronate, dark green above, paler green below; petioles pubescent, up to 10 mm. long; flowers in dense terminal and axillary spikes; calyx-tube short, 5-toothed, regular, persistent; corolla pinkish, funnel-form, much bearded within, 6–9 mm. long, lobed to beyond the middle; stamens exserted; style exserted, glabrous; fruit a 2-seeded berry, dull white, turning blackish; seeds straw-colored, smooth. Flowers, July; fruit ripe, September.

Rocky ground, northern Michigan and Illinois to Kansas, west to the Rocky Mountains. Michigan, rare in middle and upper portion of Lower Peninsula and Upper Peninsula.

The Wolfberry spreads freely by the root and often forms dense colonies. Its fruit frequently remains on the stems throughout the winter.

Symphoricarpos albus (L.) Blake. (Snowberry). Fig. 194. (*Symphoricarpos racemosus* Michx., Gray's Manual, 7th Edition, Shrubs of Michigan, 1st Edition.) Erect shrub, 2–10 dm. tall; twigs slender, light brown; bark on older branches gray, turning darker in age; leaves simple, opposite, deciduous, elliptic-oblong to orbicular, 2–5 cm. long, 1–3 cm. wide, thin, green both sides, pilose beneath, margin entire, or wavy-toothed, or sometimes lobed on young shoots; petiole about 4 mm. long; flowers on short pedicels, 1–2 in the axils, or in short, interrupted spikes at the ends of the branches; calyx 5-toothed, the sepals more or less ciliate; corolla campanulate, about 6 mm. long, pink and white, bearded inside, somewhat gibbous at the base; stamens and the glabrous style included; berry snow-white, globose, about 6 mm. in diameter, with a remnant of the style appearing as a black spot; seeds 2, slightly roughened. Flowers, June, July; fruit ripe, September, October, November.

Dry, rocky places and banks, Nova Scotia and Quebec to British Columbia, south to Pennsylvania, Kentucky, Minnesota, South Dakota, Montana and California. Michigan, infrequent throughout.

The nomenclature used here is that of Blake (1914). He recognized the variable character of the shrub and gives two varieties as follows, both of which are found in Michigan:

Symphoricarpos albus (L.) Blake var. *pauciflorus* (Rob.) Blake. A dwarf shrub; under surface of leaves strongly whitened, more or less pubescent. Lake Superior to Lake Winnipeg and British Columbia, south to Minnesota, North Dakota, Colorado and Oregon. Reported from the following Michigan counties: Cheboygan, Marquette, Mackinac, Ottawa and Keweenaw.

Symphoricarpos albus (L.) Blake var. *laevigatus* (Fern.) Blake. A taller shrub; under surface of leaves glabrous. Quebec to Washington, locally in the mountains of Virginia. This is the snowberry commonly used here for ornamental planting, from which source it occasionally escapes to roadsides etc. From such situations it has been collected in St. Clair and Marquette counties.

Linnaea [Gronov.] L.—TWIN-FLOWERS

Linnaea borealis L. var. *americana* (Forbes) Rehd. (Twin-flower). Fig. 195. A slender creeping and trailing little evergreen, somewhat woody; stems slightly pubescent; petioles 2–4 mm. long; leaves obovate or orbicular, thickish, evergreen, sparingly crenate, contracted at base, about 5–15 mm. wide, sometimes wider than long; peduncles slender, erect, 2-bracted at summit; 2-flowered; pedicels filiform, 6–20 mm. long; flowers nodding, about 8–15 mm. long, very fragrant; corolla whitish, tinged with rose-purple, hairy inside, slender-bell-shaped or funnel-form, nearly equally 5-lobed; calyx-teeth 5, awl-shaped, deciduous; stamens 4, inserted near the base of the corolla-tube, paired, 2 shorter, included; ovary 3-celled, 1-seeded, 2 of the cavities having abortive ovules; fruit a small globose dry pod with 1 oblong seed. Flowers, June to August, occasionally flowering in late fall; fruit, July to autumn.

[296]

Linnaea borealis var. americana

Moist mossy woods and cold bogs, Labrador to New Jersey and the mountains of Pennsylvania, westward to Michigan and Minnesota, also in the Rocky Mountains to Colorado and in the Sierra Nevada to California; also found in suitable habitats farther south. Michigan, abundant in northern part of Lower Peninsula and in the Upper Peninsula.

The Twin-flower was named by Gronovius for Linnaeus, with whom it was a special favorite, and this delicate little plant cannot fail to be a favorite with anyone who really enjoys the out-of-doors and the beauties of nature. The plant is also called Twin Sisters and Two-eyed Berries, both of which fit but perhaps are not quite as appropriate as Twin-flower.

Viburnum [Tourn.] L.—ARROW-WOODS, VIBURNUMS

1. Cymes with outer flowers large and showy
  2. Leaves pinnately veined, not lobed..*V. lantanoides*, p. 299
  2. Leaves palmately veined, 3-lobed...*V. trilobum*, p. 299
1. Cymes with all flowers small and uniform
  3. Leaves mostly 3-lobed and palmately veined
    4. Leaves glabrous; cymes 1–2.5 cm. broad; drupe red........*V. pauciflorum*, p. 301
    4. Leaves soft-downy; cymes 4–7 cm. broad;
        drupe purple-black..*V. acerifolium*, p. 301
  3. Leaves not lobed, pinnately veined
    5. Leaves coarsely dentate; veins prominent below
      6. Leaves rarely with more than 9 teeth on each side
        7. Under surface of leaves pubescent only on the mid-rib and
            principal veins, or very sparingly between the veins;
            petioles 2–12 mm. long...*V. affine*, p. 303
        7. Under surface of leaves densely pubescent over the entire
            surface; petioles 3–7 mm. long.......*V. affine* var. *hypomalacum*, p. 303
      6. Leaves mostly with more than 9 teeth on each side
        8. Leaves subsessile, under surface and petioles
            soft-downy, at least when young............................*V. pubescens*, p. 303
        8. Leaves on petioles 6–25 mm. long, entirely glabrous or
            with hairy tufts in the axils beneath.................*V. dentatum*, p. 305
    5. Leaves finely toothed; veins not prominent
      9. Cymes with peduncles 1–2 cm. long.........................*V. cassinoides*, p. 305
      9. Cymes sessile, or nearly so
        10. Petioles with a broad and wavy margin;
            leaves acuminate...*V. Lentago*, p. 307
        10. Petioles not wavy-margined; leaves
            rounded at apex or acute................................*V. prunifolium*, p. 307

[297]

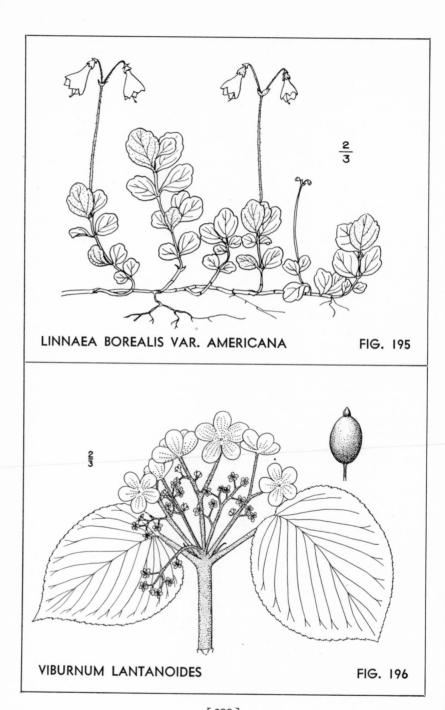

$\frac{2}{3}$

LINNAEA BOREALIS VAR. AMERICANA   FIG. 195

$\frac{2}{3}$

VIBURNUM LANTANOIDES   FIG. 196

Viburnum lantanoides Michx. (Hobble-bush, Witch Hobble, Moose-wood). Fig. 196. (*Viburnum alnifolium* Marsh., Gray's Manual, 7th Edition, Shrubs of Michigan, 1st Edition.) A low,

irregular, straggling shrub; bark on older stems smooth, purplish; twigs densely covered with a rusty-scurfy pubescence; branches often procumbent and rooting at the tips; leaves deciduous, opposite, simple, round-ovate, 1–2 dm. across, cordate at the base, abruptly pointed at the apex, finely serrate all around, strongly pinnately veined, covered with dense, rusty down both sides when young, at length glabrous and deeply corrugated above, scurfy with stellate pubescence on the veins beneath; petioles 1–3 cm. long; flowers of 2 sorts, perfect and neutral, all white and borne in sessile, usually 5-rayed cymes, 7–13 cm. broad, the marginal without stamens and pistil, about 2 cm. broad and raised on long pedicels, the inner small and perfect; calyx 5-toothed; corolla rotate, 5-lobed, the lobes spreading; stamens 5, exserted; style short; stigmas 3-parted; drupe ovoid-oblong, red, becoming purple, 10–12 mm. long; stone 3-grooved on one side, 1-grooved on the other. Flowers, May, June; fruit, September.

In low woods, New Brunswick to North Carolina, Tennessee, Ontario, western New York and Michigan. Michigan, definitely reported from only two counties in Lower Peninsula. See comments under Rare Species.

It is interesting to speculate upon the reason for some of the common names applied to the Hobble-bush. It is a straggling shrub and the long branches often take root at the end. In woods where it is abundant these loops catch the feet of the unwary, tripping them up. It is not hard to see where it would get the name Trip-toe from this character, as well as Hobble-bush, or Witch Hobble.

This viburnum is interesting in both flower and fruit. The large neutral flowers are very effective in combination with the leaves, while the fruit in its change of color through coral and crimson to purple is equally attractive.

Viburnum trilobum Marsh. (High-bush Cranberry, Cranberry-tree). Fig. 197. (*Viburnum Opulus* L. var. *americanum* (Mill.) Ait., Gray's Manual, 7th Edition, Shrubs of Michigan, 1st Edition.) A shrub 1–4 m. tall, with upright smooth gray branches; twigs glabrous; leaves opposite, simple, deciduous, 3–5-ribbed, strongly 3-lobed, broadly wedge-shaped, rounded, or slightly cordate at the base, the lobes spreading and sharply pointed, mostly dentate on the sides, entire in the sinuses, 3.5–10 cm. long, 3.5–12 cm. wide, more or less pubescent on both surfaces or becoming almost glabrous; petioles 1–2.5 cm. long, bearing two glands at the apex; cymes flat-topped, 5–10 cm. in diameter; peduncles 1–3.5 cm. long; flowers white, the outer row sterile, about 2 cm. broad; corolla rotate, deeply 5-lobed; the inner flowers fertile, about 4 mm. broad; calyx attached to the ovary, border 5 toothed; stamens 5, elongate;

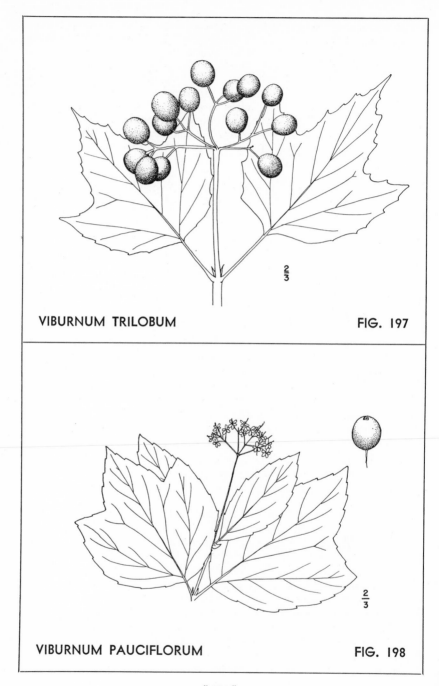

VIBURNUM TRILOBUM

$\frac{2}{3}$

FIG. 197

VIBURNUM PAUCIFLORUM

$\frac{2}{3}$

FIG. 198

stigma 3-parted; drupe globose or ellipsoid, about 10 mm. in diameter, red, sour and bitter; stone orbicular, flat, not grooved. Flowers, May, June; fruit ripe, September.

In low grounds, Newfoundland to British Columbia, south to New Jersey, Pennsylvania, Michigan, Indiana, Wisconsin and South Dakota. Michigan, common throughout.

The High-bush Cranberry is a familiar shrub in low grounds throughout Michigan. Although it is very interesting when in bloom because of having two sorts of flowers in its clusters, its greatest beauty comes in the fall when the fruit has ripened and the leaves turned a brilliant scarlet. The berries often remain on the branches through the winter. They are acid and bitter, but make an acceptable substitute for market cranberries (Vaccinium) when cooked and are frequently used for jelly.

Viburnum pauciflorum Raf. (Squashberry). Fig. 198. A straggling shrub 0.6–1.8 m. tall; bark grayish on the older stems; young twigs reddish-brown,

glabrous or nearly so; leaves simple, opposite, deciduous, broadly oval, obovate, or broader than long, 5-ribbed, rounded or semi-heart-shaped at the base, the summit with 3 shallow lobes coarsely and unequally dentate, glabrous above, pubescent on the veins beneath, 3–8 cm. broad; petiole 1–2 cm. long; cymes peduncled, few-flowered, about 2 cm. broad; flowers white, all perfect, small and uniform; calyx 5-toothed; corolla spreading, deeply 5-lobed; stamens 5, shorter than the corolla; stigmas 1–3; drupe ovoid or globose, light red, acid, 8–10 mm. long; stone flat, orbicular, not grooved. Flowers, June; fruit, August, September.

Cold woods, Newfoundland to Alaska, south to Maine and New Hampshire, Pennsylvania, northern Michigan, Minnesota, Colorado and Washington. Michigan, Upper Peninsula and Isle Royale only, rare.

Viburnum acerifolium L. (Mapleleaf Viburnum). Fig. 199. A shrub 1–1.5 m. tall; branchlets pubescent; leaves opposite, simple, deciduous, ovate, orbicular or sometimes broader than long, cordate or truncate at base, 3-lobed, 5–14 cm. long, coarsely and unequally dentate, lobes divergent, acuminate at the apex, pubescent on both sides; petioles 1–3 cm. long, downy; stipules bristle-form; flowers perfect, cream-white, in 3–7-rayed, pedunculate, pubescent cymes, 4–7 cm. broad; calyx with 5 obtuse teeth; corolla wheel-shaped, 4–6

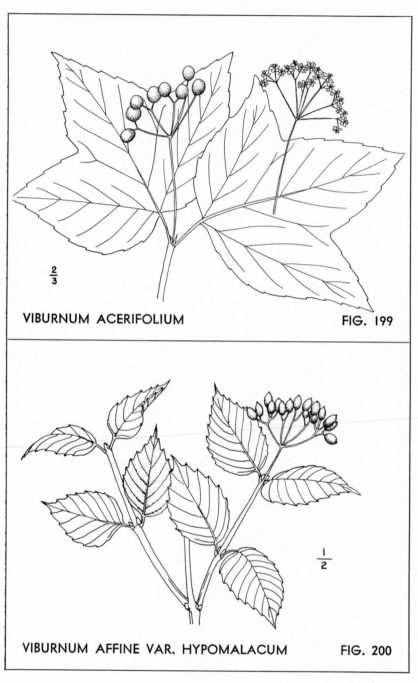

$\frac{2}{3}$

VIBURNUM ACERIFOLIUM   FIG. 199

$\frac{1}{2}$

VIBURNUM AFFINE VAR. HYPOMALACUM   FIG. 200

mm. broad; stamens 5, exserted; style 3-lobed; drupe deep purple-black, globose, 8–9 mm. in diameter; stone lenticular, faintly 2-ridged on one side, 2-grooved on the other. Flowers, May, June; fruit ripe, September.

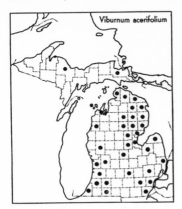
Viburnum acerifolium

Rocky woods, New Brunswick to Michigan, Minnesota, Kentucky and Georgia. Michigan, throughout, but more common in Lower Peninsula.

The Mapleleaf Viburnum appears to thrive best in deep shade and is a familiar little shrub in our deciduous woods. Its fruit remains on the branches most of the winter.

A form of this viburnum, with leaves ovate, remotely dentate and subcordate, has been separated as var. *ovatum* Rehd. It is reported by Hanes from Kalamazoo County, and no doubt may be found in other localities.

Viburnum affine Bush var. *hypomalacum* Blake. Fig. 200. A branching shrub 6–14 dm. tall; bark dark gray; twigs brownish-yellow; leaves ovate or oblong-ovate, acute to acuminate, 3.5–7 cm. long, 2.3–4.2 cm. wide, base cordate, occasionally rounded or narrowed, dentate with 4–9 teeth on each side, upper surface sparse-pilose to glabrate, densely pilose over the entire surface beneath; veins 5–7; petiole 3–7 mm. long with 2 conspicuous stipules at base; cymes peduncled, 7-radiate; flowers 6 mm. broad; drupe oval, dark purple, about 6 mm. long; seeds compressed, with slightly bi-sulcate faces. Flowers, May, June; fruit ripe, August, September.

Viburnum affine var. hypomalacum

Woods and thickets, Vermont and Ontario to Georgia, Michigan and Manitoba. Michigan, fairly frequent in both peninsulas.

In this bulletin it is the usual practice to illustrate the species, mentioning varieties in the text. In this case, however, it seems that the variety is much the more abundantly distributed within the state, and it is therefore given the first place. The species, *Viburnum affine* Bush, is the same general type of plant but has the under surface of its leaves pilose only on the veins, and the petioles are generally longer, up to 12 mm. It has been recorded from only one station, in Keweenaw County, but should be looked for wherever the variety is found. The general range is given from Ontario to Minnesota, south to Illinois and Missouri, also in Virginia.

Viburnum pubescens (Ait.) Pursh. (Downy Arrow-wood). Fig. 201. A low shrub, 1–1.5 m. tall; bark gray; twigs brownish, glabrous or sometimes

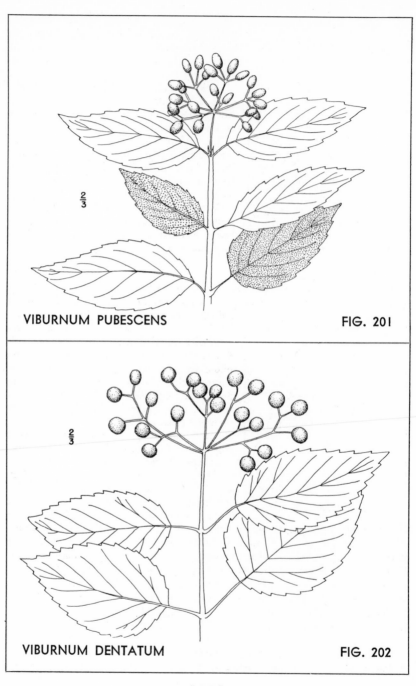

$\frac{2}{3}$

VIBURNUM PUBESCENS   FIG. 201

$\frac{2}{3}$

VIBURNUM DENTATUM   FIG. 202

Viburnum pubescens

slightly pubescent; leaves opposite, simple, deciduous, ovate or oblong-ovate, 4–8 cm. long, 1.5–4.5 cm. wide, rounded or slightly cordate at the base, acute or taper-pointed at the apex, margin coarsely and irregularly dentate, glabrous above, densely velvety-pubescent below, or sometimes glabrate on the surfaces; petioles very short, soft-downy when young; cymes peduncled with mostly 7 rays about 1 cm. long, 3–7 cm. broad, numerous; flowers perfect, white; calyx-border 5-toothed, acute; corolla rotate, with 5 spreading lobes; stamens 5, exserted; style short, 3-lobed; drupe oval, nearly black, about 8 mm. long; stone slightly 2-grooved on both faces. Flowers, May, June; fruit, August, September.

In rocky woods and on ridges and banks, Quebec and Ontaria to Georgia, west to Michigan and Iowa. Michigan, common throughout.

The autumn coloring of this viburnum is very fine, varying from deep purple to red.

Viburnum dentatum L. (Arrow-wood). Fig. 202. A shrub 1–4.5 m. tall; bark ash-colored, smooth; branches obtusely angular; leaves opposite, simple,

Viburnum dentatum

deciduous, broadly oval or orbicular, 5–8 cm. long, rounded or slightly cordate at the base, acute or short-acuminate at the apex, prominently veined, coarsely and sharply serrate, glabrous, or with hairy tufts in the axils of the veins beneath; petioles 0.5–3 cm. long; cymes flat, 5–8 cm. broad, long-peduncled; flowers perfect, white; calyx-limb 5-toothed; corolla wheel-shaped with 5 spreading lobes; stamens 5, exserted; style short, 3-lobed; fruit globose-ovoid, 6 mm. long, dark blue, somewhat acid; stone grooved on 1 side, rounded on the other. Flowers, May, June; fruit, August, September.

Found in low moist places, New Brunswick to Ontario, Georgia, Michigan and Minnesota. Michigan, infrequent throughout.

The Arrow-wood takes kindly to cultivation and is extensively planted. It is a most attractive shrub both in flower and in fruit. The young shoots are slender and very straight and are said to have been generally used by the Indians for arrows, which fact gives rise to its common name.

Viburnum cassinoides L. (Withe-rod, Wild Raisin). Fig. 203. Erect shrub 0.5–3 m. tall; branches gray; branchlets scurfy or sometimes glabrous; leaves opposite, simple, deciduous, thickish and dull, ovate to oblong, 2.5–10 cm. long,

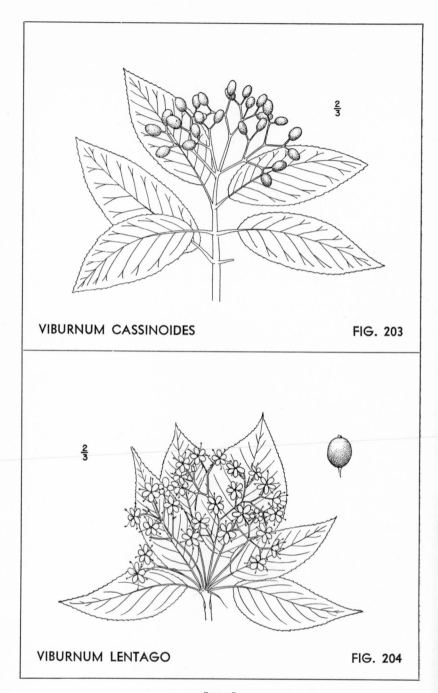

VIBURNUM CASSINOIDES

$\frac{2}{3}$

FIG. 203

VIBURNUM LENTAGO

$\frac{2}{3}$

FIG. 204

Viburnum cassinoides

obscurely veined, narrowed or rounded at the base, acute or rounded at the apex, margins irregularly crenulate-denticulate or sometimes entire, young leaves scurfy, soon becoming glabrous or nearly so; petioles 6–10 cm. long; flowers perfect, white, borne in broad, flat, usually 5-rayed, peduncled cymes up to 8 cm. in diameter; calyx-border 5-toothed; corolla rotate with 5 spreading lobes; stamens 5, exserted; style short, 3-lobed; drupe ellipsoid to spherical, 6–9 mm. long, blue-black with a bloom when ripe; stone round or oval, flattened. Flowers, June, July; fruit ripe, September.

In swamps and wet soil, New Brunswick to Manitoba, New Jersey, Georgia, Wisconsin, Minnesota and Alabama. Michigan, frequent throughout.

This viburnum is easily cultivated and becomes a compact symmetrical shrub, an ornament to any garden.

Viburnum Lentago L. (Nanny-berry, Sheepberry, Sweet Viburnum). Fig. 204. A shrub or small tree, 2–6 m. tall; twigs glabrous; leaves simple, opposite, deciduous, ovate or oval, rounded at base, acuminate at the apex, 5–10 cm. long, glabrous on both sides, closely and very sharply serrate; petioles 1–2.5 cm. long, often winged and wavy-margined; cymes sessile, 3–4-rayed, 6–10 cm. broad; flowers perfect, white, 6–7 mm. broad; calyx 5-toothed; corolla rotate, 5-lobed; stamens 5, exserted about half their length; style short, 3-parted; drupe ovoid or ellipsoid, bluish-black, 10–12 mm. long; stone oval to oblong, flat and smooth. Flowers, May, June; fruit, September.

Viburnum Lentago

In rich soil, woods and banks of streams, Quebec to Manitoba, south to Ohio, West Virginia, Wisconsin and Colorado. Michigan, frequent throughout.

This viburnum is valuable for ornamental planting and does well in cultivation. Its fruit is variable and an extreme form with spherical drupes has been separated as var. *sphaerocarpum* Gray, which is reported from Oakland County. The fruit is edible.

Viburnum prunifolium L. · (Black Haw). Fig. 205. Shrub or small tree; bark furrowed, reddish-brown on older stems; leaves simple, opposite, deciduous, ovate or broadly oval, obtuse or slightly pointed, 2–8 cm. long, narrowed at the base, finely serrulate, at length glabrous or nearly so; petioles glabrous,

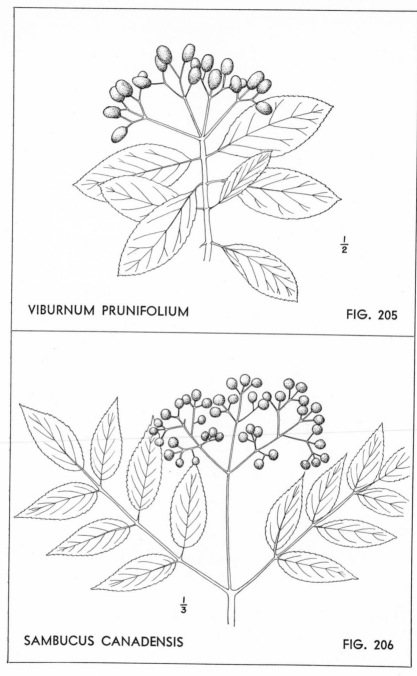

VIBURNUM PRUNIFOLIUM

$\frac{1}{2}$

FIG. 205

SAMBUCUS CANADENSIS

$\frac{1}{3}$

FIG. 206

slender or slightly winged; cymes sessile, 3–5-rayed, 5–10 cm. broad; flowers

Viburnum prunifolium

numerous, perfect, white, expanding with, or a little before the leaves, about 5 mm. in diameter; calyx 5-toothed; corolla spreading, deeply 5-lobed; stamens 5, exserted; style short, 3-parted; drupe ellipsoid, ovoid or nearly globose, 1–1.4 cm. long, blueblack with a bloom; stone oval, flat on one side, convex on the other. Flowers, May, June; fruit ripe, September and October.

The Black Haw is found in dry soil Connecticut to Georgia, west to Michigan, Kansas and Texas. Michigan, infrequent, southern portion.

This viburnum is very variable in the shape of its leaves and fruit. A form with smaller globose fruit has been reported and named var. *globosum* Nash.

Sambucus [Tourn.] L.—ELDERBERRIES

Sambucus canadensis L. (Common Elder). Fig. 206. Shrub 1–3.5 m. tall; glabrous or nearly so; stems with large white pith and grayish-brown bark, rank

Sambucus canadensis

smelling when bruised; leaves opposite and deciduous, pinnately compound; leaflets 5–11, ovate to ovate-oblong or lanceolate, shortstalked, 7–15 cm. long, 3–6 cm. wide, mostly smooth or with slight pubescence on the veins beneath, the lower sometimes 3-parted, margins sharply serrate, occasionally with stipels; petiole 4–5 cm. long, stipules few; flowers white, 5–6 mm. wide in a flat terminal compound cyme, about 10–20 cm. broad; peduncles 6–12 cm. long; calyx-tube 3–5-lobed or toothed; corolla open-urnshaped, regular, 3–5-lobed; stamens 5, inserted on the base of the corolla and reflexed with the petals; fruit globose, black, about 4 mm. in diameter; seeds, 3–5, roughened. Flowers, June, July; fruit ripe, September, October.

Distributed from Nova Scotia to Florida, west to Manitoba and Texas. Michigan, common throughout.

The Common Elder prefers rich, moist ground and, as its name implies, is widespread and abundant. To many the elder is a nuisance, but there can be

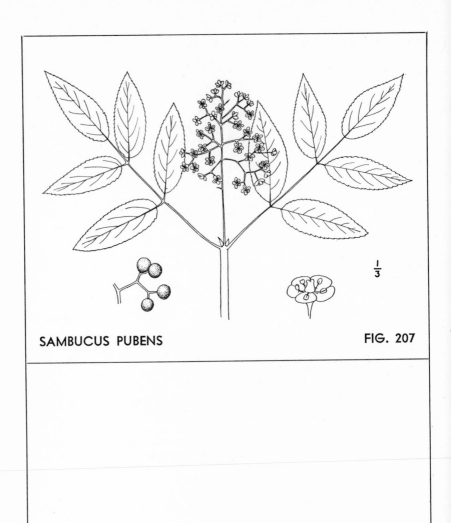

$\frac{1}{3}$

SAMBUCUS PUBENS   **FIG. 207**

little division of opinion as to the value of its fruit as food for the birds. The robins especially seem to be very fond of it. As for human consumption, elderberry pie is not at all bad. Elderberry wine is also made from the berries and is said to have a decided medicinal value.

The native elder is not much used in ornamental planting, doubtless because it is so common and cheap. Many shrubs are used, however, the flowers of which do not equal in beauty the large cymes of the elder. It comes into bloom late in the season when most shrubs are through blooming, which is an added attraction.

Sambucus pubens Michx. (Red-berried Elder). Fig. 207. (*Sambucus racemosa* L., Gray's Manual, 7th Edition, Shrubs of Michigan, 1st Edition.)

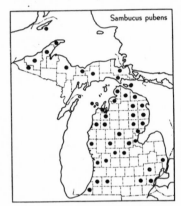

A shrub 0.5–4 m. tall; bark gray and warty; twigs usually pubescent, with dark brown pith; leaves deciduous, opposite, odd-pinnate; leaflets 5–7, ovate-lanceolate, 4–13 cm. long, 2–4 cm. wide, downy underneath, serrate, base narrowed, rounded or sub-cordate, usually unequal, apex acute or acuminate; petiole 2.5–5 cm. long; flowers in convex or pyramidal panicled cymes, yellowish-white, 3–4 mm. broad; petals reflexed; stamens 5, short; stigmas nearly sessile; fruit ripening in June, bright red, berry 4–5 mm. in diameter, acid, inedible; seeds dark brown, minutely roughened. Flowers, April, May; fruit, June, July.

Rocky woods, Newfoundland to British Columbia, south to Georgia, Michigan, Iowa, Colorado and California. Michigan, common throughout.

In the first edition attention was directed to the fact that some authors regarded *S. racemosa* L. as applicable to the European species of Red-berried Elder only, ours being *Sambucus pubens* Michx. Present-day usage tends to accept this interpretation and therefore in the second edition the Linnaean name is superseded by that of Michaux.

Sambucus pubens Michx. forma *calva* Fern., with glabrous leaves, pedicels and branchlets is reported by Hanes from Kalamazoo County. The species is usually more or less pubescent, and it may take quite a search to locate a glabrous specimen.

Our two native elders make an interesting team. The Red-berried is one of the earliest shrubs to bloom and its fruit is fully ripened before the Common Elder comes into flower in late summer. The fruit of the Common Elder ripens in the fall and remains until frost, so that between the two with flower and fruit they span the entire growing season from frost to frost.

Glossary

Achene. A dry 1-seeded fruit.

Acrid. Biting; unpleasant to the taste.

Acuminate. Gradually tapering to a long point.

Acute. Sharp-pointed.

Acutish. Somewhat sharp-pointed.

Adherent. Referring to the union of parts that are usually separate.

Adhesive. Having the quality of sticking to.

Adnate. Grown to, united.

Aerenchyma. Spongy tissue of thin-walled cells and large intercellular spaces found in stems of some marsh plants.

Aerial. Growing in the air.

Albumen. Any deposit of nutritive material stored in the seed, in many cases surrounding the embryo.

Alluvial. Referring to soil deposited by running water.

Alternate. A single leaf at each node; not opposite.

Ament. A catkin; a spike of flowers usually with bracts and frequently deciduous.

Anatropous. Having the ovule inverted, so that the opening through which the pollen tube enters the ovule is near the seed's point of attachment.

Angled. Having an edge formed by the meeting of 2 planes.

Annular. In the form of a ring.

Anther. The portion of the stamen containing the pollen.

Anthesis. The time of expansion of a flower; blossoming time.

Apetalous. Without petals.

Apex. Upper end or tip (of a leaf).

Appendaged. Having an addition or projection.

Appressed. Lying flat and close against.

Aquatic. Living in the water.

Arborescent. Tree-like.

Arched. Curved in the shape of a bow.

Arching. Growing in a graceful curve, or arch.

Aril. A fleshy, often bright-colored appendage to a seed.

Armed. Bearing thorns, spines or prickles.

Aromatic. Having a spicy smell or taste.

Articulated. Jointed, separating freely by a clean scar, as in a leaf fall.

Ascending. Growing upward at an angle, not perpendicular; upcurved.

Atoms. In botanical parlance, a very small division or particle of a substance.

Attenuate. Slenderly tapering, growing very narrow.

Awl-shaped. Attenuate from the base to a slender or rigid point.

Awn. A slender bristle-like appendage.

Axil. The angle formed by a leaf or branch with the stem.

Axillary. Situated in the axil of a leaf.

Axis. The central support of a group of organs, a stem, etc.

Bark. The covering of the stems, branches and roots of a shrub or tree.

Basal. At the base of an organ or part.

Base. The lowest portion (as of a leaf).

Beak. An elongated, tapering structure.

Beaked. A projection ending in an elongated tip.

Bearded. Bearing long, stiff hairs.

Berry. A fleshy fruit having a thin skin or outer covering, the seeds surrounded by the pulp.

Biennial. Requiring two years to complete its life-cycle; growing one year, flowering and fruiting the next.

Bipinnate. With both primary and secondary divisions (of a leaf) pinnate.

Bladdery. Thin and inflated.

Blade. The flat, expanded portion of a leaf.

Bloom. A fine powdery, waxy substance, causing the glaucous appearance of certain fruits.

Bog(s). A soggy marsh; wet spongy ground where a heavy body is apt to sink.

Bony. Hard; bone-like.

Border. Referring to the margin of a petal, sepal, or other part.

Bract. A small leaf subtending a flower or belonging to a flower cluster.

Bracteate. Having bracts.

Bracteole. A small bract or scale on the pedicel below the flower.

Bractlet. A secondary bract, as upon a flower pedicel.

Bramble. Any plant of the genus *Rubus*, which includes the raspberry and blackberry.

Branch. A secondary stem of a shrub or tree, older than the current year.

Branchlet. A secondary stem of the current year.

Bristle. A stiff hair.

Bristleform Having the form of a stiff, coarse hair or bristle.

Bristly. Beset with long spines.

Bud. An undeveloped stem, branch or shoot; an unexpanded flower.

Bundle-scars. Dots on the surface of a leaf-scar left at the time of leaf-fall by the breaking of the vascular bundles that pass from the stem into the petiole.

Caducous. Dropping off early.

Calcareous. Referring to soil impregnated with lime.

Calyx. The outer of the two series of flower envelopes, mostly green, but occasionally colored and petal-like.

Campanulate. Shaped like a bell.

Cane. The new shoots of certain shrubs, as the raspberries.

Canescent. Covered with gray, or hoary, fine pubescence.

Capillary. Fine, hair-like.

Capitate. Knob-like; arranged in a head, or dense cluster.

Capsule. A dry fruit of two or more carpels, usually opening by valves or teeth.

Carpel. A simple pistil, or one unit of a compound pistil.

Catkin. A scaly, spike-like inflorescence of small flowers, as in the willow.

Cavity. A hollow place.

Cell. The cavity of an anther or ovary.

Chlorophyll. The green coloring matter of plants.

Ciliate. Having hairs on the margin.

Ciliolate. Minutely ciliate.

Cinereous. Ashy; ash-colored.

Circumboreal. Entirely around the world in the far north.

Clammy. Soft and sticky to the touch.

Claw. The very much narrowed lower part of a petal.

Cleft. Cut about half-way to the middle.

Cluster. A group, or bunch, as of flowers or fruits.

Coalescent. Growing together, uniting.

Coherent. United or clinging together.

Colonial. Forming colonies; growing in patches.

Column. The combination of parts into a solid central body.

Compact. Closely joined or pressed together.

Compound. Containing two or more similar parts united to make one whole, as a compound leaf, which is composed of several leaflets.

Compressed. Flattened.

Conduplicate. Folded together lengthwise.

Cone. A dry multiple fruit, composed of scales arranged around an axis and enclosing seeds, as a pine cone.

Conic; Conical. Cone-shaped.

Coniferous. Producing or bearing cones.

Connate. Referring to like organs that are more or less united.

Connivent. Coming into contact; converging.

Constricted. Drawn together at regular intervals.

Contiguous. Referring to neighboring parts that are in contact.

Convex. Having a more or less rounded surface.

Convolute. Rolled up longitudinally; rolled around.

Cordate. Shaped like a heart.

Coriaceous. With the texture of leather.

Corolla. The inner of the two series of floral envelopes, usually colored.

Corrugated. Wrinkled.

Corymb. A flat-topped or convex flower-cluster, the outer flowers opening first.

Corymbiform. In the form of a corymb.

Corymbose. Like a corymb, or borne in corymbs.

Creeping. Running along the ground and rooting at intervals.

Crenate. Having much-rounded teeth.

Crenulate. Finely crenate.

Crescent. The shape of the new moon.

Crown. The head of foliage in a tree or shrub.

Cuneate. Shaped like a wedge.

Cuspidate. Tipped with a sharp rigid point, called a cusp.

Cut. Incised or cleft.

Cylindric. Shaped like a cylinder.

Cyme. A convex or flat flower-cluster, the central flowers unfolding first.

Cymose. Cyme-like, or bearing cymes.

Cytological. In reference to the science of the cell, its life history, nuclear divisions and development.

Deciduous. Not persistent; falling away at the close of the growing period.

Decumbent. Stems in a reclining position, but with the end ascending.

Decurrent (leaf). Extending down the stem below the place of attachment.

Deflexed. Bent or turned abruptly downward.

Dehiscent. Opening to discharge the contents.

Deltoid. Triangular.

Dense. Crowded closely together.

Dentate. Toothed, with the teeth projecting outwardly.

Denticulate. Minutely dentate.

Depressed. Flattened from above.

Dichotomous. Forking regularly into 2 nearly equal divisions.

Diffuse. Widely or loosely spreading.

Dilated. Distended, inflated.

Dioecious. Having staminate flowers on one plant and the pistillate on another of the same species.

Disk. An enlargement of, or extension of, the receptacle of a flower around the base of the pistil.

Dissected. Cut or divided into numerous segments.

Distinct. Separate from each other.

Divergent. Turning in different directions.

Down. Soft pubescence.

Downy. Having soft pubescence.

Drooping. Inclining downwards.

Drupe. A fleshy fruit with a pit or stone; such as the peach, plum or cherry.

Drupelet. A small drupe.

Ecology. The study of plant life in relation to environment.

Edaphic. The term for the influence of the soil on the plant growing upon it.

Eglandular. Destitute of glands.

Ellipsoid. A solid each plane section of which is an ellipse or a circle.

Elliptic. Having the outline of an ellipse, oval.

Elongated. Drawn out in length.

Embryo. The rudimentary plant formed in a seed.

Entire. Without divisions, lobes or teeth.

Epigynous. Growing on the summit of the ovary, or apparently so.

Erect. Upright, perpendicular to the ground.

Erose. Margin irregular, as if gnawed.

Exfoliating. Peeling off in layers, as the bark of certain shrubs and trees.

Expanded. Spread out; the condition of a flower or leaf in full perfection.

Exserted. Projecting beyond the surrounding parts, as the stamens from the corolla.

Face. The surface of the organ or part, as opposed to the back.

Family. A group of related plants, usually several genera that resemble each other in prominent characteristics. A single genus, however, if it differs sufficiently, may constitute a family.

Farinose. Covered with meal-like powder.

Fascicle. A close cluster or bundle of flowers, leaves, stems or roots.

Fascicled. Borne in dense clusters.

Fertile. Capable of bearing fruit; bearing seed.

Fibrous. Having much woody fibre.

Filament. A stalk; the part of the stamen which supports the anther.

Filiform. Thread-like; long and slender.

Fleshy. Consisting of pulp; succulent.

Floccose. Having loose tufts of wool-like hairs.

Foliaceous. Leaf-like; similar to leaves.

Foliate. Having leaves.

Follicle. A dry one-carpel fruit, opening only on one side.

Forked. Separating into two divisions more or less apart.

Form; Forma. A slight variation; less than a variety.

Free. Not joined to other parts.

Fringed. Bordered with hair-like appendages.

Fruit. The seed-bearing product of a plant of whatever form.

Fulvous. Tawny; orange-gray-yellow.

Funnel-form. Shaped as a funnel.

Fuscous. Dusky, too brown for a gray.

Genus. A group of species resembling each other so distinctly that a relationship is indicated.

Germinate. Sprout; to begin to develop into a higher form.

Gibbous. Swollen or enlarged on one side.

Glabrate. Without hairs, or nearly so.

Glabrescent. Inclined to be smooth; smoothish.

Glabrous. Entirely smooth; not pubescent or bearing hairs of any kind.

Gland. A small appendage or projection; a structure secreting resin, oil, etc.

Glandular. Gland-like, or bearing glands.

Glaucescent. Somewhat bluish or whitish; less than glaucous.

Glaucous. Covered with a fine bluish or whitish bloom.

Globose. Spherical or nearly so, globular.

Glutinous. Glue-like, sticky.

Habitat. The situation in which a plant grows naturally.

Hair. An outgrowth of the epidermis, either of one or several cells.

Hastate. Shaped like an arrow, but with divergent basal lobes.

Head. A dense cluster of sessile or nearly sessile flowers.

Hemispheric. Resembling a hemisphere, or half-sphere.

Herb. A plant without a persistent woody stem; one that dies annually, at least down to the ground.

Herbaceous. Herb-like.

Hip. The fleshy ripened fruit of the rose.

Hirsute. Bearing rather coarse, stiff hairs.

Hispid. Bearing bristles, or beset with rigid hairs.

Hoary. Grayish-white with a fine pubescence.

Hooded. Having a concave expansion of an organ resembling a hood.

Hooked. Curved or bent back at the tip.

Hybrid. A cross between two species.

Hypanthium. An enlargement of the flower receptacle which bears the sepals, petals and stamens.

Imbricated. Overlapping, as the shingles of a house.

Impressed. Furrowed, or hollowed as if by force.

Incised. Cut sharply and irregularly into lobes.

Included. Not extending beyond the surrounding parts.

Incurved. Bent inward.

Inferior. Below or lower; as an inferior ovary, which is attached below the calyx.

Inflated. Puffed out; bladdery.

Inflorescence. The flowering portion of a plant.

Inserted. Growing out of or attached to, as stamens inserted on the corolla tube.

Interrupted. Broken or separated.

Involucre. A whorl of leaves or bracts surrounding a flower or flower cluster.

Involute. Rolled inward.

Irregular. Applied to a flower in which one or more parts of the same kind are not alike, as when the petals are different.

Jointed. Two or more parts joined together, articulated.

Juice. The liquid contents of any plant tissue.

Keel. The two fused lower petals of the flower of the pea family.

Laciniate. Slashed; cut into narrow lobes.

Lanceolate. Long and narrow, tapering upward from the middle or below; lance-shaped.

Lateral. Arising or proceeding from the side.

Lax. Loose, not firm or tense.

Leaf. A lateral organ borne by the stem, usually flat and green in color.

Leaflet. One of the divisions of a compound leaf.

Leaf-scar. The scar left on a twig at the time of leaf-fall.

Leathery. Tough, resembling leather.

Legume. A simple dry fruit, opening along both sides, as pea and bean pods.

Lenticel. A corky pore in the stem of a woody plant.

Lenticular. Shaped like a double-convex lens.

Lepidote. Bearing small, scurfy scales.

Limb. The expanded part of a petal or sepal or of a corolla with united petals.

Linear. Long and narrow, with the sides nearly parallel.

Lip. The upper and lower divisions of an irregular corolla or calyx, as in the mints.

Lobe. Rounded division of any organ, as of leaves, stigmas, petals, etc.

Lobed. Divided into lobes.

Lustrous. Bright, shining; having lustre.

Margin. The border or edge, as of a leaf.

Mat. Closely intertwined vegetation.

Mealy. Having the quality of meal; soft, dry.

Membranous. Thin, papery; like a membrane.

Midrib. The central vein of a leaf.

Milky. With opaque white juice.

Minute. Exceedingly small.

Monoecious. Having stamens and pistils on the same plant, but in different flowers.

Mucro. A sharp and small abrupt point.

Mucronate. Having a sharp, abrupt point.

Mucronulate. Tipped with a very small point.

Mucus. A viscid, sticky secretion.

Mutation. A change; alteration in form or qualities.

Naked. Without enveloping organs or parts.

Naturalized. Of foreign origin but established and reproducing itself as though a native.

Nerve. An unbranched vein of a leaf.

Nodal. Pertaining to a node.

Nodding. Bending downward, as hanging on a bent peduncle or pedicel.

Node. The joint of a stem; the part that normally bears a leaf or leaves.

Notched. Nicked, indented.

Nut. A dry, one-seeded non-opening fruit with a hard, bony shell or covering.

Nutlet. A small nut.

Obconic. Conical, but attached at the narrower end.

Obcordate. Inverted heart-shaped.

Oblanceolate. Reversed lance-shaped, widest above the middle.

Oblique. Having the sides unequal, slanting.

Oblong. Considerably longer than broad and having nearly parallel sides.

Obovate. Inversely ovate.

Obovoid. Inversely ovoid.

Obsolete. Not evident; rudimentary.

Obtuse. Having the end blunt or rounded.

Opaque. Not transparent.

Opposite. Arranged in pairs, as leaves directly across from each other at the same node.

Orbicular. Circular in outline.

Oval. Broadly elliptical.

Ovary. The part of the pistil' that contains the ovules.

Ovate. Having the shape of a longitudinal section of a hen's egg in outline.

Ovoid. Egg-shaped.

Ovule. The rudimentary seed as found in the flower.

Palmate. Having the appearance of an open hand, with the fingers spread, as a leaf with the leaflets arising from a common center.

Palmately. In a palmate manner.

Panicle. A loose, compound, racemose flower cluster.

Paniculate. Resembling a panicle; borne in a panicle.

Parasite. An organism subsisting on another living organism.

Parasitic. Deriving nourishment from some other organism.

Parted. Deeply cut.

Pedate. Palmately divided or parted.

Pedicel. The stem of a single flower in a flower cluster.

Peduncle. Stem or stalk of a cluster of flowers, or a single flower.

Pellucid. Transparent, clear.

Peltate. Having the petiole attached to the lower surface of the leaf instead of the edge.

Pendulous. Hanging.

Perennial. Lasting year after year.

Perfect. Flowers with both stamens and pistils.

Perfoliate. With the leaf clasping the stem so that the stem appears to pass through it.

Perianth. The floral envelopes, sepals and petals, considered together, whatever their form.

Persistent. Remaining attached after the growing period.

Petal. One of the divisions of the corolla

Petaloid. Petal-like.

Petiolate. Having a petiole.

Petiole. The stalk or stem of a leaf.

Petiolule. The stalk or stem of a leaflet.

Phylogeny. Ancestral history of a group of organisms.

Pilose. Having long, soft hairs.

Pinnate. Leaves divided into leaflets or segments along a common axis.

Pinnatifid. Pinnately cleft.

Pistil. The seed-bearing organ of a flower, the ovary, stigma and style when present.

Pistillate. With pistils, but without stamens.

Pith. The soft, spongy tissue in the center of the stems and branches of certain plants, as the elder.

Pitted. Having small depressions.

Plumose. Feathery; plume-like.

Pod. A dry dehiscent fruit.

Pollen. The fertilizing grains contained in the anthers.

Pollination. The transfer of pollen from the anther to the stigma.

[317]

Polygamo-dioecious. With perfect and imperfect flowers on different plants.

Polygamo-monoecious. With the perfect and imperfect flowers on the same plant.

Polygamous. Referring to plants bearing pistillate, staminate and perfect flowers.

Polymorphic. Having many forms; variable.

Pome. A fleshy fruit, of which the apple is a typical example.

Pomological. In reference to edible cultivated fruits; dealing with the cultivation of fruits.

Prickle. A sharp needle-like growth from the bark or rind.

Primary. Of the main divisions; of the first rank.

Procumbent. Lying upon the ground or trailing, but not rooting at the nodes.

Prostrate. Lying flat upon the ground.

Protruding. Exserted; thrust out.

Puberulent. Minutely pubescent.

Pubescent. Covered with soft hairs, downy.

Pulpy. Soft, succulent.

Punctate. Dotted with depressions, or translucent dots or pits.

Pyramidal. Having the shape of a pyramid.

Pyriform. Shaped like a pear.

Raceme. A more or less elongated cluster of pedicelled flowers borne upon a common axis.

Racemose. Resembling a raceme, or in racemes.

Rachis. The axis of a compound leaf, spike or raceme.

Radiate. Spreading from or arranged around a common center.

Rank. A row.

Rays. One of the branches of an umbel. The marginal flowers of an inflorescence when distinct from the disk.

Receptacle. The end of the flower stalk bearing the floral parts.

Recurving. Curved downward or backward.

Reflexed. Bent sharply backward.

Regular. Having all the members of each part alike in size and shape.

Reniform. Shaped like a kidney.

Repand. With somewhat uneven margin; less than sinuate.

Resinous. Having resin.

Reticulate. Arranged in the form of network; net-veined.

Retrorse. Facing backward or downward.

Revolute. Rolled backward from the edge.

Rhizome. An underground stem.

Rhombic. More or less in the shape of a lozenge.

Rib. A prominent vein of a leaf.

Ridge. An elevated line.

Rigid. Tending to be stiff.

Root. The underground part of a plant which supplies it with nourishment.

Rootlet. A very slender root; the branch of a root.

Rooting. Producing roots.

Rosette. A cluster of leaves or other organs in a circular form.

Rostrate. Bearing a beak.

Rotate. Flat and circular in outline; wheel-shaped.

Rugose. Roughened; wrinkled.

Rugulose. Somewhat wrinkled.

Rusty. Having the color of iron rust.

Salver-shaped. Having a slender tube abruptly expanded into a flat top.

Samara. A simple indehiscent winged fruit.

Sap. The juice of a plant.

Satiny. With the appearance of satin.

Scabrate. Rough or roughened.

Scabrous. Rough to the touch.

Scale. A minute rudimentary leaf.

Scaly. Bearing scales.

Scar. The mark left on the stem by the separation of the leaf.

Scarious. Thin, dry and membranaceous; not green.

Scurfy. Having minute scales.

Seed. The ripened ovule.

Segment. One of the divisions of a leaf or other organ.

Sepal. One of the divisions of a calyx.

Serrate. Having teeth pointed forward.

Serrulate. Finely serrate.

Sessile. Without a stalk or stem.

Setose. Bristly.

Sheath. A tubular envelope, as the portion of the leaf base that clasps the stem.

Shoot. New growth, as a young branch or sucker of a plant.

Shreddy. In small irregular strips.

Silky. Covered with close-pressed soft and straight pubescence.

Silvery. Having the appearance of silver.

Simple. All in one piece; not compound, as a leaf.

Single. As opposed to double.

Sinuate. Having the margin wavy.

Skin. The thin external covering, as of fruit.

Smooth. Without pubescence or other roughness.

Solitary. Single, only one from the same place.

Sordid. Dirty in color; not pleasant.

Spatulate. Having the shape of a spatula; oblong with an attenuate base.

Species. A group of like individuals.

Spherical. Shaped like a sphere; globular.

Spicate. Resembling a spike.

Spike. An elongated cluster of flowers which are sessile or nearly so on the common axis.

Spine. A sharp woody outgrowth from the stem.

Spiral. As though wound around an axis.

Stalked. Borne on a stalk.

Stamen. The part of the flower that bears the pollen grains.

Staminate. Bearing stamens, but without pistils.

Standard. The large upper petal of a flower of the pea family.

Stellate. In the shape of a star.

Stem. The main body or stalk of a plant.

Sterile. Without seed; unproductive, as a flower without a pistil.

Stigma. That portion of the pistil which receives the pollen to accomplish fertilization.

Stipel. A stipule of a leaflet.

Stipitate. Having a stipe, or special stalk.

Stipulate. Having stipules.

Stipule. Appendages at the base of the petiole, sometimes attached to it.

Stolon. A basal branch rooting at the nodes.

Stoloniferous. Sending out or propagating itself by stolons.

Stone. The hard, bony seed of some fruits, as the cherry, plum, etc.

Strigose. Beset with sharp-pointed, appressed straight and stiff bristles.

Style. The portion of the pistil connecting the stigma and the ovary.

Sub-. Latin prefix denoting a lower degree; nearly, somewhat.

Subcordate. Somewhat heart-shaped.

Subglobose. Somewhat globe-shaped.

Subsessile. Almost sessile.

Subtend. To extend under, or be opposite to.

Subulate. Awl-shaped.

Succulent. Juicy.

Sucker. A shoot of subterranean origin.

Sulcate. Grooved or furrowed.

Summit. The apex; the top or highest point.

Symmetrical (flower). Regular as to the number of its petals; having the same number of parts in each circle.

Tapering. Regularly diminishing in diameter.

Tawny. A dull brownish-yellow color.

Taxonomic. Referring to classification, as of plants.

Teeth. The projections of various shapes and sizes along leaf margins.

Tendril. A slender coiling organ of a plant that attaches itself to another body, supporting the plant in climbing.

Terete. Circular in cross section.

Terminal. Borne at the end of a stem or branch, as a flower cluster.

Thorn. Usually an aborted branch, simple or branched.

Throat. The opening of a corolla having its petals united.

Tomentose. Densely covered with tomentum.

Tomentulose. Only slightly tomentose.

Tomentum. Dense woolly matted hairs.

Toothed. Having teeth, as the margin of a leaf.

Trailing. Creeping along the ground.

Translucent. Semi-transparent; allowing the transmission of light.

Tribe. A group superior to a genus, but less than an order.

Trifoliate. Having three leaflets.

Trimorphous. The occurrence of three distinct forms of organs on plants of the same species.

Truncate. Ending with a nearly straight edge, as if cut off squarely.

Trunk. The main stem.

Tube. Any elongated hollow part or organ, as a corolla or calyx having the segments united.

Tuberculate. Having rounded projections.

Tubular. In the form of a tube.

Tufts. A bunch of small, elongated, flexible parts held together at the base, as hairs in the axil of a leaf-vein.

Twig. A small shoot or branchlet of a shrub.

Twining. Winding spirally.

Two-ranked. In two rows.

Typical. Having the distinguishing features of a type.

Umbel. A flower cluster with all the pedicels arising from the same point.

Umbellate. In, or like an umbel.

Unarmed. Without thorns, spines or prickles.

Undulate. Having a wavy margin, or surface.

Unequal. Of different lengths; not alike.

Unifoliate. With one leaf.

United. Joined together.

Urceolate. Having the shape of an urn; hollow and cylindrical and contracted below the mouth.

Valvate. Meeting by the edges and not overlapping; opening by valves.

Valve. One of the parts into which a capsule splits.

Variable. Not constant in appearance; changeable.

Variety (ies). A group of lower rank than a species.

Vascular. Furnished with vessels or ducts.

Vegetative. Growing, or causing to grow.

Vein. Thread of fibro-vascular tissue in a leaf or other organ.

Velutinous. Velvety; like velvet.

Ventral. Referring to the inner face (of a carpel).

Verticillate. Whorled; arranged in a whorl.

Vessel. In botany, a tube or duct.

Villous. With long, soft unmatted hairs.

Vine. Any trailing or climbing stem or runner.

Viscid. Glutinous; sticky.

Warty. Bearing warts or hard, firm excrescences.

Wavy. Undulate; marked by shallow curves, as the margin of a leaf.

Waxy. Resembling beeswax in consistency or appearance.

Whorl. A group of three or more leaves or similar organs arranged in a circle around a stem, and arising about the same point on the axis.

Whorled. Borne in a whorl.

Wing. Any thin expansion surrounding an organ, or bordering it.

Winged. Bearing a wing.

Woody. Approaching the nature of wood.

Woolly. Having a growth of long wool-like hairs.

Bibliography

* Items marked with an asterisk have been abstracted for local distribution records.

ASHE, W. W.
   1902 New East American thorns. Jour. Elisha Mitchell Sci. Soc., 18th yr., Pt. 1, pp. 17–28.

BAILEY, L. H.
   1932 Gentes Herbarum, The Blackberries of North America. The Bailey Hortorum, The New York State College of Agriculture, Cornell University, Ithaca, N. Y. Pp. 153.
   1933 How plants get their names. Macmillan Co., New York. Pp. 209.
   1941–1945 Gentes Herbarum, Vol. 5. The Genus *Rubus* in North America. The Bailey Hortorum, The New York State College of Agriculture, Cornell University, Ithaca, N. Y. Pp. 918.
   1947 Gentes Herbarum, Species *Batorum*. Addendum 1. *Ibid.*, pp. 181–348.

BALL, CARLETON R.
   1924 Extension of range and a new variety in *Salix*. Rhodora, Vol.26, pp. 135–144.
   1948 *Salix petiolaris* J. E. Smith, American, not British. Bull. Torrey Bot. Club, Vol. 75, No. 2, pp. 178–187.

BEAL, W. J.
   *1904 Michigan flora: a list of the fern and seed plants growing without cultivation. 5th Rept., Mich. Acad. Sci., pp. 1–147.
   *1908 Additions to the Michigan flora. 10th Rept., *Ibid.*, pp. 85–89.

BEALS, KATHERINE M.
   1917 Flower lore and legend. Henry Holt & Co., New York. Pp. 245.

BILLINGTON, CECIL
   *1925 The flowering plants and ferns of Warren Woods, Berrien County, Michigan. Papers, Mich. Acad. Sci. Arts and Lett. for 1924, Vol. 4, pp. 81–110.
   *1930 The flora of two acres of farm land in Oakland County, Michigan. *Ibid.* for 1929, Vol. 11, pp. 51–73.

BINGHAM, MARJORIE T.
   *1945 Flora of Oakland County, Michigan. Cranbrook Inst. Sci. Bull. No. 22. Pp. 155.

BLAKE, SIDNEY F.
   1914 The earliest name of the Snowberry. Rhodora. Vol. 16, pp. 118–119.
   1917 Varieties of *Chimaphila umbellata*. Rhodora, Vol. 19, pp. 237–244.
   1918 On the names of some species of *Viburnum*. Rhodora, Vol. 20, pp. 11–15.

BLANCHARD, W. H.
   1905 The yellow-fruited variety of the Black Raspberry. Rhodora, Vol. 7, pp. 143–146.

BRITTON, NATHANIEL LORD, AND BROWN, ADDISON
   1913 An illustrated flora of the northern United States, etc. 2nd Ed. 3 vols. Pp. 680, 735, 637.

BROWN, CLAIR A.
   *1937 Ferns and flowering plants of Isle Royale, Michigan. U. S. Dept. Interior, National Park Service. Pp. 90.

CAMP, W. H.
   1944 A preliminary consideration of the biosystematy of *Oxycoccus*. Bull. Torrey Bot. Club, Vol. 71, pp. 426–437.
   1945 The North American Blueberries with notes on other groups of Vacciniaceae. Brittonia, Vol. 5, pp. 203–275.

CLARK, HUBERT LYMAN
   *1901 Notes on the flora of Eaton County. 3rd. Rept., Mich. Acad. Sci., pp. 51–52.

COLE, EMMA J.
   *1901 Grand Rapids flora. Published by the author. Grand Rapids. Pp. 170.

COLEY, MAY, AND WEATHERBY, CHARLES ALFRED
   1915 Wild flower preservation. Frederick A. Stokes Co., New York. Pp. 197.

COOPER, WILLIAM S.
*1914 A catalog of the flora of Isle Royale, Lake Superior. 16th Rept., Mich. Acad. Sci., pp. 109–131.

DACHNOWSKI, ALFRED
*1907 Flora of the Marquette Quadrangle. 9th Rept., Mich. Acad. Sci., pp. 88–97.

DANIELS, FRANCIS POTTER
*1902 Ecology of the flora of Sturgis, Michigan and vicinity. 4th Rept., Ibid., pp. 145–159.
*1902 The flora of the vicinity of Manistee, Michigan. Ibid., pp. 125–144.

DARLINGTON, HENRY T.
*1920 Contributions to the flora of Gogebic County, Michigan, Pt. 1. 22nd Rept., Ibid., pp. 147–176.
*1923 Contributions to the flora of Gogebic County, Michigan, Pt. 2. Papers, Mich. Acad. Sci. Arts and Lett. for 1921, Vol. 1, pp. 74–82.
*1937 Vegetation of the Porcupine Mountains, Northern Michigan, Pt. 2. Ibid. for 1936, Vol. 22, pp. 33–68.

DAVIS, C. A.
*1898 A contribution to the knowledge of the flora of Tuscola County, Michigan. Bot. Gazette, pp. 454–458.
*1900 Botanical notes on Huron County, Michigan. Geol. Surv. Mich., Vol. 7, Pt. 2, pp. 234–245.

DEAM, CHARLES C.
1924 Shrubs of Indiana. Ind. Dept. Conservation, Publ. 44. Pp. 351.
1932 Shrubs of Indiana (2nd Ed.). Ibid., Pp. 380.
1940 Flora of Indiana. State of Indiana, Department of Conservation, Division of Forestry, Indianapolis, Indiana. Pp. 1236.

DODGE, CHARLES KEENE
*1899 Flora of St. Clair County, Michigan. 29th Ann. Rept., Mich. Horticultural Soc., pp. 231–314.
*1911 Results of the Mershon Expedition to the Charity Islands, Lake Huron. 13th Rept., Mich. Acad. Sci., pp. 173–190.
*1913 The flowering plants, ferns and their allies of Mackinac Island. 15th Rept., Ibid., pp. 218–237.
*1918 Observations on the flowering plants, ferns and fern allies growing wild in Marquette County, Michigan, in 1916 and 1917, especially in the vicinity of the Huron Mountain Club. Univ. Mich., Mus. Zool., Misc. Publs. No. 5. Pp. 43.
*1921 Observations on the flowering plants, ferns and fern allies growing wild in Schoolcraft County and vicinity in the Upper Peninsula of Michigan in 1915. Mich. Geol. and Biol. Survey, Publ. 31, Biol. Ser. 6, pp. 75–123.
*1921 Observations on the flowering plants, ferns and fern allies growing without cultivation in Tuscola County, Michigan. Ibid., pp. 165–222.
*1921 Observations on the flowering plants, ferns and fern allies on and near the shore of Lake Huron from Linwood Park near Bay City, Bay County, to Mackinaw City, Cheboygan County, including the vicinity of St. Ignace, Mackinac and Bois Blanc Islands, Mackinaw County, Michigan. Ibid., pp. 15–74.
*1921 Observations on the wild plants at Whitefish Point and Vermillion, near the South Shore of Lake Superior, and other parts of Chippewa County, Michigan, in 1914. Ibid., pp. 125–164.

DYER, T. F. THISELTON
1889 The folk-lore of plants. D. Appleton and Company, New York. Pp. 328.

EMERSON, GEORGE B.
1894 A report on the trees and shrubs growing naturally in the forests of Massachusetts. Little Brown & Co., Boston. 2 vols. Pp. 624.

ERLANSON, EILEEN WHITEHEAD
1926 The wild roses of the Mackinac region of Michigan. Papers Mich. Acad. Sci. Arts. Lett. for 1925, Vol. 5, pp. 77–94.
1928 Ten new American species and varieties of Rosa. Rhodora, Vol. 30, pp. 109–121.

FARWELL, OLIVER ATKINS
*1900 A catalog of the flora of Detroit. 2nd. Rept., Mich. Acad. Sci., pp. 31–68.
*1904 Contributions to the botany of Michigan, No. 8. 6th Rept., *Ibid.*, pp. 200–214.
*1913 The flora of Parkdale Farm, with special reference to Stony Creek Valley. Contributions to the botany of Michigan, No. 9. 15th Rept., *Ibid.*, pp. 150–192.
 1915 Contributions to the botany of Michigan, No. 14. 17th Rept., *Ibid.*, pp. 167–182.
 1915 Range extension of *Ceanothus Sanguineus.* Rhodora, Vol. 17, pp. 229–230.
*1918 Notes on the Michigan flora, I. 20th Rept., Mich. Acad. Sci., pp. 161–195.
*1919 Notes on the Michigan flora, II. 21st Rept., *Ibid.*, pp. 345–371.
*1923 Botanical gleanings in Michigan. Amer. Midl. Nat., Vol. 8, No. 12, pp. 263–280.
*1923 Notes on the Michigan flora, Part IV. Papers, Mich. Acad. Sci. Arts Lett. for 1921, Vol. 1, pp. 85–100.
*1923 Notes on the Michigan flora, Part V. *Ibid.* for 1922., Vol. 2, pp. 11–46.
*1924 Notes on the Michigan flora, Part VI. *Ibid.* for 1923, Vol. 3, pp. 87–109.
*1925 Botanical gleanings in Michigan, II. Amer. Midl. Nat., Vol. 9, No. 7, pp. 259–282.
*1927 Botanical gleanings in Michigan, III. *Ibid.*, Vol. 10, No. 1, pp. 19–48.
*1927 Botanical gleanings in Michigan, IV. *Ibid.*, Vol. 10, No. 7, pp. 199–219.
*1928 Botanical gleanings in Michigan, V. *Ibid.*, Vol 11, pp. 41–71.
 1930 Botanical gleanings in Michigan, VII. *Ibid.*, Vol. 12, pp. 44–78.
 1935 Two western plants of the Keweenaw Peninsula. Rhodora, Vol. 37, p. 164.
*1938 Notes on the Michigan flora, VII. Papers, Mich. Acad. Sci. Arts Lett. for 1937, Vol. 23, pp. 123–139.
*1941 Notes on the Michigan flora, VIII. *Ibid.* for 1940, Vol. 26, pp. 3–20.

FERNALD, M. L.
 1904 The northeastern allies of *Salix lucida*. Rhodora, Vol. 6, pp. 1–8.
 1905 *Symphoricarpos racemosus* and its varieties in eastern America. Rhodora, Vol. 7, pp. 164–167.
 1905 Some lithological variations of *Ribes*. Rhodora, Vol. 7, pp. 153–156.
 1909 *Salix Pedicellaris* and its variations. Rhodora, Vol. 11, pp. 157–162.
 1911 The variations of *Ribes Hirtellum.* Rhodora. Vol. 13, pp. 73–76.
 1913 The genus *Empetrum* in North America. Rhodora. Vol. 15, pp. 211–217.
 1919 *Rubus Idaeus* and some of its variations in North America. Rhodora, Vol. 21, pp. 89–98.
 1922 The American variations of *Linnaea Borealis*. Rhodora, Vol. 24, pp. 210–212.
 1923 The identities of the Sand Cherries of eastern America. Rhodora, Vol. 25, pp. 69–74.
 1925 The American representatives of *Lonicera caerulea*. Rhodora, Vol. 27, pp. 1–11.
 1935 Critical plants of the Upper Great Lakes Region of Ontario and Michigan. Rhodora, Vol. 37, pp. 197–222, 238–262, 272–301, 324–341.
 1939 New species, varieties and transfers, IV. Rhodora, Vol. 41, pp. 423–461.
 1945 Eastern North American representatives of *Alnus Incana*. Rhodora, Vol. 47, pp. 333–361. Pls. 976–989.
 1946 Technical studies on North American plants. Rhodora, Vol. 48, pp. 27–40, 41–49. Pls. 995–1000.

FERNALD, M. L., AND GRISCOM, LUDLOW
 1935 Variations of *Rhus Copallina*. Rhodora, Vol. 37, pp. 167–168.

FERNALD, M. L., AND MACBRIDE, J. F.
 1914 The North American variations of *Arctostaphylos Uva-ursi*. Rhodora, Vol. 16, pp. 211–213.

FERNALD, M. L., AND WEATHERBY, C. A.
 1931 Some new plants from the Gaspé Peninsula. Rhodora, Vol. 33, pp. 231–240.

FRIEND, HILDERIC
 1884 Flowers and flower lore. W. Swan Sonnenschein and Co., London. 2 vols. Pp. 704.

GATES, FRANK C.
*1912 The vegetation of the region in the vicinity of Douglas Lake, Cheboygan County, Michigan, 1911. 14th Rept., Mich. Acad. Sci., pp. 46–106.

[323]

GATES, F. C., AND EHLERS, J. H.
   *1925 An annotated list of the higher plants of the region of Douglas Lake, Michigan. Papers, Mich. Acad. Sci. Arts Lett. for 1924, Vol. 4, Pt. 1, pp. 183–284.
   *1928 Additions to an annotated list of the higher plants of the region of Douglas Lake, Michigan, I. *Ibid.* for 1927, Vol. 8, pp. 111–120.
   *1931 Additions to an annotated list of the higher plants of the region of Douglas Lake, Michigan, II. *Ibid.* for 1930, Vol. 13, pp. 67–88.

GLEASON, H. A.
   1935 Plants of the vicinity of New York. New York Botanical Garden, New York, Pp. 198.

GRAY, ASA
   1887 Gray's lessons in botany, American Book Co., New York. Pp. 226.
   1908 *See* Robinson and Fernald.

HANES, CLARENCE R., AND FLORENCE N.
   *1947 Flora of Kalamazoo County, Michigan. Publ. by the authors, Schoolcraft, Michigan. Pp. 295.

HARNED, JOSEPH E.
   1931 Wild flowers of the Alleghanies. Publ. by the author, Oakland, Md. Pp. 670.

HEDRICK, U. P.
   1908 The grapes of New York. State of N. Y. Dept. Agric., 15th Ann. Rept., Vol. 3, Pt. 2. Pp. 564.
   1911 The plums of New York. State of N. Y. Dept. Agric., 18th Ann. Rept., Vol. 3, Pt. 2. Pp. 616.

HERMANN, FREDERICK J.
   1935 A mutation in *Rubus parviflorus.* Rhodora, Vol. 37, pp. 59–61.

HOUGH, ROMEYN BECK
   1924 Handbook of the trees of the Northern States and Canada. East of the Rocky Mountains. Romeyn B. Hough Co., Lowville, N. Y. Pp. 470.

JACKSON, BENJAMIN DAYDON
   1916 A glossary of botanic terms. Duckworth & Co., London; and Lippincott's, Philadelphia, Pp. 428.

JONES, GEORGE NEVILLE
   *1946 American species of *Amelanchier.* Illinois Biol. Monographs 20, No. 2. Pp. 126.

KEELER, HARRIET L.
   1928 Our northern shrubs. Scribner's, New York. Pp. 521.

KENOYER, L. A.
   *1924 Distribution of the Ericales in Michigan. Papers, Mich. Acad. Sci. Arts Lett. for 1923, Vol. 3, pp. 166–191.
   *1924 Distribution of the Umbellales in Michigan. *Ibid.,* pp. 131–165.

LINNAEUS, CARL
   1753 Species plantarum. Holmiae. 2 vols. Pp. 1230.

LITTLE, ELBERT L. JR.
   1945 Miscellaneous notes on nomenclature of United States trees. Amer. Midl. Nat., Vol. 33, pp. 495–513.

MACBRIDE, J. F.
   1918 A new species of Bladdernut. Rhodora, Vol. 20, pp. 127–129.

MATHEWS, F. SCHUYLER
   1915 Field book of American trees and shrubs. Putnam's, New York. Pp. 465.

MITCHELL, ANN MARIA
   1899 The White Blackberry. Rhodora, Vol. 1, p. 205.

MUENSCHER, W. C.
   1936 Keys to the woody plants. Published by the author at Cornell Univ., Ithaca, N. Y. Pp. 105.

NEWHALL, CHARLES S.
   1893 The shrubs of northeastern America. Putnam's, New York. Pp. 249.

NIELSEN, ETLAR L.
1937 The identity of *Amelanchier florida* Lindley. Madrono, Vol. 4, No. 1, pp. 17–21.
1939 A note concerning the identity of *Amelanchier florida* Lindley and *A. alnifolia* Nuttall. Amer. Midl. Nat., Vol. 22, pp. 207–208.
1939 A taxonomic study of the genus *Amelanchier* in Minnesota. *Ibid.*, Vol. 22, pp. 160–206.

NIEUWLAND, J. A.
*1912 Notes on our local plants. Amer. Midl. Nat., Vol. 2, pp. 267–286.
*1913 Notes on our local plants, V. *Ibid.*, Vol. 3, pp. 217–243.
*1914 Notes on our local plants, IX. *Ibid.*, Vol. 3, pp. 346–351.
*1915 Notes on our local plants, XI. *Ibid.*, Vol. 4, pp. 53–71.
*1915 Notes on our local plants, XIII. *Ibid.*, Vol. 4, pp. 276–280.

OTIS, CHARLES HERBERT
1931 Michigan trees, 9th Ed. University of Michigan, Ann Arbor. Pp. 362.

REHDER, ALFRED
1934 Manual of cultivated trees and shrubs. Macmillan Company, New York. Pp. 930.

ROBERTSON, BETTY M.
*1941 Distribution of Ranunculaceae in Michigan. Papers, Mich. Acad. Sci. Arts Lett. for 1940, Vol. 26, pp. 31–59.

ROBINSON, BENJAMIN LINCOLN, AND FERNALD, MERRITT LYNDON
1908 Gray's new manual of botany, 7th Ed. American Book Co., New York. Pp. 926.

ROSENDAHL, CARL OTTO, AND BUTTERS, FREDERIC
1928 Trees and shrubs of Minnesota. Univ. Minn. Press, Minneapolis. Pp. 385.

ROULEAU, ERNEST
1947 *Ribes hudsonianum* versus *Ribes ringens*. Rhodora, Vol. 49, pp. 217–219.

SARGENT, C. S.
1907 *Crataegus* in southern Michigan. Rept. State Bd. Geol. Surv., Mich., 1906, pp. 515–565.

SKINNER, CHARLES M.
1911 Myths and legends of flowers, trees, fruits and plants. J. B. Lippincott Company, New York. Pp. 302.

STEARNS, FRANCES L.
*1905 A study of plants in ravines near Adrian. 7th Rept., Mich. Acad. Sci., pp. 68–72.

SUTTON, JOHN M.
*1917 Flora of the Detroit Zoological Tract. 19th Rept., *Ibid.*, pp. 263–271.

WALP, RUSSELL LEE
*1935 Shrubs of Cheboygan and Emmet counties, Michigan. Amer. Midl. Nat., Vol. 16, pp. 230–247.

WALPOLE, BRANSON A.
*1924 The flora of Washtenaw County, Michigan. Dept. of Natural Science, Mich. State Normal College, Farm and Garden Project Club, Ypsilanti, Michigan. Pp. 80.

WATERMAN, W. G.
*1922 Development of plant communities of a sand ridge region in Michigan. Bot. Gazette, Vol. 74, No. 1, pp. 1–31.

WHITNEY, W. D.
*1851 Botany, pp. 359-381. In Foster and Whitney, 'Report on the Geology of the Lake Superior Land District, Part 2.' Washington, D. C.

WIEGAND, K. M.
1912 The genus *Amelanchier* in eastern North America. Rhodora, Vol. 14, pp. 117–161.
1913 The genus *Empetrum* in North America. Rhodora, Vol. 15, pp. 211–217.
1920 Additional notes on *Amelanchier*. Rhodora, Vol. 22, pp. 146–151.

ZIMMER, GEORGE FREDERICK
1923 A popular dictionary of botanical names and terms. George Routledge & Sons, Ltd., London; and Dutton, New York. Pp. 122.

Index

INDEX

Betula, 89
  glandulosa, 9, 88, 90
  pumila, 9, 88, 89
    var. *glandulifera,* 90
Betulaceae, 87
Bilberry, 259
  Bog, 10, 269, 271
  Dwarf, 22, 271
  Oval-leaved, 273
  Tall, 10, 273
  Thin-leaved, 271
Birch, 89
  Black, 259
  Dwarf, 9, 90
  Family, 87
  Low, 89
  Running, 261
  Swamp, 9, 89
  Sweet, 261
Bittersweet, 4, 277, 279
  Climbing, 9, 207
  Shrubby, 207
Blackberry, 4, 7, 119, 151, 159
  amber-colored, 155, 161
  Bristly, 165
  Cut-leaved, 163
  High-bush, 10, 159, 161
  Hispid, 10, 165
  Leafy-flowered, 161
  Low Running, 166
  Millspaugh's 10, 163
  Running Swamp, 165
  Thornless, 163
  White, 153, 161
Bladder Nut, 3, 4, 208
  American, 208
  Family, 208
Blueberry, 4, 263
  Black High, 269
  Canada, 266
  Dryland, 267
  Early Sweet, 265
  High-bush, 10, 203, 267
  Late Low, 10, 267
  Low Sweet, 10, 265
  Sour-top, 266
  Swamp, 267
  Tall, 267
  Velvet-leaf, 266
Blue Tangle, 9
Box-berry, 280
Bramble, 151
Brier
  Horse, 61
Broom
  Witch's, 97

Buckthorn, 211
  Alder, 10, 211, 213
  Common, 213
  Family, 211
Bush
  Benjamin, 104
  Burning, 9, 205
  Deer, 215
  Fever, 104
  Pearl, 117
  Running Strawberry, 9, 207
  Shad, 117
  Snow, 215
  Spice, 4, 10, 103
  Steeple, 121
  Strawberry, 9, 205
Buttonbush, 4, 280, 281
  Common, 280

C

Capillaire, 261
Caprifoliaceae, 281
Cashew Family, 193
Cassandra, 256
Ceanothus, 215
  americanus, 216, 217
  ovatus, 216, 217
    var. *pubescens,* 217
  sanguineus, 21, 214, 215
Cedar-apples, 136
Cedar, Red, 136
Celastraceae, 205
Celastrus, 207
  scandens, 9, 206, 207, 279
Cephalanthus, 280
  occidentalis, 280, 282
Chamaedaphne, 256
  calyculata, 254, 256
    var. *angustifolia,* 256
Checkerberry, 9, 257, 280
Cherry, 4, 119, 180
  Appalachian, 10, 181
  Choke, 10, 180
  Indian, 10, 134
  Sand, 10, 181
Chicken-berry, 280
Chimaphila, 247
  maculata, 248, 249
  umbellata, 247, 249
    var. *cisatlantica,* 246, 247
      occidentalis, 249
Chiogenes, 259
  hispidula, 2, 259, 260

INDEX

Chokeberry, 122
  Black, 9, 123
  Purple, 9, 122
  Red, 122
Cinquefoil, 149
  Shrubby, 119, 149
Cistaceae, 229
Clematis, 97
  verticillaris, 21, 96, 98
  virginiana, 2, 96, 97
Clover
  Winter, 280
Club
  Devil's, 235
  Hercules', 9, 233
Comptonia, 85
  peregrina, 84, 85
Coral-berry, 295
Cornaceae, 237
Cornel
  Silky, 9, 239
Cornus, 237
  alternifolia, 9, 243, 246
  Amomum, 239, 241
  asperifolia, 9, 240, 241
  Baileyi, 27, 242
  circinata, 239
  obliqua, 9, 238, 239
  paniculata, 243
  racemosa, 9, 243, 244
  rugosa, 9, 238, 239
  stolonifera, 9, 242, 244
    var. *Baileyi*, 240, 242
Corylus, 87
  americana, 86, 87
  avellana, 89
  cornuta, 86, 89
  rostrata, 89
Cotoneaster, 117
Cotton-woods, 63
Cowberry, 10, 280
Cranberry, 263
  American, 275
  Cape Cod Bell, 277
  High-bush, 11, 299
  Large, 10, 275
  Mountain, 273
  Rock, 23, 273
  Small, 10, 273, 275
Cranberry Tree, 299
Crataegus, 7, 134
  Groups, 136
  Coccineae, 145
  Crus-galli, 137
  Douglasianae, 147
  Intricatae, 139

Macracanthae, 147
Molles, 145
Pruinosae, 143
Punctatae, 139, 141
Rotundifoliae, 141
Tenuifoliae, 143
Species
  chrysocarpa, 141
  coccinea, 139
  Crus-galli, 9, 137, 138
    var. *oblongata*, 139
      pyracanthifolia, 139
  Dodgei, 141
  Douglasii, 146, 147
  intricata, 139, 140
  macrosperma, 142, 143
  Margaretta, 140, 141
    var. *angustifolia*, 141
  mollis, 9, 144, 145
    var. *sera*, 147
  pedicellata, 144, 145
    var. *albicans*, 145
  pruinosa, 142, 143
    var. *conjuncta*, 143
      latisepala, 143
      philadelphica, 145
  punctata, 9, 138, 139
  rotundifolia, 141
  succulenta, 146, 147
Crowberry, 192
  Black, 9, 19, 192
  Family, 192
Crowfoot Family, 97
Currant, 104
  American Black, 109
  Common Red, 113
  Fetid, 113
  Indian, 10, 295
  Northern Black, 111
  Red Garden, 113
  Skunk, 113
  Swamp Black, 111
  Swamp Red, 115
  Wild Black, 10, 109
Custard Apple Family, 98

D

Dangleberry, 9
Decodon, 232
  verticillatus, 2, 232, 234
    var. *laevigatus*, 233
Deerberry, 10, 263, 280
Dewberry, 10, 151, 166
Diervilla, 281
  Lonicera, 281, 282
Dirca, 229
  palustris, 229, 230

INDEX

Honeysuckle, 283
  American Fly, 10, 287
  Bush, 281
  Douglas', 291
  European Fly, 293
  Family, 281
  Glaucous, 293
  Hairy, 10, 291
  Involucred Fly, 10, 289
  Mountain Fly, 285
  Old World, 285
  Smooth-leaved, 10, 293
  Swamp Fly, 10, 287
  Tartarian, 285
  Trumpet, 289
Huckleberry, 3, 4, 9, 151, 261
  Black, 9, 261
  Blue, 267
  Squaw, 263
Hudsonia, 229
  Woolly, 229
Hudsonia, 229
  tomentosa, 228, 229
    var. *intermedia*, 229
Hyeble, 235
Hypericaceae, 225
Hypericum, 227
  Kalmianum, 227, 228
  prolificum, 226, 227

I

Ilex, 201
  verticillata, 10, 200, 201
    var. *padifolia*, 203
        tenuifolia, 203
Indian-cherry, 10, 134
Indian-pear, 134
Indigo
  False, 185, 187
Ivy
  Five-fingered, 219
  Poison, 2, 4, 193, 199
  Three-leaved, 199, 220

J

Juneberry
  Lake Huron, 125
  Low, 9, 127
  Northern, 129
  Northwestern, 134
  Oblong-fruited, 133
  Round-leaved, 125, 134
Juniper, 3, 4, 57
  Creeping, 10, 59
  Prostrate, 10, 59

Juniperus, 6, 57
  communis var. *depressa*, 10, 58, 59
  horizontalis, 10, 59, 60

K

Kalmia, 27, 251
  angustifolia, 250, 251
  polifolia, 250, 253
King's-cure, 249
Kinnikinnick, 259

L

Lambkill, 251
Lauraceae, 103
Laurel, 251
  Family, 103
  Ground, 256
  Mountain, 215, 253
  Pale, 251, 253
  Sheep, 251, 253
  Swamp, 253
Leatherleaf, 256
Leatherwood, 3, 229
Ledum, 249
  groenlandicum, 248, 249
Leguminosae, 185
Lewis and Clark, 134
Liliaceae, 59
Lily Family, 59
Lindera, 103
  Benzoin, 10, 102, 103
Linnaea, 296
  borealis, 27
    var. *americana*, 296, 298
Locust, 187
  Clammy, 187
  Bristly, 189
Lonicera, 283
  caerulea var. *villosa*, 285
  canadensis, 10, 286, 287
  canadensis, 10, 287
  caprifolium, 293
  dioica, 10, 292, 293
    var. *glaucescens*, 290, 291
  glaucescens, 291
  hirsuta, 10, 290, 291
  involucrata, 10, 23, 288, 289
  Morrowi, 293
  oblongifolia, 10, 286, 287
  sempervirens, 288, 289
  tatarica, 284, 285
  villosa
    var. *Solonis*, 284, 285
  Xylosteum, 293

[331]

INDEX

INDEX

[335]

INDEX

INDEX

Exemplum Ad Imitandum

It is furthest from my desire to intrude too much of myself into this volume. After all it is a treatise on a segment of our flora and is not in any way an anthropological work. It is the aim of any such effort to be of help to others, and if my own experience can aid this effort it may be worth calling attention to.

When the first edition was written I was actively engaged in business, and the work was carried on in my spare time. I am now retired from the major portion of my business connections, and if I had not years ago taken up systematic botany purely as a hobby I might now be without any sort of useful occupation. Therein lies the suggestion to others who may read this bulletin and who may wish to profit by my experience. Systematic botany, with its many field excursions and contact with nature generally, furnishes relief and relaxation from the daily exactions of business and adds immeasurably to the joy of living. Later on in life if pursued consistently it may furnish a worthwhile escape from the deadly monotony of old-age retirement.

On one of my numerous visits to the University of Michigan Herbarium Dr. McVaugh expressed the wish that he had a number of persons to help with the work there. Here would be a delightful way of relieving the monotony of retirement for any capable worker, at the same time achieving a most worthwhile end-result. The Cranbrook herbarium welcomes such assistance and already has the help of an enthusiastic group. There is room for more, however, and no doubt other institutions need and would welcome similar support. Not all places have herbaria to work in, but information and specimens are always welcome, and the director of any such institution would be more than glad to supervise the efforts of capable workers.

The opportunities are almost numberless, and there could be no greater reward than to feel that my experience, which has been most satisfactory in every way, had influenced others to pursue the same profitable line of endeavor.

CECIL BILLINGTON

[339]

Q
11
C95
1950
C3
Billington
Shrubs of Michigan

Glen Oaks Community College
Library
Centreville, Michigan